# Symbiosis and Ambiguity

*Symbiosis and Ambiguity* is the first English edition of the classic study of early object relations by influential Argentinian psychoanalyst José Bleger (1922–1972). It is rooted in Kleinian thinking and rich in clinical material.

Bleger's thesis is that starting from primitive undifferentiation, prior to the paranoid-schizoid position described by Klein, autism and symbiosis co-exist as narcissistic relations in a syncretic 'agglutinated' nucleus. In symbiosis part of the mind is deposited in an external person or situation; in autism it is deposited in the patient's own mind or body. The nucleus is ambiguous and persists in adults as the psychotic part of the personality.

Symbiosis tends to immobilise the analytic process, so the analyst must mobilise, fragment and discriminate the agglutinated nucleus, whose ambiguity tends to 'blunt' persecutory situations. The psychoanalytic setting functions as a silent refuge for the psychotic part of the personality, where it creates a 'phantom world'. At some point, therefore, the setting itself has to be analysed and the analytic relationship de-symbiotised, as Bleger observes in a celebrated chapter on the setting.

José Bleger's work demonstrates the need to analyse early narcissistic object relations as they arise clinically, especially in the setting. More widely, he regards undifferentiation and participation as operating throughout life: in groups, institutions, and society as a whole.

**José Bleger** was born in Argentina in 1922. An active member of the *Asociación Psicoanalítica Argentina*, he was also a highly-regarded Professor of Psychology and a well known intellectual. Author of many books and papers, his reputation grew steadily after his early death in 1972. He is now considered a major figure of Argentinian psychoanalysis.

**John Churcher** is a psychoanalyst in private practice in Manchester, and a member of the British Psychoanalytical Society. Until 2002 he was a Lecturer in Psychology at the University of Manchester.

**Leopoldo Bleger**, born in Argentina, has lived in Paris since 1976. A Training Analyst of the *Association Psychanalytique de France*, he is currently General Secretary of the European Federation of Psychoanalysis.

THE NEW LIBRARY OF PSYCHOANALYSIS
General Editor: Alessandra Lemma

The New Library of Psychoanalysis was launched in 1987 in association with the Institute of Psychoanalysis, London. It took over from the International Psychoanalytical Library which published many of the early translations of the works of Freud and the writings of most of the leading British and Continental psychoanalysts.

The purpose of the New Library of Psychoanalysis is to facilitate a greater and more widespread appreciation of psychoanalysis and to provide a forum for increasing mutual understanding between psychoanalysts and those working in other disciplines such as the social sciences, medicine, philosophy, history, linguistics, literature and the arts. It aims to represent different trends both in British psychoanalysis and in psychoanalysis generally. The New Library of Psychoanalysis is well placed to make available to the English-speaking world psychoanalytic writings from other European countries and to increase the interchange of ideas between British and American psychoanalysts. Through the *Teaching Series*, the New Library of Psychoanalysis now also publishes books that provide comprehensive, yet accessible, overviews of selected subject areas aimed at those studying psychoanalysis and related fields such as the social sciences, philosophy, literature and the arts.

The Institute, together with the British Psychoanalytical Society, runs a low-fee psychoanalytic clinic, organizes lectures and scientific events concerned with psychoanalysis and publishes the *International Journal of Psychoanalysis*. It runs a training course in psychoanalysis which leads to membership of the International Psychoanalytical Association – the body which preserves internationally agreed standards of training, of professional entry, and of professional ethics and practice for psychoanalysis as initiated and developed by Sigmund Freud. Distinguished members of the Institute have included Michael Balint, Wilfred Bion, Ronald Fairbairn, Anna Freud, Ernest Jones, Melanie Klein, John Rickman and Donald Winnicott.

Previous general editors have included David Tuckett, who played a very active role in the establishment of the New Library. He was followed as general editor by Elizabeth Bott Spillius, who was in turn followed by Susan Budd and then by Dana Birksted-Breen.

ALSO IN THIS SERIES

*Impasse and Interpretation* Herbert Rosenfeld
*Psychoanalysis and Discourse* Patrick Mahony
*The Suppressed Madness of Sane Men* Marion Milner
*The Riddle of Freud* Estelle Roith
*Thinking, Feeling, and Being* Ignacio Matte Blanco
*The Theatre of the Dream* Salomon Resnik
*Melanie Klein Today: Volume 1, Mainly Theory* Edited by Elizabeth Bott Spillius
*Melanie Klein Today: Volume 2, Mainly Practice* Edited by Elizabeth Bott Spillius
*Psychic Equilibrium and Psychic Change: Selected Papers of Betty Joseph* Edited by Michael Feldman and Elizabeth Bott Spillius
*About Children and Children-No-Longer: Collected Papers 1942–80* Paula Heimann. Edited by Margret Tonnesmann
*The Freud–Klein Controversies 1941–45* Edited by Pearl King and Riccardo Steiner
*Dream, Phantasy and Art* Hanna Segal
*Psychic Experience and Problems of Technique* Harold Stewart
*Clinical Lectures on Klein & Bion* Edited by Robin Anderson
*From Fetus to Child* Alessandra Piontelli
*A Psychoanalytic Theory of Infantile Experience: Conceptual and Clinical Reflections* E Gaddini. Edited by Adam Limentani
*The Dream Discourse Today* Edited and introduced by Sara Flanders
*The Gender Conundrum: Contemporary Psychoanalytic Perspectives on Feminitity and Masculinity* Edited and introduced by Dana Breen
*Psychic Retreats* John Steiner
*The Taming of Solitude: Separation Anxiety in Psychoanalysis* Jean-Michel Quinodoz
*Unconscious Logic: An Introduction to Matte-Blanco's Bi-logic and its Uses* Eric Rayner
*Understanding Mental Objects* Meir Perlow
*Life, Sex and Death: Selected Writings of William Gillespie* Edited and introduced by Michael Sinason
*What Do Psychoanalysts Want?: The Problem of Aims in Psychoanalytic Therapy* Joseph Sandler and Anna Ursula Dreher
*Michael Balint: Object Relations, Pure and Applied* Harold Stewart
*Hope: A Shield in the Economy of Borderline States* Anna Potamianou
*Psychoanalysis, Literature & War: Papers 1972–1995* Hanna Segal
*Emotional Vertigo: Between Anxiety and Pleasure* Danielle Quinodoz
*Early Freud and Late Freud* Ilse Grubrich-Simitis
*A History of Child Psychoanalysis* Claudine and Pierre Geissmann
*Belief and Imagination: Explorations in Psychoanalysis* Ronald Britton

*A Mind of One's Own: A Psychoanalytic View of Self and Object* Robert A Caper
*Psychoanalytic Understanding of Violence and Suicide* Edited by Rosine Jozef Perelberg
*On Bearing Unbearable States of Mind* Ruth Riesenberg-Malcolm
*Psychoanalysis on the Move: The Work of Joseph Sandler* Edited by Peter Fonagy, Arnold M. Cooper and Robert S. Wallerstein
*The Dead Mother: The Work of André Green* Edited by Gregorio Kohon
*The Fabric of Affect in the Psychoanalytic Discourse* André Green
*The Bi-Personal Field: Experiences of Child Analysis* Antonino Ferro
*The Dove that Returns, the Dove that Vanishes: Paradox and Creativity in Psychoanalysis* Michael Parsons
*Ordinary People, Extra-ordinary Protections: A Post Kleinian Approach to the Treatment of Primitive Mental States* Judith Mitrani
*The Violence of Interpretation: From Pictogram to Statement* Piera Aulagnier
*The Importance of Fathers: A Psychoanalytic Re-Evaluation* Judith Trowell and Alicia Etchegoyen
*Dreams That Turn Over a Page: Paradoxical Dreams in Psychoanalysis* Jean-Michel Quinodoz
*The Couch and the Silver Screen: Psychoanalytic Reflections on European Cinema* Andrea Sabbadini
*In Pursuit of Psychic Change: The Betty Joseph Workshop* Edited by Edith Hargreaves and Arturo Varchevker
*The Quiet Revolution in American Psychoanalysis: Selected Papers of Arnold M. Cooper* Arnold M. Cooper. Edited and Introduced by Elizabeth L. Auchincloss
*Seeds of Illness and Seeds of Recovery: The Genesis of Suffering and the Role of Psychoanalysis* Antonino Ferro
*The Work of Psychic Figurability: Mental States Without Representation* César Botella and Sára Botella
*Key Ideas for a Contemporary Psychoanalysis: Misrecognition and Recognition of the Unconscious* André Green
*The Telescoping of Generations: Listening to the Narcissistic Links Between Generations* Haydée Faimberg
*Glacial Times: A Journey through the World of Madness* Salomon Resnik
*This Art of Psychoanalysis: Dreaming Undreamt Dreams and Interrupted Cries* Thomas H Ogden
*Psychoanalysis and Religion in the 21st Century: Competitors or Collaborators?* David M. Black
*Recovery of the Lost Good Object* Eric Brenman
*The Many Voices of Psychoanalysis* Roger Kennedy
*Feeling the Words: Neuropsychoanalytic Understanding of Memory and the Unconscious* Mauro Mancia
*Constructions and the Analytic Field: History, Scenes and Destiny* Domenico Chianese

*Projected Shadows: Psychoanalytic Reflections on the Representation of Loss in European Cinema* Edited by Andrea Sabbadini

*Encounters with Melanie Klein: Selected Papers of Elizabeth Spillius* Elizabeth Spillius

*Yesterday, Today and Tomorrow* Hanna Segal

*Psychoanalysis Comparable and Incomparable: The Evolution of a Method to Describe and Compare Psychoanalytic Approaches* David Tuckett, Roberto Basile, Dana Birksted-Breen, Tomas Böhm, Paul Denis, Antonino Ferro, Helmut Hinz, Arne Jemstedt, Paola Mariotti and Johan Schubert

*Time, Space and Phantasy* Rosine Jozef Perelberg

*Rediscovering Psychoanalysis: Thinking and Dreaming, Learning and Forgetting* Thomas H. Ogden

*Mind Works: Techniques and Creativity in Psychoanalysis* Antonino Ferro

*Doubt Conviction and the Analytic Process: Selected Papers of Michael Feldman* Michael Feldman

*Melanie Klein in Berlin: Her First Psychoanalyses of Children* Claudia Frank

*The Psychotic Wavelength: A Psychoanalytic Perspective for Psychiatry* Richard Lucas

*Betweenity: A Discussion of the Concept of Borderline* Judy Gammelgaard

*The Intimate Room: Theory and Technique of the Analytic Field* Giuseppe Civitarese

*Bion Today* Edited by Chris Mawson

*Secret Passages: The Theory and Technique of Interpsychic Relations* Stefano Bolognini

*Intersubjective Processes and the Unconscious: An Integration of Freudian, Kleinian and Bionian Perspectives* Lawrence J. Brown

*Seeing and Being Seen: Emerging from a Psychic Retreat* John Steiner

*Avoiding Emotions, Living Emotions* Antonio Ferro

*Projective Identification: The Fate of a Concept* Edited by Elizabeth Spillius and Edna O'Shaughnessy

*Creative Readings: Essays on Seminal Analytic Works* Thomas Ogden

*The Maternal Lineage* Edited by Paola Mariotti

*Donald Winnicott Today* Edited by Jan Abram

*Symbiosis and Ambiguity: A Psychoanalytic Study* José Bleger Edited by John Churcher, and Leopoldo Bleger

*Psychotic Temptation* Liliane Abensour

*The Theory and Technique of Psychoanalytic Supervision: The Sao Paulo Clinical Seminars* Antonino Ferro

## TITLES IN THE NEW LIBRARY OF PSYCHOANALYSIS TEACHING SERIES

*Reading Freud: A Chronological Exploration of Freud's Writings* Jean-Michel Quinodoz
*Listening to Hanna Segal: Her Contribution to Psychoanalysis* Jean-Michel Quinodoz
*Reading French Psychoanalysis* Edited by Dana Birksted-Breen, Sara Flanders and Alain Gibeault
*Reading Winnicott* Lesley Caldwell and Angela Joyce
*Initiating Psychoanalysis: Perspectives* Bernard Reith, Sven Lagerlöf, Penelope Crick, Mette Møller and Elisabeth Skale
*Infant Observation* Frances Salo
*Reading Anna Freud* Nick Midgley

## TITLES IN THE NEW LIBRARY OF PSYCHOANALYSIS 'BEYOND THE COUCH' SERIES

*Under the Skin: A Psychoanalytic Study of Body Modification* Alessandra Lemma
*Engaging with Climate Change: Psychoanalytic and Interdisciplinary Perspectives* Edited by Sally Weintrobe

THE NEW LIBRARY OF PSYCHOANALYSIS

General Editor Alessandra Lemma

# Symbiosis and Ambiguity
## A Psychoanalytic Study

José Bleger

Edited by John Churcher and Leopoldo Bleger
with a Preface by R. Horacio Etchegoyen

Translated by Susan Rogers, Leopoldo Bleger
and John Churcher

Routledge
Taylor & Francis Group
LONDON AND NEW YORK

First published in Spanish as
*Simbiosis y ambigüedad: estudio psicoanalítico*
in 1967 by Paidós, Buenos Aires.

This English edition first published 2013
by Routledge
27 Church Road, Hove, East Sussex BN3 2FA

Simultaneously published in the USA and Canada
by Routledge
711 Third Avenue, New York, NY 10017

*Routledge is an imprint of the Taylor & Francis Group, an informa business*



*British Library Cataloguing in Publication Data*
A catalogue record for this book is available from the British Library

*Library of Congress Cataloging in Publication Data*
Bleger, José.
[Simbiosis y ambigüedad. English]
Symbiosis and ambiguity : a psychoanalytic study/José Bleger, John Churcher, Leopoldo Bleger.
p. cm. — (The new library of psychoanalysis)
Includes bibliographical references and index.
ISBN 978-0-415-46463-5 (hardback) — ISBN 978-0-415-46462-8 (paperback) 1. Psychoanalysis. 2. Ambiguity I. Churcher, John. II. Bleger, Leopoldo. III. Title.
BF173.B62132013
150.19'5—dc23

2012014043

ISBN: 978-0-415-46463-5 (hbk)
ISBN: 978-0-415-46462-8 (pbk)
ISBN: 978-0-203-09398-6 (ebk)

Typeset in Bembo by RefineCatch Ltd, Bungay, Suffolk UK

MIX
Paper from responsible sources
FSC www.fsc.org FSC® C004839

Printed and bound by CPI Group (UK) Ltd, Croydon, CR0 4YY

# Contents

1 An earlier translation of Chapter 6 was published in the *International Journal of Psycho-analysis* as 'Psycho-analysis of the psycho-analytic frame' (Bleger, 1967a)

# Preface

*R. Horacio Etchegoyen*

With the exception of 'Psycho-analysis of the psycho-analytic frame' which appeared in 1967 in the *International Journal of Psychoanalysis*, and a contribution titled 'Ambiguity: a chapter of psychology and psychopathology', published in volume II of *The World Biennial of Psychiatry and Psychotherapy* edited by Silvano Arieti, English-speaking readers have had few opportunities for contact with the work of José Bleger, undoubtedly one of the most lucid and original thinkers in Latin-American psychoanalysis.

José Bleger was born in Santa Fe (Argentina) in November 1922. He took his medical degree in the Faculty of Medicine of Rosario, as did his wife Lily. Later on they moved to Santiago del Estero, around 1947. They lived in La Banda, one of the poorest districts of the province, where they both practised general medicine. Her interests were more in gynaecology and his in psychiatry.

There José began to use sodium pentothal for exploration and psychotherapy of the numerous neurotic patients who came to his consulting room. From this experience emerged his first book *Teoría y Práctica del Narcoanálisis* (*Theory and Practice of Narcoanalysis*) which was published in 1952, where his clear understanding of the human mind was already apparent.

Having decided to pursue a serious psychoanalytic training the Blegers both commuted to Buenos Aires for some time, before finally settling there. They joined the Asociación Psicoanalítica Argentina (APA), which had been founded in 1942. José became a member at the end of the 1950s and his personal development was steady and rapid.

Like many young practitioners of that period, myself amongst them, Bleger came under the beneficent influence of Enrique J. Pichon Rivière, and went on to become one of his most outstanding disciples. From Pichon Rivière, Bleger learned not only psychiatry and psychoanalysis but also the intimate relationship of psychoanalysis with culture and society at large, and the need to review and re-elaborate Freudian hypotheses within the framework of epistemology. To do this he chose the powerful instrument of dialectical materialism, which he understood better than most.

The reading of Georges Politzer and his example as a militant in the Resistance, who was shot by the Nazis in 1942, were decisive in Bleger's intellectual development. His reflections were crystallised in his *Psicoanálisis y Dialéctica Materialista* (*Psychoanalysis and Dialectical Materialism*), a book of lasting value which was published by Paidós in 1958.

In his *Critique des Fondements de la Psychologie* (*Critique of the Foundations of Psychology*) (1928), Politzer takes 'drama' as the object of study of psychology, as it includes at the same time behaviour and the inner life. Convinced that what behaviourism studies is a mere physiology, and that the inner life of the psychology of introspection is only a matter of ontology or essence, a myth, Bleger takes as his starting point Politzer's dramatics. Unlike Politzer, however, he doesn't think that inner life is necessarily a myth; rather, it only *becomes* mythical 'when it is extracted and isolated from the dramatic totality and is converted into a thing with its own nature and existence' (Bleger, 1958, p. 36). If it is recognized in the dramatic unity to which in fact it belongs, inner life is the raw material of psychology and psychoanalysis; however, if it is torn out and turned into an entelechy, into 'second nature', then indeed does inner life give birth to myth and start to become part of the ideological arsenal of the dominant class.

Bleger understood from the beginning, and he never abandoned the thought, that one of Freud's greatest merits was to have broken away from the psychology of faculties of the soul and from fleshless behaviourism. 'It is precisely Freud who inspired in Politzer his vision of a concrete psychology' (Bleger, 1958, p. 32), although 'the concrete is submerged in a theoretical structure completely rooted in philosophical idealism, if not in abstractionism' (Bleger, 1958, p. 34).

Psychoanalysis, Bleger asserts, examines the psychological event as a function of the subject's life; but it goes astray when it abandons the dramatic for the dynamic and reduces explanation to a play of forces, extrapolated from Newtonian physics, that are called 'instincts'. With his habitual precision, Bleger puts it thus: 'In other words, to explain the difference between the dramatic and its dynamic transposition, it could be said that in the former the drives derive from object relations, while Freud argued in his dynamic theories that object relations derive from the interplay of the drives' (Bleger, 1958, p.118) There are clear Fairbairnian resonances here.

The dramatic, as a legitimate field for psychology and psychoanalysis, leads Bleger to become more and more interested in the study of interpersonal relationships by Fairbairn and by Melanie Klein. At that time, most scholars in Buenos Aires and Montevideo were feeling strongly drawn to these authors and were putting the psychoanalytic session at the centre of their interest in studying the field of the analyst-patient interaction.

The studies that culminated in the major work that the reader now has in his or her hands began to be written simultaneously with, or shortly after, *Psicoanálisis y Dialéctica Materialista.* In 1960 there appeared his 'Estudio de la dependencia-independencia en su relación con el proceso de proyección-introyección' ('Study of dependence-independence in relation to the process of projection-introjection') and in the following year 'La simbiosis' ('Symbiosis'), which form part of the first chapters of this book.

*Symbiosis and Ambiguity* was published in 1967, in a beautiful edition by Paidós, at a time when Bleger's huge personality as a psychoanalyst, as a committed intellectual and university teacher, and as a true master in his field, shone in his speaking, his writing and his example.

Bleger conceived symbiosis as a state of primitive undifferentiation, which includes the subject and his/her environment, although not yet as separate entities. *Homo sapiens* is not born as an isolated being who acquires the status of being social by abdicating isolation and adapting to culture, as proposed paradigmatically by the Freudian theory of primary narcissism (and also the autistic stage of Margaret Mahler). For Bleger, on the contrary, the human creature is by nature a social being, who passes through a period of primitive undifferentiation that will later be transformed into other types of relationship, and which will lead into the development of identity and of the sense of reality. Bleger emphasises in the Prologue of this book, and he repeats it throughout his work, that this stage of undifferentiation is a *structure*, a specific organization, which always includes the subject and his/her environment in a unique relationship.

To this primitive stage, which is prior to the Kleinian positions, Bleger gives the name *glischro-caric position*; it is where primary identification reigns and the syncytium is formed which is the seat of *ambiguity* – a vertebral concept in Bleger's thinking. The paranoid-schizoid position that follows later operates with the mechanism of dissociation that Fairbairn and Melanie Klein studied. As long as objects are partial and the anxieties persecutory, Bleger uses the Pichonean concept of *divalence* to characterize this type of object relation. Only when the subject can integrate the good and bad parts of the object and of the self in the depressive position is ambivalence finally established. Before then, there is only ambiguity.

If it is true that every vigorous work emerges both out of and in reaction to other, similarly vigorous works, which it extends and to which it presents itself as agonistic, it could be said that when Bleger wrote he was always thinking of Freud and Marx, of Politzer, of Fairbairn and Melanie Klein, although the scope of his reading in fact had no limits.

Bleger was influenced in the first place by Pichon Rivière, who was his teacher, and teacher to the whole of Latin American psychiatry and psychoanalysis. Pichon's work found expression in those who carried it further: Liberman, Bleger, Baranger, Fiasché and Rolla, amongst others. On the other hand, Bleger is undoubtedly a Kleinian analyst, who debates with Bion and with Rosenfeld; he is also someone who takes issue with Margaret Mahler and with Searles. The title of the book sufficiently illustrates its Ferenczian roots, that Mahler was later to develop masterfully. These conceptual debts in no way diminish the originality of Blegerian thinking: they are simply the bases on which it was established and which made it possible.

*Ambiguity* and *symbiosis* are key concepts in Bleger's attempt to explore the earliest levels of the psyche, prior to the dynamics described by Melanie Klein. It is fundamental to understand that for Bleger, the primitive mental levels dominated by subject-object undifferentiation are only partially resolved during the rest of life, and they constitute the foundation for many phenomena which permeate the analytic situation, groups, institutions and society as a whole.

The brilliant application that Bleger makes of his theories in accounting for the muteness of the setting is well known. His paper 'Psycho-analysis of the psycho-analytic frame' (1967a) has become a classic and is part of this book.

Although Bleger's ideas open up an attractive road towards the understanding of psychosis, they also apply to neurotic patients and are at the same time the substrate of a good part of what is happening in our social and institutional life. Bleger's strongest thesis is probably that the phenomena of undifferentiation related to the early psyche operate both in clinical psychoanalysis and in processes of societal and cultural change.

*Warrior's Rest*, the novel by Christiane Rochefort, published in Buenos Aires in 1959, gave Bleger an opportunity to apply his ideas to understanding a work of literature. The relationship between the protagonists, Geneviève and Jean Renaud, may validly be understood from the perspective of symbiosis and the nature of the link with the agglutinated or glischroid object. The agglutinated object corresponds to a very early stage in the development of the ego, in which there is no differentiation or discrimination between ego and non-ego, and which is dominated by ambiguity and fusion (not confusion). The symbiotic link is a pact between the dead parts of the participants, which starts from a crossed identification. This hypothesis explains the relationship between Geneviève and Jean Renaud, a failed suicide, with whom Geneviève becomes involved through the dead part of her. The two parties configure an agglutinated object in which the dead parts of the man and the woman are crystallized, and crossed over in a desperate effort to rescue themselves from a symbiotic relationship and from the catastrophic anxieties that bind them together.

More than thirty years after his premature death, Bleger's research is still completely relevant today.

* * *

The publication in English of *Symbiosis and Ambiguity*, which is added to the French version published years ago by Presses Universitaires, is proof of the enduring vitality of Bleger's thinking. The book has also been published in Portuguese and Italian. By overcoming the barriers of language, furthermore, it offers a singular opportunity through the contact with a larger audience for new conceptual bridges to emerge between analysts in the diverse areas of international psychoanalysis.

In short, a wonderful book.

*Buenos Aires, 11 January 2009*

# Editorial Introduction

*Leopoldo Bleger & John Churcher*

*Symbiosis and Ambiguity*, which is here made available in English translation for the first time, was originally published in Spanish more than forty years ago. In the English-speaking world, knowledge of José Bleger's work has until now been based largely on a single paper: 'Psycho-analysis of the psycho-analytic frame', which was published in 1967 in the *International Journal of Psychoanalysis* (Bleger, 1967a). One of only three pieces by Bleger hitherto published in English, it had appeared earlier that year in Spanish as an integral chapter in this book. The paper has become a classic among writings on the psychoanalytic setting, but its isolation from the clinical and theoretical context of the book as a whole, as well as some deficiencies in the published translation, mean that English readers have long been denied an opportunity to make a proper assessment of José Bleger's distinctive contribution to psychoanalysis.

## The value of this book for psychoanalysts today

In recent years there has been a steady growth of interest in very early object relations and their clinical manifestations. In *Symbiosis and Ambiguity* José Bleger made important and original contributions to this area, but the unavailability in English of most of his writings has had the consequence that when related ideas have subsequently been put forward by others they have often appeared without reference to his work.

For example, when Thomas Ogden published his work on the 'autistic-contiguous' position (Ogden, 1989), he cited pioneering work by Esther Bick, Frances Tustin, Donald Meltzer and others, but appeared to be unaware of José Bleger. Noting this, in a letter to the *International Journal of Psychoanalysis*, the Spanish psychoanalyst Rafael Cruz Roche pointed out that thirty years earlier

Bleger had proposed 'concepts which were practically identical' to Ogden's, and he made a plea for more of Bleger's work to be translated (Cruz Roche, 1992). Bleger's ideas were discussed in Horacio Etchegoyen's book *The Fundamentals of Psychoanalytic Technique*, which first appeared in English in 1991, including briefly his views on early adhesive identification, and on symbiosis (Etchegoyen, 1991, pp. 525–534, 622, 755). No further English translations of Bleger's writings appeared, however, and a few years later Rachel Blass and Sidney Blatt could publish a wide-ranging review of the psychoanalytic literature on symbiosis without mentioning him (Blass and Blatt, 1996); the same is true of Judith Mitrani's review of the evolution of the theory of adhesive identification (Mitrani, 2001, Chapter 2).

The motive for publishing this book now is not simply to correct these historical omissions. We think that its value for psychoanalysts today lies in a distinctive view that it offers of early object relations, as these are manifested in the psychoanalytic situation in everyday clinical practice, and in its illustration of a particular way of thinking about this situation 'in the session'. Although written almost a lifetime ago, its combination of theoretical innovation, detailed clinical illustration, and 'clinical thinking' (Green, 2005), makes this book as relevant today as it was when it was first published.

## The context in which the book was written: Argentinian psychoanalysis in the 1950s and 1960s

*Symbiosis and Ambiguity* was written at a time when major events were occurring both in Argentinian society at large and in the world of Argentinian psychoanalysis. José Bleger was personally involved in these events, and deeply affected by them, so that a proper understanding of their part in determining the directions taken by his work would involve a detailed consideration of historical and biographical material. We have avoided any attempt at this, partly for reasons of time and space, but also because our main aim in publishing this translation is to make available to the reader something in José Bleger's work that we believe is of general value to psychoanalysis today as a clinical practice, a method of enquiry and a body of theoretical ideas. Nevertheless, a very brief account of some trends in the Argentinian psychoanalytic movement in the 1950s and 1960s will help to situate the work for the English reader.[2]

The *Asociación Psicoanalítica Argentina* (APA) was founded in 1942. Almost from the beginning, this group was interested not only in 'classical'

2 More detailed surveys can be found in Wender et al. (1992), Plotkin (2001), Etchegoyen and Zysman (2005a, 2005b), Arbiser (2003), Bernardi (2002), Ungar (2005), Taiana (2006). For discussion in Spanish, French and Italian see: Aberastury et al. (1967), Cesio (1981), Cucurullo et al. (1982), Mom (1982), Vezzetti (1996), Civitarese (2004). See also Moreno (1995), Tylim (1996). These lists are not exhaustive.

psychoanalytic practice, but also in problems of psychosomatic illness, the treatment of psychoses, child analysis, problems of groups and of mental health institutions. This may be one of the reasons for the sustained interest of many Argentinian psychoanalysts in the work of Melanie Klein and her school, and their development of a strong current of Kleinian thought. Klein's investigations of early development, her stress on the importance of problems of psychoanalytic technique and the tools that she was able to construct, mainly with the concept of projective identification, were quickly taken on board by the young Argentinian movement.

Problems of countertransference became a focus of interest from early on, so that a preoccupation with countertransference is now for many readers a defining characteristic of Argentinian psychoanalysis. Heinrich Racker's first paper on this subject appeared almost simultaneously with that of Paula Heimann,[3] and his book on technique, which is widely read in English translation (Racker, 1968), became quickly known in Argentina and elsewhere, and was a major point of reference at the end of the 1950s. Racker was one of José Bleger's supervisors during his training.

Interest in countertransference was accompanied by increasing emphasis on the session as the most important 'reality' of psychoanalytic activity, and by a gradual concentration on the here-and-now of the situation, rather than on developmental considerations. One of José Bleger's first psychoanalytic papers was on 'The psychoanalytic session', and we discuss this paper below.

An important influence on José Bleger was that of Enrique Pichon Rivière, a founder member of the APA. Pichon Rivière published little but his teaching became an enduring point of reference for many of the most creative psychoanalysts in Argentina, including Willy and Madeleine Baranger, David Liberman and Salomón Resnik. Some of his ideas and his way of thinking are exemplified and developed by Bleger in this book, in particular his notion of the 'link' (*vinculo*), which is not quite the same as Bion's; his distinction between 'depositor', 'depositary', and 'deposited' in the process of projection; and his conception of the three concentric 'areas' of mind, body, and external world (see below, p. xxxiii, n. 13).

## Structure and composition of the book

*Symbiosis and Ambiguity* is divided into three parts. Part One, comprising Chapters 1–4, is titled 'On Symbiosis'. Part Two, comprising Chapters 5 and 6, is titled 'On Ambiguity'. Part Three comprises Chapters 7–9 and is titled 'Appendix'. The paper on the psychoanalytic setting forms Chapter 6,

3 Racker's paper was delivered to the APA in September, 1948 (Racker, 1953); Heimann's was read at the 16th IPA Congress, Zürich, 1949 (Heimann, 1950).

which is thus the final substantive chapter of the book. It represents a culmination and synthesis of work described in the preceding five chapters, as well as its application to a particular problem in psychoanalytic technique.

From the way in which the book is structured, and from the quantity of original material included in it, it is evident that it was intended as an integrated whole and not simply as a collection of papers. The first four chapters had already appeared separately between 1960 and 1964, but the remaining five, which make up about half of the book, had not been previously published. The fifth and sixth chapters were written in parallel, probably in 1965–66.

As its title suggests, the book explores the relationship between symbiosis and ambiguity as psychological phenomena, in normal mental life and in psychopathology. An exploration is not simply an exposition, however. In the 'Prologue', written shortly before the book was published, José Bleger invites the reader to join him in retracing a journey that has been undertaken over a period of some years, during which he was trying to gain a better understanding of certain problems that he had already grasped intuitively, and to find a way of formulating and conveying them. He writes:

> Since the reader will be following the course of an investigation, I think it will be easily confirmed that between the first chapter and the later ones there are certain conceptual modifications to which I was led by the investigation itself...
>
> (pp. 3–4)

One aspect of this journey is a progressive displacement of emphasis in the investigation, *from* symbiosis *to* ambiguity (which could have been an alternative title for the book), and this is reflected in the labelling of Parts 1 and 2. However, things are not quite so straightforward, for in Chapter 6 symbiosis reappears as a central concept, while ambiguity is mentioned explicitly only once, its theoretical elaboration in the preceding chapters being taken as read.

The following synopsis is intended to help orient the reader. However, those who prefer to approach the text more directly may wish to skip this section.

## Synopsis

Bleger argues in the 'Prologue' that the beginning of human development is characterised by a primitive undifferentiation, and that the primary syncretic structures of psychological life have their roots in corporeal relationships rather than in mental ones. These two points are presented not as vague assertions but rather as hypotheses that imply a radical choice of perspective, an attempt to think about development in a particular way. For Bleger, 'undifferentiation' is not a negative concept defined by the absence of differentiation; instead, undifferentiation has a specific structure and organisation that are evident in the analytic situation, and which can be observed in everyday analytic experience. With the concepts of symbiosis and ambiguity, '... it is not a matter of giving a new name to phenomena that are already familiar, but of re-situating them on the basis of a concept that comes closer to reality' (p. 3). By 'reality' here he means, primarily, the reality of the psychoanalytic session.

## *Chapter 1*

The first chapter is a clinical study of dependence and independence in relation to the process of projection-introjection in the case of a young woman, Maria Cristina, who is suffering acute difficulties in separation from her family. Bleger shows how a disturbance in the process of projection-introjection is evidence of her excessive dependence, and how 'dependence' and 'independence' can be defined in terms of stagnation or mobility of this process.

The case illustrates the co-existence of autism and symbiosis in the transference, both of which are viewed as narcissistic relations with internal objects, in which a part of the mind is 'deposited' by projection. In symbiosis the receiver of the projection, the 'depositary', belongs to the external world, whereas in autism it belongs to a zone of the patient's own mind or body. Massive projection by the patient implies a need to establish a symbiotic transference relation with the analyst, but this relation is narcissistic in character. The patient 'needs to control the analyst (depositary) so that he does not get "inside" her, into her autistic formation, as much as she has to control him from getting into what has been deposited' (p. 12). Re-introjection by the patient is only possible slowly and in small doses, a process in which the body functions as a 'buffer', limiting the disequilibrium.

Maintaining the distinction between depositary and deposited, which he borrows from Pichon Rivière,[4] allows Bleger to distinguish between merely projecting a role, which may have no impact on the depositary, and promoting the acting of a role by the analyst, or delegating one which is already present in the analyst. He argues that in every analysis there is 'a continuous assignment of roles' which needs to be clearly understood by the analyst in order to be able to interpret. The symbiotic relationship 'is a highly

4 In Bleger's own words, Pichon Rivière 'uses the term depositary for the external object into which the projection is made, depositor for the person who makes the projection, and deposited for what is projected'. He adds: 'Discrimination between deposited and depositary makes possible the withdrawal of the projection, and thereby a better understanding of reality' (Bleger, 1963, p. 188).

condensed relation with very complex and contradictory aspects that need to be "broken up" in order to be introjected and worked through by degrees' (p. 24). But strictly speaking, he writes, 'we should speak of symbiosis only when the projections are crossed, and each person acts according to the compensatory roles of the other' (p. 14).

## *Chapter 2*

The limitations of what can be published about symbiosis in the transference and countertransference for reasons of confidentiality, and the advantages of studying it in a situation where it is free to follow its course instead of being modified by the 'fundamentally "antisymbiotic" task' of psychoanalytic treatment (p. 32), lead Bleger to study the symbiotic relationship portrayed in a novel: *Warrior's Rest*, by the French author Christiane Rochefort (1958). It tells the story of Geneviève Le Theil, a student who takes a twenty-four hour trip from Paris to a nearby city to take possession of a legacy from an aunt. At the hotel, she mistakenly enters the room next to hers and finds the body of a man, Jean Renaud, who has evidently attempted suicide. She intervenes to save his life, and from that moment on she feels herself tied to his fate. She visits him at the hospital the following day, and as he is discharged they embark on a symbiotic relationship in which compulsive sexual activity is a way of communicating in which the roles are stabilised. Some time later she returns to Paris with him, and through a series of crises they eventually manage a kind of separation.

Bleger shows how the relationship is established as a 'pact' between the protagonists, each using the other as a depositary for parts of themselves by which they are threatened, and this is experienced by Geneviève as a bodily metamorphosis. Each functions as the other's sole depositary, to the exclusion of other relationships:

> The symbiotic link is thus a pact with the dead, destroyed and dangerous parts of its members, who 'pledge themselves to each other' in order to carry a corpse they hold in common. However, it is a pact for life and for the possibility of continuing to live. *The secret of symbiosis is that of a living corpse that needs to be kept, controlled and immobilized by the participants*; if control is lost, destruction or at least the risk of it ensues.
>
> (p. 46)

One day they quarrel, Renaud walks out, and from then on the symbiosis becomes progressively more disequilibrated. Eventually Renaud leaves altogether, Geneviève contracts tuberculosis, she enters a sanatorium and waits for death.

In the second part of the novel, the situation is reversed: Renaud returns to save Geneviève's life and the pact is renewed. By now other parties have become involved, and the relationship breaks down again, but this time more quickly. The novel ends with Renaud in an asylum, and Geneviève pregnant and alone.

Elaborating on the conclusions of the preceding chapter Bleger describes the symbiosis as a relationship with a unitary 'agglutinated' object, characterised by syncretism and lack of discrimination, and subject to immobilisation and control, including by the use of compulsive sexuality. Loss of this control results in massive, paroxistic mobilisation, with catastrophic anxiety and a risk of psychotic disintegration. Contact with other people, and a shift towards a more perverse-polymorphous sexuality, result in a partial fragmentation of the agglutinated object, and the beginning of a slow working-through, with some awareness.

The agglutinated object is also described as *glischroid* (from the Greek *γλισχροσ*, meaning 'viscous'), and in a footnote Bleger explains that this term was introduced by F. Minkowska in her discussion of viscosity and adhesiveness as characteristic of epileptoidia (Minkowska, 1956).[5] 'Viscosity', he writes, 'is the phenomenon resulting from the link with an agglutinated object' (p. 34).

## *Chapter 3*

This brief and schematic chapter outlines a central thesis of the book: that prior to the paranoid-schizoid position as described by Melanie Klein there is a position, whose characteristic anxiety is confusional rather than persecutory, and in which the object relation is one of symbiosis with a primitive 'agglutinated nucleus'. Bleger calls this the *glischro-caric* position (from *γλισχροσ* meaning 'viscous', and *καρυον* meaning 'kernel' or 'nucleus'). In support of this thesis he refers in the first page of this chapter to passages

5 Minkowska wrote: 'When in 1923, on the basis of my genealogical research, I presented to the Medico-Psychological Society [in Paris] my first paper on epileptoidia, the point that was most discussed was viscosity and adhesiveness, which were relatively new elements . . . To mark the importance of viscosity we have introduced, following a suggestion by Pichon, the term glischroidia. We wanted to introduce this term definitively into our nomenclature in order to avoid . . . any imprecision or misunderstanding attached to the term epileptoidia.' (Minkowska, 1956, p. 110, our translation). She is referring to her first published paper (Minkowska, 1923). Her husband refers to 'the viscous and adhesive affectivity of the epileptoid or glischroid – from *γλισχροσ* – described by Mrs Minkowska as the constitutional basis of the manifestations of epilepsy' (Minkowski, 1953, pp. 67–68, our translation). (The Pichon mentioned by Minkowska here is the French psychoanalyst Edouard Pichon, and not Enrique Pichon Rivière.)

in Klein's work, as well as in Fairbairn's, which mention an incomplete differentiation between the good and bad objects in the first months of life (p. 72).

He also shifts in this chapter to using the term 'agglutinated nucleus' instead of agglutinated object, because:

> there is, strictly speaking, no real object relation between the objects and the ego nuclei therein, but a true 'primary identification', which is the term Fairbairn used for those states in which differentiation has not occurred between the object and the part of the ego that is related to it. (p. 74)

This nucleus persists in adults as the psychotic part of the personality, whose vicissitudes will be explored in the following chapter through clinical illustrations. It also constitutes the earliest form of the Oedipus complex, characterised by fusion and non-discrimination of the parents.

The chapter ends with a summary table indicating the characteristic anxiety, object, defences and fixation point of the glischro-caric position in comparison to those of the paranoid-schizoid and depressive positions.

## *Chapter 4*

At the beginning of this chapter, which is titled 'Study of the psychotic part of the personality', Bleger writes that an advantage of preserving the clinical autonomy of symbiosis is that it enables him to understand in a unified way a number of clinical phenomena that are dynamically related. He links this observation to psychoanalytic technique, stating that his discussion of the handling of the agglutinated nucleus is not innovative, but rather an attempt to 'define precisely, understand and ground in a unitary manner various technical alternatives that are largely implicit in what every psychoanalyst does to some extent in the course of a treatment' (p. 81).

The agglutinated nucleus is equated with the psychotic part of the personality, as Bion had described it some years previously in two papers (Bion 1956, 1957). In keeping with mainstream psychoanalytic practice in Argentina in the 1950s and 1960s, Bleger thinks of the psychotic part of the personality primarily in bodily terms, and he considers that its analysis requires 'mobilisation, fragmentation and discrimination' (p. 89). *Mobilisation* because the symbiotic transference implies immobilisation of important parts of the personality; *fragmentation* because these parts tend to function in a massive (quasi-psychotic) way; and *discrimination* because the elements are undifferentiated. All three steps depend on the capacity of the analyst to introduce a split between himself and what is deposited in him. The agglutinated nucleus has to be 'broken up' before discrimination and schizoid division will be possible. This requires the alternating and complementary use of two types of interpretation:

> In the first case – the split interpretation – we show patients their relation with themselves, or what they do with a part of themselves to another part of themselves, while in the latter case – interpretation without splitting – we include ourselves in the interpretation without differentiating the internal object of the depositary.[6]
>
> (p. 91)

At the end of this theoretical introduction to Chapter 4 Bleger links the discrimination that is involved in naming these 'technical alternatives' to the discrimination that is promoted in the patient by psychoanalysing the symbiosis. Both involve 'giving names to things that we already know', but that this is only possible 'when they acquire a certain identity as a result of discrimination' (p. 93). The recommendations in this chapter are thus not simply indications for technique but part of a broader methodological approach.

This approach is illustrated by clinical material from the case of a woman patient, Ana Maria, who was in the process of separating from her husband. Her abandonment of her medical degree when she married, and her difficulty in later resuming it, were symptoms of the blockage of an agglutinated nucleus replete with oedipal conflicts whose protagonists have remained undiscriminated. Attempts to mobilise this part of her personality by interpretation are met by heavy silences and tension which for a long time tend also to immobilise the analyst. When the analysis succeeds in dispersing the agglutinated nucleus to some extent, she experiences this as being left in pieces between the sessions, like the pastry that she tries to make for a dessert but which won't hold together. In a detailed account of three consecutive sessions Bleger shows how, in a rhythmical alternation of re-projection and re-introjection, the agglutinated nucleus is analysed little by little and the various identifications of the oedipal situation become more discriminated, leading gradually to a capacity for more mature independence. Using further clinical material from the same patient, and building on observations by Klein and by Rosenfeld, he shows how the successive re-introjections are marked by various kinds of confusion that indicate regression to the glischro-caric position, and a return to the fusion of an original non-discrimination.

6 He relates this distinction to Strachey's (1934) paper, and it can be seen as anticipating Steiner's (1993, 1994) distinction between patient-centred and analyst-centred interpretations.

## Chapter 5

This chapter explores both the concept of ambiguity and its presentation in manifestations of the agglutinated nucleus, with numerous clinical examples. Although Bleger realized quite early that the agglutinated nucleus was ambiguous in character, it was only gradually that he fully understood the significance and the implications of this fact. An important shift of focus between Chapters 4 and 5 is from the study of the split-off psychotic part of the personality, which functions as a nucleus of symbiotic dependence and which is ambiguous due to its lack of discrimination, to the multiple personalities by virtue of which the ego itself is ambiguous; that is, to a particular kind of identity or 'granular' organization of the ego as a multiplicity of non-integrated nuclei (p. 165).[7] Whereas in the previous chapter Bleger studies the agglutinated nucleus as split off from the more integrated part of the ego, in Chapter 5 it is the ambiguity of the symbiotic nucleus itself which is in the foreground. He writes:

> Up until my most recent work on the theme of symbiosis, I studied its persistence (as dependence) in subjects who had reached a more integrated ego, in whom these nuclei of symbiotic dependence were managed by maintaining a strong splitting from the more integrated ego. In this way I studied the agglutinated nucleus and the glischro-caric position. I want to suggest that in these cases the symbiosis persists *as a nucleus* and to some extent also this exists in every human being, because of deficient discrimination in the split-off part of the more integrated ego. In these studies I identified the eminently ambiguous character of this agglutinated nucleus. What I want to do now is to examine the inverse situation, in which the more integrated ego is only a minimal part of the personality and the latter functions totally or predominantly with an organisation that keeps the symbiosis to the fore. This requires me to study ambiguity *per se*, as it presents in different personality types or traits, unlike the earlier studies in which I studied the dynamics of the agglutinated nucleus in its different manifestations (hypochondria, epilepsy, mania, melancholia, etc.). Strictly speaking, these latter manifestations depend on the defence of the more integrated ego against the possibility of invasion by the agglutinated nucleus.
>
> (p. 208)

Ambiguity is carefully distinguished from ambivalence, contradiction, divalence, dissociation, and confusion, and equated instead with undifferentiation,

7 See pp. 165, 167, 172. The notion of a 'granular' ego is similar to Glover's (1943) concept of a primitive 'multinuclear' ego. Bleger cites this paper by Glover in a different context (p. 133, n. 106).

in which different terms co-exist without contradiction or conflict because they have never been discriminated. The agglutinated nucleus is present in everyone, and is normally split off from the more mature ego. In an 'ambiguous personality', where this split is absent or reduced, the personality is a direct expression of the agglutinated nucleus.

Bleger distinguishes four ways in which this typically happens. The ambiguous personality may persist as a '*syncretic ego*', lacking firm attachments and characterised by a constantly shifting identity, shallowness and inconsistency, giving rise to an impression of 'fictitiousness'. Or it may be partly organized as a '*factic ego*': attached to an institution, group, or person from which it has not yet distinguished itself, the ego exists only *in* the action, the job, etc., without interiority.[8] A similar absence of interiority is found in *psychopathy*, but whereas the factic ego 'accepts' the ambiguity and makes it central, in psychopathy the ambiguity is split off and deposited destructively in the external world through psychopathic acting. A fourth possibility is when the syncretic ego becomes extremely and rigidly polarised around just one of its nuclei of ambiguity, giving rise to the '*authoritarian personality*' as described by Brunswick and Adorno. These main types were previously situated in a wider panorama of vicissitudes of symbiosis and ambiguity (see p. 171).

In distinguishing the various forms of ambiguous personality Bleger remarks that he is 'describing a typology and not necessarily a pathology' (p. 176, n. 128). He points out that although ambiguity may involve contradiction for the observer, 'there is no contradiction for the subject, since this has not yet come into play' (p. 175). As well as comparing each type with the mature ego, he maintains that we should 'study each structure in itself and its own organisation'. This point is elaborated towards the end of the chapter, where he urges that instead of regarding illness as an entity, as in Kraepelin's nosology, we study the mobile and changing organisations or structures of behaviour and personality, with their dynamic interrelations (p. 224).

It is a methodological principle of Bleger's writing to avoid thinking solely in pathological terms with the normative notion of 'deficit', and to allow for other kinds of identity and other senses of reality. In using the expression 'syncretic ego', for example, he seeks to define the ambiguous personality 'in terms not of what it is lacking but of what it is'. The syncretic ego is understood as an ensemble of personal relations, and Bleger compares this to the way the anthropologist Maurice Leenhardt understood personal identity in a Melanesian society (pp. 181–2).

The implication for Bleger's contribution to Kleinian theory becomes clear when he writes:

> If we accept primary undifferentiation, the statement that the first psychological mechanism is projection (as postulated by Melanie Klein)

8 For Bleger, 'factic' (*fáctico*) means based on doing, on action.

> is also placed in doubt, and the same applies to projective-introjective identification. It is a question of primary identification (Fairbairn); both projection-introjection, and massive projective-introjective identification appear as phenomena of a more integrated ego (although still in its earliest forms) which uses them to 'manage' ambiguity by keeping it split. (pp. 185–6)

The syncretic ego operates in a simpler way that Bleger, borrowing a term from Levy-Bruhl, calls 'participation':

> The phenomenon of participation does not inevitably require the hypothesis of projective-introjective identification; instead, participation consists in the mobilisation and actualisation of levels of the personality that function directly with that structure. Having to accept, as we are in the habit of doing, the existence of projective-introjective identification in all cases, requires that we consider each subject a 'closed system' that communicates with other human beings through diverse channels; whereas, accepting participation as an originary phenomenon implies the hypothesis that human beings begin or start out from an organisation that is an 'open system', gradually becoming individualised and personified. (pp. 186–7)

By now it is clear that he has moved from the theoretical position developed in Chapters 1 and 2, in which symbiosis involves massive projection into a depositary, to one in which ambiguity results from syncretic participation in an activity or group, without the use of defences characteristic of the paranoid-schizoid position. This amounts to a revision and clarification of the scheme presented in Chapter 3, and is an example of the 'conceptual modifications' referred to in the 'Prologue'.

The clinical material in this chapter also illustrates a defensive function of regression to the ambiguity of the glischro-caric position during psychoanalytic sessions, as a way of 'blunting' or 'taking the edge off' persecutory situations. Similarly, it can serve as a shock-absorber against the impact of insight.

Chapters 5 and 6 were written in parallel, and where the discussion in Chapter 5 touches on questions of psychoanalytic technique and treatment it anticipates the discussion of the setting in Chapter 6. The persistence of an ambiguous personality in the adult is due, Bleger suggests, to a lack of 'trustworthy' depositaries in early childhood, and he concludes that one of the functions of psychoanalytic treatment is to provide a symbiosis that was lacking or distorted, this function being provided by the setting. The therapeutic aim, however, is not a permanent restoration of the symbiosis, as if this were a kind of idyllic fusion. Rather, it is the temporary provision of a good-enough symbiosis as a prerequisite for a lasting escape from symbiosis into maturity: 'Children need a secure symbiosis that permits them to count on a depositary or 'supplementary ego' so that they may face their greed and destructive envy' (p. 209).

## Chapter 6

In this chapter Bleger considers the psychoanalytic setting from different conceptual viewpoints: as a 'non-process', as the background of a *Gestalt*, as a social institution, as part of the body schema, as a non-ego or meta-ego, etc. This allows him to characterise the setting more fully than hitherto but it is the preceding work on symbiosis and particularly on ambiguity which provides him with the basis for a new theoretical understanding of the nature of the setting.

The chapter begins by defining the psychoanalytic situation as comprised of an analytic process and a 'non-process'. The 'non-process' is the setting, which is held constant and within which the analytic process occurs. Sometimes the setting does change, 'from the background of a *Gestalt* into a figure, that is, into a process' (p. 229), but only when something happens to make us aware of its existence. Such changes are usually temporary, because as clinicians we seek to maintain or restore the setting, to return it to the background, so that we can continue to observe and analyse the process that is occurring within it.

Bleger points out that a psychoanalytic relationship is itself a particular kind of social institution and he argues that institutions actually form parts of our personalities, so that personal identity is at least partly constituted by belonging to, and participating in, a group, an ideology or an institution. This radical position has been anticipated by clinical material in Chapters 1 and 5, and by the discussion of the ambiguous personality in Chapter 5, particularly the 'factic ego'.

Since this participation is partly syncretic, and lacking in mind-body discrimination, social institutions also partly determine the body schema. In other words, our body schemata, the internal representations of our own bodies, partly consist of internalised versions of the institutions in which we participate.

Just as in neurology the body schema reveals itself in the phenomenon of the 'phantom limb' following an amputation, so the psychoanalytic setting makes its presence known only when it is broken. As long as the setting is *not* broken, it remains unnoticed. The normal, silent, continuous, background presence of the setting thus furnishes the patient with an opportunity for repeating the original symbiosis of the infant with the mother. The psychotic part of the patient's personality, the undifferentiated and unresolved part of the primitive symbiotic relationship, is deposited in the setting, where it silently persists as a 'phantom world', undetected but nonetheless psychically real. The primitive organisation that was studied in Chapter 5 as an aspect of the personality is now found to be inhabiting the session itself.

Because in psychoanalysis much of the symbiosis resides in the setting, and is not present in the analytic process where it might be observed 'in action', the setting forms a persistent, tenacious, and invisible 'bastion',[9] a refuge for the psychotic part of the personality, which demands that nothing shall change. Precisely because the setting is so much respected and preserved in psychoanalysis, much of this area of the mind may never be analysed.

The implications for psychoanalytic technique are that at some point the setting itself has to be analysed, and the analyst–patient relationship has to be 'de-symbiotised', but this will meet strong resistance because the symbiosis is something which has never before been recognised by the patient.

The final part of Bleger's argument involves his recognition that the patient brings his or her own setting, which is not the same as the analyst's. Among the examples he gives is that of a patient, whose treatment he supervised, who proposed to use the familiar form of address when speaking to the analyst.[10] Only by eventually interpreting this, was it possible to reveal the narcissism and omnipotence of the patient, and his use of the familiar form to suppress the person and role of the analyst. Bleger concludes:

> The analyst needs to accept the setting brought by the patient . . . because within it will be found in summary form the primitive unresolved symbiosis. However, we need to state at the same time that accepting the patient's meta-ego (his setting) does not mean giving up the therapist's own, as a function of which it is possible to analyse the process and the setting itself when this has been transformed it into process . . . In sum, we may say that the patient's setting is his most primitive fusion with the mother's body and that the psychoanalyst's setting must serve to re-establish the original symbiosis, but only in order to change it. Both the disruption of the setting and its ideal or normal maintenance are technical and theoretical problems, but what fundamentally disturbs the possibility of thoroughgoing treatment is the disruption introduced or accepted by the psychoanalyst in the setting. *The setting can only be analysed within the setting*; in other words, the patient's dependence and most primitive psychological organisation can only be analysed within the analyst's setting, which should be neither ambiguous nor changing, nor altered.
>
> (pp. 240–1)

9 The concept of 'bastion' (*baluarte*) is borrowed from Baranger, M. and Baranger, W. (1961–62).

10 In Spanish, when addressing another person, use of the informal *tú* in place of the more formal *Usted* may, depending on the context, be experienced as excessively familiar or disrespectful.

## Chapters 7–9

The remaining chapters form an Appendix which reviews the literature on ambivalence and ambiguity, and discusses two relevant articles by Freud.

Chapter 7 reviews the history of the psychoanalytic literature on ambivalence and ambiguity, beginning with Bleuler's introduction of the term 'ambivalence', and Freud's use of both concepts. Following Pichon Rivière, Bleger distinguishes ambivalence from 'divalence', which is developmentally prior to ambivalence and refers to antinomic elements (feelings, tendencies or attitudes) which are kept apart by schizoid division, whereas ambivalence implies the co-existence of elements in relation to the same object at the same time, and thus a degree of integration in the depressive position.[11] Ambivalence always indicates conflict, whereas divalence always indicates potential or avoided conflict, and both are distinguished from reaction-formation. The implications of these distinctions and the use of related terminology are traced in some detail through Freud's work, and then in work by Klein, Fairbairn, Abraham, Glover, Sterba, Langer, Bose, Stephen, Scott, Wisdom, Kris and Kaplan, and Tarachow. The review gives Bleger an opportunity to test the utility of his classification by mapping it onto the ideas of these authors, to extend it in places, and to develop a capacity to distinguish more accurately between analytic situations that might be seen as similar.

Chapter 8 is a commentary on Freud's (1910b) paper, 'The antithetical meaning of primal words', and argues that the hypothesis of primitive undifferentiation offers a simpler explanation than Freud's for the appearance in dreams and in language of elements that apparently express contradictory meanings. Benveniste's (1956) critique of the etymological speculations by Abel, which Freud had used to support his argument, is included.

Chapter 9, the last of the book, is about Freud's (1919) paper 'The "Uncanny"'. What interests Bleger here is the appearance of the uncanny when something ambiguous mobilises the 'syncretic ego', *i.e.* the non-ego, and the chapter elaborates ideas in Chapters 5 and 6 concerning the phantom world created and inhabited by the 'factic' personality, and its presence in the psychoanalytic setting. What for Freud is a return of the repressed, Bleger regards as a breakdown in the normal splitting between the ego and the non-ego.

In some ways the three final chapters simply extend many passages earlier in the book in which Bleger sifts through the psychoanalytic literature on undifferentiation, and in part this is done in acknowledgement of the influences on his work and in recognition of his debts to other authors. However, these chapters also demonstrate that undifferentiation and ambiguity

11 What Bleger calls 'divalence', Fairbairn (1941, p. 257) called 'dichotomy' (see p. 271).

have been present in psychoanalytic thought from the beginning. Moreover, they help to make clear a radical inversion, resulting from the gradual introduction of the idea of participation or syncretism, in Bleger's way of thinking these concepts. By the end of the book, symbiosis and ambiguity are no longer simply aspects of the transference-countertransference but ubiquitous features of mental life.

## The relation between this book and the rest of José Bleger's work

José Bleger wrote on a wide range of issues. Besides his practice and teaching as a psychoanalyst in the *Asociación Psicoanalítica Argentina*, he was a well-known and reputable Professor of Psychology at the University of Buenos Aires. In this context he wrote many papers and three other books: *Psicología de la Conducta* [*The Psychology of Behaviour*] (1963), *Psicohigiene y Psicología Institucional* [*Psychohygiene and the Psychology of Institutions*] (1966) and a compilation of five important papers, *Temas de Psicología* [*Psychological Themes*] (1971b). The first of these books became a classic in Argentina and other Latin American countries and is now in its nineteenth reprinting.

A thorough study of his writings would require careful consideration of the importance of his psychoanalytic views in other fields of his work, mainly in the teaching of psychology but also in the work on groups and institutions which informs some of the ideas in Chapter 6. But such a study is beyond the scope of this Introduction. We confine ourselves here primarily to papers that have some connection with *Symbiosis and Ambiguity,* only briefly mentioning other psychoanalytic papers and giving a brief account of those in other fields. Our intention is to give the reader only an overview of the development of Bleger's ideas. A definitive bibliography is not yet available, but the list compiled by David Maldavsky, although incomplete, gives a good idea of the range of Bleger's work (Maldavsky, 1973).

One of Bleger's first psychoanalytic papers was on 'La sesión psicoanalítica' ['The psychoanalytic session'], written in 1957 and published as a chapter of his book *Psicoanálisis y Dialéctica Materialista* [*Psychoanalysis and Dialectical Materialism*] (Bleger, 1958). The title of the book is somewhat misleading as it is a critical study of the epistemological presuppositions or assumptions of psychoanalysis, starting from the work of the French Marxist philosopher Georges Politzer and arguing that these should be understood in terms of dramatics rather than dynamics.[12] The paper develops Pichon Rivière's idea of the transferential interaction between patient and analyst as a 'dialectical spiral' in the 'here and now' of the session. It was written as an introduction to a clinical presentation at the APA which considered in

12 See the comments by Horacio Etchegoyen in the 'Preface', p. xiii.

detail all of the implications for the patient *and the analyst* of just *one* session, which could not be published in its entirety. But the paper is also a methodological reflection on the evolution of psychoanalysis and on the importance gradually acquired by the psychoanalytic session, its setting and the field that it represents, which finally became transformed into an object of investigation. The 1957 paper is clearly a precursor to the one on the setting that later appeared as Chapter 6 of the present book and in the *International Journal of Psychoanalysis*.

During the period in which the various chapters of *Symbiosis and Ambiguity* were written, José Bleger published two other papers directly related to symbiosis, both of them presented to the internal Congress of the APA in 1964 and published in 1966: 'Psicopatía como deficit de la personificación' ['Psychopathy as a deficit of personification'] written with L. S. de Bleger, G. R. de García Reinoso and D. García Reinoso (Bleger et al., 1966), and as sole author, 'Simbiosis, Psicopatía y Manía' ['Symbiosis, psychopathy and mania'] (Bleger, 1966b). In the first of these psychopathy is considered as a developmental disorder and not as a defensive one, *i.e.* essentially as an early deficit of symbolization. Following Freud's idea of the ego as initially a bodily ego and using Pichon Rivière's concept of the three areas[13] the authors consider that the process of symbolization, which pertains to the construction of the mind (*i.e.* of 'area one') in the relationship with the earliest figures, is lacking or seriously limited. This primitive relationship is syncretic; more precisely, there is a 'syncretic organization' rather than a 'syncretic relationship' (Bleger et al., 1966, p. 265). In the second paper Bleger considers psychopathy and mania as a way of controlling the agglutinated nucleus and as a primitive deficit in the installation of the symbiosis. This view of psychopathy as a vicissitude of symbiosis was overtaken by the shift between Chapters 4 and 5 of *Symbiosis and Ambiguity*, away from the splitting of the symbiosis or psychotic part of the personality, to the study of the ambiguous personalities built on the syncretism, including psychopathy.

In one of Bleger's three papers already available in English, 'Schizophrenia, Autism and Symbiosis', written in 1970 and therefore some time after the publication of *Symbiosis and Ambiguity*, he considers the psychoanalytic therapy of schizophrenics (Bleger, 1974). There are, he states, three

13 In *Psicología de la Conducta* Bleger writes: 'Following Pichon Rivière, we represent the three types of behaviour by three concentric circles, numbered one, two and three, and corresponding respectively to mental phenomena, bodily phenomena, and the phenomena of action in the external world . . . He calls these circles "areas of behaviour"' (Bleger, 1963, p. 29, our translation). In an important footnote to the present work (p. 199, n. 152), Bleger also refers to his own 'principle of equivalence of the areas' and briefly outlines his view that the earliest psychological phenomena are not mental, and that the child's psychological organisation starts out as an 'open system' that gradually closes up, and not (as Margaret Mahler supposed) as a 'closed system' (autism) that gradually opens up.

fundamental technical positions: one which 'allows neither deposition[14] or symbiosis', another which supports the inclusion of the therapist in a truly psychotic symbiosis (Searles, 1965) and 'a third (Rosenfeld, 1965; Bion, 1957; Pichon Rivière, 1961) which admits and uses deposition but does not enter into a symbiotic relationship as a technical aim'. If the aim is 'to build a symbiosis which is different from the pathological one on which the personality was based', then it must be a symbiosis for the patient and not for the therapist 'who must "withdraw", counter-transferentially, from the pathological symbiosis reproduced in the therapeutic relationship' (Bleger, 1974, pp. 20–21). In this paper he mentions an important distinction which may have led him to take further the investigation pursued in *Symbiosis and Ambiguity*. He writes:

> 'Syncretism' defines a structure in which there is no discrimination (the paranoid-schizoid position has not been established). When this indiscrimination belongs to, or is a remnant of, the first stages of development, I call it *syncytial structure*.[15] Syncretism can be found in both normal and pathological symbiosis, in the psychotic restoration, whereas the *syncytial structure* is normally found in the very beginnings of the development of the personality and in a certain type of symbiosis (or part of a symbiosis) which is not established by projective identification.
>
> (Bleger, 1974, p. 22)

With this distinction and considering that in all schizophrenics there is a co-existence of autism and symbiosis, it is possible for Bleger to reconsider the different clinical presentations of schizophrenia in a unitary way. The psychoanalytic treatment of psychosis, a problem which interested many Argentinian psychoanalysts, is not examined in *Symbiosis and Ambiguity* where the main concern is with psychotic aspects of the transference, *i.e.* in clinically non-psychotic patients, and not the transference of psychotic patients. The syncytium is briefly mentioned in the book, however, when describing a patient (Ana Maria) who for a while was unable to distinguish between her own body and that of the analyst (p. 101).

In a paper on psychoses published in 1971, he takes up once more the difference between 'the syncytial structure' as the most primitive organization and 'syncretism' as that part of the personality which still functions in an undifferentiated way and which hasn't developed towards discrimination (Bleger, 1971a). This distinction allows him to consider the fundamental concepts with which psychoanalysis has tried to understand the psychotic process. He suggests that we should distinguish between psychotic

14 *Depositación*, which in the present book we translate by 'depositation'.

15 In biology, a syncytium is a cell-like structure filled with cytoplasm and containing multiple nuclei.

disintegration, psychotic restitution, the psychotic part of the personality and psychotic personality. This conceptual reformulation permits a more adequate approach to understanding the psychotic process and its various clinical manifestations.

In 1971, Bleger wrote a paper for the *World Biennial of Psychiatry and Psychotherapy*, edited by Silvano Arieti, in which he manages to present in less than twenty pages, in a clearly articulated way, the hypothesis developed in *Symbiosis and Ambiguity* (Bleger, 1973a). It is evidently an after-effect (an *après-coup*) of the book and in it he reconsiders the importance of the 'factic personality'. As in the book, he uses Leenhardt's scheme to convey the general structure of ambiguous personalities, of which the factic personality is one variety.[16] He writes:

> The factic personality's dependency on obsessive fixation to objects and persons shows a lack of discrimination between the ego and the object. They *are* the relation. No true interpersonal relation is established. His identity is formed by these relations or functions that he establishes with the objects. He does not speak about himself or his experiences; he speaks about others. But this is the only way he can refer to himself. He has a group or institutional identity; this does not mean that he depends on or belongs to a function, a group or an institution: he *is* the function, the group, or the institution. This is or may be all the identity he has. He defines himself or is identified by what he does or by his membership in groups. If these fail his ego is actually disorganized.
>
> (Bleger, 1973a, p. 460)

Describing the different types of personality already considered in Chapter 5, he introduces a further consideration:

> Although some of these personalities may become openly pathological, I believe they should not be entirely included in pathology, but in varieties of personification. In this sense, all ambiguous personalities are included in one chapter[17] for which a term suggested by E. Pichon Rivière seems adequate: dispersonalisation.... This term 'dispersonalisation'[18] also includes ambiguity processes that appear in normal development, such as in adolescence and in period of crisis.
>
> (Bleger, 1973a, pp. 464–465)

16 Unfortunately, in the version included in Arieti's volume, the wrong diagram appears in the text at this point due to a publishing error, and the correct diagram appears in a different paper elsewhere in the same volume.

17 *i.e.* 'under one heading'.

18 On 'dispersonalisation' see p. 167, n. 119.

These two points, the clear description of the factic personality and regarding it as a process which also appears in normal development, allow him to write at the very end of the paper:

> It is possible to assume, as a hypothesis derived from the above concepts, that the factic structure is a pattern of the most primitive psychological organization, which is followed by a gradual 'interiorisation' of primary identifications leading gradually, under normal conditions, to individuation and personification. All the alternatives for the agglutinate nucleus discussed in this chapter appear normally in the course of development, and it is these alternatives that enable a partial working through of the normal symbiotic situation.
>
> (Bleger, 1973a, p. 468)

The hypothesis of the primitive organization of the personality as factic is consistent with Bleger's idea of the construction of the infant's world in the relationship with external figures, *i.e.* in Pichon Rivière's 'area three'.[19] This helps to explain Bleger's interest in groups and institutions and why his papers on psychoanalysis cannot easily be separated off from his papers on these subjects.

In Bleger's view, identity is not principally sustained by the most developed and consolidated aspect of the personality (which is of course a part of identity), but by the most primitive fusion and by states of non-discrimination, the 'syncytial structure' referred to above. It is the persistence of this primitive structure on which identity essentially depends throughout life.

In a paper written in 1971 for a congress on adolescent identity, he suggests that the crisis of adolescence is precisely a crisis of the 'syncytial structure', which accounts for its importance and its radical character, a crisis of the foundations on which the whole of the personality is structured. The identity of the adolescent may then be considered as a poly-identity or 'multiple identity', mixing up different levels with 'the mobilization, disorganization and superposition of all of them at the same time' (Bleger, 1973b, p. 11, our translation). In this paper, as in the 'Prologue' to *Symbiosis and Ambiguity*, Bleger takes up once more the problem of which approach to adopt: whether to consider early mother-infant relations as an interaction between two autonomous beings, or as a symbiotic situation from which eventually two differentiated personalities may emerge. Pushing his hypothesis further, he writes at the end of the paper:

> There remains the task of rethinking the relations between the individual, society and culture, since we no longer can speak of an ego-culture

19 See p. xxxiii, n. 13.

> relation as between two autonomous and independent entities that are interacting, but rather that from the psychological point of view, what is not included in the ego is the non-ego or syncretic ego and that is just as psychological as what we call the ego.
>
> (Bleger, 1973b, p. 14, our translation)

One of Pichon Rivière's most important contributions had been his concept of the 'single illness', which arose from his search for a psychoanalytic theory capable of encompassing the illness itself, the processes of falling ill and of recovery, and the therapeutic process. In a paper written as a homage to Pichon Rivière, Bleger characterizes this approach in a very clear way:

> The theory of the single illness allows us to understand in a unified way the dynamic relation between normal and pathological processes, as well as the transitions and relations between neurosis, psychosis, perversions, psychopathies and psychosomatic illnesses. At the same time, it allows us to follow step by step the onset and course of an illness, as well as the alternatives of a psychiatric or a psychoanalytic treatment.
>
> (Bleger, 1967b, p. 348, our translation)

Several other papers by Bleger, most of them unpublished, are part of a project to build a psychoanalytic psychopathology by taking symbiosis and ambiguity, and particularly the agglutinated nucleus, as starting points in a search for a unified theory. What would be specific to each variety of psychological illness would be, on the one hand, the way in which the splitting is maintained to preserve the most integrated ego, and on the other hand the relationship between the agglutinated nucleus and the ego once this splitting has collapsed or disappeared. A third important element would be the loss of a depositary and the consequent danger of ego disintegration.

Thus, in 'Perversiones' ['Perversions'], written in collaboration with N. Cvik and B. Grunfeld, perverse acting is characterised as an egodystonic manifestation of this splitting but with a particular handling of the situation: 'during the perverse acting the more integrated ego is submitted to and in the service of the display of the identifications of the psychotic part' (Bleger, Cvik and Grunfeld, 1973, p. 355, our translation). Although the more integrated ego, during the perverse acting, retains the sense of reality there exists a 'transaction' which makes him accept another reality, as already pointed out by Freud.

In 'Duelo y sus vicisitudes' ['Mourning and its vicissitudes'], published posthumously in 1973 and probably in the same series, Bleger considers two kind of sociability, one syncretic and the other interactive, depending on the degree of discrimination between subject and object (Bleger, 1973c). If every mourning implies a certain proportion of depression and melancholia, as is usually accepted in the classical psychoanalytic theory, the proportion will depend on the nature of the relationship to the object *before* its loss: the more the relationship was one of a syncretic sociability, asserts Bleger, the more the result will be melancholia; and conversely, the more the relationship was characterised by a sociability of interaction, the more the outcome will be the possibility of normal mourning and its resolution.

During the period in which he was writing *Symbiosis and Ambiguity*, Bleger also prepared the three-volume edition of the *Psychological Writings of Georges Politzer* in Spanish, with long prefaces and appendices (Politzer, 1965–66). Horacio Etchegoyen, in his preface to the present work, clearly brings out the importance of Politzer's critique of psychoanalysis for José Bleger's ideas. Bleger used Politzer's critique as a basis for clarifying the presuppositions of psychoanalysis and the relationship between its theory and its practice.

In 1969 there was a crisis in the relationship between the theory and practice of psychoanalysis in Argentina, when two groups of psychoanalysts who were members of the APA, some of them prominent members (and including one of its founders, Marie Langer), resigned from the institution because in their view, its organisation and ways of functioning were incompatible with the political commitment required in the political and social situation that had developed in Argentina. Despite his Marxist orientation, Bleger was in complete disagreement with their position and did not resign. He partly explains his position in a paper written at this time, in which he reconsiders once more the relationship between the theory and practice of psychoanalysis, but now from the standpoint of what he called 'psychoanalytic praxis': he argues that the 'institution' (not only as an organization but taking also into account the way in which psychoanalysis is taught), must be viewed as an important part of this praxis, informed by an implicit theory, and not simply as an excrescence or something external to psychoanalysis itself.

In a trenchant assessment of the situation and development of psychoanalysis in the same paper, he wonders whether the criticism that we make of some 'wild psychoanalysts', is not a 'criticism that we spare ourselves when it concerns our own theory. We are possibly carrying a legacy from a time when all psychoanalysis was "wild psychoanalysis"' (Bleger, 1969). In another paper written at the same time (Bleger, 1971c), he states that psychoanalytic institutions have on the whole tended to bring about an impoverishment of investigation: instead of using psychoanalysis clinically as a research method, they have merely 'applied' existing knowledge: 'they look for what they already know, and they don't try to find out what they don't know' (p. 122). In his view, psychoanalysis has not yet really developed its own epistemological procedures and this represents a challenge for the methodology of science.

We have omitted many other papers by José Bleger, and the various papers and books that he was working on at the time of his death. This brief survey may be sufficient, however, to give the reader a view of the way in which he saw his work in the different psychoanalytic fields of clinical practice, work in institutions and with groups, theoretical work, and teaching, as all interrelated.

## Commentary on José Bleger's work in the psychoanalytic movement

At the time of his death in 1972 José Bleger was one of Argentina's best-known psychoanalysts and his reputation extended to other Latin-American countries such as Uruguay, Brazil and Venezuela. Many Argentinian and Latin-American analysts recognize his influence in their own work, among them Elsa Rappoport de Aisemberg, Luis Allegro, Silvia Amati Sas (in Italy), Raúl Jorge Aragonés (in Spain), Ricardo Bernardi (Uruguay), Emiliano del Campo, Allan Poe Castelnuovo, Haydée Faimberg (in France), Hector Fiorini, Yolanda Gampel (in Israel), Beatriz Grunfeld, Hernán Kesselman, Mauricio Knobel, Blanca Montevechio, Janine Puget, David Rosenfeld, Marcelo and Maren Viñar (Uruguay), Juan Carlos Volnovich, and Benzion Winograd. *Symbiosis and Ambiguity* was translated into Portuguese and published in Brazil in 1977. Discussion of Bleger's work by various Latin-American authors may be found in three special issues of the *Revista de Psicoanálisis*: 'Homenaje a José Bleger' (Vol. 30, No. 2, April-June 1973); 'El analista trabajando' (Vol. 60, No. 4, October-December 2003); and '150 años del natalicio de Sigmund Freud' (Vol. 63, No. 2, June 2006).

Maud Mannoni met Bleger during her first visit to Buenos Aires in 1971, and her commentary on his work was probably the first mention of his work in the French psychoanalytic world. Jean-Luc Donnet began to discuss Bleger's ideas (Donnet, 1973), and in 1975 André Green referred to the paper on the setting in a paper given at the IPA congress in London and published in the *International Journal* (Green, 1975). The paper on the setting was translated into French in 1979 in a book edited by René Kaës (Kaës, 1979), and a French translation of the whole of *Symbiosis and Ambiguity* appeared in 1981. Since then a number of French psychoanalysts have engaged with aspects of Bleger's work, including Didier Anzieu, René Roussillon, and in particular René Kaës. A new edition of the French translation of *Symbiosis and Ambiguity* is currently in preparation with a preface by Daniel Widlöcher.

In Belgium, Jacqueline Godfrind, André Alsteens and others have made a careful study of this book (Godfrind, 1983, 1991; Alsteens, 1984, 1987). The *Revue Belge de Psychanalyse* has recently published a French translation of Bleger's 1957 paper on the psychoanalytic session (Bleger, 2009).

In Italy the work of the Argentinian psychoanalyst Armando Bauleo, and other colleagues including Silvia Amati Sas, Aurelia Galletti, Claudio Neri,

Maria Elena Petrilli and Mauro Rossetti, has resulted in Bleger's work becoming well known in Italy where *Symbiosis and Ambiguity* was first published in 1992, a second edition appearing in 2010. In 1989 an anthology of other papers by Bleger was also published in Italian and a second edition is now available (Bleger, 1989, 2011).

A survey of references to José Bleger's work in the most important psychoanalytic reviews in English suggests that although the paper on the setting was read and quoted soon after its publication in 1967 in the IJP, and despite a detailed discussion in 1992 by the Australian psychoanalyst O.H.D. Blomfield based on the French translation of *Symbiosis and Ambiguity* (Blomfield, 1992), it is only since the late 1990s that it has been frequently referred to. Perhaps this coincides with a certain opening of Anglo-Saxon psychoanalysis recently to Latin American currents. It seems likely that Horacio Etchegoyen's book *The Fundamentals of Psychoanalytic Technique*, published in English in 1991, and his Presidency of the IPA, the first by a Latin-American psychoanalyst, had a beneficial influence. In his book Etchegoyen integrates the work of the Argentinian and Latin-American psychoanalysts with other currents of the psychoanalytic movement and he has a thorough knowledge of José Bleger's work, which he quotes and discusses in his book. More recently, an appreciation by Rogelio Sosnik has appeared in the *Journal of the American Psychoanalytic Association* (Sosnik, 2011).

## About the present translation

An English edition of *Symbiosis and Ambiguity* was commissioned in 1987 by Robert Young of Free Association Books, and for a time this was advertised as 'forthcoming', under the title *Symbiosis and Ambiguity: the Psychoanalysis of Very Early Experience*. The translator was Christine Trollope, who became ill while working on it and who later died. The contract subsequently lapsed, and by the time we approached Routledge in 2007 with a proposal for the present edition, twenty years had passed since the initial agreement with Free Association Books.

The present translation is the result of a collaboration between three psychoanalysts. Although we had an opportunity to read the draft translation by Christine Trollope, we decided at an early stage to start afresh. Susan Rogers made a primary draft translation of the entire book, and we as the Editors then went through her draft, revising and annotating it in detail. It soon became clear that the task was much bigger than we had realised, and that without the sustained efforts of all three of us it would not have been possible to complete it. Responsibility for the remaining errors and infelicities, however, rests with us as the Editors, who made the final decisions.

Some problems of translation were solved very simply. For example, in the previous English version of Chapter 6 (Bleger, 1967a), the phrase 'ghost member' makes no sense as a translation of *miembro fantasma*. When correctly translated as 'phantom limb', however, not only does it have a clear meaning in English, but it also restores the pivotal connection that Bleger draws attention to, between the body and the setting, and the parallel consequences of injury to either.

In general, however, the difficulties we faced were of a different order. A number of terms in the Spanish are used in specifically psychoanalytic ways which do not have exact equivalents in English psychoanalytic usage. This is in part due to distinctive aspects of Latin American psychoanalysis, in particular of the *rioplatense* group of Argentinian and Uruguayan psychoanalysts. At the same time, the pre-eminent influence of Kleinian psychoanalysis, as developed largely in England in the 1950s and 1960s, is evident on every page of this book, as is the fact that José Bleger was immersed in and familiar with the psychoanalytic literature in English, as well as in French, German and Spanish. Further complications arise when terms used originally in German by Freud have been differently translated into English, Spanish and French, and where the Spanish or French is then retranslated into English. Similarly, some terms used by Melanie Klein were translated into Spanish in ways that cannot always be back-translated into English without some loss. Specific examples of such problems are discussed below.

In her editorial article 'Is translation possible?', which introduces a special issue of the *International Journal of Psychoanalysis* titled 'Papers on Translation', Dana Birksted-Breen characterises this situation as follows:

> Translation is 'site-specific'. The setting defines and delineates specific meanings and is an integral part of the work of translation. Outside the setting of psychoanalysis, the same 'language' would not take on the same meaning. Moreover it is the setting which calls forth and 'asks' for a translation.
>
> (Birksted-Breen, 2010, p. 687)

She goes on to consider this problem as it arises also between different local cultures or 'dialects' within psychoanalysis, as do many of the papers that she is introducing.

The word 'setting' itself is an example of this problem. Bleger begins Chapter 6 by referring to Winnicott's use of the word, which he reproduces in English, but thereafter he uses the Spanish *encuadre*. The 1966 English translation renders *encuadre* as 'frame'. However, as part of his definition of this concept Bleger also uses the word *marco*, for which the 1966 translation has 'bounds' (in the sense of boundaries, or limits). As Saussure (1916) pointed out, it is precisely because any language is a system of differences like that between *encuadre* and *marco*, or between 'setting', 'frame' and 'boundary', that perfect equivalence between expressions in different languages is impossible. Following the predominant usage in psychoanalytic discussions in English of recent decades, and confining ourselves to what is merely possible, we have decided to translate *encuadre* consistently by 'setting', and *marco* in this context by 'framework'.

A different kind of example is presented by the word *vínculo*, which we translate variously as 'link', 'tie', 'connection', 'relation' or 'relationship', depending on the context, and this choice is complicated by a number of considerations. *Vínculo* is a term used by Pichon Rivière to refer specifically to the ensemble of the object, the subject and the relation between them; Bleger sometimes uses the term in this Pichonean sense, and sometimes more loosely. Secondly, 'link' is a well-known concept of Bion's, and Bleger makes frequent reference to Bion's writings but he does not employ this concept directly. Thirdly, there is a degree of semantic overlap between this word and *relación*, which we usually translate as 'relation', for instance *relación de objeto* as 'object relation', but sometimes as 'relationship', as in *la relación social*: 'social relationships'.[20]

A particularly complicated issue arises with a group of terms which are all in some way semantically the opposite of *vínculo*, since they refer to various kinds of *dis*connection, but which carry different theoretical connotations: these include: *disociación, clivaje, escisión, división, fragmentación, disgregación, disolución*. There is some inconsistency in the use of the first four of these terms in the initial chapters of the book, and we think this is at least partly due to two main difficulties: first, for the German *Spaltung*, which Strachey translates as 'splitting', the Spanish translators of Freud use *escisión*; secondly, the Spanish translators of Melanie Klein's principal works into Spanish use *disociación* for 'splitting',[21] whereas Argentinian analysts have generally preferred *clivaje*. Although different Spanish words may be used for the same concept, it is clear that when discussing Freud's and Klein's work, Bleger is referring to the German concept *Spaltung* and the English concept 'splitting'. This usage occurs in the context of the contrast that Bleuler made between *Spaltung* and *Zerspaltung*, which in the English edition of his book (Bleuler, 1911) were rendered as 'splitting' and 'irregular fragmentation' respectively, as Bleger discusses on p. 36 and in footnote 48 on p. 61.

In any case, for Bleger the introduction of a new position involved a distinction between the mechanisms of the glischro-caric and paranoid-schizoid positions. For the characteristic defence of the glischro-caric position, which keeps the agglutinated nucleus separated from the rest of the personality, he generally uses *clivaje* ('splitting'), while for the mechanism of the paranoid-schizoid position he generally uses *disociación* ('dissociation'), but also sometimes *división esquizoide* ('schizoid division') or simply *división* ('division'). Following his remarks at the beginning of Chapter 2 (p. 37),

20 See also Scharff (2011).

21 See also footnote 84 on page 102, and our commentary.

where he discusses the use of these terms by Bion and Rosenfeld, we could represent Bleger's view approximately by the following table:

| | *glischro-caric* | *paranoid-schizoid* |
|---|---|---|
| Bleuler (1911) | *Zerspaltung*<br>('irregular fragmentation') | *Spaltung*<br>('splitting') |
| Bion (1958) | 'splitting' | 'dissociation' |
| Rosenfeld (1958) | 'abnormal splitting' | '(normal) splitting' |
| Bleger | *clivaje*<br>('splitting') | *disociación, división esquizoide*<br>('dissociation', 'schizoid division') |

A further complication arises when, for theoretical reasons that are gradually elaborated in the book, Bleger goes on to apply this distinction also to the difference between a process that operates within a given level of organisation and one that operates between different levels of organisation. Thus in Chapter 6 he writes:

> Between ego and non-ego (or between the neurotic and the psychotic parts of the personality) there is no dissociation but instead a splitting, in the sense that I have used this term in a previous text.
>
> (pp. 234–235)

In Chapter 7, discussing Breuer's case of *Anna 'O'*, he writes:

> Strictly speaking, the dissociation of consciousness in cases of '*double conscience*' does not correspond to divalence but to what we now term splitting between the neurotic and the psychotic part of the personality. I reserve the word dissociation for divalence, in which what are dissociated are not two states of consciousness, two parts of the personality or two different egos, but the antinomic terms of the same conflict that the subject directs toward different objects that, for the subject, are not integrated into a single one.
>
> (pp. 255–256)

A few pages later he writes:

> A fundamental difference is that dissociation is a separation of antinomies within the same level of ego structure, while splitting is a separation between two organisations with different structures or between different levels of organisation (maturity and immaturity).
>
> (p. 259)

*Desmenuzar* we translate as 'break up', as in breaking up a lump of material into smaller pieces. In everyday Spanish it refers typically to a physical action such as crumbling a piece of bread between the fingers, but Bleger uses it for the activity or process, within a psychoanalysis, of breaking up the agglutinated nucleus, or a symptom, or a symbiotic relationship.

The primary meaning of *embotar* is to blunt, as in taking the edge off a sharp instrument, and metaphorically it is used meaning to make dull or stupid, or to numb the mind. Bleger uses it to describe the effect of ambiguity in reducing the sharpness of persecutory feelings, or of greed or envy, which we translate by 'blunting'.

Bleger uses *facticidad* and *fáctico* in a way which cannot be translated as 'factual', both because in modern English this word no longer carries a strong enough connotation of action, of 'doing', and because Bleger clearly indicates that he is borrowing his use of the terms from Existentialism. We follow the translators of his 1966 and 1973 articles in translating them as 'factic' and 'facticity'. Bleger contrasts these with *ficticidad*, which we translate as 'fictitious' (*cf.* 'fictive personality' in Bleger, 1974).

Pichon Rivière's triad of *depositante*, *depositado* and *depositario* we translate as 'depositor', 'deposited' and 'depositary' respectively; for the noun which names the process, *depositación*, we have opted for 'depositation' which, though less common, is more correct than 'deposition'.

There is a group of related terms in Spanish (*actuar, actuación, actualisar, actualisación, acción*), whose English equivalents share the same root ('act', 'acting', 'actualise', 'actualisation', 'action'), as does the German *Agieren* used by Freud in the sense of 'acting out', and here too important distinctions of meaning can easily be lost. One of the common meanings of *actuar* in Spanish is to 'act', in the theatrical sense of playing a role. We translate *actuación* usually as 'acting', only occasionally as 'enactment', and *actuación psicopática* as 'psychopathic acting'. We have avoided the usual translation of *actuación* as 'acting out' because Bleger tends to use the word in a wider sense, and when he means 'acting out' in the strictly psychoanalytic sense he generally uses the English phrase. He also differentiates clearly between psychopathic acting and the 'action' (*acción*) of the factic ego. For *actualisar* and *actualisación* we decided to use the equivalents 'actualise' and 'actualisation', although these words are not so commonly used in English.

Following Strachey's convention, for better or for worse, we translate *yo* where appropriate by 'ego', and therefore Bleger's concept of *no-yo* by 'non-ego'.

Finally, the different requirements of Spanish and English concerning grammatical gender and sex create difficulties with personal pronouns that are not always soluble without either changing the meaning or making excessive use of expressions such as 'he or she'. We have not succeeded in approaching this problem consistently, but have tried to deal with it in an *ad hoc* way each time it arises.

## Editorial conventions

Wherever possible bibliographic references are to original or translated works in English, quotations have been replaced by corresponding passages from these, and in most cases we have added page references. Quotations from Freud are from the *Standard Edition* unless otherwise indicated.

Where we have added editorial material in footnotes, or occasionally in the text, this is in square brackets. Footnotes not in square brackets are by the author.

The original text was punctuated at intervals by the Greek letter $\psi$ appearing alone in the middle of a line. We have retained these marks which seem intended to indicate places where the reader might wish to pause for thought.

# Acknowledgements

We would like to thank the following:

Susan Rogers, for laying the foundations of the translation.

Dana Birksted-Breen, Alessandra Lemma, and the Editorial Board of the New Library of Psychoanalysis, for their patience and support.

Horacio Etchegoyen for agreeing to write the Preface and for being so accessible and generous with his time and knowledge.

Arturo Varchevker, Gregorio Kohon, and Robert Young, for encouragement at various times over the years.

Nenuca Amigorena-Rosenberg and Eduardo Vera Ocampo, for their friendship and for all the work done in the Seminar on 'Psychoanalysis in the *Río de la Plata*'.

Kate Hawes, Camilla Barnard and colleagues at Routledge, for practical guidance and for allowing us the time that we needed.

Kate Fox, for a machine-readable version of the Spanish original that proved to be invaluable.

The librarians whose meticulous and professional assistance we have relied upon: Jill Duncan, Andrea Chandler, Saven Morris, Hélène Martin, and Peter Cox at the Library of the Institute of Psychoanalysis, London; Diego Baracat at the 'Biblioteca Profesor Willy Baranger' of the *Asociación Psicoanalítica Argentina*, and the staff of the 'Bibliothèque Sigmund Freud' of the *Société Psychanalytique de Paris*.

Giselda Batlle and Malba – Fundación Costantini, Buenos Aires, for permission to reproduce on the cover of the paperback edition a painting by Juan Batlle Planas: *Radiografía paranoica*, *c.* 1936, from the eponymous series, tempera and pencil on paper, 26 × 19.5cm.

Taylor and Francis Books (UK) for permission to reproduce an extract from Fairbairn, W. R. (1952). *Psychoanalytic Studies of the Personality*. London: Tavistock Publications, pp. 42–43.

The Institute of Psychoanalysis and the publishers of *The Standard Edition of the Complete Psychological Works* of Sigmund Freud, translated and edited by James Strachey, published by Vintage Books, for permission to reproduce the excerpts from various articles in *The Standard Edition* that appear on pages 99, 161, 216, 233n. 179, 249ff., 286ff. and 293ff. Copyright © 1946 James Strachey. Reprinted by permission of Basic Books, a member of the Perseus Books Group; by permission of The Marsh Agency Limited on behalf of Sigmund Freud Copyrights; and by permission of The Random House Group Limited.

University of Chicago Press, for permission to reproduce the diagram on page 181.

Lowell Bair, for permission to reproduce excerpts from his translation of the novel *Warrior's Rest* by Christiane Rochefort, and Christian Gehman for his assistance. Penguin Books do not warrant that this use does not infringe any third party rights.

Editions Paidós, for permission use the selection of material in the Table on page 77.

Two anonymous reviewers who read the final typescript and made valuable comments.

Klara and Eric King for their careful and evenly-hovering attention to the typescript and the index.

Karen Clarke and Marie-Christine Bleger, for putting up with this, and us, for so long.

# Symbiosis and Ambiguity

*José Bleger*

# Prologue

Symbiosis, under that name, is a relatively new theme in psychology and psychopathology. However, there is no doubt that it has been included in very diverse ways in psychoanalytic writings, by different authors and on various topics, especially in studies referring to the earliest stages of personality development. The present publication is an attempt to take further the investigation of this question, which I consider of the greatest importance for a better understanding of problems in both normal psychology and psychopathology, and in individual psychology as well as in group, institutional and community psychology. Such is, in short, the range of fields and problems covered by the investigation of symbiosis.

However, even considering the precedents in the literature, it is not a matter of giving a new name to phenomena that are already familiar, but of re-situating them on the basis of a concept that comes closer to reality. Symbiosis places us fully, and from the outset of personality development, in the area of human interrelation, which then presents very particular features. Its study leads us to an understanding of other phenomena of adult life and its pathology, since it demands that we re-consider certain hypotheses and theories, as will become clear in reading the various chapters.

The study of symbiosis has also led me to another crucial point: the theme of ambiguity in normality, in pathology and in daily life. The bridge between these two themes, of symbiosis and ambiguity, is for me provided by the hypothesis that the nucleus, or the fundamental reason, for which the link or symbiotic interdependence is formed or persists, is by its very nature ambiguous. When I reached this latter conclusion, the study of ambiguity became unavoidable and I therefore had to re-consider concepts that were already in use, especially with reference to autism, primary narcissism, identification, etc.

Since the reader will be following the course of an investigation, I think it will be easily confirmed that between the first chapter and later ones there are certain conceptual modifications to which I was led by the investigation itself, as I have indicated. For now, it seems important to highlight some basic and general assumptions that gradually emerge, since they provide unity to the entire book and point to fundamental issues that touch on the very essence, not only of the phenomena studied, but also of the theories and hypotheses that I intend to apply to them.

One of these is the rejection of the assertion that the initial stages of human life are characterized by isolation, starting from which the subject gradually begins to relate to other human beings. This assertion is the quintessence of individualism imported into the scientific field, in the sense that individuals are not born as *isolated entities,* nor do they, from that point on, gradually structure their social nature by loss of this isolation in favour of the assimilation of culture. To replace this hypothesis, I was led to conceive a state of *primitive undifferentiation* as the starting point of human development. This means, among other things, that we no longer have to search and investigate how children, in the course of their development, gradually make connections with the external world, but how a certain type of relationship (undifferentiated) undergoes a modification which results, under optimal conditions, in a development of the child's identity and sense of reality. George Bernard Shaw was right when he once said that 'independence is a prejudice of the middle class';[22] but this would lead us into the field of the sociology of scientific thought.

Furthermore, this state of primitive undifferentiation is a *particular organization of the ego and of the world*, so that we are obliged to make an effort and face a new injury to our narcissism, as Freud put it, which occurs with each scientific advance: that *our* identity and *our* sense of reality are not *the* identity and sense of reality but only one of their many possible organizations. Therefore, we need to recognize that what differs from our own ways, structure or organization is not *always* a defect or a distortion but often a *different organization* that we need to study in its own right.

For some, this latter conception may seem simplistic and trite; for others it may seem absurd and nonsensical. In any case, I consider this one of the basic points for psychoanalytic theory, since it overturns one of the fundamental scientific 'models' or suppositions of psychology and psychoanalysis, and questions, re-evaluates and re-formulates them on a different basis.

This primitive undifferentiation is not actually *a state* of undifferentiation but a different *structure* or organization that always includes the subject and the subject's environment, though not as differentiated entities. The remnants of the nuclei of this primitive undifferentiation in a 'mature' personality is responsible for the persistence of symbiosis; I have therefore termed it the agglutinated nucleus, which can be observed in normal development (in adolescence and periods of crisis or change) and in pathology (in epilepsy,

22 [A reference to Shaw's *Pygmalion*, Act V: 'Independence? That's middle-class blasphemy. We are all dependent on one another, every soul of us on earth'. (Shaw, 1916).]

melancholia, etc.). If all or most of the personality is structured according to one of the modalities of this primitive undifferentiation, we encounter the ambiguous personality or a personality with ambiguous features. On the other hand, this primitive undifferentiation and its two most salient phenomena (symbiosis and ambiguity) are normal, not only by virtue of their quantity but also of their dynamics; for which reasons they may also involve or imply pathological clinical pictures or pathological moments, some of which are even *necessary* for normal personality development. I hope that all this, at least in some measure, has been reflected in this book and conveyed to the reader. I have discussed some of these clinical and theoretical considerations to a certain extent in other publications that were written or elaborated in parallel; I refer to my book, *Psicohigiene y Psicología Institucional* (Bleger, 1966) and to the Prologue and Appendices to *Escritos psicológicos de George Politzer* (Politzer, 1965–66).

A second fundamental hypothesis, to which I have already alluded, is the abandonment of the belief that psychological phenomena are mental from the outset: that psychological phenomena, in order to be psychological, have to be mental from the beginning, and that if this quality of being mental does not appear manifestly, it must exist or pre-exist in unconscious form. Instead of this hypothesis that, as I have said, is more of an assumption or conceptual model of psychology than a hypothesis, I postulate that mental phenomena are *a* modality of behaviour, one that appears later than the others, and that the first undifferentiated, syncretic structures are fundamentally bodily relations. This hypothesis has also been taken up and developed in the publications mentioned above and will not be discussed here in detail; however, I consider it important enough to at least bring it up in this Prologue. In the course of the different chapters of this book, I include various bibliographical references which show that these two hypotheses are not, strictly speaking, completely new in the field of psychoanalytic investigation, but that they have not been sufficiently emphasized and particularly that their necessary and inevitable consequences were never developed, an objective that I hope to realise here, at least to some extent.

The presentation of a theme having these characteristics (since symbiosis and ambiguity are a single theme, though they are different clinical phenomena), and whose investigation is not far advanced, plus their relation to hypotheses that are so broad, makes it impossible to discuss in a volume that has the characteristics of a textbook. However, in this sense I think that the reader will agree that although it may be easier to read a textbook (and it isn't always), it is no less true that it is also easier to 'mummify' the knowledge in it. What I am trying to do is just the opposite. In this sense, although I allude to other authors' contributions to the subject, I do not present the literature systematically, since my objective is to document my own investigation and its results, although this does not preclude citing the investigations and conceptions of other authors. I must point out especially that, for the same reasons, I do not enter into consideration of the similarities and differences in relation to other conceptions that are somehow related to the theme, such as the 'dead-alive' object postulated by W. Baranger (Baranger and Baranger, 1961–62), A. Rascovsky's 'fetal psychism' (Rascovsky, 1957) or the 'lethargic nucleus' postulated by F. Cesio (Cesio, 1958).

In this book, I have had to make a considerable effort to exclude approaches to symbiosis from a biological perspective and to ambiguity from artistic, aesthetic and philosophical vantage points. I have expressly left them out, even though I felt quite attracted to them. I wanted to focus, as strictly as possible, on clinical work and on the theories and hypotheses deriving from it, and to leave aside those fields: biology, philosophy and aesthetics, which would assuredly have led me far from clinical issues.

A minimal acquaintance with the theme of symbiosis in biology shows us very interesting, or at least very attractive, relations in regard to symbiosis, parasitism, commensalism, saprophytism, mutualism, etc. and to the fascinating study of lichens and the spectacular phenomenon of neoteny. It is especially the latter that has most frequently drawn my attention, because the intensely symbiotic subject and the person with profound ambiguity have always seemed to me to be intimately related to the phenomenon that biology terms neoteny. I simply note that these relations are subjects for further development.

The second and third parts of this book have not been published previously, while the chapters in the first part that deal with symbiosis have been: the first chapter in the *Revista de Psicoanálisis*, Vol. XVII (Bleger, 1960); the second chapter, presented in the Argentine Psychoanalytic Association in April, 1961, was published in the *Revista de Psicoanálisis*, Vol. XVIII (Bleger, 1961) and Vol. XIX (Bleger, 1962a); the third chapter, presented in the Symposium on the Work of M. Klein in 1961, was published in the *Revista de Psicoanálisis*, Vol. XIX (Bleger, 1962b) and the fourth chapter was published in the *Revista Uruguaya de Psicoanálisis*, Vol. VI (Bleger, 1964a).

*Buenos Aires, January 1967*

# PART ONE

# On Symbiosis

# 1

# Study of dependence-independence in relation to the process of projection-introjection

> The process of differentiation of the object derives particular significance from the fact that infantile dependence is characterised not only by identification, but also by an oral attitude of incorporation. In virtue of this fact the object with which the individual is identified becomes equivalent to an incorporated object, or, to put the matter in a more arresting fashion, the object in which the individual is incorporated is incorporated in the individual. This strange psychological anomaly may well prove the key to many metaphysical puzzles. Be that as it may, however, it is common to find in dreams a remarkable equivalence between being inside an object and having the object inside ... Such then being the situation, the task of differentiating the object tends to resolve itself into a problem of expelling an incorporated object, i.e., to become a problem of expelling contents.
>
> (Fairbairn, 1952, pp. 42–43)

## Objective

The aim of this chapter is to study, in a female patient whom I will call Maria Cristina, some aspects of her dependence and her development in psychoanalytic treatment.

Between *total dependence* as the starting point, and independence or *mature dependence*, there is a very long period that may last a lifetime; Fairbairn calls it the 'transitional period', when features of infantile dependence intermingle, co-exist and alternate with those of mature independence and reaction formation to the dependence.

In my patient, development toward mature dependence was blocked by a modification of the process of projection-introjection, giving rise as a result to phenomena of autism and symbiosis that tended to stabilize or balance the fluctuations. More specifically, I develop in this chapter two conclusions or basic theses very closely related to the works of Fairbairn and the Kleinian school:

(1) Disturbances of the process of projection-introjection are at the root of conflicts of dependence-independence;
(2) The patient's analysis required the study of the formation of autistic and symbiotic types of behaviour that are intimately connected to phenomena of projection-introjection and of course to the management of paranoid and depressive anxieties.

## Autism and symbiosis in the transference

Beginning with the latter thesis, and in reference particularly to my patient, I found not only an alternating presentation of autistic and symbiotic types of behaviour, but *the co-existence of autism and symbiosis in the transference relation*, the latter appearing on two levels at once, or two fronts. On the one hand, she remained distant and controlling, preventing the therapist from crossing the 'barrier' and penetrating into her inner life (autism); at the same time, she established another type of relationship characterised by the reduction of the therapist to the role of a depositary into which the patient projected intensely, in an attempted symbiotic relation that she also needed or could not do without.[23]

## Background

Bleuler (1911) introduced the term 'autism' to name what Janet had studied as a 'loss of the sense of reality', which Bleuler defined as: 'withdrawal from reality, together with relative or absolute predominance of internal life'.

Autism is nowadays considered a defensive behaviour in reaction to persecutory situations in which the relation with internal objects predominates and relationships are therefore essentially narcissistic.

Kanner (1935) described the clinical picture of early infantile autism whose fundamental characteristic is withdrawal and removal from the external world, which is kept as a dividing barrier. Everything that signifies forcing or breaking through this barrier is experienced with great anxiety. Pichon Rivière, in seminars and classes, affirmed that autism is a normal and necessary stage in child development and that the clinical picture described

23 The concept of autism and its re-formulation in relation to symbiosis is developed in the chapter in which we study ambiguity (Chapter 5).

by Kanner appears as a result of fixation or regression to that autistic formation. Autistic remnants from this period of development ('nature reserves')[24] provide elements for the construction of neuroses, psychoses and character disorders; we also need to recognise the intervention of autistic nuclei in normal life (dreams, fantasies, etc.).

M. Mahler (1952, 1958) studied a clinical picture that is different and seemingly totally opposite to Kanner's: the symbiotic psychoses characterised by a relationship of very close dependence on an external object. The symptomatology is quite manifest when this symbiosis breaks down, in panic attacks or catastrophic crises. In these massive projections into an object, a large part of the subject's ego is estranged or alienated[25] in the object. It also entails fixation or regression to a primitive mother-child symbiotic relation, which is normal during development. Just as the symptoms typical of schizophrenic disintegration appear when autism is breached, symbiotic psychosis appears when symbiosis is broken.

M. Mahler differentiates three types of psychosis in childhood: first, Kanner's early infantile autism and second, Mahler's psychotic syndrome of infantile symbiosis. A third group of more benign infantile psychoses was described by Mahler, Ross and De Fries (1949), as well as by Geleerd (1946), characterised by the ego's simultaneous or alternating use of neurotic mechanisms, autism and symbiosis. These three types evidence disturbances of the sense of reality, sense of identity and body schema.

M. Mahler describes more benign cases, but in psychoanalytic practice I am interested in being able to *detect the very slightest expressions of all these disturbances*, even in non-psychotic patients of course.

In this sense, D. Liberman (1956, 1958) studied what he termed transference autism, which he defined as: 'the manifestation of the narcissistic phase in the analytic situation. Autism opposes the establishment of a reciprocal relationship, and of a certain objective connection with the analyst' (Liberman, 1958, p. 372).

G. Racker[26] (1958) also worked on this topic, especially from the technical perspective, and agreed with D. Liberman's theoretical formulations.

## Transference narcissism

With my patient, Maria Cristina, it was evident that the transference relationship corresponded to the characteristics described by D. Liberman

24 [*parques naturales*, the image used by Freud (1917, p. 372)]

25 [*enajenada o alienada*, from *Entfremdung* and *Entäusserung* in Karl Marx; for the English translation of these terms as 'estrangement' and 'alienation' respectively see Marx (1844, p. 588, n. 1)]

26 [Génèvieve T. de Racker, later G.T. de Rodrigué]

in the definition above: the absence of an objective connection with the analyst and opposition to the establishment of a reciprocal relationship. On the one hand, she set up a barrier and would not allow me to penetrate into her inner life: I was supposed to work only on what she gave me: parts of herself, in relation to persons in her family environment. On the other hand, she treated me, not as a separate person, differentiated from her, but as an object that she would make into the depositary of a large quantity of objects and relationships for which she could not take responsibility. This is not merely control of re-introjection but a more general control to bar me from disturbing the entirety of her narcissistic relations.

If we observe this closely, we can see that both the autistic and the symbiotic links in the transference are narcissistic relations; both are relations with internal objects that aim to preserve the pleasure principle and defend those objects from intrusion by external reality.[27]

The massive projection thus produced, which makes it difficult for her to separate from me, establishes a symbiotic transference relation. But this relation and dependence on what is projected does not constitute a relationship with the other; it is still largely a narcissistic relation. For this reason, I consider it important to differentiate, as Pichon Rivière does, between depositor, deposited and depositary. Maria Cristina needs to control the analyst (depositary) so that he does not get 'inside' her, into her autistic formation, as much as she has to control him from getting into what has been deposited.

Like the symbiotic transference relationship, the autistic transference relationship is equally narcissistic. The difference is that in the former, the depositary belongs to the external world, while in the latter it belongs to a zone of her own mind or body.

If we momentarily broaden the field of our inquiry, we see that in every analysis we encounter some degree of projection of internal objects or parts of them into the analyst, and with this a continuous assignment of roles and a ceaseless search for a relationship of symbiotic dependence that simultaneously involves the maintenance and control of a barrier that must not be crossed (autism).

Autistic and symbiotic transference are in both cases narcissistic relations: that is, with internal objects, among which a vigorous process of splitting and dissociation has been established, with the projective expulsion of some of them. For this reason, autism and symbiosis are the two extremes of the splitting between the projected and the introjected. There can be no autism without symbiosis and vice versa, whatever form these phenomena may take and at whatever level. Diagnosis is made on the basis of whatever is manifest or predominant. The co-existence of autism and symbiosis explains the apparently paradoxical and contradictory character of the transference in psychotic patients. At the time when the emphasis was placed only on

27 [This point is returned to at the end of Chapter 5, on p. 226]

autistic behaviour, the lack of transference relationship in psychotics was deduced (as postulated by Freud). It was subsequently discovered that psychotic transference is installed rapidly and massively, a finding that was possible when attention was drawn to the symbiotic relationship established by the psychotic. This aspect was discovered only later because the symbiosis is 'mute', with a noticeable display of symptoms appearing only in cases of its rupture; but in psychotics the symbiosis was also cloaked by the withdrawal into autistic defence. Pichon Rivière said of the psychotic transference: 'The tendency to establish contacts with other persons is as intense as the tendency to isolation as a defence' (Pichon Rivière, 1952, p. 255). We can now reflect that complete autism without symbiosis is incompatible with life.

Symbiotic transference also explains epileptic viscosity, as one of its variants.

Our subject now is basically that of dependence in relation to the phenomena of projection-introjection. In studying this, I came across autism and symbiosis, and for this reason I include them here, although I will reserve these subjects for a specific and special discussion below.

## Symbiosis and psychopathic acting

Symbiosis rests upon the process of projective identification; in this process, the relation between the depositor and the deposited has been studied in depth (impoverishment or evacuation of the depositor, dependence on the deposited, etc.), but not so the relation between the deposited and the depositary. In the clinical material I am presenting, however, this difference is fundamental.

In projection, everything occurs within the subject. Even its definition refers to the depositor with the deposited. The relationship with the depositary is a simple depositing that neither changes, influences nor modifies the behaviour of the depositary; it is possible to be the depositary of internal objects of another subject without ever knowing about it or one's behaviour being influenced by it.

In the relationships of our patient's family group, projection presented quite different consequences: the depositary *acts* the role corresponding to the deposited, (takes on the role). For example, in the first interview, the mother takes on the daughter's controlling function. In these cases, the distance between the deposited and the depositary disappears. In some way (the pre-verbal communication accompanying verbal communication), this acting or assumption of the projected role is *promoted* by the projection; alternatively, in the already existing behaviour of the depositary, a role may be *delegated* or, most probably, both of these happen: the promotion of acting as well as the delegation of a role in the other's already current behaviour. In my patient's transference relationship there was a constant attempt to promote and delegate a role in the therapist.

Strictly speaking, we should speak of symbiosis only when the projections are crossed, and each person acts according to the compensatory roles of the other. Thus, symbiosis is a type of dependence or interdependence in the external world. The need to promote the acting out of roles is an indicator of deficient communication on the symbolic level.

These considerations lead me to define family groups like that of our patient Maria Cristina as a narcissistic and/or symbiotic group, in the sense that each member is a depositary and acts out roles that belong to relations with the internal objects of other members. All this occurs in a complementary and mutually involved manner. In these cases, the narcissism is group narcissism. Group narcissism indubitably coincides with the phenomenon of endogamy. These are family groups that Mme. Minkowska defines as agglutinated or epileptoid. The rupture of this symbiotic interplay of roles produces a disintegrated or dispersed (schizoid) group.

## The patient's history

Maria Cristina was eighteen when she started her psychoanalytic treatment, slightly over three years ago (October 1956). She was living with her parents in the city of Santa Fe, from where she came to Rosario at the beginning of 1956 to study medicine. Her brother Juan, five years older than she, had already been here for several years, studying for the same degree.

Thus, the family group had dispersed slowly and progressively. A fundamental event in the break-up and change in the family structure occurred when, one year previously, the father had had a stroke and 'was now like a baby', his personality radically changed. Maria Cristina remembered him as an aggressive and tyrannical man, affectively blocked and distant from his children and wife. Because of his illness, her mother 'took the reins of the household' and from then on, the patient's conflicts with her increased. Her mother is described as a mild but very resentful woman; her cultural level higher than her husband's, she always lamented that her marriage had ruined her career as a concert musician.

With the father's illness, a certain family organization was permanently destroyed and Maria Cristina was overtaken by moments of disorientation, confusion and uncertainty in relation, among other things, to the economic situation in which they found themselves. Even so, she decided to move to Rosario to study medicine. Her relationship with her brother Juan had always been very good for her; she had found support in him and he was a source of hope for Maria Cristina. But the relationship with Juan had also changed; among other factors, he now had a girlfriend. She also had to face the disappointment that her brother had fallen behind in his studies and had not taken exams for several years. At the same time, she embarked on a relationship with a young man who had great difficulties with his studies, and with whom she had frequent arguments.

What made her decide explicitly that she needed treatment were three nervous breakdowns in 1956. One of these occurred when she was on the street with her boyfriend: she heard about a revolutionary movement in the country and, when she saw planes that were going to bomb a military base, she experienced great anxiety and believed that they were going to bomb them; she felt dizzy and fainted. She was taken to a clinic where she sobbed and shook, and for a number of nights afterwards she was afraid to go to sleep and afraid to dream. The two later breakdowns occurred following arguments with her boyfriend. Later, she remembers that she had had a nervous breakdown years before, when she was ten, and another one in 1955, the latter following an argument with her mother; she had stood up and fallen onto the table in a fit of weeping.

## Dependence-independence

In the first consultation with mother and daughter, the fundamental problem for which she was coming to analysis was sketched out: dependence-independence. Her mother seemed to notice a change in her, while Maria Cristina complained that her parents rejected her relationship with her boyfriend (her independence).

> (1) In her first session, she tells me that the night of the day of her consultation with me, which was also the first night she slept in the boarding house, she does not know whether she was dreaming or whether it was a fantasy: when she turned over in bed, she thought she saw her roommate naked, and this reminded her of her mother.
> (2) I interpret that she remembers this now because it is a way to facilitate her relation with the unknown: the new boarding house, me and the treatment. It means being accompanied by her mother so that she can feel protected.
> (3) She answers 'Exactly' and goes on, telling me how her mother found out about her relationship with her boyfriend, and how her father reacted to this and, through her mother, forbad her to continue seeing 'that loafer'. Once, when she went to Santa Fe for a short holiday, her mother forbad her from going out with her boyfriend and sent her on an errand; since she was afraid, she went where her mother had sent her.

With (3) she shows me the counterpart of her mother. When in (2) I pointed out how she uses her mother's protective aspect in situations that are new and therefore unknown and dangerous, she shows me (3), the counterpart: the possessive aspect of that protection, a reflection of the possessive and controlling character of her own affection for her mother.

When she came to the first consultation with her mother, in order to feel protected against the unknown, the paranoid anxiety about the unknown was such that the symbiotic couple needed to come: the protective mother *had to be* with her. In the first session, when she remembers her mother in order to relate to the unknown, the protective mother is brought in as an internal object and thus there was a passage from the symbiotic relationship to the autistic relationship, which she projects into to me in order to re-construct the symbiosis with me. Between the first and the second time she sees me, the extent to which I am unknown and dangerous decreases, thus allowing introjection of the protective object. But the projection of the protective mother onto the analyst, onto the unknown, also involves certain risks. Therefore the possessive mother comes to the fore so that she can defend herself and avoid surrendering fully. The persecutory (possessive) object is the superego that also acts as a protector. These two objects (protective and possessive) are cathected – separately – with her own need to be protected and the absorbing character of her own affects (her greed). They co-exist as internal objects, their predominance alternating. However, when her fears were more intense (the first consultation) it was not enough for her to come accompanied internally: she actually came with her mother, as a symbiotic unit, and each of them acted by taking on a role that, separately, was one aspect of the problem that existed in both: the mother took the dominant, possessive, accusing, curious and controlling role, saying that her daughter had changed, and brought it up as a reason to start her treatment; that is, she personified Maria Cristina's super-ego. The daughter took the independent role, accusing her parents of holding on to her and not allowing her to have a boyfriend. The *projection and delegation* (Weiss, 1947)[28] to her mother of her own dependence and need of protection enable Maria Cristina to insist on her independence. On the other hand, her relationship with the boyfriend also confirmed the conflictive character of this independence, since she carried her relationship with her mother into this new relationship, even though this went unnoticed: she was also protective of her boyfriend in an all-absorbing way and tended to help him to study; that is, the symbiotic relationship was re-structured.

The session continues:

(4) I interpret that she is posing a question: whose side am I on: hers or her mother's?

(5) She answers 'Exactly so' and goes on to tell me that when her parents were in Rosario, they moved her out of the boarding house and her mother took her with them to the hotel 'and it caused me great anxiety when she

28 [In the Spanish version of Weiss' paper (Weiss, 1948) 'proxy' was translated as *delegación*, a term independently used by Bleger, following Pichon Rivière, which we translate throughout by 'delegation'.]

> took me away with her, because I feel quite irritated with my father as soon as I'm with him. I have to leave. The night before last, when I was talking to my brother's girlfriend, I remembered that when I was small, I used to call him old banana, and I remember that my father liked that.'

With this, and in response to my interpretation, Maria Cristina is showing the erotic relationship with her healthy father that has now revived with me, and this is why she brought in her mother (maternal superego) at the beginning of the session: her mother defends her from her genital impulses while at the same time she uses these impulses to defend herself from the consuming relationship with her mother (oral superego).

> (6) 'I remember a dream I had two years ago. I was walking down a sidewalk and felt very lonely. I went into a house with a garden like a park. I sat down on a stone bench and a shadow like a ghost sat down beside me. I felt calm. When I left, the ghost became a fellow I liked. When we left, his friends, sitting on the ground, said hello to him. And when we both left, daddy's car was there. He crossed the street at right angles and he had a bushy beard. He didn't say anything to me, he just looked at me, and then I said to Jorge, "We're done for", and we started to run and Jorge disappeared, and on the corner up the hill my father was smoking a cigarette and looking at me. I went down the other hill and he ran after me. There was nobody on the street and after that I don't remember anything else. I remembered this dream once when mamma was very angry because Juan – to demonstrate the value of psychoanalysis – asked me to tell a dream and I told it in front of mamma and when I did, I remembered that when I was little, I entered the bathroom and saw dad urinating. It goes without saying that mamma was shocked.'

In (3) she emphasises her parents' attempt to separate her from her boyfriend, thereby concealing her own desire to separate her parents and her discomfort regarding her father, onto whom her own oedipal phantasies, which become persecutory, are projected.

When an affectionate and erotic relationship is reactivated in the transference, persecutory phantasies about her mother are also awakened.

Both she and her father and all the boys in the house belong to her mother, are inside her (the house in the dream), and behind her relationship with men is the incestuous relationship with her father (5). Her difficulty in separating from her mother, in leaving her insides, is the difficulty of facing the oedipal conflict and her envy of her mother because of her contents. If she is inside her mother, she is protected, and is not afraid of the ghosts; the symbiotic relationship with her mother protects her from persecutory situations. For this reason, she stays tied to her mother in a relationship of symbiotic dependency. If they separate, she must introject and manage tensions inside of herself that exceed the capacity of her own ego to confront or work through these anxieties.

> (7) Because of what she relates in front of her mother (the dream and the memory), the mother blames Juan for the wayward relationship and the 'things' that Maria Cristina is learning. She goes on to say: 'She (the mother) always mixes us up and calls Juan dear girl and calls me dear boy, and this bothers him as much as it does me. She used to dress me in trousers when I was small and put a skirt on my brother'. She tells me that it was Juan who had discovered all this by asking their mother questions and that she had said, 'You're already analysing me'.

Just as she feels threatened by her parents' union, she inverts the situation and projects the anger, arousing it in her mother by forming a couple with her brother. Just as her mother uses her father against her, in (3): 'Your father doesn't want you to go out with that loafer', she uses her brother by projecting into him her active part that tends toward separation from her parents. Separation is also conflictive because it is a separation from her parents joined together, or rather against her mother, who possesses the father inside of her. This is a compulsive and combative separation. She needs the relationship with me in order to defend herself and to satisfy her rivalry with her mother. Her own aggression is displaced onto her father, thus hiding her oedipal conflict from her mother and herself. When she does this she takes over her own mother's hostility toward her husband.

She defends her brother from her mother: it's not his fault but her mother's, who confused him, and confused her regarding her gender and did not allow her to be a woman, thus projecting her own destructive envy onto her mother. She defends her brother from her mother because this defends him from her own aggression and rivalry in taking the place of a man (brother/father) in order to penetrate her mother. Her brother replaces her father and with Juan she forms a less dangerous couple in relation to her mother than if she were to form a couple with her father. This would be as dangerous as she feels the union with me is now, considering that it provokes her mother's envy.

Each member of her family is not a person with whom she relates in an objective way; instead they are all depositaries of her tensions and internal objects. She herself, on the other hand, internalizes and acts out roles corresponding to tensions in the others. We can say that although it was she who came to the analysis, she was in some ways sent or brought, and that she also brought her family to the treatment. As long as she remains inside her mother, she can use her mother's contents (father and brother) *as if they were hers* without entering into conflict, while also concealing her desire to appropriate everything contained in her mother.

(8) She narrates, at the end of the session, how she and her brother swore that they would always join forces against their parents, but now she is desperate because her brother no longer backs her up.
(9) Since I remained silent, she says, 'Just now it seemed to me that you had left. I was afraid that I would find myself alone, the same fear that I felt during the breakdowns, especially the last two. During the first one it was more fear that Dad might come into the room. It seemed to me that day that I was attending a burial. And what mainly provoked the breakdown were the planes flying past.'
(10) I interpreted at that time that she was afraid that I would leave her on her own just as she felt left on her own by her father and her brother Juan.

The fear of finding herself on her own is the fear of re-introjecting everything that she had projected previously into me. When she talks directly to me ('Just now it seemed to me that you had left'), it is an attempt to exert a much more direct and strict control on me and on what has been deposited in me.

(11) To interpretation (10) she answers: 'Of course, after Dad's stroke I started to talk about Dad in the past tense. One day I said, "When he died . . ."'
(12) At this moment I interpret that it is harder for her to see her father ill than to see him dead. So much so that it is hard for her to feel that I don't leave her completely on her own, but neither do I accompany her as much as she needs.
(13) 'Yes. As things are, it's as if he were my son and not my father. He's like a child, except when he gets violent. I now prefer him when he's more violent than the way he is almost all of the time'. And she immediately adds, 'Just now it seemed to me that you were going to cut[29] me in half. As if you were going to sentence me and cut me in two with a sword. And that doorbell I heard, it seemed to me that my father was going to arrive and ask me whether I forgot something. I always have the image of my mother spying behind doors. She has that habit. Yesterday, during the examination, something strange happened to me. When I went to take the exam I was ready for them to fail me, although I knew I was going to pass'.

In (8) she is preparing for the separation from me. She is afraid of loneliness as a re-introjection of her destroyed father, her own aggression and her envious and controlling part projected into her mother. She recalls her breakdowns as a defence against re-introjection. She has felt subjected to an

29 [The Spanish *partir*, here used transitively meaning to 'cut', also evokes its intransitive use meaning to 'leave' or 'separate', as in 'we must part'.]

examination of her insides (13) and seductively tries to reassure herself that I accept her and accept everything that she has projected onto me. She would prefer me to be violent with her because then she would be sure, more than she is now, that I care for her and am interested in her things. Waiting for the outcome is also a technique she uses in order to control whether I will accept the role of depositary and to promote this role in me. The fantasy of being cut in two by a sword is the projection onto me of her own violent mechanisms of dissociation, with which she divides her ego and her objects.

Listening to the doorbell is an indication of how she has remained alert, controlling what was happening around her and in me. Her curiosity emerges, personified by her mother, while the control is personified by her father.

## Summary

Before continuing, it might be a good idea to recapitulate briefly.

We have seen that Maria Cristina presented the problem of her dependence-independence. On the basis of the data that we have up to now, we can add that this problem is a conflict between two levels of development: orality and genitality.

I have mentioned the dissociation or separation between the terms of this conflict and the 'depositing' of each part of the conflict in each member of the couple (her parents). Her father is the depositary of her own genital tendencies (independence and separation from her mother) and of her oral tendencies projected onto her mother (dependence). In the session she feels united with me as a healthy, potent father whereas the mother is left out as a third party, excluded and envious.

Her phantasy of separating her parents is a necessity imposed by the dissociation of this conflict. This is why she leaves her home to study in Rosario when her mother takes over the reins of the household and everything else. In other words, when the mother assumes both roles (mother-father), the control fails and confusion and disorientation appear.

We may wonder why Maria Cristina's segregation occurs at this point and why these tensions are not worked through. Let us observe that the need to renew relationships arises not only for Maria Cristina but for all the members of the family group. For Maria Cristina the orality-genitality conflict remains unresolved and no decisive choice is made for one or the other because each level of development is used as a defence against the other, since each is also conflictive in itself. Why? Because the oral dependence is tinged with her own greed and therefore by the dangers of being absorbed and destroyed. The independence encapsulated in her genital impulses involves her own aggression and rivalry with men, with the consequent guilt and the vicious circle of connecting with objects in order to make reparation, but then, once they have been repaired she herself takes up the rivalry and tends to destroy them or be destroyed in retaliation.

We shall stop at this point because this summary is intended only to orient the reader for the developments on the pages below.

## Comments on the initiation of the treatment

The request for treatment and an initial interview is made by her brother Juan. She comes to the first interview with her mother. They both enter the office and while they are together the mother speaks and, summing up her narration, says that she notices her daughter has changed. When I ask the mother to wait for us outside, she leaves without any difficulty and Maria Cristina does not protest. Her history is gathered, during which she places the emphasis on her parents' rejection of her relationship with her boyfriend. Only for deciding the arrangements for paying the fees and the frequency of session does she ask her mother to be present.

Throughout the first session she demonstrates her total denial of the new situation and the new relationship with me. She talks to me as if she knew me and as if I knew her and knew all about her affairs. In the session she includes her mother, father, brother, boyfriend and even Jorge, a boy who appears in a dream, whose identity I learn in subsequent sessions. She does not talk to me about herself but about her objects. Or rather, the only way she talks to me about herself is through her objects. She has, it seems, nothing inside herself; part of her is in each of her objects. She is herself as long as the family nucleus holds together; if it disintegrates, she herself disintegrates. She talks to me, but not as a differentiated person with her own identity. She answers all my interpretations with 'yes', 'exactly' or 'of course', but does not really make contact with me directly. I am a depositary of her objects. Her failure to recognize me as a differentiated, different person implies a deficit in her own personification and sense of identity. Her way of remaining free of anxiety is to re-create her family in the relationship with me and thus to re-create herself inside of me. When she leaves the session, she gets trapped in the lift, between two floors that are above the one I occupy.

We can say that in this first session – and it continued in this way for a long time – there are some very important circumstances to consider:

(a) The verbalization is easy and flowing. The material she gives is copious. She 'deluges', with the result that her material is 'invasive'. The transcription of the session above preserves this character, to help the reader experience the corresponding countertransference.
(b) At the same time, she keeps me at a distance and doesn't let me really get inside her concerns; that is, she keeps herself at a distance.

(c) What she expresses verbally is not really just saying something, but *a way of acting* or of doing something with me and with herself: trying to fill me up with contents that she cannot keep inside herself, and controlling me so that I will act according to her needs, while at the same time avoiding re-introjection. This is to make me a depositary of her objects.
(d) All this requires that she keep parts of herself divided and separated.

There has been an intense and massive projection into me of objects that she had previously projected in a fragmentary manner into each member of her family group. The distance she keeps from me and the distance at which she keeps me tends to prevent re-introjection and to protect her inner world. She tries to re-create her dependence on the family group in the transference relationship, because the family is no longer functioning successfully as a depositary of her projected objects. Fear of re-introjection was all the greater because I only acted as a depositary and Maria Cristina was not sure whether I fully took on those roles.

We see fragmentation and dissociation of the very process of projection-introjection, but with a consequent organization of what is projected and introjected; this organization is what actually gives stability and continuity to the dissociation. I want to emphasise that the process of projection-introjection is not paralysed but instead dissociated.

When Maria Cristina left the first session she got trapped in the lift. The process of projection, of 'depositing' her objects had been so massive that at the end of the session she finds herself trapped in the re-introjected depositary object. When she entered the lift she pressed the button to go up, as if she were still on the ground floor and had just arrived for the session. Depositing was unsuccessful: it had not resulted in delegation or acting. At the end of the session this claustrophobic episode occurs as an attempt to protect herself from the danger of dispersion and of losing control of her objects and – therefore – of her own ego. We recall in her history other defences against re-introjection: the fainting spell during her nervous breakdown. The bombing involved the danger of massive and sudden re-introjection, its characteristics the same as in the previous projection. The fainting was a flight from and an avoidance of this danger; the convulsions were an expulsion of what had been re-introjected. The fear of sleeping is also accounted for as fear of losing control of dissociation (equivalent to a return of the repressed).

## The course of the treatment

Although it is very difficult to give a succinct account of Maria Cristina's entire psychoanalytic treatment up to the present, it can be said schematically that it has included three major fundamental stages: the first, in which she would answer my interpretations with 'yes', 'of course' or 'exactly'; a second phase, in which a short silence on her part followed my interpretations, after which she would either take up the thread of what she had been talking about or else change the subject in the manifest content while responding unconsciously to the interpretation. In a third period, she would respond to many of my interpretations with a meaningful 'Mmmmm ...' of surprise and discovery. We see that these three types of response are related to a progressive reduction of distance and an increased 'permeability' in the transference relationship, with some greater degree of insight, correlative to a gradual decrease in anxiety and a relative re-establishment of the process of projection and introjection.

The first period was characterised by a continuous effort to keep situations immobile, with fear of and defence against re-introjection, fear of any kind of change and fear of the examination of the contents of her own mind. In one of the first sessions she talked about her fear of the dark and her fear that when opening the door of the closet she might discover something in three parts inside. She immediately fell silent and said that she had the fantasy of a head inserting itself into her mouth. I interpreted this to her as a fear that I might force her to see the things she had inside, formed of three parts: mother, father and brother. As it was later possible to confirm and interpret using different material, she feared the examination of her insides; she was not sure of me as a depositary because she feared that, at any moment, I might return everything to her violently (put it through her mouth).

Paranoid anxieties appear basically in connection with her aggression and greed, projected respectively onto her father and mother. The former appeared in connection with the fantasy of Frankenstein and the latter with Dracula; dreams of dead persons and spiders – nightmares – were frequent, and dreams were sometimes in colour.

The second period of her analysis began when a symbiotic relation was established, with acting out in the transference. She constantly tried to get her boyfriend to have analysis with me, although she never said so or asked for it explicitly, but accepted it when it was interpreted in this way. However, on the other hand, she displaced it by urging her brother to have analysis with a female analyst who was a friend of mine. This accomplished various objectives or needs: to make her brother well again and, due to her oedipal phantasies, to control and appease my wife. The conflict regarding her parents' union, with the consequent aggression and guilt, moved wholly into the transference relationship. With this advance, the theme of her brother's analysis disappeared from the material of her sessions. When her brother improves and progresses in his studies, her guilt in relation to her desire to surpass him decreases, and at this point she enters into open rivalry with me. At that moment, the theme of academic work disappears from the material of analysis.

A long transition period covering a large portion of the second and third periods of her analysis, and which to a large extent she is still in, gives rise to two particular phenomena which I will discuss in greater detail: fragmentation and control in space of paranoid anxieties, and the participation of her body as a 'buffer' in re-introjection.

## Fragmentation, dissociation and control in space

Due to rupture of the primitive family organisation, the different cities (Santa Fe, Rosario and Buenos Aires) become, by displacement, depositaries of different relationships: Santa Fe represents her dependence (orality), Buenos Aires her attempt at independence and maturity (genitality) and Rosario her rivalry. Each of these cities is used as a defence and refuge from the conflicts that surface in the others. Consequently, her symptoms appear predominantly during journeys (the connection between one place and another) and the analysis therefore largely centres on them. This produces a further consequence, which is dissociation and fragmentation in each of the cities. For example, when she is in Santa Fe, she stays at home and refrains from going out or seeing her girlfriends or relatives, here again dissociating dependence (her home) from independence (her friends). In Buenos Aires, she is late for her sessions, while in Rosario a phobic avoidance of the hospital emerges. On one occasion, when I travel to Rosario for the first time to give classes, she faints in the hospital, a place where her rivalry with me is concentrated and which, because of my presence, is connected with her attempts at independence and genitality.

This fragmentation of space is a projection of the fragmentation of her conflicts, which enables progressive, fragmented and controlled re-introjection, with gradual working through of the 'fragments'. This patient labour lasted for months that seemed totally unproductive but which nonetheless led ultimately to a condensed and explosive breakthrough of insight, as described below. In Maria Cristina, this major fragmentation of her conflicts (of her objects, her ego and the relations between them) was useful for their gradual working through. We consider that the reason for this may be that the symbiotic relationship is a highly condensed relation with very complex and contradictory aspects that need to be 'broken up' in order to be introjected and worked through by degrees.

## Re-introjection and the body as a 'buffer'

Re-introjection can be done only in small 'doses' and at an appropriate pace, so that when a certain 'threshold' is passed, the re-introjection functions as an abrupt return of the repressed. In this case re-introjection may occur on the bodily level which already involves the possibility of a certain degree of re-introjection but also means using the body as a 'buffer' that tends to prevent alterations of equilibrium on the mental level. I call this function a 'buffer' because this word originally refers to solutions that counter or damp down any change in the acidity or alkalinity of a medium. (The body 'buffers' as a homeostatic mechanism.)

I shall illustrate this process with a session nearly two years into analysis, which I have chosen because circumstances created conditions that placed the phenomenon in greater evidence. This session takes place on a Monday following two missed sessions, one cancelled by me and the one after it, cancelled by her. On the Saturday immediately before the day of the session, she had attended a class of mine in Rosario. She also knows that after this session I will be absent for a week.

> (1) She arrives punctually. She folds her arms and then grasps her left wrist, saying, 'Now I have the same feeling as on Saturday: a slight feeling of confusion'. She tells me that on Saturday she encountered a girlfriend and her brother in a coffee shop and they spent about two hours studying the drawings of a schizophrenic patient, and 'suddenly I started to feel badly; confusion and a feeling that pressed on my brain. I couldn't breathe and wanted to run out. I calmed down but kept feeling that my brain wasn't mine. The same feeling when I entered the classroom. When you came in I calmed down. Afterwards, we took the tram and I was very confused: I was alone and felt I was sitting there and at the same time that I was outside the tram, running alongside it. At that point I felt frightened and got off. I cooled off because it was raining. Compared to before, when I was crying and shaking, I wasn't afraid of going mad'.

The confusion when she comes to the session is the same as when I went to Rosario; two parts that she kept divided and separated become intermixed. Additionally, while retaining me, on the one hand, as a very frustrating object (I cancelled a session and will now be absent for a week), on the other hand, she internalises me as a libidinal and idealised object by using my knowledge to interpret the schizophrenic's drawings. Since I travel to give classes in Rosario, the spatial separation no longer controls this division of the object (frustrating and idealised), which also causes confusion.

Introjection fails and cannot be maintained because the encounter between the frustrating and the idealised object provokes madness when she feels oppressed inside (she can't breathe). She calms down when she is able to divide and control the introjected part in her body: 'I calmed down but I kept feeling like my brain wasn't mine'. That her brain wasn't hers implies denial of introjective identification: the knowledge was mine and she was unable to accept it inside because the introjected object was cathected with her own greed and need to control. She calms down when she sees me enter the classroom because this proves that I am not inside her, I am outside, and therefore unable to control or destroy her, as she too has not destroyed me with her rage at the frustration.

The brain functions in the body-mind division in the same way as the spatial division, controlling the separation of two different affects or two parts of the divided object.

She herself points out that when she shook and had convulsions everything was easier and less anguishing whereas now, when they are absent, she is afraid of going mad. The trembling and convulsions served as 'barriers' against experiencing the 'fear of going mad'. When the body-mind division is about to fail again, a total splitting in two occurs: she felt she was sitting inside the tram and at the same time running alongside it. This is an attempt to re-establish the division between persecutory and protective objects: on the one hand, autism (sitting without me, with her internal objects) and on the other hand symbiosis (running alongside the tram as if running away with me). This phenomenon of the 'double' emerges as an escape from her confusion in finding that she was very much confused with her psychoanalyst.

(2) I interpreted that she was confused because of the anger she felt when I cancelled a session and was now about to abandon her for a week, and that she was trying to prevent her anger from destroying everything good and valuable she had got from me.

(3) She answers, 'Yes. Because Thursday night I had a dream. I've been nervous for several days in a strange way and conversation relieves me but now it's just the opposite. On Thursday night I lay down to sleep and was very nervous and I suddenly saw the clinical examination room and saw a man lying down who looked like my father. I didn't see his face, and that person was dying and all the doctors were coming in. It's the first time I've seen a man die. I woke up choking'.

She is pointing out that when there is confusion re-projection does not function well as a defence (conversation fails to relieve her now). Her aggression kills the objects of her love (her father and me). The narration of the dream also involves some confusion, a failure of the control (separation) between waking and sleeping; she doesn't quite know whether it is a dream, a fantasy or a hallucination ('I lay down to sleep and . . . suddenly I saw' and 'it's the first time I've seen a man die').

(4) I interpret that because of her anger a part of her dies that is connected to her relationship with me.

(5) She tells me that she woke up feeling quite anguished and tried in every possible way to get in touch with her boyfriend.

(6) I interpret that she is trying to contact her boyfriend in order to replace me during my absence so that she won't be left alone with dead things inside her.

(7) She smiles, answers 'yes' and talks again about Saturday, when 'what most bothered me was that I didn't have any conversion symptoms; as if it were all in my head'.
(8) I tell her that in her head she had all my knowledge; she had me with everything she envies in me.
(9) She goes on talking as if she hasn't heard me: 'Other times I even started to do something or took a sedative and it would go away, but . . . I didn't feel nervous, it was quite strange, it was confusion'. She folded her arms and said she feels like going to Santa Fe this weekend.
(10) When I show her the denial of what I interpreted and the reasons for it, she says that she met a girlfriend and her friend said she had also dreamed that her father was dying.
(11) I interpret her attempt to share the guilt for my destruction, just as she shared it with her brother and mother for her father's destruction.

When she answers 'yes' and smiles (7), this is a moment of insight, but when I go on interpreting what might represent a threat of re-introjection, at that point she goes on talking as if she hasn't heard me. The danger of introjection provokes the return of division and separation between the contents of her autistic relationships and everything related to me as a depositary in the symbiotic relationship, and she adds that she wants to go to Santa Fe. The latter is her attempt to regain spatial control when faced by the danger of introjecting the good that I possess (knowledge) which she envies.

It is interesting to note that autism does not always mean that the subject remains inside with what is good and idealised and that the bad and the persecutory, from which there is a tendency to flight and defence, remains outside. As in the material I have just transcribed, in autism what is mad, destructive and dead remains, while the good that cannot be re-introjected is preserved outside. When control and separation between the external and the internal are being lost in the face of a threat of re-introjection and the consequent confusion, the body acts as a 'buffer'.

## Some characteristics of the emergence of insight

I have mentioned a third period in Maria Cristina's analysis, characterised by the development of insight. This is not to say that there was not some degree of insight before this third period, but what it does mean – and what most characterises this stage – is more frequent emergence of moments of insight in an abrupt, almost explosive way; it is only in the latest months of treatment that all the previous years of analysis may be seen to have 'crystallised'. It is also undoubtedly appropriate to make explicit that I by no means consider this as a definitive insight in which all of my patient's difficulties are resolved. Up to now, there had been small 'nuclei' of insight that remained isolated or encysted then suddenly came together and crystallised. This was more noticeable now and was also reflected in her influence on and behaviour toward the persons around her.

This third period started to take shape more firmly when her brother improved and resumed his studies, and when Maria Cristina began to pay for her own treatment.

The process of projection-introjection was partially though not yet firmly re-established. This implied – among other things – a steadily improving contact with reality, because on the basis of her relation with internal objects (a narcissistic relation), projection-introjection involves an imperceptible but continuous 'contamination' by the real characteristics of the depositaries and objects of the external world. That is, in projection-introjection and re-projection and re-introjection, although it happens little by little, new experiences are always rectifying the internal image. The break with stereotyped behaviour that this involves very often generated a feeling of bewilderment in Maria Cristina, preceded by and alternating with fear of change and the fissuring of the affective blockage and of the stable and rigid defensive organisations of autism and symbiosis.

Whenever the rupture of the defensive organisation was excessively abrupt, two very particular phenomena followed: one was a need or fantasy of attacking someone or attacking herself, and the other was the fear of looking at herself in the mirror. Although I will not go into these fascinating topics extensively, let us recall that the rupture or confusion of the symbiotic relationship entails a certain degree of loss and disorganisation of the body image, providing an opportunity for re-organising both this image and the feeling of identity, two very closely related processes.

She used aggression in an attempt to control and restore the boundaries of her body, configuring them anew through abrupt contact with external objects. In the studies of M. Mahler I have also found a description of this phenomenon in symbiotic psychoses, which she interprets similarly. Auto-aggressive activity (head-hitting, biting oneself, etc.) is an attempt to sharpen knowledge of the boundaries of the body, the ego and the non-ego. This is also expressed in the well-known phrase, 'to pinch oneself to see whether one is awake or asleep'. To illustrate, I shall present the following fragment of a recent session:

> The patient tells me that her parents are in Rosario and that she was able to see, for the first time, that they actually loved each other and that she had to rectify her image of parents always being in discord. She also found it very strange that her mother demanded nothing of her. While she repeats these ideas over and over again, *she pinches* the back of her hand, and at another moment says that she fancied that a car was going to hit her.

In these periods, there also appeared a fear of the dark and various phenomena or manifestations on going to sleep. One of these was a feeling that she was 'dissipating', and she had to turn on the light immediately, or alternatively, she would react with a muscular jerk.

The fear of looking at herself in the mirror is her fear of discovering that she has changed so much that she is now unrecognisable and of finding a strange person there when her feeling of identity is not yet firmly anchored. The psychological perception of a still unsecured change of identity extends to the mirror image.

Zazzo (1953) describes how children are only able to recognise their image in the mirror when they are two or two years and two months old, this being preceded by a special behaviour of disorganisation. Towards the end of the third year some anxiety appears in association with the child's pleasure of looking at his or her own image in the mirror.

This disorganisation, previous to the possibility of looking at oneself in the mirror and accepting a change in identity and the body image (personification), is the consequence of a certain rupture of the symbiotic relationship, and it is this that provoked Maria Cristina's temporary fear of looking at herself in the mirror.

Now, I shall present material that illustrates another very peculiar phenomenon in relation to insight and change: the fantasy of pregnancy and childbirth:

> She has gone to Santa Fe, and when she returns, she phones me from Rosario during the hour of her session to say that she has just returned from her trip and that she will not have time to come to her session today, but will come to the next one. It is the first time that she has called to let me know that she will be absent but that she wishes to come.
>
> She arrives at the following session quite punctually, and when she sees painters working in my house she says that this has provoked a feeling of great bewilderment in her since when she left her house in Santa Fe it was all in a jumble because painters were working there. On the way to my office, she was thinking about how she would find me.
>
> I interpret that she was thinking about how she would find her things that she left in me during her absence, because now that all her things in relation to her parents and Santa Fe have got into a jumble, she is completely bewildered if she doesn't find her things here exactly as she left them when she went away.
>
> 'Mmmmm . . .'. She touches her temple and is silent for a moment. Then she tells me that yesterday and today she felt very depressed and that in an outing with her boyfriend she lost her handbag where she had money to pay me, her father's pen, her identity documents and a photo of her boyfriend. Since she was going to take an examination, she phones her mother asking her to mail her an old identity card, and her mother thought

she was calling her because it was her mother's birthday, which she had forgotten. And she says how this time everything was so different in her house; they knew about her relationship with her current boyfriend, and not only accepted it but showed friendly interest in her things.

Faced with the changes in her home and in herself, she attempted to regress to an old identity (to be as she was before) and to return everything to its former state; all this was accompanied by a loss of all the current and new connections that threatened the dependent relationship with her mother.

I interpreted her bewilderment regarding these changes and told her that this is why she needs something fixed and unchanging and that she had delegated this to me. It was I who could restore to her all of her old way of being.

She replies that today she was thinking about suddenly discovering herself with a child, since the changes happen so quickly that she is hardly aware of them. She sighs. She says that now she doesn't understand what she reads very well and that she doesn't want to take the exam. 'I don't know why I feel that this year my courses have been like giving birth'.

At another moment when very important changes occurred in her real life and relationships, the expression she used was that she felt she was in labour, trying to expel her mother.

When changes are abrupt and take place rapidly and unexpectedly, the fantasy of pregnancy signifies an attempt to control changes in a more familiar area (the body) and in the shape of another commonplace event (pregnancy).

The fantasy of childbirth and of trying to expel her mother implies separation from the symbiotic object that she was holding inside her and that was also holding her inside it.

## Summary and conclusions

Based on the works of W.R. Fairbairn concerning the problem of dependence-independence and of M. Klein and her school regarding projection-introjection, I have developed and deepened the knowledge of these processes through a study of the analysis of a patient, demonstrating:

(1) the dependence-independence conflict is based on a disturbance of the projection-introjection process;
(2) blockage of the projection-introjection process (concomitant with blockage of the dependence-independence conflict) attains a degree of stability through the formation of autistic-like relationships on the one hand and symbiotic relationships on the other;

(3) these autistic and symbiotic relationships are organised by the dissociation of projection and introjection;
(4) proof of the constant co-existence of autism and symbiosis in which one or the other predominates absolutely, relatively or alternately;
(5) by studying the transference, the emergence of even minimal expressions of autism and symbiosis, and in this regard: (a) I review the salient points of development in the literature on these topics; (b) I extend the concept introduced by Liberman of transferential autism to include transferential narcissism; (c) transferential narcissism encompasses the character of the relationship in both autism and symbiosis; (d) I explain how knowledge of this co-existence of autism and symbiosis explains the character of transference in psychotics; (e) I postulate that transferential autism and symbiosis co-exist in all analyses.
(6) I discuss the group character of the conflict and of the processes studied and also relate projective and introjective identification to psychopathic behaviour by specifically analysing the relation between 'the deposited' and 'the depositary' and the difference between projecting, delegating and promoting roles.
(7) Attempts to re-establish the projection-introjection process are sometimes expressed as particular phenomena attempting to recover control when there is danger of losing it: (a) presentation of phobic attacks, fainting, etc.; (b) fragmentation of objects and relationships and their control in space; (c) the body acting as a 'buffer' when re-introjection is abrupt or massive; (d) appearance of the phenomenon of the double; (e) auto-aggression as an attempt to restore the body's boundaries and identity when there is danger of losing it; (f) fear of looking at oneself in the mirror as fear of confirming a bewildering change; (g) a feeling of 'dissipation' occurring in the dark, and recovery by turning on the light or by means of a muscular jerk; (h) attempts to give up everything new that is bewildering and to revert to 'the way things were'.
(8) Re-introjection is facilitated when it occurs in a fragmented and controlled way, with gradual working through of 'fragments' preceded by fragmentation of what initially appeared in very 'condensed' form.
(9) Insight appears sporadically in an 'explosive' way, associated with fantasies of pregnancy and childbirth in which independence and maturation are reached by expelling the object as well as by emerging from inside the object.

# 2

# Symbiosis in *Warrior's Rest*

My aim at this time is to deepen the study of symbiosis by undertaking an essay in applied psychoanalysis. I examine a novel of great psychological subtlety by Christiane Rochefort, *Warrior's Rest* (Rochefort, 1958). Although this novel can be studied for its own sake, it also serves to illustrate and apply what I have deduced from clinical work, although it does not specifically include material of a clinical nature. The advantage of choosing a novel is that the material studied is easily accessible for anyone who wishes to compare opinions; another, even stronger reason is that the study of symbiosis involves the analysis of the intercrossing of roles. In clinical material the field would be that of the transference and countertransference, which would therefore have to be limited to what is publishable, with evident impoverishment of the original material and disadvantages in relation to the clarity of the exposition. I was also interested in studying symbiosis that is allowed to follow its course in the interpersonal relation, whereas psychoanalytic therapy is, in this sense, a fundamentally 'antisymbiotic' task.

In my previous study on the problem of dependence-independence in relation to processes of projection-introjection, in studying symbiosis as a form of dependence using some clinical material, I made the following observations:

(1) autism and symbiosis are always coexistent, with an absolute, relative or alternating dominance of one of them;
(2) both are narcissistic object relations, the difference being whether the depositary is another person or the subject's own mind;
(3) both are intimately connected to the phenomena of projection-introjection or, more precisely, to a dissociation between projection and introjection, autism and symbiosis being the two extremes of this split;
(4) in symbiosis the projected role coincides with role of the depositary. Strictly speaking, we should refer to symbiosis when we observe a crossed projective identification in which each depositary acts according to complementary roles of the other, and vice versa;

(5) symbiosis is based on massive projections that are immobilized inside the depositary, in such a way that a large part of the subject's ego is estranged[30] in the latter;
(6) symbiosis is 'mute'; the symptomatology only appears with noticeable clarity when the symbiosis ruptures. I pointed out its involvement in psychotic transference and to some degree in all analyses, as well as its relation to psychopathy and hypochondria;
(7) rigid control of the symbiotic link aims to prevent the depositary from breaking the narcissistic object relation and to avoid its re-introjection;
(8) the symbiotic link is a highly condensed relation between very complex and contradictory elements that need to be 'broken up' and discriminated to enable their re-introjection and working through. The re-introjection can only occur in small doses and at an appropriate pace. Small 'nuclei' of insight are produced which remain isolated and encysted and which at a certain moment come together and crystallize giving rise to insight that appears in an 'explosive' way;
(9) when a certain 'threshold' is passed, re-introjection acts as a sudden return of the repressed, sometimes manifesting as specific phenomena which tend towards recovery of control when there is a risk of losing oneself: phobic attacks and fainting spells, fragmentation of objects and their control in space, the body acting as a 'buffer', the phenomenon of the double, auto-aggression, fear of looking at oneself in the mirror, a feeling that one is fading away, a return to something previous and familiar;
(10) in symbiosis there are deficits in personification, in the sense of identity and in the body schema, as well as confusion between feminine and masculine roles, and a communication deficit on the symbolic level with increased communication on the pre-verbal level: even speaking is a way of acting.

## Symbiosis and the nature of the object relation

This study of symbiosis has led me to confirm my observations in the previous chapter. There I asserted that 'the symbiotic link is a highly condensed relation between very complex and contradictory elements that need to be 'broken up' and discriminated to enable their re-introjection and working through.' Although it was not my specific aim at that time, the present contribution basically relates to this point: the nature of the symbiotic object and its vicissitudes.

Symbiosis is a link or relationship with an object which because of its characteristics I call an *agglutinated* or *glischroid* object. The latter term,

30 [*enajenada* – see p. 11, n. 25]

introduced by F. Minkowska in the study of epilepsy, originates etymologically from the Greek and means viscous.[31] Viscosity is the phenomenon resulting from the link with an agglutinated object.

Symbiosis is a relation which permits the *immobilization and control* of the agglutinated object. The latter is a conglomerate or condensation of very early outlines or formations of the ego in relation to internal objects and to parts of external reality, on each and every level of integration (oral, anal and genital), all *without discrimination* but also *without confusion*. Confusion arises when discrimination is lost, whereas in agglutination there is strictly speaking no confusion, since discrimination has not yet been attained. The agglutinated object includes the most primitive psychological structure, in which there is a fusion of internal and external (a state of syncretism: Wallon), and its persistence constitutes the psychotic nucleus of the personality. The intensity and character of the symbiotic dependence depends on the magnitude of this psychotic (agglutinated) nucleus.

Loss of the immobilization and control of the agglutinated object and consequently its mobilization, is produced in a *massive, accessive, paroxistic* way, provoking or threatening to provoke *the total and immediate annihilation* of the subject's ego, accompanied by the most intense, massive and primitive *catastrophic anxiety*, which surpasses the possibilities of the kind of defensive techniques found in the paranoid-schizoid and depressive positions. The defensive techniques that act against the agglutinated object are the most primitive ones, but they also appear violently and massively at their maximum intensity: *dissociation, projection and immobilization*.

In the establishment and stabilization of the symbiotic link (immobilization and control of the agglutinated object), self-regulation is accomplished basically through communication on a regressive, concrete level where words have the immediate sense of actions. A similar role is played by sexual relations, reinforcement of the persecutory situation and aggression, psychopathic acting and hypochondria. They are used to juggle and balance many dangers, such as the danger of losing the depositary or of being shut in. The vicissitudes of a symbiotic relation may be understood entirely as a function of a fluctuation between claustrophobia and agoraphobia.

In these cases, sexual relations have a compulsive character and are a form of acting which stabilizes roles and establishes a control over the distance between the two participants (feedback). As for persecution, not all persecution is by a bad object but also by fragments of undiscriminated (agglutinated) objects or by objects the discrimination of which has been lost. Reinforcement of persecution by an agglutinated object may be a very useful defence mechanism, in the sense that at least the dangerous object is thereby given a location. Paranoid anxiety may function as an alarm signal, unlike catastrophic anxiety provoked by threat from an agglutinated object

31 [See Introduction, p. xxiii]

whose immobilization and control has been lost. In the latter situation, the reaction is massively disruptive. Confronted with paranoid anxiety, neurotic defences may be used, but this is not possible in the face of catastrophic anxiety provoked by the agglutinated object. Of course, we are speaking of typical situations, without considering variations of degree or transitional cases.

Throughout our study of symbiosis, it seemed to be fundamental to differentiate between object and depositary (following concepts introduced by Pichon Rivière), since one of the characteristic features of symbiosis is coincidence between the projected internal object and the role taken on by the depositary. *All symbiosis is always group symbiosis* and consequently involves two or more interrelated individuals. The symbiotic group as a whole has the characteristics of an agglutinated object: it moves *en bloc* in a massive and rigid way; the unit is the entire group, with no differentiation or discrimination between its members; roles are fixed and rigid; they are allotted rather than shared,[32] having been taken on by its members in a complementary and solidary manner. The lack of differentiation or discrimination between members of the symbiotic group lies in the fact that *even though roles are fixed, the depositaries who take them on may rotate or alternate, although this rotation is also done* en bloc *or massively.* In a symbiotic group there are at least three roles which are fixed and always present: the protected, the protector and the observer-controller. The third is the group's hypochondriac, who has converted self-observation and control into observation and control of the group, whose other members are like his own organs. These three roles may be distributed among two or more persons.

Symbiosis is established and operates first and foremost in the area of the body and the external world. *The mental area is severely dissociated or split off* from the other two and is present as a spectator at the events and vicissitudes of symbiosis, unable to intervene in them or channel them. However, the area of the mind is also sometimes invaded by or involved in the alternations of symbiosis, with the most varied consequences.

Separation from the depositary requires the working-through of the symbiotic relation, which is to say the working-through of the agglutinated object. This is quite gradual and is brought about in fragments that are split off from the rest of the agglutinated object through a *diversification of links* with other objects and other depositaries, as well as a *reactivation of the perverse-polymorphous stage,* in which different zones of contact with the same agglutinated object or one of its fragments are diversified, alternately and jointly. These diversifications allow progressive discrimination and gradual and controlled re-introjection. Everything that contributes to fragmenting and discriminating the condensation of the agglutinated object also helps to

32 [*i.e.* as parts are allotted to actors when casting a play]

re-establish the process of projection-introjection and the working-through of the agglutinated object.

The link with an agglutinated object is not specific or exclusive to symbiosis, since we also find it in epilepsy and in all the states that we include in epileptoidia, in intense emotional blockages, in sleep and dreaming and in the phenomenon of negative therapeutic reaction. The transference relation also tends constantly to be structured as a symbiotic link, since at the same time as it is a regression the agglutinated object (the psychotic part of the personality) is reactivated, which is also due to the fact that very different experiences, involving very diverse objects and parts of the ego with very distinct characteristics, are accumulated and condensed in a single depositary (the analyst).

When symbiosis is broken suddenly (that is, when the depositary is suddenly lost), the agglutination may be weakened, and then there is a danger of psychotic dissolution with dispersion. In this regard, we highlight a difference, introduced by Bleuler, between *Spaltung* and *Zerspaltung*,[33] which it now seems important to take up again, since *Spaltung* is a dissociation that separates already distinct parts, while *Zerspaltung* corresponds to irregular fragmentation and disordered dispersion of the agglutinated object, in other words to psychotic dissolution. If this difference postulated by Bleuler and emphasized by Minkowski has practically gone unnoticed, I believe it is because our knowledge of schizophrenia derives from studies based primarily on pictures of psychotic restitution in which *Spaltung* is more evident than the *Zerspaltung* of the agglutinated object, which is present in moments of psychotic dissolution. I believe that these considerations may help us better to establish the dynamic relations between epilepsy, schizophrenia and symbiosis.

When control of the agglutinated object is lost and it invades the mind, confusion may result. One defence that permits immobilization of the agglutinated object to protect the ego by using the body as a buffer is hypochondria, studied by Rosenfeld as a defence against confusional states. What I wish to point out is that confusion is not a feature of the agglutinated object itself but that *it appears when the ego is invaded*. The agglutinated object is not confused; rather, it is undiscriminated. However, when it is no longer immobilised or controlled, *it is an object that confuses*.

Aside from this relation between hypochondria (control of the agglutinated object in the body) and confusion, we see that, at some point, all phenomena related to the dynamics of the agglutinated object modify the clarity of consciousness (sleep, dreaming, the negative therapeutic reaction, rupture in the symbiosis) and may even abolish it entirely as in the case of epilepsy. This suggests that the different degrees of this decrease in clarity of consciousness (whether normal or abnormal) depend on the invasion of the

33 [See p. 61, n. 48]

ego by an agglutinated object of variable magnitude. The maximum effect is *total annihilation of consciousness and of the ego*, a danger which inspires catastrophic anxieties (with maximum intensity and massivity), since the agglutinated object is massive and undiscriminated. In these conditions the ego is unable to use any defences since its destruction is total. Everything is in danger, not only the good internal objects or parts of the ego. The instrument of defence itself is destroyed. In this sense, psychotic fragmentation (*Zerspaltung* of the agglutinated object) saves the ego from a total, deadly annihilation.

ψ

The suggestion or working hypothesis at which I have arrived is that, in addition to the two basic positions postulated by M. Klein (each with its own characteristic anxieties, objects and defences), we may identify a third, previous to both, characterized by an agglutinated object relation, catastrophic anxiety, and defences such as splitting, projection and immobilization, functioning with maximum intensity, massivity and violence. Whereas the paranoid-schizoid and depressive positions constitute fixation points for the schizophrenias and for depression, respectively, this new stage which I am suggesting as a possibility is the fixation point for epilepsy and epileptoidia. I suggest that we refer to it as the *glischro-caric position*.

Transition from the glischro-caric to the paranoid-schizoid position takes place by means of slow and progressive fragmentation and discrimination inside the agglutinated object, which coincides with a gradation of splitting and projection, all of which leads to the establishment of the process of projection-introjection and the appearance of new defences that are capable of operating in the paranoid-schizoid position but would be totally insufficient in the glischro-caric. *The paranoid-schizoid position is thus built on ground reclaimed from the glischro-caric position.* W. Bion suggested a difference between splitting and dissociation, which I think coincides with the perspective I am presenting here and it could therefore be inserted into my hypotheses. Dissociation takes place in the paranoid-schizoid position while splitting takes place in the glischro-caric position in order to separate or to preserve the ego from the agglutinated object and also to operate against the agglutinated object, fragmenting it or separating a part of it in order to immobilise or control it, or so that it may eventually be worked through. This operation against the agglutinated object (which Bion calls splitting and Rosenfeld calls abnormal splitting), at its maximum level corresponds to what Bleuler called *Zerspaltung*; what Bion calls dissociation corresponds to Bleuler's *Spaltung* and to Rosenfeld's normal splitting.

The same may be said for projection as we have said for dissociation. The difference in its intensity in the glischro-caric and paranoid-schizoid positions makes these two processes qualitatively different, with consequences that are also different. In the glischro-caric position the intense, sudden and accessional projection of an agglutinated object or its fragment is not accompanied by re-introjection, and does not alternate with re-introjection; instead it is accompanied by, and alternates with, immobilization. This difference in the projection paralyzes learning throughout this entire sector of the personality.

Just as for the two types of dissociation, so for the two types of projection, I believe that it is preferable to avoid labelling them with the adjectives 'normal' and 'abnormal'. I consider it advantageous to use Bion's terms: dissociation and splitting (or dissociation and fragmentation), and in the case of projection, I think that it is better to speak of projection and agglutinated projection.

ψ

In order to explain to the reader all these points on symbiosis, I have brought forward the material that I present below, thereby reversing the order in which they became evident to me. This is because for the purposes of explanation there is no need for the reader to retrace every vicissitude of the investigation and of the deduction. However, it is an important point, because in the course of studying the novel one can see the deduction of this knowledge rather than its application, and this is also how the process originally occurred. The reader's work is made easier by first hearing about what has been deduced and bringing forward the conclusions, as I have done here.

## The material

The novel is in two parts and its narrator is the protagonist, Geneviève Le Theil, a student who takes a twenty-four hour trip from Paris to a nearby city to take possession of legacy from an aunt. 'There was nothing to indicate that my life was about to be disrupted.' (p. 5)[34]

At the hotel, she mistakenly enters the room next door to hers and sees the body of a man who has visibly attempted suicide. She takes the necessary precautions for his assistance, but from that moment she feels herself tied, linked to that person's fate. The link is consolidated when she goes to visit him at the hospital the following day and in this way the symbiotic relation is established. She returns to Paris only some time later with Renaud. The entire novel is concerned with the vicissitudes of this symbiotic relation, which we shall study in detail in the first part and very briefly in the second part.

34 [Page numbers in Rochefort's novel, which have been added to this translation, refer to the English edition (Rochefort, 1962 [1960]), from which the quotations are also taken unless otherwise specified.]

## Conditioning of the symbiotic link

Geneviève arrives from Paris to claim the legacy of an aunt, showing no signs of grief for this 'relative I hadn't seen since my First Communion.' (p. 7). She came only to claim her legacy, planning to stay for twenty-four hours. Then she would return to Paris, where her fiancé awaited her.

When she arrives in the station, nobody is waiting for her to 'warn me, advise me' (p. 5); that is, she suddenly feels that here there is no one to protect her. It is raining, and as she sees the train that brought her drawing away she feels a *shiver* (p. 5). She reflects that in Paris the weather was fine and that was why she didn't bring a raincoat; she thinks that one should not rely on that, since 'we always think the weather will be the same everywhere' (p. 5).

Through this material and as a function of the total context of the book, we now understand that here Geneviève feels that she is missing the protection she had in Paris (not enough clothes). Neither did she bring any internal object that would protect her and she thinks that she had better mistrust the belief that feeling protected by external objects also means that there are internal protective objects ('that the weather will be the same everywhere').

She reacts with loneliness and abandonment when she sees the train that brought her moving away: it is the link with everything protective contained in Paris and the part of her that is tied to it. She overcomes this situation by immediately organizing all the details for her return: 'Everything was mapped out. I like everything to be mapped out' (p. 6).

Our first encounter with Geneviève allows us to deduce that, when she is separated from the city and the persons by whom she feels protected, she has no objects left inside her by which she can feel protected. Separation and the loss of the protective external object produce her reaction of *loneliness and abandonment* (schizoid depression). However, when the train that brought her leaves, she also has a *shiver*: it is a moment when she feels threatened by very dangerous internal objects and the shiver functions as a defence mechanism which is *massive and paroxistic or accessional, that prevents re-introjection and reinforces the dissociation* between a dependent and protected part and another part that is protective but is *dangerous to re-introject*. This defence is then consolidated by the obsessional control.

Afterwards, she leaves the station and walks '*as I might have expected*, into an ugly, wind-swept square' (p. 6). The repression of surprise here serves a defensive function similar to that of the shiver she felt before, preventing the return of the repressed.

She chooses one of two hotels at random: 'The Peace' instead of 'The Station' (p. 6), names which also symbolize what she was seeking and what she was repressing (the station: loneliness and abandonment).

She is irritated when the hotelkeeper asks her if she wants a room for one or two persons: 'Couldn't he see I was alone? I confirmed it for him.' (p. 6).

Her irritation stems from the reminder in the hotelkeeper's question that she is alone, unprotected and divided. The hotelkeeper gives her 'an unnecessarily suspicious look' (p. 6), in which we see the projection of her own mistrust because of her perception of her splitting. Thus there is very actively functioning *a part of her ego as self-observation and to control immobility* and of what must on the one hand remain introjected and on the other hand be projected.

> I went upstairs escorted by a bootboy of doubtful cleanliness. The wash basin had a sluggish drain, and the hot water wasn't hot. I made the best of it. I changed my blouse and went downstairs; the hotelkeeper took his nose out of his newspaper and watched me as though my conduct amazed him. It was quite unremarkable, however; it was nearly one o'clock and I was going to have something to eat before going to see the lawyer.
>
> (p. 6)

This unremarkableness is the schizoid experience that Fairbairn describes as futility, and it shows us how Geneviève acted towards everything new with a certain distance or detachment. The doubtful cleanliness of her interior is projected on to the servant who takes her up to her room. The washbowl with a sluggish drain symbolizes the deficit in projection of her dirty internal objects, and the lack of hot water her emotional helplessness. She herself is amazed by everything which is happening to her and tries to deny it or slow it down by seeing it all as unremarkable.

That day she visits the lawyer and when she leaves his office she is the owner of two properties and other possessions that would ensure her a comfortable life. Then, 'I gave free rein to the daydreams I'd sensibly refrained from till then, for fear of disappointment – with old people there are sometimes surprises: bad investments, devaluations. ... Aunt Lucie had apparently avoided these pitfalls.' (p. 7). Aunt Lucie was up to then *a doubtful object*: she might frustrate her or gratify her, but now that the doubt had been dissipated, she could let go the control, be happy and make plans: the property would be dedicated to needy children: 'I loved children, especially since my health might never allow me to have any of my own.' (p. 7). She has to use the money for others in order to avoid feeling guilty and she will repair in others her own unhappy childhood. If Aunt Lucie turned out to be a good object, the problem of guilt and doubt is displaced onto her own insides: she doesn't know whether she will be able to have children.

Aunt Lucie was a doubtful object up to then. When she is *discriminated* as a gratifying object and is introjected, internal persecution and a reactivation of doubts about her own insides (hypochondria) ensue. Then her mental block recurs: when she returns to the hotel she 'felt vaguely that [she] had already wasted too much time.' (p. 7). In the hotel she mistakenly goes to the room next to hers and opens the door: this is a search for an external object, for company, to reassure or defend her from her persecutory (doubtful and confused) interior.

## An encounter and the return of the repressed

When she opens the door of the room next to hers, she sees a man lying on the bed fully dressed, his mouth open and snoring irregularly. 'In the fading daylight there was something *sinister* about the whole picture.' (p. 8). She touches his hand and it is cold; she shakes him and gets no reaction. 'It was horrible.' (p. 8). She sees two empty phials next to a glass and realizes that it is a suicide. She runs out and calls the hotelkeeper who looks at her with suspicion 'as though I'd painted the whole picture myself.' (p. 9). She explains that her key opened the wrong door,

> 'And it's lucky it does! Lucky *for you*,' I stressed, with a heavy emphasis which I thought not out of place. . . . Finally he got onto the police station and announced to me, as though I were *a member of the family*, that they'd be there right away.
>
> (p. 9)

This encounter with a dying (dead and alive) man breaks the immobilization and repression which had been maintained with a certain equilibrium up to then. The return of the repressed makes her experience the scene of the dying man as sinister and horrible. There is some confusion or coincidence of internal and external (she feels that the hotel attendant looks at her as if she had painted the whole picture) because of the projection on to the dying man of her own internal objects, and she struggles against this confusion or coincidence by making it clear that the discovery is lucky for the hotelkeeper rather than for her. This discrimination (putting things into place) is oscillatory, and the coincidence returns in experiencing the event as if she were a relative (an experience akin to *déjà vu*). 'I started resentfully when I heard myself associated with that dying wreck.' (p. 13). Her start is a violent and massive dissociation that is opposed to the coincidence of the internal with the external: that is, a dissociation opposed to re-establishment of projection-introjection. Her start has the same defensive function as the shiver she felt when she got off at the station, and both have the same paroxistic or accessional and massive character.

## The process of accepting the depositary

On the hotel registration card, he is registered as Jean Renaud, student (later she learns his real name: Sarti). His baggage is no more than a briefcase containing neither money nor identification. The police inspector comments: 'He probably ... tore it up and flushed it down the lavatory.' (p. 10). 'He'll be in a fine mess when he wakes up in the hospital with no papers and no money. And he thought his troubles were over.' (p. 12). When she hears these words from the police inspector, Geneviève is confused and doubts: 'Till that moment I'd been convinced I'd done a good deed. I suddenly realized that "Jean Renaud" might look at it differently.' (p. 12). She understands the coincidence in having saved Jean Renaud in order to save her dying internal objects. She saved him as a depositary of her internal objects. This is why she subsequently acts in a repeatedly reparatory and masochistic manner.

At times she totally forgets what has happened:

> I owned some premises let out in flats and a house with beautiful grounds; for a moment I'd forgotten about them. I regained my footing. 'I'm going out to dinner,' I said happily ... 'After all that excitement,' said the hotel-keeper, 'you need a good meal.' Excitement? What excitement? Oh, yes, the dead man. I remembered him with embarrassment. That long, cold hand which I'd touched. I went upstairs to make myself more presentable.
>
> (p. 14)

Denial also has a defensive function, but this is viable when the splitting between the internal and the external is successful.

> I didn't do much justice to my 'dinner for gourmets'. Sitting alone, surrounded by sumptuous dishes, I felt ill at ease; I hurried back to the hotel.
>
> (p. 14)

She again feels lonely but tends to immobilise the projection-introjection: she cannot eat.

Before going to sleep: 'I sat down in front of the table and tried to get down to essentials' (p. 14); in this way, she tries to use obsessional control (get down to essentials) to establish a discrimination amidst the confusion. But this attempt is unsuccessful:

> Not a sound, except for the hoarse rumbling of trains, which passed out of earshot leaving a still deeper silence behind them. I was alone in the middle of the night.
>
> (p. 14)

Alone in the night, she feels overwhelmed by her internal confusion, there are no protective objects. Confusion spreads and erases the boundaries of her identity, ideas escape her and she experiences madness and loss of control. Everything is accentuated when she hears the trains that, like the one that brought her, leave her behind and disconnect her from the protection of Paris.

She stops feeling lonely and everything falls into place when she remembers that

> on the other side of town a man was struggling as they snatched him back from the peace he'd found for himself. In his hospital bed, what was happening to 'Jean Renaud'?
>
> (p. 14)

When she accepts the depositary and the projection into him, she no longer feels lonely and oppressed: there is someone to take in her dying objects. If she accepts Renaud inside her, everything becomes orderly and calm. And she can sleep.

That night, she has a nightmare:

> I'm looking for someone; I come into a public place, I'm greeted by the laughter of men and I realize I'm wearing a nightgown that's too short and not very clean. This scene haunted my childhood in various forms, made a brief reappearance after my father's death, then vanished. I'd hoped it had lost track of me. But no. Here it was again. I decided that the man I'd seen the day before had died at last.
>
> (pp. 14–15)

If Jean Renaud has died and the depositary has disappeared, during sleep the repressed returns as a nightmare. She seeks help from men but fails, since she is soiled by her incestuous tendencies. In sleep, splitting of the projected from the introjected also fails.

When she wakes up she realizes that she is having a bilious attack. If Renaud has died, his place is taken by hypochondriacal control due to a previous re-introjection ('The simple fact was that I'd eaten too much for dinner the night before, there was no mystery about it.') (p. 15). However, this hypochondriacal defence is unsuccessful and she feels a compulsive need to find out about Renaud, which is a search for or re-encounter with the depositary for re-projection. She cannot evade her need to go to the hospital to ask for information, but once she is there she is also unable to avoid an encounter with Renaud.

## Recapitulation

Up to this point, we have met only one of the protagonists and have followed her for a few hours of her life in detail, beginning at a moment when she tended to deny any change at all and made an effort to hold rigidly onto her psychological organization (her distribution of objects).[35] The dangers begin when she feels separated from her protective external objects (Paris and her fiancé), provoking loneliness and abandonment. Her defence against the danger of disorganisation is achieved with mechanisms that intensively and massively reinforce dissociation or splitting: the start and the shiver paralyze and block projection-introjection and this blocking is consolidated by denial and obsessional control.

This situation continues with different oscillations and alternations and she might have been able to return to Paris and her fiancé and regain her links of protection and security, of dependence.

Her encounter with the suicide, a dying man, suddenly interrupts the *status quo*: the repressed returns brusquely, with a rapid alternation of massive projections-introjections. At different moments this produces an experience of something sinister, something familiar, an erasure of boundaries between internal and external and the consequent confusion. She can no longer re-establish the original immobility and mental block. Dangerous internal objects are now operating that threaten her with confusion, madness and annihilation. The need for a depositary is pressing and there is a pre-configured compulsion to re-establish immediately a link that will keep her free and protected from her dangerous objects: *symbiosis as a defence against confusion and annihilation: estrangement*[36] *of a part of herself in order that she can go on living.*

Her entire interior is uncertain, and her objects as well: her father (about whom other details are given later in the novel) is stained by her incestuous tendencies. Her aunt might equally gratify or frustrate her. She also learns from the hotelkeeper that on the grounds of her property a motel was going to be constructed: 'the motel, you know, one of those road-side barracks that are getting to be so fashionable . . .' (p. 14). Renaud is dead and alive at the same time.

## The configuration or establishment of the symbiotic link

Geneviève goes looking for her depositary and now we need to follow her and observe, in her encounter with Renaud, the projective intercrossing with which symbiosis, the 'pact' between them, is established.

Compulsively, she goes to see him at the hospital and is guided to him by a nurse, who 'dragged me along against my will, in a flood of explanations.' She follows her, 'dazed and bewildered.' (p. 15). This is the automaton-like

35 We note a first coincidence with the negative therapeutic reaction: the need for 'nothing to happen' and for this, the rigid control and immobility in the distribution of objects.

36 [*enajenación* – see p. 11, n. 25.]

state in which she is going to be 'symbiotised', the condition in which she offers herself passively as a depositary of Renaud's projections. It is not a question of simple introjection but of introjection that will mobilise or promote roles similar to those that are introjected, and that the two of them will fuse together. Renaud as a real object is a necessary object for her, but one that is unknown and dangerous, 'doubtful' (one of Geneviève's expressions), and for this reason she carries on 'dazed and bewildered', in a mixture of confusion, panic and paralysis.

The nurse functions as an intermediating object. She tells her in advance that Renaud is expecting her, 'He wants to see "the woman he owes his life to, after his mother" . . .' ; that when he came out of his comatose state 'he opened one eye and said, *"Merde!"* . . . Ever since he started feeling better it's been like a circus around here.' (p. 16). As predicted, Renaud receives her with a flood of pompous, mocking and cynical words, but the content is a bitter complaint about his fate and a request for protection. *This contradiction between form and content* (the 'two fronts' in the transference) provokes bewilderment in Geneviève. In these circumstances, Renaud slips in a 'There, there, don't cry.' (p. 17) when she is not crying at all, with which he also deepens her disorientation.

She thinks that Renaud evidently does not feel the slightest gratitude towards her for having saved his life, which is the opposite of what she consciously expected. When she asks him if he needs anything, Renaud answers, 'Nothing at all, thank you. You've already done far too much for me.' (p. 17). Renaud cannot be grateful. His envy of the woman who can give life prevents him.

With all the intrapsychic process that occurred in Geneviève (projection into Renaud of her dead and dangerous objects), in her meeting with him she is *paralyzed and invaded*. Renaud makes her feel responsible for his having stayed alive and this makes her feel guilty because, for her, Renaud stayed alive in order to carry her dead objects. Geneviève will have to go on injecting life into him in order to avoid re-introjection, but not too much life or she might lose him. As a depositary Renaud needs to be living and dead, like her projected objects.

The dialogue with Renaud is on two fronts: on the one hand it is disparaging, but on the other it promotes in Geneviève the need to continue to take care of him like a child who hangs on his mother's neck and makes her feel guilty for having given birth to him. This has also inverted the original formula. Geneviève went looking for a protective situation, whereas with Renaud a situation is configured in which she is the protector, with the result that she is protected to the extent that she projects her own crippled parts into Renaud. His lack of gratitude reinforces her own feeling that she is not protected or taken care of in this new relationship, since she does not find this reassurance in her good internal objects. To achieve this, she is destined to continue repeatedly and compulsively giving and constantly 'saving him'. If she were to fail or to stop doing it, she would be invaded by her own dead and dangerous objects. To survive, she needs to feed Renaud's greed in order to avoid succumbing to her own; she has nobody to protect her in the way that she is going to protect Renaud. In protecting him she shelters herself.

To her surprise and in an indirect way she feels obliged to return to the hospital the next day (Renaud has 'involved' and obligated her and she has 'involved' herself and has promoted and reinforced Renaud's 'involving' of her) although her original project had been to return to Paris that day. She is already locked inside the depositary and cannot leave. She has an attack of phobia: 'I was ill at ease. And it was too warm in that hospital. I should have taken off my raincoat. It was a real diving suit; I was sweating abundantly.'[37] (p. 18).

The fate of this symbiosis is sealed and the 'pact' has been consummated.[38] Before leaving the hospital, she feels *pity* for him and nostalgia for the parts of herself that she has deposited in him.

> He seemed to want me to come. He must be terribly lonely. It showed, in spite of the way he was braving things out. I'd felt a little sorry for him, in fact. After all, I could spare one day for a man who'd just killed himself. (p. 18)

He is not a man who had just been saved by her intervention. Because of what she had projected into him, he was '*a man who had just killed himself*' and she was a mother who had given birth to a dying son, who had to go on living while dead for her and because of her. He accepted this role in exchange for someone who would take charge of his life, which he was unable to do: death in exchange for dependence: this is his chance to live. The symbiotic link is thus a pact with the dead, destroyed and dangerous parts of its members, who 'pledge themselves to each other' in order to carry a corpse they hold in common. However, it is a pact for life and for the possibility of continuing to live. *The secret of symbiosis is that of a living corpse that needs to be kept, controlled and immobilized by the participants*; if control is lost, destruction or at least the risk of it ensues.

When she leaves the hospital, she feels relieved. She has left all her dead and dangerous objects inside Renaud, and that day she makes all the

37 The phobic attack appears frequently at two typical moments: when the symbiosis is installed (claustrophobia) or when the symbiotic link is broken or weakened (agoraphobia). It may be replaced permanently or temporarily by attacks of asthma.

38 Fairbairn, commenting on 'A Seventeenth Century Demonological Neurosis', says, '... the whole point of a pact with the Devil lies in the fact that it involves a relationship with a bad object.' What Christoph was seeking from Satan '... pathetically enough, ... was not the capacity to enjoy wine, women, and song, but permission, to quote the terms of

arrangements in relation to her inheritance. Under these conditions she can also think about being happy: she would buy an automobile, a fur coat, she would go to the south (on holiday), would live well and get married to Pierre, her fiancé. 'I'd be happy' (p. 18).

She thinks about all this, but when she says 'I'd be happy', the dissociated part of her returns: she does not know what to do with the house she has inherited, 'an old residence without style' (p. 18), and she returns to her decision to stay in order to resolve what to do with the house. This rationalization screens her compulsion to take care of Renaud, not to separate from her dissociated part, projected into Renaud. It functions with the same structure as the phenomenon of the negative therapeutic reaction:[39] if she accepts happiness she also has immediately to take charge of her dead and dangerous parts that threaten to destroy her. It is a circle of iron. Her object relation *functions en bloc* with no dispersion or discrimination. It is a reaction that functions in terms of the law of *all or nothing*: if she wants to take on her life, she has to take on her death instantly and simultaneously. *If she wants to live, she must also repair and give life to her dead objects, in which case the ego and all its good objects run the risk of succumbing.*

> I stayed. That ridiculous resolve seemed to have been made without me, and in easy stages. One of these was a sentence thoughtlessly spoken under the influence of the heat and now holding me prisoner.
>
> (p. 19)

The decision to stay had been made by another part of her, dissociated from this one that now fantasises being happy. She was a prisoner of one part of herself projected into the depositary. She is thus a victim of one of her 'fragments', a part of her own ego linked to her dead and projected objects.

the pact itself, "sein leibeigner Sohn zu sein" ("*for to be unto him euen as a sonne of his bodie*"). What he sold his eternal soul to obtain, accordingly, was not gratification, but a father, albeit one who had been a bad object to him in his childhood.' (Quoted by E. Pichon Rivière in 'The Uncanny' (Pichon Rivière, 1947)). The pact (symbiosis) is control and pacification of dangerous objects in order to remain inside oneself 'euen as a sonne of his bodie.' (Fairbairn, 1952, p. 71). [The Spanish version has: *para estar dentro de él como hijo de su propio cuerpo*, literally 'to be inside him as the son of his own body']

The study of symbiosis takes us deep into the psychology of 'pacts' with the devil (Christoph Haizmann, Faust, etc.) and of *folie à deux*, as well as the negative therapeutic reaction, which is also a pact. In all these phenomena, a part of oneself is sacrificed *in order to go on living with the rest inside oneself.*

39 Negative therapeutic reaction is not entirely a quality of any particular type of neurosis, but results from a certain relation between analyst and patient. Negative therapeutic reaction is a symbiosis in which there is a crossed projection; it is a 'pact'. The 'lethargic object' described by F. Cesio (1958) is an agglutinated object which is not lethargic but instead 'induces lethargy' when it is mobilized and invades the ego.

She fantasises a way she might get rid of symbiosis or at least mitigate it: she would help Renaud financially:

> I'd make it possible for him to get out of there, because, after all, it was my fault he still had to take trains (that is, it was her fault that he had to go on living). I'd pay for his ticket and even give him enough to live on until he had – whatever it was that he wanted. Furthermore, wouldn't it be an excellent first use of the money I'd inherited? A good deed. The idea was taking shape. Then I'd be even with that Jean Renaud who'd come along to commit suicide on my path and had been disturbing my mind since yesterday, no matter what I thought about him. At bottom, I felt *remorse*; I'd have to *pay a price to get rid of it*.
>
> (p. 19)

## Derision and pity

With this fantasy of bribing her persecutors she returns to the hospital:

> And so the next day, carefree because I felt certain I'd solved all the problems, I walked into B Block. I found my victim sitting on a bench, chatting with his nurse.
>
> (p. 19)

She strikes up a conversation, in which her fantasy of a bribe totally fails and instead of ending the relation their connection becomes closer; her need to repair Renaud and her dead objects in him is reinforced. It is no longer only a process of projection and control, for to this is added in a fundamental way a compulsion to make amends, to give life to her depositary and keep him alive. This strengthening of the symbiosis is takes place through an intercrossing of derision and pity.

With his derision, Renaud makes her feel her weakness in relieving his own, and he promotes guilt in her, and the role of protector. With her pity she relieves her guilt and makes him feel her protection, promoting and intensifying in him the role of being the weak one who is burdened by the death of both of them. With derision and pity, the symbiotic circle intensifies itself in a distribution of roles. *What is most typical of symbiosis is that roles are not shared but allotted*. The allotment of roles implies a stricter dissociation in order to avoid destruction and confusion. For role sharing, it is necessary to have reached a discrimination, and therefore a successful schizoid division. Sharing is creative while allotment demands immobilization and indicates a paralyzing vicious circle. In the symbiotic relation (or symbiotic group) the individuals who take on these roles may rotate or alternate, but the roles themselves are fixed and unmovable. There are also symbiotic groups in which no rotation in role-taking is possible. On the other hand, *in a symbiotic group, one role that is always present is that of observing and controlling the group (the hypochondriac role)*, for which the other parties to the link are like organs or parts of the body which need to be observed and controlled.[40]

ψ

Renaud surrenders the living parts of his healthy ego:

> 'You see? My little soul is still here,' he said, pointing with precision to the middle of his chest. 'You'll have to make the best of it; it's yours, it belongs to you, it no longer concerns me. Do whatever you like with it, it's your possession.'
>
> (p. 23)

Renaud also allots and does not share:

> 'And now you've got a soul on your hands. But you can always throw it away. It's not asking you for anything; it doesn't ask anything at all of anyone at all. It doesn't give a damn about anything. It was very nice of you to help me get out of there. Thanks. But now it's every man for himself.'
>
> (p. 23)

Renaud asks for nothing from anybody. But he will make the other give to him without having to ask or, to put it more clearly, by promoting in the other the role of giver or the need to give 'He wasn't begging. He was at most consenting to receive.' (p. 25). He shows neither that he is receiving nor that anyone is giving to him.

Now it is Renaud in this dialogue who reinforces his dissociation and the projection of his dissociated part, and this dissociation and projection of his 'soul' is experienced as a death. He asks for a glass of rum as a 'last wish' (p. 23), while he has an attack of phobia: 'There really were beads of sweat on his forehead; he was probably more exhausted than he was willing to show. He had a stubborn, anxious expression.' (p. 24).

Here, language has an important function in the communication: it is what basically establishes symbiosis. However, language does not exert this function by operating at the level of full symbolic value but on a regressive level as acting and also as agent of the other's acting. Instead of promoting a symbol or meaning in the recipient, it directly promotes acting. The symbolic level is not in the fore and words have their literal, concrete sense.

40 These observations on group psychology were developed later in *Psicohigiene y psicología institucional* [*Psycho-Hygiene and Institutional Psychology*], Buenos Aires, Paidós. (Bleger, 1966).

Renaud asks her for a glass of cognac:

> 'you'll have to treat me', he said brusquely, 'I'm broke.' 'Of course', I said, smiling, 'Isn't that my duty?' It was extremely imprudent. No doubt about it, that man was able to deprive me of every shred of common sense.
>
> (p. 23)

After drinking his cognac, he says, 'I'm all yours.' (p. 24). Geneviève thinks, 'Let the heavens fall, I'd picked up the devil. Why did *an ordinary figure of speech sound like a literal reality in his mouth?*' (p. 24).

Words are acts and generate acts directly in the other. Geneviève perceives this and thinks: 'You had to have a dictionary to understand that man. . . . I felt as though I'd been talking gratuitously all my life and had just heard someone really talking for the first time.' (p. 25). Symbiosis functions and is stabilized on the concrete level. Words do not generate thoughts prior to action in the other but acts that are dissociated from the mental area and from its symbolic content. Communication is direct and literal, from action to action. The mind is dissociated. In any case, it is present as an *excluded spectator* of the drama that is being played out.[41]

## Metamorphosis

In the establishment of symbiosis a change occurs which is centred fundamentally on the body schema and which is experienced as a metamorphosis. The centre of the personality is no longer the more mature part of the ego: the repressed returns, displacing it and inhabiting its place.

Geneviève no longer resists symbiosis and she surrenders to it. The ego nuclei (up to then strongly repressed) involved in symbiosis are now the centre of her personality. Change is experienced as madness:

> I was mad. My body underwent an intense metamorphosis, I was going to come to myself as a caterpillar or a white whale, I was going to scream, weep, yelp, or bray. I loved him. I loved that man. And I had from the start.
>
> (p. 26)

41 This spectator, the excluded part (the mind), which acts as observer and which as a role, as we said, is always present in every symbiotic bond, although its depositary (whoever assumes the role) may rotate or alternate, is related to manicheism, which was introduced into psychiatry by Magnan and taken up later by Dide & Guiraud to characterize delusional pictures in which there is a struggle between coexisting persecution and protection or rather between persecutors and protectors. This struggle seems to operate outside the patient or without the patient, who is present as observer or mere spectator. The latter is most characteristic of the picture of delusional manicheism according to Dide & Guiraud.

This sudden actualisation and dominance or breaking through of a part of her regressive ego, until now strongly repressed, is experienced as madness, but a madness which is controlled and fixated in the bodily metamorphosis. We could say that it is like a generalized, massive, *en bloc* hypochondria, since it takes over the entire body – not just a segment of it – in an intense and sudden way. This saves her from psychosis. From that moment onwards a severe dissociation between mind and body is established. The regressive symbiotic level operates and is installed principally in the body schema, whereas the mind can operate at the logical level of reality and adjustment to it, *in an observing function*, where it is often perplexed and does not understand why the body does not obey and even seems to be independent of it.

When she accepts the symbiosis, the change, the metamorphosis, and she no longer struggles against it, a certain peace or at least relief arrives; the phenomenon is similar to the relief felt by psychotics when they accept and submit to their delusions or hallucinations and in general their persecutors. 'I felt relief, as though I'd just given birth. It was done. I'd confessed. He knew.' And at the same moment:

> My whole being ached. A warm animal had been living inside me for the past minute and it was already taking up all the room; the monster was expanding and it was myself. The self that had always denied love at first sight and had just been struck dead by it.
>
> (p. 26)

Displacement from the centre of the personality towards the regressive and symbiotic ego nuclei is perceived as being in labour, a birth, a revival full of life, but also as an invading monster, a pregnancy that takes over the entire personality. The fantasy of labour and pregnancy are simultaneous and arise as attempts to control anxieties by referring the unknown to what is most familiar and concrete.

After the metamorphosis she is a different person. They were eating but now she is no longer hungry. 'The other girl had been hungry. In the girl I now was, the hunger had been distributed differently' (p. 26).

*ψ*

Metamorphosis derives from Greek and means 'complete change'; the word and its etymology correspond quite accurately to what occurs in reality and to what we have seen in Geneviève. This 'complete change' of personality presents a problem and an answer. The problem we face is why in these cases an actualization of links (always involving a segment of the ego and an object) leads to a complete change of personality when other changes take place only within the continuity of the same personality. The answer is that if there had been good schizoid division, or in other words a sufficient fragmentation and discrimination of ego and objects, no change of link would be experienced as a global and massive change of personality; no fragment of the ego (or of the object) would condense or polarize such a large quantum of the total ego that its actualization could be considered a metamorphosis.

This naturally brings us to a second answer or at least to a logical consequence: a metamorphosis may occur, as in the symbiosis which we are studying, only if *the ego is displaced in massive, condensed segments which have not been sufficiently fragmented or differentiated*, in which case the passage from one fragment of the ego to another is a real change of personality, a metamorphosis. This is what I call the *agglutinated object or agglutinated object relation*.

ψ

'He magnanimously gave me time to get settled in my new skin and to put my new world in order.' (p. 27). This change is experienced on the one hand as a disaster, the collapse of her former ego and the break-up of all the organisation corresponding to that ego. Now, everything is reorganised and has new meaning. In this reorganisation everything is arranged or adjusted to a different ego (until now repressed) on a regressive, magical level.

> Everything was becoming clear to me: why I'd walked under a ladder, why I'd chosen the Hôtel de la Paix, why I'd hurried back to it at six o'clock, why I'd opened the wrong door and why my key had unlocked it: because I loved Renaud Sarti.
>
> (p. 27)

The consequences give order to the events that preceded them and everything is integrated on a magical, teleological level full of meaning. 'That I was meant to love that man was as plain as the nose on his face, for all eternity.' (p. 27). This predestined *coup de foudre* is a phenomenon akin to *déjà vu* from the dynamic viewpoint; the *coup de foudre* is a sudden encounter with an internal, idealized image and thus it appears to have the characteristics of predetermination.

## Dangers of the symbiotic relation

Symbiosis is a relation whose equilibrium may at times be very unstable, especially during its installation.

'I was a white whale and completely mad, ready to burst out of my skin.' (p. 27). The metamorphosis is not only the establishment of a new bodily ego, but an invasion that tends to break through the boundaries of the ego and the body schema that are operating up to that moment. In the face of this danger of 'bursting' or suddenly losing boundaries, bodily contact is indispensable, a new kinaesthesia that re-configures the boundaries of the body scheme: 'I wanted those hands to touch me.' (p. 26).

If regression risks becoming too intense, there is danger of 'fading away' and contact with the other becomes indispensable in order to limit regression and re-configure personification by 'looking at oneself in the other' in a search for limits:

> But it was essential, essential, to be alone with him, between walls, sheltered from everything, away from everything, alone with him for a moment, just to be able to look at him, as you must have still water to throw back your reflection; it seemed to me that there, outside, even though the streets were nearly deserted, everything prevented me from seeing him; I did not have him, he was far away.[42]
>
> (p. 28)

Another risk is that of staying dependent on and submitted to the object:

> Those hands, that face, that hard mouth, that long body . . . had become closer to me than my own, my flesh itself, a physical extension of myself; or rather, it was I who was an extension of them; I depended on their slightest movement . . . The whole world arranged itself around that newcomer; he was already my master and was ordering me to do things I would never have dared to do.
>
> (p. 28)

We may reduce the fundamental risks to three: one, that of remaining shut inside the object and/or depositary (claustrophobia); another, that of losing control of the object and/or depositary: 'incompleteness anxiety'. The third is that of confusion with the object and/or depositary. These three dangers alternate rapidly and may even co-exist. Symbiosis may be understood entirely as a stabilized defence against the dangers of alternating or oscillating from claustrophobia to agoraphobia and *vice versa.*

## Time

Symbiosis was finally configured over lunch. Few words passed between them. 'You can't do everything at once.' (p. 27). Geneviève suggests that they go to her house, the one she has just inherited. '"As you like," he said. "I'm all yours."' (p. 28). He presses her arm and Geneviève feels dizzy: danger of confusion. She is very impatient to arrive. It is a reaction of impatience to escape the danger of confusion; until they arrive everything is kept paralyzed.

42 The role of the gaze in the personification has been emphasized by Sartre. He also makes interesting suggestions about 'pastiness' (viscosity).

'The time was endless . . . The next minute seemed inaccessibly remote. I'd never each it.' (p. 28).

Time stops when the paralysing of projection-introjection becomes necessary to control the confusion. Time also stops when the relation is massive and has only one object, when there is maximum reduction in diversification of object relations. The experience of time corresponds to displacement in space towards different objects. 'Temporalization can only emerge where the body differentiates real feelings of gratification and frustration.' (Koolhaas, 1958. p. 412).

If there is only one link and one uniform experience, then no experience of time is possible.

> [Renaud] couldn't even keep the days straight. How could he tell when it was Thursday? What indication was there? He didn't know the method. He would say glibly, 'All right then, Thursday at four'. But he had no way of recognizing that privileged moment amid the homogeneous flow of time . . .
>
> (p. 161)

> There was no sky for him, no outside. Time didn't flow, the days didn't follow one another, there was only one homogeneous, continuous day, one indefinite hour that was forgotten as soon as it passed; his life left no marks of its passing, he was always dying and forgetting himself along the way.
>
> (p. 58)

## Sexuality

The sexual relation is fulfilled as a compulsive kind of need. It is a link imposed as a communication technique in the interpersonal relation when all other techniques have become uncertain. Words and attitudes are no longer enough as techniques for the distribution of roles and for regulating the symbiosis.

Their first relation is a cunnilingus in which a distribution of roles between mother and child, protector and protected, mouth and breast, is configured and reaffirmed by what they do, by the act. The genital relation is thus a complete technique which consolidates the link and overcomes 'anxiety of incompleteness'.

Renaud makes an effort for her to reach orgasm and he requires her to confirm it verbally and explicitly. She is the depositary of life and the one who must have an orgasm responding with gratitude, tenderness and protection. His anxieties around his fear of destroying are calmed. *The sexual relation stabilizes the roles and establishes control of the distance between the two partners,* in the sense that they do not get lost because they are near one another, and they also do not fuse or become blurred because the contact and opposition of their bodies reinforces the boundaries of each as a separate individual.[43]

This experience of 'completeness' with concrete control of the various dangers of symbiosis will result in compulsive sexual relations:

> As soon as he left me I began to suffer. . . . 'I'm all yours,' Ah, but he didn't say till when. Maybe he'd leave me the next day, the next moment. . . . With Renaud beside me I constantly thought of losing him . . . Anxiety had taken up residence within me at the same time as its twin, desire.
>
> (pp. 29–30)

This anxiety of losing the object is also her safety valve against the dangers of symbiosis and it includes her own fear of fleeing from Renaud.

Sexual relations also imply reparation and gratification for both of them: 'We lay naked in the bed Aunt Lucie had died in' (p. 30) in an attempt to inject life into Aunt Lucie, her father and Renaud himself.

## Equilibrium in the symbiotic link

The symbiotic relation has been established. The roles are distributed and well configured and the instrument of control or balance (feedback) is principally the sexual relation.

They are now in Paris, in Geneviève's apartment. She takes care of everything and Renaud undergoes a schizophrenic regression: he never goes out, stays in bed all the time, reading detective novels, smoking, drinking and having sex. He does not speak. Geneviève thinks, 'I'd been reduced to facts: he was there.' (p. 35). Renaud's life is reduced to the minimum.

> His attentions to me, although they took up a good part of the day and the night, were confined to my body. . . . I had only a material existence. He didn't listen to what I said, he looked at it; it gave me a very strange sensation, as though another self existed side-by-side with me. Ensconced in his litter, he observed me and, oblivious to the circumstances or the time of day, he grabbed me whenever I passed within reach, even if I was pushing the vacuum cleaner or carrying the four ash trays.
>
> (p. 36)

He is part of her (her 'double') and there is no need to speak. Communication functions on a very regressive level, body to body. Although he has never

43 I mention in passing the role of coitus in discharging tension and anxiety and the similarity, established long ago, between orgasm and epileptic discharge.

said it, 'he had no "affairs" to get back to'; he is free: 'Such is the freedom of the dead.' (p. 32).

> He lived on my bed. To make that bed, I had to seize brief opportunities. Around him was a circle of ash trays. . . . he filled them, I emptied them; the cycle was constantly repeated. I kept the window open as much as I could; it's hard for me to breathe stuffy air. He said nothing, but I could tell he didn't like it.
>
> (pp. 35–36)

He is the living corpse, her own dead part that needs to be kept alive, just enough so that it does not die completely but not too much, to avoid losing him. He fills her with the stench of corpses (the poisonous atmosphere described by M. Klein) and she empties and periodically purifies herself.[44]

Renaud, the living dead (the maximum of death compatible with the minimum of life), is the corpse of Geneviève's father and Aunt Lucie (a dead couple) whom she needs to keep alive. They are in the same apartment as her father kept to which he used to take his lovers. The bed was ordered to measure especially by her father, because he was tall, as tall as Renaud, who is satisfied with the bed because before they were always too small for him.

Geneviève feels like a little animal who allows herself to be trapped, 'a continually devoured and willing victim.' (p. 37). This is in contrast with her discovery of her body as a source of pleasure, which she learns with Renaud's skilful guidance.

> That monster of selfishness, who cared nothing about loving, was the most generous of lovers: in love he never thought of himself, he took his own pleasure as a by-product, after all the pleasures he could give me had been exhausted.[45]
>
> (p. 38)

Geneviève oscillates from one extreme to another, and cannot clear up her confusion. The link pacifies her relation with her dead objects, but creates new conflicts, and new confusions which she cannot discriminate:

44 In a play by Ionesco (*Amédée*), an inward-looking couple also takes care of a dead person who constantly keeps growing, and poisonous mushrooms grow in the rooms, invading everything. The corpse which occupies more and more space, and other allusions, point to a lack of genital potency to repair and control or immobilize this progressive invasion by the corpse.

45 Renaud's 'generosity' when he showers her with pleasure 'without thinking about himself' is not of course generosity, but heavy obsessional control due to fear of becoming disorganized or dissolved in the orgasm itself.

> I didn't know whether I was being corrupted or developed ... Wasn't I a slave? Or was I a real woman? ... was it natural sensuality or perverse deviation? In short, was I normal or already depraved? My intense though partial pleasure, the only kind I could yet attain, was a drug and an obsession to me. ... I was almost afraid of him. Wasn't he trying to ruin me? Whither was he leading me? And my brain began to harbour irrational notions of sin, falls from grace, vice and perdition.
>
> (pp. 38–39)

Confusion appears because at that point the symbiotic link has fractured.

She feels absorbed by Renaud, by 'that timeless world ... I'd entered into the dark kingdom of Renaud, who was dead. *I was living with a dead man who kept dragging me down towards him*. ... I was almost afraid I'd lost the world.' (p. 39). Either she loses the world or she loses Renaud. Both are parts of herself and she cannot escape the dilemma. The drama played out with Renaud is the drama of her internal conflicts. However, she feels increasingly absorbed by the greediness of the death that she has to keep alive to prevent it from destroying her.[46]

Renaud has become a greedy and demanding dead man by whom Geneviève feels subjugated, attracted and absorbed. The progressive regression tends to search for an optimal point of equilibrium, *but each regressive level produces in turn new conflicts.*

> Monsieur Sarti ... in me had an income, a maid and someone to go to bed with into the bargain. He never lifted a finger in the place. The cleaning, cooking and shopping were for me. He no doubt thought it was all done automatically, together with all the complications of banking and withdrawing money. Monsieur Sarti lay sprawled on the bed, smoking the cigarettes I brought him at the rate of forty a day, drinking the whisky I handed him in a glass he never washed, and occasionally doing me the special favour of leaving the bed for an armchair while I changed the sheets, which I never seemed to do fast enough. He probably didn't know that rubbish accumulates in a flat, didn't understand how dustbins filled, or what arrangements existed for emptying them. He was oblivious to all that. But he was in good health now. He ate without appreciation – though he never complained – the food I prepared, consenting to move as far as the table to ingest it; I delivered his breakfast to him at his home, in bed. I sometimes felt weary, and it may have showed in my face, but he never saw anything in my face but desire. He noticed only what suited him, and then only if he had to make no

46 In reference to encysted dead objects kept alive inside, one patient spoke of 'sequestra', equating them to the 'sequestra' of bone in osteomyelitis.

> particular effort; if he'd had to exert himself in the slightest ... There were times when ...
>
> (pp. 42–43)

However, this internal rebellion is immediately pacified:

> I usually repressed 'someone's on velvet' with the aid of the following argument: Renaud had asked for nothing; everything I did was voluntary; if I didn't do it, he'd get along without it; he had nothing to lose; he had, with no half-measures, killed himself.
>
> (p. 43)

Renaud has reduced himself to the minimum compatible with life. This regression implies the minimum relation compatible with survival; minimum in the sense of remaining tied to one human being, Geneviève, and moreover in the sense that the relation with her is also reduced to the minimum of communication, on the most regressive level.

Geneviève has also withdrawn with him and she begins at times to feel 'almost afraid I'd lost the world; it was almost as though I were living in a convent.' (p. 39). She excludes all relationships, whether they are old or recent: her mother and her former fiancé.

For both of them, the installation of symbiosis has meant breaking up the diversification of objects and links. Everything centres on one depositary. Beyond it, the entire world does not exist.

This concentration on only one depositary is a regression which implies preverbal communication that is also very primitive in a link with an agglutinated object, as described above. In this sole object are concentrated love and hate, aggression and reparation, life and death, and on all levels: oral, anal and phallic.[47] For this reason, it is an object that has to be rigidly controlled.

This predominant relation with the agglutinated object (symbiotic dependence) and its strict immobilization and control involves the paralyzing of projection-introjection and the paralyzing of time with some loss of the sense of reality, deficit in ego integration and confusion between what belongs to one person and what to the other. Therefore, we find in the symbioses deficits in personification and identification, confusion between homo- and heterosexuality, and a deficit in the integration of the body schema.

47 We also find this concentration – the link with an agglutinated object – under normal conditions: in the adolescent's ideal of having a partner who would be his mother, girlfriend, sister, lover, wife, etc.

## Vicissitudes of the symbiotic link

Geneviève has had a very short interview with her former fiancé and they agree to end their relationship. She returns to the apartment fearing that Renaud will not be there, 'the logic of life required that Renaud disappear just after I'd made my last remaining sacrifice for him; sudden disappearance fitted him like a glove.' (p. 42). She is also afraid that he might have poisoned himself during her absence. 'What could he have used? I'd thrown out everything in my medicine chest, nothing had seemed innocent to me, not even the aspirin. I felt he was capable of changing a chocolate bar into poison.' (p. 42). (Projection of her own hypochondria into Renaud.)

She has broken one more link with the world and now only Renaud is left. She is afraid that he too may disappear. Her total dependence on him would make his loss catastrophic. But this fear co-exists contradictorily with her fantasy that he may leave or poison himself: a reaction to her fear of depending completely on him and of being shut in; also a reaction to the exclusive tie with one single object, which she fears may fill her with Renaud's poison and death. *The symbiotic tie is regulated fundamentally to some extent by sexual activity on the one hand and on the other by reinforcement or increase of persecution*. Just when she fears complete absorption in dependence, *looking for and provoking a quarrel* introduces some distance or some control of the relationship and of the fears.

Renaud only asks her whether she has brought something to drink. He asks nothing about her meeting with Pierre. 'I've just broken with my past. And even with my future.' Renaud replies: 'Good. You still have the present.' 'What present?' First of all, Renaud

> laid down his book, sat up on the edge of the bed, grabbed his shoes and put them on. Went into the bathroom, came back with his toothbrush, put it into his brief case. There was panic in my belly. He was leaving!
> (pp. 43–44)

Renaud has left. Since the relationship is for him one mass, any minimal frustration affects the whole in a catastrophic manner. Nothing is left. His agglutinated object relation functions *en bloc*, with no discrimination possible. It is the law of all or nothing.

Geneviève, angry and resentful, accepts his departure.

> Meanwhile my body was pressed up against the door, howling, and I was howling, too, like a dog. My body – I'd forgotten about that. My mouth opened, gasping for air, like a fish. And yet that aching flesh was part of me, too. It was stronger than all the rest, in fact. My mind was in a turmoil, my reasonable argument, or the distaff side of it, disintegrating.
> (p. 44)

Geneviève tries to make a mind-body division: her fantasy that he might not be there is her wish that Renaud go away, a way of going away herself when only the relation with him remains. Her fantasy is enacted by Renaud: he leaves. In her mind she accepts the separation, it frees her from the fear of the exclusive, absorbing relationship with Renaud. But it is her body that manifests the emptiness, the 'anxiety of incompleteness'. There, her symbiotic link functions very intensely and her body imposes itself: she goes out to look for him.

She finds him standing on a street corner, 'his face was dead, unlit by hope.' (p. 45). Without his protective object, Renaud is paralyzed and hopeless on a street corner. This is the panic of being left at the mercy of death. He is incapable of becoming depressed or of activating graduated defences: *loss of the protective object with which he has a massive (agglutinated) relation is catastrophic.* Loss of an object with these characteristics cannot be worked through in the depressive position. On the other hand, this lost object transcends the characteristics of a persecutory object that could be managed with defensive techniques of the paranoid-schizoid position. The reaction is one of annihilation and panic.

Geneviève implores him to return. A very sober and dense dialogue develops between them, in which there is an attempt at *rapprochement* and at a re-structuring of the distribution of roles. Everything hinges on the emphasis that it is she and only she who needs him to return. The link can be re-established only on the basis that she is the only one who derives something from the relationship. Renaud can accept nothing inside himself or receive anything from her. For Renaud, receiving something would involve his destructive voracity and revive his guilt for his mother's death: he already killed her with his voracity.

Renaud agrees to return, but first he asks for a drink and starts to talk about himself and about love:

> 'the mortal doesn't die, he survives. Just as he survives the atomic bomb, with his body made radioactive for good, and his soul hovering over the abyss of *potentially disintegrating molecules,* over the essential void.' 'not even love protects' 'Love is a bandage for blindfolding, that's common knowledge.'
>
> (pp. 47–48)

In this way, Renaud promotes in her the need to protect him from the threat of internal destruction. We also observe in passing the metaphysical character of his anxiety, similar in adolescents and epileptics.

'It was always when he was terrible unhappy and lost that he began raving. As though his despair drugged him. And right away he'd think of a bistro.' (p. 48). Drinking, and afterwards compulsive sexual relations. When he feels unhappy and lost (on the verge of a situation that would annihilate him) he needs to start raving and to feel desperate (anguished) because to feel anguish means to feel alive. This anxiety in turn is fought off by drinking and once again, in the face of the danger of annihilation, sexual relations are a technique to calm and pacify his anxieties. It is a vicious circle with feedback.

## Agglutination and dispersion

Following Renaud's experience of annihilation, when he returns to his link with Geneviève, the symbiosis is re-ordered and it is then, when he feels more protected, that he is able to recognize that he is on the verge of internal destruction ('potentially disintegrating molecules, over the essential void'), of schizophrenic dispersion, and this danger is so great that no love can save him. Renaud rejects life and runs away from it and by means of this flight and his rejection he saves his life. Symbiosis is his chance to go on living at the best level possible. It is no longer a question of saving himself entirely, but of *not destroying himself totally.*

This total destruction is schizophrenic dispersion, by which we mean psychotic dissolution rather than schizophrenic restitution, which already indicates some order and re-adjustment to the environment.[48] The state of 'potentially disintegrating molecules' does not yet correspond to schizophrenic dispersion but to agglutination. *Symbiosis, which is ultimately the immobilization and control of the agglutinated object, protects against destructive, annihilating, psychotic fragmentation (Zerspaltung).*

Dispersion is the characteristic of schizophrenia, while agglutination is that of epilepsy. 'In schizophrenia everything is dissociated, everything is dispersed, everything is disintegrated, while in the epileptic everything accumulates, condenses, agglutinates . . .' (Pichon Rivière, 1943–44, p. 367). This characteristic of epilepsy (agglutination, viscosity or glischroid ) was studied by F. Minkowska and corresponds to what we call the agglutinated object.

48 Bleuler distinguished '*Spaltung*' from '*Zerspaltung*' and says in this respect: 'The splitting [*Spaltung*] is the prerequisite condition of most of the complicated phenomena of the disease. It is the splitting which gives the peculiar stamp to the entire symptomatology. However, behind this systematic splitting into definite idea-complexes, we have found a previous primary loosening of the associational structure which can lead to an irregular fragmentation [*Zerspaltung*] of such solidly established elements as concrete ideas. The term, schizophrenia, refers to both kinds of splitting which often fuse in their effects.' [Bleuler, 1911, p. 362]. (Quoted by E. Minkowski: *La esquizofrenia* (Minkowski, 1960).) (In the English edition of Bleuler's book, the word *Zerspaltung* does not appear as such, but as 'an irregular fragmentation.') According to the terminology used in psychoanalysis, *Spaltung* would correspond to schizophrenic restitution, while *Zerspaltung* would be psychotic dissolution ('explosion' or fragmentation of the agglutinated object).

We have already emphasised the accessional, paroxistic, sudden and massive character of the defences when the protective link in symbiosis is lost, and now we highlight the similarity of the symptomatology to that in epilepsy (starting, shaking, shivering).

Therefore, we find the phenomenon of the agglutinated object relation not only in symbiosis but also in epilepsy and also as I have already indicated in the phenomenon of negative therapeutic reaction. The differences between these diverse phenomena may possibly be due in part to differing amounts of the psychotic or regressive nucleus that are involved in the agglutinated object.

We may further add that Renaud's difficulties in waking up are described frequently in the novel. They consist of a resistance to renewing contact with the real world. This orients us to consider that sleeping involves not only disconnection from the real world but also the concentration or limitation of the link to just one object and perseverance in this concentration. This would therefore show us another phenomenon in which the agglutinated object relation occurs. If this is so, it would explain the facilitation of epileptic manifestations that are produced by sleep. The mechanism of condensation in dreams is yet another case of a relation with an agglutinated object.

## Fragmentation of the agglutinated object through diversification of object relations

After they have sex a dialogue follows in which it is basically Renaud who speaks. He accepts Geneviève but not her love or any love. If he accepted and recognized love, he would destroy the object as he destroyed his mother: 'I never knew my mother, . . . She died when she gave birth to me. Too late: it was already done.' (p. 55).

His ability to speak also indicates a different link at this moment. He is able to verbalise now that he has experienced his capacity to separate from Geneviève and rejoin her. Assurance that he can separate and reunite is the safety valve that also allows him to integrate their relationship on a higher level of development (that of speech) and this assurance of the possibility of reunion is the guarantee that he will be able to effect separation. Speech itself is a recovery of the object and a control over it.

Now that the symbiotic link is renewed, it no longer functions with its previous stability. It is confinement for both of them. Geneviève defends herself from this claustrophobic anxiety with division:

> I realized there were two Genevièves: Mademoiselle Le Theil and Sarti's mistress, with a ditch dug by a bulldozer between them. The two didn't

> know each other, despised and denied each other. 'I'm a real woman,' said one, and the other said, 'You have a sexual obsession.'
>
> (p. 56)

Now Renaud can no longer remain shut in: he goes out constantly to drink. Both have learned something in the rupture and re-structuring of the relationship. Something has moved in both of them and the roles can no longer be so definitively dissociated. Now, each one has inside some link with his or her self. Claustrophobia is also present in both of them. Symbiosis shuts in and is dangerous since now each of them is carrying a bit of life and a bit of death inside.

'I was crushed to see our affair turning into a physiological case-history.' (p. 63). Renaud was drinking and was always drunk. Geneviève was nauseated, vomited and had liver attacks. Each of them had to control and immobilise internal persecution. Part of the drama which previously was played out only outside, between depositaries, had now been introjected and each of them now had to handle it inside. In the experience of separation each had introjected *a small fragment of the massive and agglutinated object relation* that had previously existed as an exclusive relationship. *The motor of this learning* was and continues to be the fear of being locked up inside the other. Each of them operated with internal defences on the bodily level.

Sexual relations are now more compulsive, faster and more aggressive:

> He slipped his hands under my skirt and caressed me, then he took me brutally, in the kitchen, making me lean over the table among the dirty dishes. He wanted to shove me down into the triteness of our situation and force me into a scene. When he was saturated – with him I could distinguish only between saturation and concealed intoxication – he was animal in his methods and swift in his gestures, unconcerned with my pleasure.
>
> (p. 62)

The genital relation is also dangerous now because of its contamination with oral greed, which was a displacement (on the table among the dirty dishes). For this reason sexual relations have a counterphobic character. They are also handled in a way that may lead to a quarrel (a scene) that will place distance between them.

The symbiotic link needs to be controlled. It constantly threatens to shut in, swallow and annihilate. It cannot be dissolved: projections are still massive. A small fragment of the projected had been re-introjected by each of them and as long as the internal working through of that 'fragment' lasted, each needed the other to keep massive, agglutinated, and still undiscriminated objects in a state of immobilisation.

Geneviève proposes a deal and she buys a car. Travelling together in it, they will be together without being alone and will be alone without being too much together. It's a deal between agoraphobia and claustrophobia. When they go to buy the car, they are still distributing the claustrophobic and agoraphobic roles: Renaud wanted 'a 1935 Voisin hearse, with vases for flowers, which made me think of Nosferatu the Vampire. I pulled him away from it, horrified. The thought of rolling through the streets in that catafalque, which delighted him, made me shudder.' Geneviève chooses . . . 'A glass-roofed Aronde' . . . and Renaud refuses to accept this 'moving showcase in which you ride around almost undressed, like a hermit crab without its shell'. 'Actually, he said, he'd like a car, provided you could sleep and make love in it and close the windows; better still, it should have no windows at all; whether it ran or not was a secondary matter.' (pp. 66–67).

They went out into the countryside together in the car, but everything was reduced to drinking and having sex. Geneviève accompanies him to bars and taverns. 'To maintain a balance, I mingled Renaud with my own friends and organized little parties in my flat . . . But Renaud gave them a tone that made me regret my initiative.' (p. 68). Going out and relating with people was the counterphobic struggle taken on by Geneviève. To overturn this initiative was the struggle against agoraphobia taken on by Renaud.

Contact with people also included advances in learning and development of the symbiosis. It implied an attempt to diversify object relations and fragment the massive and agglutinated relation with a single, exclusive object.

In this struggle for a stable or at least not dangerous equilibrium in the relationship, sexuality again plays a very important role together with aggression. Renaud forces Geneviève into exhibitionistic episodes, especially to show her breasts in bars and taverns; 'I engaged in exhibitionistic excesses of the kind he liked, and I added some of my own invention.' (p. 77). Then, with active induction by Renaud, she participates in sexual play with a lesbian. Psychopathic acting frees relations between Renaud and Geneviève of very destructive tensions. Renaud is also more and more aggressive with her and Geneviève increasingly passive and submissive.

When the genital relation can no longer control symbiosis, the perverse-polymorphous phase is activated and thereafter plays a very important part in fragmenting the agglutinated relation and in diversifying links. The perverse-polymorphous phase thus prepares the possibility of separation and of re-structuring the relationship on an ultimately more integrated level. *The perverse-polymorphous phase, by diversifying links, fragments the agglutinated object* and subsequently permits entry into the depressive position (following an earlier passage through the paranoid-schizoid position).

## Separation

'While I was sacrificing everything for him he went on sinking deeper, as if I was sacrificing nothing for him.'[49] To sacrifice everything, to submit to all his demands, in order to get Renaud to come to her or to make him feel that she loved him. Renaud demanded and demanded as a way of demonstrating that there is nothing for him or for anyone. Neither of them finds relief, whether in aggression or in promiscuity.

However, in this process of disequilibration of the symbiotic link, a moment comes when Renaud gains some insight. For the first time he complains:

> 'I feel ill,' said Renaud. 'Speaking doesn't mean anything. Ever. It doesn't explain anything. There's only seeing. Or not seeing. *You are very kind. But I feel ill.* There's absolutely nothing you can do. You're no use.'

Geneviève asks him to get treatment to be detoxified of alcohol. Renaud answers:

> As though alcohol were a cause; you take it away from the man and that's all there is to it. And what do you think you'll find afterwards? A man who's going to drink, or his ghost. So be logical. Put me back in my mother's womb.'
>
> (p. 78)

Renaud knows it is not the alcohol, that if he does not drink he meets his ghost, that drink pacifies the internal persecutor in the area of the body. Nothing can return him to his mother's womb and therefore he has to admit his mother is definitively lost and he cannot recover her. Not in the relationship with Geneviève either, because symbiosis is not regression to intrauterine life, even though that is the fantasy, as protection against the dangers of destruction. Symbiosis does not reissue or realize the fantasy of extreme protection like that which is supposed to obtain in intrauterine life. Even feeling unconditionally protected by Geneviève has made him feel bad and destructive.

'You're stupid. Stupid and useless. Lost like all of us.' (p. 79). Renaud finds insight in his destroyed objects and sees that not only he but she too is contaminated. However, Geneviève does not know it and that is why she is stupid. Everything that Renaud has put into her for protection is also contaminated.

49 [This passage is missing from the English version of the novel, and the following one has been mistranslated so both are here translated directly from the Spanish.]

> 'I'm alone, alone in the world.' . . . 'But while I'm doing it, dear Madam, I'm alone. . . . Living, maybe . . . Who knows? But how? . . . That's the whole problem. Actually, I'd like to live, I'm sure of it. If you have any ideas . . .'
>
> (p. 80)

After this dialogue, Renaud leaves. He has gained some insight into his illness. Geneviève's behaviour has taught him that his frustration and lack of pleasure in life does not come from what he is not being given but from his internal conditions: from his unrealizable ideal of extreme protection inside another's body, like returning to his mother's womb and recovering her alive. He demanded and demanded ever more of Geneviève, hoping that she would frustrate him, so that he would be able to attribute his unhappiness to external frustrations. Geneviève is now dangerous: she has made him feel ill and made him feel the danger of his voracity. In order to preserve her and to preserve himself, to avoid destroying both of them, he leaves. They must separate.

Geneviève is left in a crisis. Her attempt at reparation has failed and she accepts the separation from Renaud:

> Let him go: at long last the whole business was more than I could cope with. All incomprehensible, granted. All I knew was that he didn't love me and that I was powerless. *I'd have had to be super-human and I wasn't*, that was all.
>
> (pp. 80–81)

This is what Geneviève learned in the relationship with Renaud: that she could not repair his destroyed and dead objects. 'Stupid and useless' are his words that most affect her. 'With that phrase, Renaud had rejected me, cancelled me, annihilated me.' (p. 82). She had to take charge of her own internal destruction and the ineffectiveness of her omnipotent phantasy of reviving her dead objects.

She drinks like Renaud, coughs and has a fever. She calls Alex, the physician who moved into the office that had been her father's. She is admitted to a hospital for tubercular patients. She has time to leave a message for Renaud with a cheque 'payable to the bearer, to pay for his board and lodging and living expenses for several days.' (p. 85).

They have separated. 'What I don't like is that we're heading towards different cemeteries.' (p. 86). There is nostalgia for Renaud and she has left a letter, a connection to make a reunion possible. Her tuberculosis is the fixation of the psychosis in the body; 'It was a good thing I'd collapsed; I'd have gone mad otherwise.' (p. 88).

Both of them have learned something in the symbiotic relationship and this same learning is what has made it possible for them to separate.

## Summary of the subsequent course of the symbiosis

The second part of the narration begins with a description of Geneviève in the sanatorium. She contracted tuberculosis instead of having a psychotic episode. She is depressed (schizoid depression) and willing to die and has made her will. She awaits death.

> I hated the world and felt no pain at leaving it, I waited peacefully, completely pacified, for the end of that useless journey. I'd been a dead loss . . . It was a good thing I'd collapsed; I'd have gone mad otherwise.
>
> (pp. 87–88)

One day she finds Renaud at her side, speaking to her. He has done all he could to find her, has even sold a case of whisky instead of drinking it to raise money for the trip. During their separation he has acquired some insight into the character of their relationship, and to some extent their roles are now reversed. It is he who does everything possible to keep Geneviève from dying and he admits that he needs her to go on living. (The roles as such are relatively fixed, but their depositaries have changed.)

> And then, I've had enough of never seeing you come after me. . . . Then *I* made a tour of the bistros, *looking for you looking for me*, and I didn't find you; I was furious with you, you were a traitor, I hated you, it was almost love.
>
> (p. 90)

> I wasn't so complete as I thought, I'd caught a dependency, I'd weakened. There was a lost child in me, too. . . . The fact was that I was suffering from your abandonment of me . . .
>
> (p. 92)

Nourished now by his affection, Geneviève improves, and in Renaud's care she is able to leave the sanatorium. When their life together recommences and they have their first sexual relation since leaving the sanatorium, the ghost of destruction returns. Renaud says, 'Either I'll be the end of you or you'll be the end of me. That's human love.' (p. 101).

It is this presence once more between them, of the dangers of destruction, which leads them to multiple relations, to sexual promiscuity, and Sarti to alcohol as a way of diversifying the links and attempting to decrease the risks of destruction for both of them.

> 'You have no idea how hard it is for a man of my era to live among you. I drink only because I can't kill everyone . . .'
>
> (p. 108)

Geneviève is again the one who has to take care of him. Renaud, given up to drink and inertia, begins to suffer from anginas, rheumatism, chilblains and polyneuritis. When he feels emotionally close to Geneviève, he tries to break the phobic circle with aggression and sexual compulsion. Alex, the physician who cured Geneviève, follows the couple closely and it is he who understands the conflicts raging in Renaud:[50]

> When love finally touches fellows like him, they're often the hardest hit. Maybe it will save him.
>
> (p. 116)

The affection also has a massive quality, just like the aggression. It swings abruptly from one to the other without gradation or transition. Because of this massive quality, the affection is also dangerous; it shuts in and asphyxiates. The other danger is that, once love has appeared, in its release it is not possible to control the sudden, dangerous emergence of aggression. Aggression and love are thus massive and mutually excluding extremes. Both are dangerous and each is used alternately as a defence against the other.

The fear of losing her leads Renaud to the fantasy of marrying Geneviève and he tells her so. Afterwards, as a defence, he starts to direct a strong, silent hostility towards her:[51]

> I had to make up my mind to it: I was going to be mistreated for a period of indeterminate duration, until he'd digested his kindness.
>
> (p. 120)

50 At this point roles have been distributed among more participants, since the role of observation (the hypochondriac role) is now taken by the physician, Alex.

51 The use of increased persecution, aggression and traumatism, in order to avoid fusion and loss of boundaries – loss of personification – is quite frequent. I pointed this out in relation to the patient Maria Cristina, studied in the previous chapter. This was also described by M. Mahler in her patients (Mahler, 1960). In regard to the frequent loss of identity by schizophrenics, H. Rosenfeld (1950) describes the case of a male patient for whom it was extremely difficult to differentiate himself from his analyst and who dreamed that a German professor riding a motorcycle was trying to split himself in two by colliding with a lamp post. Dividing himself in two meant separating from the analyst with whom he felt mixed up. The analyst was of German origin and the patient had just applied for a professorship. Minkowski (1960) also refers to schizophrenics who complain that they cannot feel and who try to procure the feelings that they are missing through violent and sometimes dangerous acts. Cesio (1958) described the same phenomenon in negative therapeutic reactions in which the analyst-patient dissociation may be achieved through an accident. Aggression serves to separate as well as to unite in, respectively, cases of fusion with the object and of dissociation or separation from it.

A new character comes between them now, contributing some equilibrium to the relationship: Rafaele, a woman who 'resembled him like a sister'. (p. 122). Geneviève fulfils the role of mother for the two of them, who play like siblings at very childish or rather pre-pubertal games:

> They had codes and signals that were in perpetual mutation. They were as tiring as children.
>
> (p. 129)

> They instantly set up a family and a mythical birth . . .
>
> (p. 130)

Sheltered by Geneviève, Renaud learns anew with Rafaele, whom he feels is undemanding. He stops drinking, is active and even sings in the bathroom.

Geneviève is warned by a woman friend about the dangers of this relationship between Renaud and Rafaele. Geneviève has a fainting spell when faced with the risk of losing Renaud again. From that moment, the danger of Geneviève's illness reappears and he reacts to the fear that she may abandon him, fall ill or die. Now it is he who reinforces the link between them and he demands her continual presence at his side to avoid falling into depression. His relationship with Rafaele was possible as long as it kept the symbiotic relation with Geneviève immobilized. If she is in danger, he needs to reassure her. He can play with Rafaele as a child can play: as long as he is sure that he can go back to be with his mother. But the link with Geneviève without Rafaele is also dangerous:

> I want to sleep-die, and a woman is the best way to do that. Love is a kind of euthanasia. Lull me, put me back in my mother's womb, in other words, love me. What else is there to do?
>
> (p. 140)

Separated from Rafaele, Renaud returns to inertia and drinking and the circle of feeling shut in by affection and breaking it up with aggression and sexual compulsion, only to begin again to seek the emotional relationship and closeness. He has the fantasy of writing detective novels whose plots would reveal his experience of going mad (failure of agglutination and consequent psychotic dissolution). An attack of neuritis forces him to agree to see a doctor, although he does not follow any of his prescriptions afterwards.

Coinciding with this process of psychotic reactivation in Renaud and in view of his visible falling to pieces, Geneviève has a fantasy of having a baby:

> Maybe it was a secret desire to start a Renaud from scratch, and also to achieve his redemption in another way if my present means failed . . . And

> even if Renaud were to leave me some day, he wouldn't be leaving me utterly.
>
> (p. 155)

Geneviève gets pregnant and tries to immobilize herself in order to avoid damaging her child, thereby already reproducing her attitudes towards Renaud. She feels like nothing more than a receptacle or a carrier and tries to keep herself as immobile as possible in order to avoid damaging her child. In this she finds peace.

Meanwhile, Renaud worsens progressively as a reaction to abandonment and struggles with constant contradiction between complaining that he feels alone and imploring her not to leave him.

Renaud 'lived in fear . . . he no longer rebelled haughtily; on the contrary, he humbly admitted I was right and said he'd obey me if only he could.' (p. 164).

When Renaud attacks her, Geneviève throws him out in order to defend her pregnancy. Renaud implores her to take care of him and weeps. His omnipotence has collapsed:

> 'I once decided I was a god, and I've been drinking to make myself believe it . . . I want to belong to the human race at last, to that miserable, unfinished human race. . . . I'm a miscarriage of a man. But I'm sick of living as a miscarriage, I want to be nothing but a man . . . help me, you know how it's done. Help me to live. Force me to live . . .'
>
> (pp. 170–171)

Renaud is hospitalised. They separate. Before they do, they get married.

> 'He waved to me and walked through the gate. He was pale. He knew he'd never come back.'
>
> (p. 172)

## Epilogue

Renaud has achieved in symbiosis – because of it and also because of its rupture – an awareness of illness and the wish to be cured and to live, which leads to his hospitalisation. He has achieved this by going through a gradual and progressive falling to pieces of his defences, of his control, his dependence and his immobilization.

Geneviève does not attain insight into illness. She avoids psychosis at one point by contracting tuberculosis and later with a pregnancy, as an acting out. Both have learned through the evolution of the symbiosis and Renaud – who at a manifest level is the more ill - has learned more and achieved more insight.

## Summary and conclusions

A study is made of the symbiotic relation in the novel *Warrior's Rest*, by Christiane Rochefort. Conclusions from the previous chapter are verified and confirmed and a contribution is made to the study of the role of psychopathic acting, sexual relations, hypochondria, words and the phenomenon of metamorphosis in the establishment and regulation of the symbiotic relation. In view of the phenomena studied and their characteristics, the conclusion is that symbiosis is a link with an agglutinated object whose basic feature is that the elements of its structure have no discrimination or differentiation. Therefore, its mobilization takes place *en bloc*, provoking catastrophic anxiety and the acting of very primitive defences such as dissociation, projection and immobilization, which also act in an intense, massive and accessional manner.

Thus, symbiosis is a relation in which an agglutinated object is kept immobilized and controlled. The relation of dependence in symbiosis is characterized by group interdependence in which fixed and complementary roles can be recognised but with undifferentiation of the depositaries of these roles. Roles may rotate or alternate, moving *en bloc* in a redistribution.

The agglutinated object can be worked through only by 'fragments', in a slow discrimination that is achieved by diversifying links and by re-activating the perverse-polymorphous stage.

It is postulated that the link with an agglutinated object may be observed in other phenomena apart from symbiosis: in epilepsy, in intense affective blocks, in negative therapeutic reactions, in dreams, in sleep and in hypochondria. For future study, the relations between epilepsy, schizophrenia and symbiosis are pointed out, as is the relation with the agglutinated object in the processes of *Spaltung* and *Zerspaltung* (Bleuler), dissociation and splitting (Bion) and splitting and abnormal splitting (Rosenfeld). It is emphasized that the component elements of the agglutinated object are not discriminated, but nor is it confused, although when mobilised it is the agent of confusion when it invades the ego.

The agglutinated object is related to the earliest phases of development in which there is no differentiation or discrimination between ego and non-ego. A hypothesis is put forward concerning the existence during development of a stage which I call the glischro-caric, previous to the paranoid-schizoid position and characterized by an agglutinated (glischroid) object, danger of total and deadly annihilation, catastrophic anxieties and primitive defences such as dissociation, projection and immobilization, which function at maximum intensity and massivity. The glischro-caric position is the fixation point of epilepsy and epileptoidia.

# 3

# Modalities of object relations

Through her development and deepening of Freud's works, M. Klein contributed the discovery of two basic positions corresponding to two different but dynamic and co-existing modalities of the organisation and structuring of behaviour: the paranoid-schizoid and depressive positions. Each position has its characteristic anxieties, objects and defences.

Concerning the object relation, the partial object relation predominates in the paranoid-schizoid position, which encompasses the first three or four months of life, while in the depressive position the relation is with a total object. That is to say, in the former position, experiences of gratification and frustration are perceived and kept separate as corresponding to two totally different objects (good and bad).

M. Klein's recognition of these two positions, however, has not led her to fall into a simplistic schematism, since she herself provides elements that facilitate an investigation and problematisation of her own hypotheses. Thus, although she postulates that the child's world is constructed or integrated on the basis of isolated elements or experiences (partial objects), she affirms in her article 'Some theoretical conclusions regarding the emotional life of the infant' (Klein, 1952a) that

> There are, however, grounds for assuming that even during the first three or four months of life *the good and the bad object are not wholly distinct from one another in the infant's mind.*[52] . . . The mother's breast, both in its good and bad aspects, also seems to merge for him with her bodily presence; and the relation to her as a person is thus gradually built up from the earliest stage onwards.[53]
>
> (Klein, 1952a, pp. 62–63)

52 The italics are mine.

53 Fairbairn in 'Observations on the nature of hysterical states' (1954) also says in this respect (and in modification of his earlier views): 'However, I have now revised my previous opinion to the effect (1) that the differentiation of objects into categories to which the

In this chapter I attempt to point out succinctly how the study of transference in the analysis of psychotics and the investigation of symbiosis have led me to assign great importance and validity to this statement by M. Klein, which she did not develop systematically, and how I have also come to put forward a working hypothesis which I consider extends our understanding of a group of phenomena.

I have arrived at the conclusion that what characterises psychotic transference is precisely its symbiotic quality, and that we find this quality to some extent in every analysis. Thus, by focusing my study on the phenomenon of symbiosis, I observed that its object relation lacks the characteristics that strictly specify either the partial or the total object. Symbiosis involves the dynamic of an object with very complex characteristics, having good and bad parts with no discrimination or differentiation between them. There is no discrimination between the parts of the ego involved in all these experiences, that is, an absence of boundaries and discrimination between ego and non-ego and between internal and external. Moreover, this object presents the characteristic of being mobilised *en bloc* in such a way that extreme and massive anxieties (catastrophic and confusional) are provoked in the more integrated ego, to which only the most primitive defences respond. In view of all these characteristics, I call it the *agglutinated object.*

In linking the symbiotic phenomena I have studied with to the earliest mother-infant symbiotic relationship, I have suggested that the relation with an agglutinated object is a residue of the most primitive experiences and that this constitutes the psychotic part of the personality. Thus, the agglutinated object involves a part that is not differentiated or discriminated from the ego or from external reality: a conglomeration of many frustrating and gratifying experiences at different moments and with diverse intensities from the beginning of the infant's life, at all stages of development (oral, genital and anal), with no stratification or sequencing between them, with quite varied aspects of external reality, each with a small nucleus of the ego, but all agglutinated and neither differentiated nor discriminated. A residue of this primitive agglutinated formation persists in everyone, its magnitude determining the deficit in personification, sense of reality, sense of identity and body schema, and these processes are always interconnected.

In this way, we develop and set value on those remarks by M. Klein that, as in the passage quoted above, seem to differ from the characteristics of the partial object that she identified for the paranoid-schizoid position. We also find very concrete anticipation of what we are saying in isolated passages by

respective terms "good" and "bad" can be applied only arises after the original (pre-ambivalent) object has been introjected, and (2) that this differentiation is effected through splitting of an internalized object which is, in the first instance, neither "good" nor "bad", but "in some measure unsatisfying", and which only becomes truly "ambivalent" after its introjection'. (Fairbairn, 1954, p. 107. n.).

authors before M. Klein, such as Fenichel. Referring to the infant's earliest perceptions, he says that

> [o]bjects are not necessarily sharply distinguished from one another or from the ego or parts of it. The first images are large in extent, all enveloping and inexact. They do not consist of elements that are later put together, but rather of units, wholes, which only later are recognized as containing different elements. Not only are perception and motility inseparable, but also the perceptions of many sense organs overlap. The more primitive senses, especially the kinesthetic sensations and the data of depth sensibility (proprioception) prevail.
>
> (Fenichel, 1946, p. 38)

This is also consistent with studies by non-psychoanalytic authors who, like Wallon, have suggested the term 'syncretism' for this type of primitive relation.

I believe, therefore, that in the first or the earliest moments of development, there are no partial objects (good or bad) and that the delimitation and differentiation of isolated elements is acquired progressively and gradually by dissociation and discrimination operating within the agglutinated object, a process that also comes into action from the first moment of life. However, a highly variable portion of the agglutinated object always remains in which the schizoid division has not occurred. M. Klein has studied some types of interference in the dissociation of the good from the bad object and she attributes them to excessive envy, an expression of the destructive impulses. Within the agglutinated object there is, strictly speaking, no real object relation between the objects and the ego nuclei therein, but a true 'primary identification', which is the term Fairbairn used for those states in which differentiation has not occurred between the object and the part of the ego that is related to it. For this reason, I prefer now to speak of an *agglutinated nucleus* instead of the agglutinated object as I have done until now.

For all these reasons, I have also suggested the very early existence of a position prior to the paranoid-schizoid that I have termed the *glischro-caric* position (glischro: viscous; karion: nucleus), whose temporal extension or predominance, in the intra- as well as the extra-uterine period, I currently find it impossible to estimate. It is in this position that the nuclei of the ego and the partial objects become gradually differentiated; that is, the paranoid-schizoid position is formed out of or at the expense of the glischro-caric position, by means of a gradual discrimination of small fragments of the agglutinated nucleus (Bleuler's '*Spaltung*' or Bion's 'dissociation'), which is achieved by means of two basic techniques: the diversification of relations with other objects and the diversification of links with the same object, both of which depend to a large extent on the maturation process. Many of the characteristics described by M. Klein for the earliest states of the paranoid-schizoid position, we believe, correspond more strictly to the glischro-caric position.[54] In the latter, anxieties are extreme, powerful and massive because of the ego's great weakness and lack of cohesion and because the ego is threatened massively by an agglutinated nucleus that is not discriminated and that moves *en bloc*; these are confusional anxieties and in response to them the defences are primitive and violent: dissociation and projection. These defences are also used in the paranoid-schizoid position but there they are more gradated and less violent. They are primitive defences because they are the only ones that can act before the good object has been discriminated from the bad, and the ego from the non-ego, while the infantile neuroses are structured by defensive techniques (phobic, hysteric, obsessional, paranoid) that can only act on well discriminated partial objects, that is, on a previous schizoid division. I postulate that this glischro-caric position is the fixation point of epilepsy and epileptoid states.[55]

ψ

The clinical picture of the agglutinated nucleus derives from three circumstances, and in all of them what is fundamental is given not only by the vicissitudes of the agglutinated nucleus but also by its relation with the more integrated ego of the personality. Schematically, we identify:[56]

1. *Control of the agglutinated nucleus.* The healthy and more integrated ego needs to keep the agglutinated nucleus immobilised; avoiding re-introjection is the basic defence to preserve the more integrated ego (the non-psychotic part of the personality). Excessive agglutination and a basic lack of discrimination prevent a gradual and piecemeal re-introjection. This control is achieved by:
   (a) *Symbiosis*: techniques are developed to control the depositary;
   (b) *Affective blockage;*

54 In a scientific meeting of the Argentine Psychoanalytic Association (APA) during which I presented my paper, 'Symbiosis' (April 1961) [republished as Chapter 2 of this book], Dr. Liberman suggested that the glischro-caric position could actually be a modality of the paranoid-schizoid position rather than an independent position as I present it.

55 In the discussion of my paper, 'Study of dependence-independence in relation to the process of projection-introjection', [Chapter 1 of this book] presented in the APA in April, 1960, Dr. E. Pichon Rivière suggested the existence of a third position in addition to the paranoid-schizoid and depressive positions, which would be the fixation point of epilepsy. In my study on Symbiosis I arrived at the same conclusion.

56 In a later paper (Bleger, 1964b) I present the roles played by psychopathy, melancholia and mania as normal mechanisms in the course of development and in the evolution from the glischro-caric stage (and position) to the paranoid-schizoid stage (and position), as well as disturbances of this development.

   (c) *Hypochondria*: the use of the body as a 'buffer'. This includes psychosomatic illnesses (bodily relationships are the most primitive);
   (d) *Re-projection*: violent and massive.
2. *Loss of control of the agglutinated nucleus* and massive invasion of the ego.
   (a) *Prodromes*: insomnia. Intensification of observation and control. Other symptoms are 'suspense' and perplexity;
   (b) *Spasmodic*[57] *ego defences*: reinforcement of the dissociation between the more integrated ego and the agglutinated nucleus: absences and fainting fits; epileptic discharges; epileptoid states; fright, shivering, trembling, etc.;
   (c) *Invasion of the more integrated ego*: quite diverse phenomena may occur, including annihilation of the ego (loss of its integration), panic, and all the degrees of narrowing of consciousness: confusion, obfuscation, twilight state.
3. *Psychotic breakdown.* In view of this discussion and my current understanding of the topic, there may be two extreme types of psychotic dissolution, which are always found to be combined in varying degrees:
   (a) Disintegration of the more integrated ego when it is invaded by the agglutinated nucleus, as above in 2c. One example would be – among other conditions - the severe psychoses described by Mauz as schizocarias.
   (b) Loss of the agglutination and dispersion of the agglutinated nucleus (the psychotic part of the personality), which corresponds to what Bleuler termed *'Zerspaltung'* and Bion called *'splitting'*. This coincides with a certain degree of regression of the more integrated ego. In this condition, psychosis may be a step leading to the discrimination that did not occur normally in the course of development and may lead to recovery with an enrichment of the personality. French and Kasanin (1941) described this for some psychoses and we also observed the same recently, comparing them with an adolescent crisis that occurs in a psychotic, condensed and delayed manner. Psychotic restitution is a process of re-agglutination and it is here that we must locate Bion's 'bizarre object', which is therefore a form of agglutinated nucleus, but one that, as a phenomenon of restitution, is normally absent from the course of development. The bizarre object contains, together with the object, the perceptual apparatus, with intervention by the secondary process, which is of course lacking in the agglutinated nucleus.[58]

ψ

57 [*accesionales*]

58 The intervention of the secondary process in the bizarre object was suggested to me by Dr. R. Avenburg in a study group on the works of Melanie Klein and her school.

*Addenda*: In the later paper (Bleger, 1964b) mentioned above, I presented the following table that indicates the characteristics of the glischro-caric position in comparison to those of the paranoid-schizoid and depressive positions.

| *Position* | *Anxiety* | *Object* | *Defences* | *Point of Fixation* |
|---|---|---|---|---|
| DEPRESSIVE | Depressive | Total (Ambivalent) | Manic | Manic-Depressive Psychosis |
| PARANOID-SCHIZOID | Paranoid | Partial (Divalent) | Division | Schizophrenia |
| GLISCHRO-CARIC | Confusional | Agglutinated Nucleus (Ambiguous) | Splitting, Immobilisation, Fragmentation | Confusional States, Epilepsy[59] |

59 [In the Spanish edition Epilepsy is erroneously included with Schizophrenia in the row above. See also p. 75, n. 55.]

# 4

# Study of the psychotic part of the personality

## Introduction

Study of the problem of dependence-independence has guided me to the problem of those cases of extreme dependence that we recognize as symbiosis. I found that the characteristics of the transference relation appearing in the symbioses were equivalent to those of psychotic transference that I had already encountered, both in my own experience with the psychoanalysis of psychotics and in basic writings on this theme, especially those by F. Fromm-Reichmann, E. Pichon Rivière, H. Rosenfeld and W. Bion. On the other hand, I found I was dealing not only with a large quantity of clinical facts closely related to the subject of symbiosis (psychopathy, hypochondria, epilepsy, confusional states, psychosomatic affections, etc.) but also with the complex theme of narcissism and development of the ego (identity, body schema, hetero-homosexual differentiation, etc.).

Guided at first by the work of M. Mahler, I recognized the clinical existence of symbiosis in adults, as well as that of the symbiotic psychoses. Later, I studied symbiotic organization in the transference relation, particularly in connection with autism, in terms of both the dynamics and the vicissitudes of symbiosis. Preserving the clinical autonomy of this phenomenon offered certain advantages and some disadvantages. One of the advantages was that it enabled me to elaborate some hypotheses that I think clarify to some extent the problem of symbiosis and other related problems. Another advantage was that it allowed me to discover the symbiotic nuclei in the analyses of patients who did not present a clinical picture of symbiosis, at least not superficially. An equally valuable advantage was that it enabled me to understand in a unified way a number of clinical phenomena that crop up either as organisation, immobilisation and control of symbiosis (affect blockage, autism, body-mind dissociation, negative therapeutic reaction), or as defences against the rupture of symbiosis (hypochondria, phobias, psychosomatic illness, psychopathic acting , the phenomenon of metamorphosis, etc.). Thus, a number of phenomena could be seen to be dynamically related and unifiedly centred. Among the disadvantages of this independent approach to the autonomy of the theme was, first and foremost, the possibility of not having done justice to authors who worked in other areas but who in one way or another included (though not explicitly) in their investigations and conclusions some phenomena closely related to symbiosis. It may happen again in this instance, since it would be very difficult to define the degree of influence of the many works I have read, although I did not consciously relate them to 'my topic'.

ψ

Symbiosis is a close interdependence between two or more persons who complement each other in order to keep the needs of the more immature parts of the personality controlled, immobilised and in some measure satisfied. These parts demand conditions dissociated from reality and from the more mature or integrated parts of the personality. This immature and more primitive part of the personality has remained segregated from the more integrated and adapted ego and forms a whole with certain characteristics that have led me to recognise it as the agglutinated nucleus of the personality.[60] This segregation must be rigidly sustained because otherwise psychotic disintegration may ensue.

Influenced especially by the works of Bion (1956, 1957), my interest now centres on the study of the psychotic part of the personality, which is precisely the part that establishes the symbiotic relation and symbiotic transference. This psychotic part of the personality is what I have identified as the agglutinated nucleus.[61] Its basic characteristic is non-discrimination: between ego and non-ego among the different components or identifications of different experiences at different moments; between good and bad object; and between the different phases (oral, anal and genital).

As I explained in Chapter 3, I regarded this agglutinated nucleus, that in adults forms the psychotic part of the personality, as the remnant of the most primitive organisation of the personality, developmentally prior to the paranoid-schizoid position, which I termed the glischro-caric position (glischro: viscous, or agglutinated; karion: nucleus).[62] This agglutinated

60 Although I called it the agglutinated object at first, I later saw that I needed to change this term to 'agglutinated nucleus', since it can function not only as an object corresponding to the more integrated ego but also as a primitive ego or superego that may displace or replace the former.

61 Throughout this chapter I use the terms 'psychotic part of the personality' and 'psychotic levels of the personality' as synonyms.

62 'I chose the term "position" in regard to the paranoid and depressive phases because these groupings of anxieties and defences, although arising first during the earliest stages, are

nucleus is not always of the same size, since it may expand at the cost of regression from the paranoid-schizoid position due to a loss of discrimination between good and bad object and between ego and non-ego, etc. This loss or lack of discrimination was studied by M. Klein (1957) and H. Rosenfeld (1958) in [phenomena of] confusion. What I am adding to that here is recognition of the reappearance of primitively fused or undifferentiated nuclei that have remained as such, no discrimination having operated on them.

In this regard, we often find mention in psychoanalytic works (including in Freud, M. Klein, Fairbairn and Fenichel) of undifferentiation in the earliest stages of development, so that my proposals consist of a continuation and deepening of this thesis.[63] For example, M. Klein says that 'There are, however, grounds for assuming that even during the first three or four months of life the good and the bad object *are not wholly distinct* from one another in the infant's mind.' (Klein 1952a, p. 62). In another of her works she writes: 'The libidinal stages overlap from the earliest months of life onwards.' (Klein, 1945, p. 416). In *Envy and Gratitude* the theme of confusion is notably clarified and she says: 'Here again we have to consider the effects of early confusion, which expresses itself in a blurring of the oral, anal, and genital impulses and phantasies. *An overlapping between these various sources* both of libido and of aggressiveness *is normal*.'[64] (Klein, 1957, p. 195)

The remnant of this primitive organisation of primary undifferentiation[65] or fusion forms the main part of the psychotic levels of the personality, persisting in adult life segregated from the ego and from the more developed, mature and integrated part of the personality. Symbiosis is the relation that keeps this psychotic part of the personality (the agglutinated nucleus) immobilised and controlled.

not restricted to them but occur and recur during the first years of childhood and under certain circumstances in later life.' (Klein, 1952a, p. 93). The same holds true for the glischro-caric position.

63 Hartmann, Kris and Loewenstein explicitly recognise an 'undifferentiated phase', as do A. Freud and Spitz. M. Balint (1952, p. 359) also states that 'the primary, archaic, object relation is so primitive, that it cannot be called either love, hate, or narcissism, or anything; all these are contained in it in rudimentary form as yet indiscriminable from one another, and they appear and become discernible only during later development'. Lagache (1955) proposes to call this beginning of individual psychological existence not undifferentiation but primary differentiation, since this undifferentiation is relative in comparison to the subsequent stages. [Balint, in the article cited, goes on to criticise this view as being merely negative, and therefore empty. Bleger's argument here is precisely *against* the view that the conception of an undifferentiated phase is necessarily a negative one.]

64 The italics are mine. [In the Spanish, 'overlapping' is translated by *superposición*, which can also mean coinciding.]

65 [The original has *diferenciación*, but the context clearly suggests that this is a slip for *indiferenciación*.]

ψ

For present purposes I am interested not only in deepening this theme through clinical material but also in underlining the technical aspects raised by handling the psychotic part of the personality, as well as related aspects of the theory of the technique. I shall also refer to this briefly in this introduction before going into greater detail.

Theory and technique are quite closely related in psychoanalysis: new theoretical formulations lead to new technical possibilities, while the latter make possible the extension and perfection of theory and the formulation of new hypotheses with their consequent confirmation or correction. Much of what I discuss here in relation to the technique of handling the agglutinated nucleus (the psychotic part of the personality) is not innovation but an attempt to define precisely, understand and ground in a unitary manner various technical alternatives that are largely implicit in what every psychoanalyst does to some extent in the course of a treatment.

My references to psychoanalytic technique in this chapter are also based on Bion's ideas and on the conclusions of his work on the differentiation between the psychotic and the non-psychotic personality, when he affirms that just as we need to discover the neurotic personality hidden by the psychosis in the psychotic, every severe neurotic has a psychotic personality masked by the neurosis that needs to be discovered and treated. In 'On Narcissism: An Introduction', Freud identified three groups of phenomena in the psychoses: those of preserved normality, those of the pathological process and those of restitution. Now we can say that this is true not only in the psychoses, but also in the neuroses. On this basis, the present study refers to the emergence and handling in the course of the analysis – of any patient – of the psychotic part of the personality. It may occur in phenomena of very disparate clinical magnitudes: from diverse, sparse and isolated psychotic nuclei to a single, very robust psychotic nucleus co-existing as another ego alongside the more integrated ego. Thus, my present study refers more strictly to transference psychosis[66] than to the transference of psychotics (clinically recognised as such).

In relation to technique, I wish to emphasise from the outset a fundamental concept, and this relates to the *discrimination* required in the technical handling of the agglutinated nucleus. That is to say, we have to establish the schizoid division on the psychotic levels (the agglutinated nucleus) and thereby proceed to the paranoid-schizoid position. Discrimination of the

66 This theme appears in the psychoanalytic literature with different names or approached from different contexts: Abraham (1908, 1919), Nunberg (1931, 1951), Tarachow (1962), Little (1958, 1960), Rosenfeld (1964). Of particular interest and importance is M. Klein's description of schizoid object relations, which shows us the symbiosis in what she describes as 'a compulsive tie to certain objects'. (Klein, 1946, p. 13).

components of the agglutinated nucleus converts the psychotic part of the personality into a neurotic part.

Psychoanalytic technique, its theory and objectives, can be defined briefly as resulting from two interrelated aspects: (a) making conscious the unconscious and (b) integrating dissociations. The first is the technical advice that Freud formulated, while the second, although it stems from Freud, derives fundamentally from M. Klein's studies of schizoid division and of the depressive position as integrative. For Racker, these and other formulations of the aims of technique are all different aspects deriving from a single principle previously defined by Freud: to make conscious the unconscious by overcoming resistance. We shall not linger here over the interrelation of the two proposals that have been put forward, since this is not what will be studied most closely here.

Inquiry into the dynamics of the agglutinated nucleus in the clinical phenomenon of symbiosis, and now into the dynamics of the psychotic part of the personality, have led me to emphasise two formulations: (a) that making conscious the unconscious (in handling the agglutinated nucleus) coincides with or is equivalent to the re-introjection of what has been projected into other persons who are used as depositaries[67] and (b) that a necessary technical task, before integrating the dissociations, is to 'break up' the agglutinated nucleus, which then leads the more integrated ego to establish an internal discrimination among its components, that is, to establish the schizoid division.

Discrimination is thus the technically necessary step for working through the psychotic part of the personality so that it is transformed into a neurotic part. In this perspective, the immediate objective of the technique is different in handling the neurotic versus the psychotic parts of the personality. In the former, we tend to integrate the schizoid division (an already existing discrimination), while in the latter we tend to try first to help the patient to discriminate, that is, to establish the schizoid division on the basis of the agglutinated nucleus. With this, its subsequent incorporation into the neurotic part of the personality is achieved and it is then possible to tend toward integration.

In this manner, the psychoanalytic treatment elicits not only the integration of what already existed but is also able to expand the personality by incorporating elements that, as such, never existed. This expansion of the personality is not only a consequence of the resolution of conflicts (schizoid

67 The psychotic part is related to projection and the neurotic part to repression, which is genetically a later defence. In this regard, Bion (1956, p. 41) says: 'It will be clear that where the non-psychotic personality, or part of the personality, employs repression the psychotic has employed projective identification. Therefore there is no repression, and what should be his unconscious is replaced by the world of dream furniture in which I have described him as moving.'

divisions) of the neurotic part, but also of an evolution of the psychotic part of the personality.

The role of discrimination as an ego function was recently discussed in a paper by Hacker (1962),[68] but the part played by discrimination in the therapeutic process and in psychoanalytic technique has not been recognised in as fully explicit way as we are doing here.

In order to proceed to the study of dynamics and technique in the handling of the psychotic part of the personality, I need to refer to the clinical characteristics of the transference in the way in which it presents itself. For this purpose, I shall present clinical material and, since it is not possible to deal separately with each topic of interest, I shall study four interrelated aspects of the clinical material:

(a) some clinical manifestations of the psychotic part of the personality, omitting those already described in earlier works on this subject;
(b) their correspondence with the dynamics of the agglutinated nucleus;
(c) some transference and countertransference phenomena to which they may lead;
(d) technical aspects: basically, the process of discrimination and the way to bring it about.

## Technical problems

In this section, I wish to deal specifically with some of the fundamental technical problems encountered in the handling of the psychotic part of the personality. My references to the psychotic part of the personality derive from its study in the course of the phenomenon of transference symbiosis or, what amounts to the same thing, of transference psychosis.

68 Hacker (1962) notes that in disturbances of character we observe the lack, dysfunction, underdevelopment or inoperativeness of the discriminatory functions of the ego as in immature personalities characterised by confusion, inhibition of action, diffuse identity, existential hopelessness and feelings of futility; in subjects unable to sublimate but who conceal their lack of discrimination behind an apparently strong ego (inflexible, rigid and stereotyped); in what is commonly called 'lack of character'. This author says: 'Clinical conditions, so far called ego deformity, character disorders, narcissistic disturbances, and so on, cannot be satisfactorily explained, classified, or treated without such a theoretical construct as a discriminatory or selective ego function, conceptualized like all other ego functions as a specific aspect of the ego's general task'. (Hacker, 1962, p. 404).

In everything we have discussed up to this point, my position is that the deficit of discrimination intervenes in a series of phenomena beyond those in Hacker's description.

In close connection to the theme of discrimination, Peto (1961, 1963) described a 'fragmenting' function of the ego, different from splitting, 'as described by Freud in the fetishist'. (Peto, 1961, p. 239; 1963, p. 328).

The identification of a neurotic level and a psychotic level of the personality, each in turn characterised by a certain structure of the internal objects involved, by no means implies establishing two types of analysis or two totally different techniques, but it does require an emphasis on some technical aspects that become more evident or have greater impact on each level.

In the first place we have to consider the patient's timing, his or her capacity to accept and work through the psychotic part of his or her personality. Obviously, in relation to this problem, we cannot formulate strict rules because situations vary greatly and we may also need to take into account a personal countertransference coefficient in each analyst, which also imposes or demands its own timing.

In this respect, we may consider that there are three typical situations. One of these is evident in those cases in which the patient starts analysis when the boundaries separating the neurotic and the psychotic parts of the personality are already broken and therefore demand immediate attention and inclusion without delay of the psychotic levels in the analysis. In these cases it is no longer specifically transference psychosis but rather transference in a psychosis, a topic closely related to the one occupying us here but that will anyhow not be discussed specifically at this time. A second basic situation is found in patients who present neither very strict control nor immobilisation of the psychotic levels of their personality, with the result that the inclusion of the latter in the analysis depends much more on the analyst; in these cases, I believe we need to work in a way which allows time for the analysis of the neurotic levels, with the aim of consolidating as much as possible the integration of the more mature ego. We need to become trustworthy depositaries of the psychotic part and to act as tolerant parents who give it time to grow up and not to overwhelm it with problems that are premature for the patient's ego. The positive effects of dissociation of the good from the bad object were described by M. Klein as a necessary dissociation for the successful integration of the ego:

> This sounds paradoxical. But since, as I said, integration is based on a strongly rooted good object that forms the core of the ego, a certain amount of splitting is essential for integration; for it preserves the good object and later on enables the ego to synthesize the two aspects of it.
>
> (Klein, 1957, p. 192)

Similarly, I think that in certain periods of development the dissociation between the neurotic and psychotic levels of the personality is also very positive and necessary, a dissociation that preserves the ego from an overwhelming and disintegrating part and also gives it time to consolidate itself and to return at another time to confront the dissociated part. This is also what needs to occur in the technical handling of this type of patient. I believe that if we can allow time for a better consolidation of the ego, so that the patient is later able to face the psychotic part of the personality without the emergence of a clinically manifest psychosis, we should do so. We have already seen that in some cases the decision is not ours and, even in cases of this latter type, the psychotic part frequently breaks through anyway, evidently escaping our control.[69]

A third type includes patients who (as in the clinical material we study below) present a rigorous dissociation and very severe control between the neurotic and psychotic parts of the personality, thus giving themselves the time they need – and even more – which renders interpretation of the psychotic levels inoperative, at least as an immediate effect. The rigid ego of these patients should not be mistaken for a well integrated ego, and in any case we must first support the patient's need to analyse the neurotic levels, in order to be able to bring the psychotic part of the personality into the treatment later. It is this third type of patient that we shall discuss in this chapter, and they are characterised in the analytic situation or relation by seeming clinically to be autistic but establishing an intense and mute transference symbiosis.[70] To these we can apply everything that M. Klein says about those patients whose envy is constitutionally strong:

> However, the analysis of those deep and severe disturbances is in many cases a safeguard against potential danger of psychosis resulting from excessively envious and omnipotent attitudes. *But it is essential not to attempt to hurry these steps in integration.* For if the realization of the division in his personality were to come suddenly, the patient would have great difficulties in coping with it. The more strongly had the envious and destructive impulses been split off, the more dangerous the patient feels them to be when he becomes conscious of them. In analysis we should make our way slowly and gradually towards the painful insight into the divisions in the patient's self.[71]
>
> (Klein, 1957, pp. 224–225)

69 Here, we include all those cases which at consultation appear clinically to be psychosis, but which once the treatment has begun and from the first session onward appear to be neurosis due to the massive and immediate depositing of all the psychotic part into the analyst (metamorphosis). The opposite case corresponds to the first type.

70 It would of course be important to identify these patients in an initial interview. For this purpose, I consider as guiding signs the countertransference experience, produced by the patient, of feeling overwhelmed, and a presentation as 'pure', structured almost on a single structure: paranoid, phobic, hysterical, obsessional. (I later adopted the term 'systematised neuroses' for these clinical pictures.)

71 The same author adds a note: 'It might well be that a person who unexpectedly commits a crime or has a psychotic breakdown had *suddenly* become aware of the split-off dangerous parts of his self. Cases are known of people trying to be arrested in order to prevent

ψ

The analysis of the neurotic levels of the personality is characterised by the possibility of our working with objects that are definite and discriminate, and with a more integrated ego, while we tend to resolve dissociations with displaced, repressed or projected objects, promoting anxieties (paranoid and depressive) that are not overwhelming for the ego. The aim of reinforcing the ego of the neurotic levels of the personality is achieved within the framework of the interpretation of both the positive and the negative transference. For that reason, we wish to indicate the total exclusion of measures such as teaching or support, which some authors postulate for the periods around the outset of the analysis of psychotics or children.

The psychotic part of the personality is psychotic basically because at this level there is no discrimination (no splitting) between internal reality and the external world. There is no discrimination between the depositary and what is projected; that is, in this sector there is a lack of sense of reality. On the analyst's capacity to maintain this discrimination (splitting) depends in a fundamental way the patient's being able to learn it. This lack or loss of discrimination – fusion – between the internal and external worlds is the basic phenomenon characterising psychotic transference or transference of the psychotic part of the personality, configuring a symbiotic relation that we analysts need to undo countertransferentially, first for ourselves and then for the patient. Also valid for these cases are the characteristics that Bion (1957) studies in psychotic transference: it is premature, sudden and massive, tenacious and fragile. The transferential relation is narcissistic and functions on two co-existing levels: a more manifest or visible level, that of autism, which sets up a barrier that we cannot pass, and which Liberman (1958) studied using the term transference autism; and another less apparent or larval transference level, that of symbiosis; in this the patient's internal (narcissistic) world is inside the analyst. This entire phenomenon is what deserves to be called transference narcissism.[72] The patient defends the autistic world from invasion by the symbiotic part, while on the other hand defending the

themselves from committing a murder.' (Klein, 1957, p. 225, n. 1). (All the emphases are mine.) She also quotes Rosenfeld, who 'showed that "acting out" is used in order to avoid the undoing of the split'. (Klein, 1957, p. 219).

72 Fliess (1961) differentiates between transference and projection. In the former, the analyst takes the place of an object in the patient's history; in the latter, he reflects a part of the patient's ego. In this way, for Fliess the transference is object-related and the projection is narcissistic; the former results in an illusion and the latter in a delusion. Fliess adds that in the former, the patient's image of the analyst is changeable depending on what is transferred and it is corrected through the analysis; in the second, it is either unchangeable or only changeable through prolonged effort. I think that Fliess is referring here to the difference between neurotic and psychotic transference, but in this regard we follow M. Klein, for whom narcissism is also an object relation. I think that in narcissism it is a

projected symbiotic part from invasion by the depositary. The immobilisation of the depositary is a defence against both dangers of disorganisation. Paradoxically, we cannot penetrate the narcissism of autism, but instead the patient's narcissistic world has penetrated the psychoanalyst and once inside tends to behave like a parasite. The basis of this process is massive projective identification as studied by M. Klein (1946, 1957), Rosenfeld (1950, 1952a) and Bion (1955, 1958), and the dissociation of projection from introjection with the consequent organisation at each extreme, respectively, of autism and symbiosis. Autism is omnipotent denial of symbiotic dependence.

Clinically, there are two different types of symbiosis that correspond to two different types of autism: in one, the autism is clinically more relevant while the symbiosis is mute; in the other the symbiosis is what draws our attention with its obvious manifestations, while the autism is mute and has to be discovered. Up to this point I have discussed the former type more specifically.

Another characteristic of the psychotic part of the personality is the rigid and omnipotent control of both the situation and the depositary, which avoids a double danger: re-introjection of what has been projected and interference by the depositary (splitting). Any mobility in this situation is experienced as a danger of psychosis, and if we achieve the re-introjection of a fragment of the projected, we have an accurate indicator ('re-introjection index') for detecting when this has occurred: the appearance of confusion (confusional anxiety) in any of its manifestations: clouding of consciousness, dizziness, suspense, bewilderment, perplexity, etc. Just as anxiety is an alarm signal in the depressive and paranoid positions, confusional anxiety is an alarm signal when there is danger of massive re-introjection of the agglutinated nucleus with the consequent threat of psychotic disintegration of the ego. In other patients, dependence (symbiosis) is controlled by means of active paranoid rejection (in one case of paranoid psychosis I have analysed).

For understanding the phenomena of the symbiotic relation (the psychotic part of the personality), and for its technical management, we need to keep in mind that, aside from the above mentioned characteristics, there is a paradoxical threshold for stimuli: those of great intensity have a very high threshold and do not act because they are immobilised and neutralised, since they would disorganise the personality, while small stimuli have a very low threshold, so that we need to detect them constantly in the frustrations

question of a primary identification in which discrimination has not been sufficiently established between ego and object.

M. Little (1958, 1960) observes two characteristic phenomena in patients with a predominance of transference psychosis: one is the particular position that it forces the analyst to take and the other is the great importance of bodily events. However, this author considers that it is not a symbiosis, but the patient's attempt to establish a state of total identity and undifferentiation with the analyst.

and minimal changes. To this we add that quite frequently the responses are delayed and occur far removed from the moment when the stimulus acted. All this of course makes the psychoanalytic task difficult, but not impossible. The effect of the interpretation follows the course of any stimulus; in this sense its effects are cumulative and the response may appear quite belatedly; it is not infrequent to observe a true metamorphosis, that is, a sudden, explosive change due to a kind of accumulation of insight.[73] In other patients, the change is gradual, although not continuous but episodic, and this is what occurred in the patient whose material I study below. The latter category coincides with the fact that they do not immediately incorporate what they need to learn (including interpretation, of course), but first encapsulate it in a kind of autistic nucleus where they keep it as neither foreign to them nor yet totally incorporated into the personality. Gradually, and by virtue of subsequent experiences, the patient repeatedly 'feels' and examines what has been incorporated, to decide whether or not to integrate it into the personality. During the analysis, this can be seen in that they neither accept nor reject the interpretation; they need time and sometimes a long time before they eventually use these effects as their own. The accumulation of these autistic nuclei causes insight to appear sometimes in an explosive or cyclical manner.

Exaggerating slightly, I could say that the analysis of these patients does not reside fundamentally – in the periods of analysis of the psychotic part – in analysing the patients, but in the analyst being able to analyse what the patient is continually making of the analyst, with the aim of playing only the role of depositary without becoming fused with what is deposited, thereby preserving the analyst's personality or identity (analysis of the projective counteridentification); in other words, aiming to maintain consistently the split between the depositary and the deposited. Achieving this must be one of the fundamental goals of the strategy that needs to be followed in the analysis of these patients. Of course this is not the only goal, but it is a central pivot of the analysis.[74]

73 The sudden breakthrough of psychotic levels into the more integrated ego is responsible for the shock that M. Klein described in some of her cases; 'I believe that this kind of shock, which I have now reported in several cases, is the result of an important step in the healing of the split between parts of the self, and thus a stage of progress in ego-integration.' (Klein, 1957, p. 215).

74 In symbiosis, the part of the personality with the best sense of reality is not what is projected into the depositary (which as we have seen is responsible for the transference psychosis), but what is retained within the autistic nucleus. The latter, in turn, is redistributed among other external objects when the agglutinated nucleus can remain firmly deposited in the symbiotic partner. In these cases, the patient always seems to be much healthier when the patient does not need to deal with the depositaries of the psychotic part in the external world. If they relate to the latter, the loss of the sense of reality

On the psychotic level we have, then, to face one or more agglutinated nuclei whose re-introjection is overwhelming for the ego of the patient, who tends immediately to re-project and thereby to re-establish the maximum distance and most rigid control possible. For this reason, we must aim to fragment the agglutinated nucleus and discriminate its components on the basis of the fragments. Once this has been accomplished the analysis becomes an analysis of the neurotic levels. We need to discriminate because we cannot bring about the re-introjection of the projected, since it overwhelms the ego, which immediately proceeds to re-project.[75]

How is the agglutinated nucleus fragmented and discriminated? The reply must be similar to something a physician once said: 'I only take care of the patient, he cures himself'; that is, we create the possibilities, and it is the patient's ego that does the discriminating. However, in this task, the analyst's ego must also operate as the patient's supplementary ego and discriminate so that the patient may also learn to do so.

Given that in symbiosis the agglutinated nucleus is projected and immobilised in a depositary, one of the basic aims of technique is to bring about its mobilisation, and thereby the consequent re-introjection; this must be done with respect for the patient's timing, but we must often force it, although without doing so to excess, an objective that we cannot always reach to the extent and in the proportion we would prefer. In all the process we are describing, which consists of three steps (sometimes successive and at others simultaneous): *mobilisation, fragmentation and discrimination,* the central technical step is the introduction of a split between the analyst and what is deposited (projected) into the analyst. We need to split the role that we need to adopt as analyst from the role that we are obliged to play as depositary.

This splitting between the projected and the analyst leads to undoing (however temporarily) the division or separation between the neurotic and the psychotic parts of the personality. Although this confrontation (not yet integration) between the two parts of the personality is quite temporary and it immediately – by projection – turns into a re-establishment of the division, this repeatedly reactivated process causes the agglutinated nucleus gradually to fragment.

appears much more manifestly and this is why the patient avoids a direct relationship with the analyst in the analytic relation, keeping the ego very narrow.

As we have seen, the patient is autistic in relation to the depositary; however, he is not so with persons with whom such an intense symbiotic relationship is not established and with whom (since the psychotic part is immobilized in another object) a healthier part of his personality may be used, manifesting quite dissimilar behaviour in relation to different groups or persons. This is easy to observe in symbiotic patients and children or adolescents who preserve all their symbiotic dependence in the primary group (the family), while their behaviour is quite different, 'unrecognizable', in secondary groups.

75 J. Mom (1957, p. 67) also emphasized this need for discrimination in patients 'with marked projection and external dissociation'.

This process often has to be accompanied by investigation of other depositaries the patient uses, in order to analyse not only the projection but also the displacements; this other depositary may be studying, work, persons, a place, etc. On other occasions – and quite frequently – the psychotic part of the personality is concentrated in mourning. The patient keeps these depositaries segregated from the analysis, just as the analyst is kept segregated and controlled, so that any attempt by the analyst to bring these depositaries and their contents into the analysis is extremely painful and difficult for the patient; for this reason, although it needs to be done, it is necessary to proceed with the greatest possible tact. As we said earlier, the intervention of an ego that has been previously reinforced on its neurotic levels is of incalculable value. These depositaries and their contents (including the analyst) need to be analysed by following each ramification and each relation, which is often not easy, since the patient tries to keep them segregated or brings elements into different or distant sessions, which demands a great effort on the analyst's part. All this work also corresponds to the discrimination that we need to effect by including in the interpretations – as far as possible - greed, rivalry and envy at all levels of the oedipal organisation, determining the objects and anxieties involved at each moment.[76]

Our concern in the analysis of patients with autistic transference has always been formulated as the need to operate technically in such a way that we are able to pass through the barrier and reach the inside of the autistic nucleus. The finding that autism always co-exists with a symbiotic organisation, with depositaries in the external world (including the symbiotic transference) shifts the focus of the problem from how to get into the autism to how to get out of the symbiosis. Based on this point and centring the interpretation in this way, we can mobilise the patient's entire narcissistic organisation.[77] We must not only interpret how the patient keeps us outside and far away, but fundamentally how the patient holds us inside, also keeping a part of the patient inside of us, and how for the patient we are what the patient projects and not what we really are. Thus, we operate on the loss of sense of reality that the narcissistic organisation imposes on the patient.

76 We could apply to all this what J. Rivière says when she studies the negative therapeutic reaction: 'Now it might be objected here that no analyst worth his salt has failed to interpret these manifestations in precisely this way time and again in his practice and this of course is true; but in my view there is all the difference in the world between what may be called single isolated interpretations, however correct and however frequent they may be, and the understanding and interpretation of such detailed instances as part of a general organized system of defence and resistance, with all its links and ramifications spreading far and wide in the symptom-picture, in the formation of character and in the behaviour-patterns of the patient.' (Rivière, 1936a, p. 310).

77 In clinical autism we must therefore work on the latent symbiosis, while in clinical symbiosis, we need to discover and work on the autistic nuclei. This may possibly offer some interesting clarifications for the psychoanalytic treatment of schizophrenia.

The splitting between the depositary and what has been projected is also achieved and maintained through sustained and detailed analysis of the projected, making it gradually possible to achieve and establish a discrimination in the agglutinated nucleus and a discrimination between ego and non-ego. The transference interpretation must refer to what the patient does with us at each precise moment, what the patient rejects, accepts, expects, etc., including determination of the affect that is present.

Succinctly, we need to recognize that four variables are involved: patient and analyst on the one hand, and also what each has projected into the other. This considered, we distinguish between two types of interpretation, which are by no means mutually exclusive, and which refer to the existence or non-existence in the interpretation of the splitting between the analyst and what is deposited in the analyst. In the first case – the split interpretation – we show patients their relation with themselves, or what they do with a part of themselves to another part of themselves, while in the latter case – interpretation without splitting – we include ourselves in the interpretation without differentiating the internal object of the depositary.

Taking examples from the material transcribed below, we call the following an interpretation without splitting: 'You are showing me how I left you all in pieces, like the pastry, after the last session, and that you had to manage by yourself and gather everything up and put yourself back together, leaving me outside.' In these cases, for the patient, I am showing that there is 'something' outside herself, which is related to what happens to her inside herself, but by not differentiating between the analyst – external object – and the internal object projected into him, I am not showing her what this 'external something' is composed of; thus this type of interpretation tends to overcome the segregation and quashing of an external 'something' that for her does not exist in relation to her autistic world.

An example of the split interpretation is when I say: 'On the one hand, you now notice your own feelings inside yourself and on the other hand, you yourself reject them and do not allow yourself to have your own feelings'. In this case, a 'something' is left outside, which is the analyst, as an independent and discriminated person, and also, in her autistic world the affect is incorporated that, as part of the patient's ego, is segregated and projected into the analyst. The patient's response points to this internal object to which the affect was linked, which is now no longer the analyst but the internal object inside herself; thus, the patient answers: 'Okay . . . but I have got rid of them. I gave more importance to everything that was repellent to me (silence). As I was speaking about my father, saying that he didn't give us cuddles, I felt my father's warmth'.

It is with the split interpretation that we really provoke a re-introjection, while with unsplit interpretations, although we do strengthen a fusion between depositary and the deposited, we also exert an important function of connection between the patient's inside and outside; that is, a certain overcoming of the segregation that the patient maintains and controls. The problem does not reside in deciding which of the two interpretations we should use, because we need to use both, but in knowing when to use one or the other; in this sense, the interpretations without splitting function as 'feeder' interpretations, in the words of Strachey (1934), one being as indispensable as the other. They alternate and complement each other in re-establishing the mobilisation of the agglutinated nucleus, that is, in the progressive re-establishment of the process of projection-introjection, which we have indicated as the fundamental objective of our technique. The reiterated and repeated process of projection-introjection, together with the reinforcement of the central ego through analysis of the neurotic levels, make it possible to mobilise, fragment and discriminate the agglutinated nucleus.[78] For a long time, we actually need to handle the agglutinated nucleus as what it is, a conglomerate, without knowing much about its structure (the internal objects involved in it, the parts of the personality and the specific historical experience), and throughout this time we need to use the unsplit interpretation, which leads the patient to recognise an outside that allows, by a relative increment of the associations, to recognise and discriminate between its components. When the latter has been achieved to some extent, the split interpretation allows an attempt at re-introjection, which is only possible once a certain advance in discrimination has been made. We could say that re-introjection is only successful with discriminated internal objects, and we consider successful the stable re-introjection that is not followed by an immediate re-projection.

The presentation of the theory of the technique discussed here is evidently similar and related to the postulations of Strachey, who differentiates two phases in the mutative interpretation: first, the phase when patients realise that they have aimed a particular quantity of energy of the id directly at the analyst; second, the phase when patients understand that this energy is aimed at an archaic object and not a real one. However, this distinction of Strachey's cannot be made completely to coincide with the one we postulate here, because in the unsplit interpretation, what is obtained or what we try to obtain is the patients' recognition that there is something separated from and quite related to the patient; with the split interpretation we try to introduce the sense of reality, showing that what the patients have kept separate or dissociated from themselves is in reality composed of two parts, one that belongs to external reality and another that pertains to their internal world. These two modalities of interpretation would be included in the first phase postulated by Strachey and they correspond to the psychotic

78 'Selection, discrimination, etc., are based on projection and introjection'. P. Heimann (1952, p. 125). The split interpretation favours re-introjection, while the unsplit interpretation favours re-projection; this is technically important, because it is what also enables the analyst, at least in part, to control the timing.

levels of the personality. Strachey's second phase corresponds to both the psychotic and the neurotic levels of the personality because, in proceeding to the discrimination of the components of the agglutinated nucleus, we inevitably need to resort to historical (archaic) objects of the patient's internal world.

Following some of Strachey's reflections, we should ask ourselves whether the split interpretation, which interprets the patients' relation with themselves, is not an extra-transferential interpretation, and my answer is that it is not, since it is always given in the context of the present situation (in the here and now).

Another question that could be asked is whether all transference is not always a phenomenon of the psychotic levels, considering that the analyst is at a given moment experienced in function of the internal object that has been projected into the analyst. My answer to this would be that the transference phenomenon does not always correspond to the psychotic levels of the personality, since in the transference neurosis projective identification is not massive and discriminated (partial or total) objects are projected, thus facilitating re-introjection, while the process is always more plastic; also, the distortion of the sense of reality is never as intense as in symbiotic dependence. However, we must point out that there is no strict delimitation between the two and the passage from one to the other is invisible.

Because of the nature of the agglutinated object and its particular dynamic, a long time passes before we may comply with the 'principle of minimal doses', also formulated by Strachey. For the same reasons, it is much easier for the 'explosive possibilities of interpretation' to occur in the analysis of the psychotic levels of the personality.

The two types of interpretation we have discussed tend to introduce or reinforce the patients' sense of reality. In the unsplit interpretation, this is true to the extent that they incorporate more of something that exists externally, while not yet discriminating between depositary and deposited. In the case of the split interpretation, when we show patients the relation between two parts of themselves within them, even though we do not include ourselves explicitly in the interpretation, it results in more recognition of the internal world and at the same time a better recognition of the external world.

It could be said that in our discussion we have only given names to things we already know and that every psychoanalyst already uses without using the same terms. I would answer that this is undoubtedly true, and I have already said so. But I would add that giving names to things is only possible when they acquire a certain identity as a consequence of discrimination. And this process is what we have tried to demonstrate as also happening in the analysis of symbiosis, which uses many things that are implicit and bound up together until their reiterated use and enrichment results in their being discriminated and given identity.

## Study of the clinical material

### *(a) Background*

Ana Maria is now thirty years old, having started her treatment just over four years ago. A few months previously, her husband had asked me for an interview, with the result that he started psychoanalytic treatment with a woman. Months before, he had begun to have sexual relations with another person, and came to see me with the idea of separating permanently from his wife; although he had decided to do it and had told her about it, he was unable to free himself emotionally from his marriage; he was anxious and disoriented. It was he who later requested psychoanalytic treatment for his wife.

Ana Maria came to the interview very well dressed, but without grace or elegance, her hair very recently done at the hairdresser's as if preparing for a very special occasion; although she was not very expressive or attractive, she was paradoxically a pleasant person, and looked a bit younger than her real age. Her glasses were too large for her face, and the very well done coiffure looked like something superimposed on her and foreign to her intellectual appearance. Some time later, I understood that in this way she was representing two of her conflicting roles: her condition as a woman and her aspirations as a professional. At times, her face took on a tortured expression. She spoke with a certain ease, but kept her body quite rigid, with very marked limitations in her gestures and expressions. She was not anxious. She made no reference to what her husband might have informed me already and told me that he had a lover and wanted to separate, that this made her feel devalued and that she wanted to restore her marriage to normal, but that if he decided to separate she would accept it; therefore, she was now coming to analysis on her husband's advice and it was his fault. She saw no reason to have treatment, but her husband had persuaded her that she had to prepare to live alone with their three children. There was nothing else wrong with her, and she gave me the impression that she was only waiting for her husband's decision; in the meanwhile, he had told her that her analysis could be very beneficial for her. The most concrete thing she said as a direct reference to herself was that, although she didn't know why, she had stopped studying medicine in the course of the fourth year, and that she had great difficulty in improving her economic situation or her personal income; she had a very few teaching hours in two secondary schools

### *(b) General course of the treatment*

The course of her analysis could be described, very schematically, as the alternation or predominance either of the neurotic or of the psychotic part of the personality. That is, although the two levels were always present, during periods of predominance of the neurotic levels the psychotic part of the personality was kept quite segregated; my attempts to mobilise it by interpretation were fruitless, so that whatever had to be made explicit and verbalised (by her or by me) was not supposed to refer to any 'other thing'; in periods when the psychotic levels predominated, the 'other thing' could be included in some measure and the profound dissociation of the personality overcome to some extent. Although this alternation of the levels sometimes occurred in the same session, it was evident that for a very long initial period of time, analysis of the neurotic levels of the personality predominated, while in a second period rupture of the dissociation and inclusion of the psychotic levels predominated.

Throughout the entire, very prolonged initial period, Ana Maria would sit in a chair facing me, at the side of the desk, and she would stay that way the whole time, nearly motionless, never looking at me directly; she always came with 'things' in her hands (handbag, bags, books, notebooks, overcoat, etc.) and she would let them drop in disarray onto my desk. She seemed, especially at the beginning, not to assign any importance to what she said; it was rather to fill the time, waiting for her things to be mended outside of her, in her husband's analysis, while she had only to wait. Often, this dissociation was responsible for a certain atmosphere of triviality or futility in her sessions: what was important was elsewhere, not between us.[79] At other times, I had the impression that she had already handed her 'things' over to me for me to 'do something'; I often thought that this person now in analysis was different from the person I had met in the first interview, and that she gave me only an arranged or ordered part of her life, like her coiffure, and that I was not to include anything that was behind or outside, about which she would keep silent and implicitly required me to do so as well.

She spoke about her relationships with her husband, her children, her mother and siblings; the material was not hard to interpret, but there were two limitations: one was that I had to stay within the material that she gave me and the other was that I could not include myself as a person. I found that I was facing the same characteristics as I had studied in a previous paper and which, starting from the studies by Abraham (1919) of the resistance and transference of persons with a heavy narcissistic component, I came to catalogue as narcissistic transference, identifying in this a simultaneous autistic and symbiotic organisation.

79 Fairbairn (1952, pp. 5, 51) described futility and artificiality as features of the schizoid personality, which we see as more dependent on a deep splitting between the neurotic and psychotic levels. It is possible that the schizoid personality is characterized precisely by this: a deep dissociation between the neurotic and the psychotic levels of the personality and by the simultaneous presentation of autism and symbiosis.

If I failed to comply with these two demands, a very prolonged silence would follow; she grew more tense and rigid, after which she continued on a different subject in a very low, distant and sometimes plaintive tone of voice, so quiet that I had to make an effort to hear her. She would allow no reference to her husband's analysis or to his analyst; or to her abandoned studies or her difficulty in managing her economic affairs. There was a great restriction or narrowing of her ego and affective blockage with intense body-mind dissociation. It was a case of a symbiotic personality with a phobic-obsessional character.

What was immobilised or immovable in her analysis was a dissociated part corresponding to the psychotic part of the personality: she kept this in order and distributed between her husband and me and would not allow me to touch it, include or interpret it; if I did so, she blocked herself and blocked me. This often assisted me in testing her degree of tolerance or permeability, in detecting the degree of integration of her more mature or 'ordered' ego, to see whether I could yet intensify the analysis of the psychotic part of the personality. At the outset, I 'broke the rules' quite frequently, but very soon decided to follow her timing as far as possible, because I understood that she needed first to strengthen or consolidate the degree of cohesion of her more mature ego.

When I proceeded with respect for her timing, my interpretations met with a shorter silence of reflection and less blockage, which often seemed more a silence of reflection than real blockage. When I speak of periods of predominance of the neurotic or psychotic part of the personality, I refer precisely to this: to the periods when the interpretation including the psychotic part was inoperative, when I was forced to await her timing and – on the other hand – the periods when it was possible and operative to mobilise the psychotic part of the personality, at least to some extent. The *'index of increased blockage'* was a useful signal that I had to stay with the neurotic levels, while the *'index of re-introjection'* helped me to see that I could intensify the analysis of the psychotic levels.

As I have already explained, these periods were neither consecutive nor exclusive, but co-existed with alternating predominance. In any case, during the first and larger part of the treatment, dissociation and immobilisation predominated; in the second, there was a certain degree of mobilisation of the psychotic part of the personality; it is especially this second part that I shall study here in greater detail.

With the analysis following this course I began to learn – by fragments or segments and somewhat as if 'by the way' – that she had married seven years before and had three boys aged six, four and two. She came from a very poor home, and it had been her mother who supported the family by going out to work in different places all day long, while her father stayed at home and did the housework. She has three brothers, six, four and two-and-a-half years younger than she, whom she took care of when they were small while their mother was absent. They had moved quite frequently and each child had been born in a different house; actually, these weren't houses but one or two rooms that they occupied in houses that were also occupied by other families. She had few memories and the first move she really remembers dates from when she was seventeen, when they moved to a house they were able to buy, and where she also lived with her parents until approximately a year after her marriage. These situations were particularly painful for her when I included them in her analysis, relating them to other material, and she would be severely blocked for several sessions, especially when I included her parents. She felt betrayed, since if she had already said it once why would I repeat it to her? What was the point?

She occupied the greater part of many sessions with complaints about her mother: that she had always been very authoritarian and cold; even now that she was married, she always gave her orders and advice about what she had to do and not do; it was impossible to win an argument, because she was always right and acted as if she were perfect. This active complaining about and rejection of her mother was actually a cover and a way of holding on to a strong dependence on her. The projection of a severe superego into her mother put a limit on the patient's abuse of greed toward her.

In contrast with the image she presented of her mother, the patient complained that everything she did turned out badly, devaluing herself; this melancholic nucleus, which persisted for a long time, masked her guilt toward her mother and siblings for her greed, denying her envy and rivalry with them. She had been a very good student, reaching the fourth year in medicine, and when she married, she left her studies without knowing why and was unable to take them up again. Nearly four years later, she remembered another detail in connection with this: that she stopped studying during her first pregnancy, which also coincided with moving out of her parents' house into their own house where she and her husband would live alone.

Her younger brother had also studied medicine but had not finished, had married and lived with his wife and children in a poor economic situation. Her other siblings ('the middle ones') were unmarried and lived with their parents in a really parasitic situation: they could not hold down a job, nobody ever knew what work they were doing, and their parents often had to give them money, which they needed. There were periods when they spent a lot of time sleeping or lying in bed. She never referred to her siblings by name; they were just 'the middle ones' and 'the youngest'.

Her father was the most absent or almost totally absent character in the analysis. Ana Maria felt pity and contempt for him; she saw him as totally submissive to her mother and incapable of intervening or 'getting involved', since he left everything up to her mother.

Ana Maria made real her marriage with her husband in the course of the treatment, when we were able to analyse to some extent her dependence on her mother, the rivalry and submission with guilt for the phantasy of having displaced her in the home and having stolen her children. On one occasion, very much in passing, when I could not hear her very well, she remembered how she had always been her mother's favourite, the one who always had the most comfortable arrangements in the house, the only one whose birthday was celebrated and who could go away for holidays. From this derived the analysis of her guilt for having displaced her siblings and kept everything; her self-deprecation masked this guilt and her greed. To the same effect she would sometimes take a newly-formulated interpretation by becoming angry with herself for being that way or for having such a conflict.

In addition to her mother and siblings, a third theme in her analysis at this time was the analysis of her relationship with her husband and children, a relation of submission and guilt for having displaced her relationship with her siblings onto her husband.

Surprise, astonishment or bewilderment were sometimes her reactions when she was able to experience her projections as her own; but this became more intense when she began to see all that she did to induce her husband to carry the burden of the decision of separating on account of isolation and suffocation in the marriage (suffocation in her dependence and submission).[80] During this period of her analysis, a difficulty in intercourse improved somewhat: after her orgasm, she could not tolerate her husband's intra-vaginal ejaculation, so she obliged him to ejaculate between her thighs: at other times she herself could not reach an orgasm if the penis was inside the vagina. She also stopped using glasses, replacing them with contact lenses, which improved her appearance notably.

The entire analysis consisted at this time of interpreting her projections and displacements, as well as her fears. The interpretation of her dependence also occupied a good portion of her analysis, but I didn't know what that dependence was, what it was made of, and I felt that I was handling or speaking of a 'package' or a conglomerate of which it was still impossible for me to know what the components really were. As her relationship with her mother and siblings, husband and children improved, she began to make suggestions that her treatment was coming to an end and that she already felt healthy, which I would interpret but which re-appeared persistently.

In parallel, her relationship with me worsened. The silences following my interpretations became longer and heavier; she was progressively more distant and cold, and no longer looked at me when she entered or when she left, her material was increasingly scanty and monotonous, her voice dwindled. We had arrived at a relationship in which with me too, the question was divorce or separation, but she needed me to act it out as her husband had done. I was undoubtedly confronting a firmly established negative

80 Her husband's infidelity was an attempt to break out of the symbiotic enclosure by diversifying relationships with new depositaries.

therapeutic reaction. I felt increasingly ignored and frustrated and I thought that her husband must have felt this way when he tried to break the marital tie with her. The situation had become very dangerous and claustrophobic for her. I constantly had to recover from hopelessness and frustration, from the impotence she delegated to me, while I systematically interpreted what was happening between us.

This type of transference relation undoubtedly possesses, then, all the characteristics of a narcissistic link, with an organisation that is autistic and symbiotic at the same time: symbiotic in that she had massively deposited in me a part of her personality that she was unable to re-introject; autistic in that she did not let me get in and appear as a person, but only as a depositary that had to act within the limits she imposed.

I had been able to work on the neurotic levels of her personality, on the dissociated, projected and displaced objects, but I was unable to mobilise the psychotic parts; she strictly controlled her timing and had thus been able to reinforce to a degree her more integrated ego.[81] For her, the treatment was over and I frequently remembered what Freud said in 'Analysis terminable and interminable':

> Analytic experience has taught us that the better is always the enemy of the good and that in every phase of the patient's recovery we have to fight against his inertia, which is ready to be content with an incomplete solution.
>
> (Freud, 1937, p. 231)

I continued in this way, fighting against her inertia and the inertia of my countertransference reactions, and I continued to interpret systematically, trying to use my energy and mobilise hers.

At one point, she proposed to leave the treatment because of economic difficulties, since her husband helped to pay for most of the treatment. In this way and on this occasion, it was now money that was responsible for our separation and she was again a victim of the circumstances. This was the acme of a claustrophobic transference situation, in which she felt trapped and constantly threatened by the psychotic parts of her personality that she feared I would force her to re-introject. On the other hand, it was a repetition in the transference of things started and not finished (like medical school), and an enactment of her unrealised and unsatisfied infantile oedipal phantasies. Her guilt for everything that she received passively also came into it. While all this was being analysed, she began to feel depressed and to weep almost constantly for the slightest reason at home. She was greatly

81 Above, I pointed out how, because of the existence and maintenance of this dissociation or division of the personality, the more mature ego can – paradoxically – become more integrated.

surprised and incredulous when I began to interpret that this was weeping and sadness for having to separate from me. The relations between her weeping and sadness and our possible separation were totally repressed, but she was now capable of weeping and getting depressed – something that had not happened even during her husband's attempted separation – it was a consequence of greater strengthening and integration of her ego; if this had not occurred, I think that she would have separated from me, reinforced her blockage and bodily rigidity and reinforced the melancholic mechanisms. This episode, with the risk of losing me, made her aware to some extent of her affection for me, because it is quite evident that in a stationary symbiotic relationship no affection or love is felt, these appearing only once the object is lost or is in danger of being lost; they do not know that they love the object or how much they love it until they lose it. But at the same time there has to be some integration of the ego if this affection is to appear.[82]

The treatment continued in this way: my interpretations continued to be blocked with heavy silence, but she did make an effort to get more class hours and private pupils, and so her economic situation improved to some degree.

A short time after, she made a bet with a girlfriend to show her what she was capable of doing and began to lie down on the couch. Then, the phenomena corresponding to the psychotic part of the personality were even further accentuated, with their respective control and immobilisation. She is able to continue the treatment by retaining the dissociation between her neurotic and psychotic parts, as well as her dependence; her desire to continue the treatment appears as an imposition from outside, projecting her superego into a girlfriend, and thus her submission to her own dependence appears disguised as a challenge. In this way, she manages to project her dependence outside and is thus able to avoid the claustrophobic reaction with me and thereby accept the continuation of her treatment, which was also conditioned by her inability to face the sadness of our separation. Her dependence results from keeping her agglutinated nucleus (her psychotic, immature or undifferentiated part) projected in a depositary and for this very reason the relationship with the depositary (analyst) becomes claustrophobic, so that her tendency is to separate; however, if she tried to do this, she would face a new danger: that of re-introjection.

### *(c) Features of the transference and countertransference*

She no longer looked at me and she totally ignored me. Her sessions became heavier and her associations scantier, her voice weaker with long pauses

82 M. Balint (1952) identifies a type of patient who tends in the analysis to perpetuate the dependence and in whom only the end of the analysis mobilises anxieties.

even between words. My interpretation was always followed by a very long and heavy silence, and when she continued, she would talk about a different subject. The affective blockage and the rigidity of her body, kept immobile and tense, had increased. Sometimes, she grasped the edge of the couch or placed the outstretched palms of her hands flat on the surface of the couch (something I have also observed in other patients in intense symbiotic transference).

Countertransferentially, I had to make a great effort to remember, after each pause, the previous material; it was frequently 'lost' and I laboriously managed to recover it. This meant that I had to fight constantly against losing my role and against taking on the role that she assigned me: that of a simple depositary for part of her narcissistic world and objects. The invasive power of her projective identification was very strong and tended to wipe out my identity as an analyst. Whenever I was able, I began the interpretation by saying what she had just said and what she had said before falling silent or what she had just said and my interpretation previous to the silence; I tied the two segments together meaningfully. Sometimes, I had to exert self-control over a kind of compulsion to interpret and to speak more than she, to escape from the blockage she infiltrated into me, and thereby escape from the control and immobilisation.

Interpretations in terms of feelings (anxiety, love, hate, rivalry, etc.) were empty words, because all this occurred in the area of the body, with no corresponding representation in the area of the mind. In these patients, the mind has a strong logico-rational organisation and the affects are experienced directly in the body; they have to learn to discriminate them and represent them (perceive them) in the area of the mind and to do so they need to overcome the mind-body dissociation. I learned that the affects had to be pointed out in bodily behaviour (position of the hands, movement of the feet, uneven breathing, change of the position of the head, etc.), only afterwards giving this emotion a name and relating it to what was occurring in the transference relationship. For her, in this period of the analysis it had no meaning and it became unworkable for me to formulate the interpretation by saying, for example, 'you feel . . .', because she actually did not feel it; instead, the feeling only 'happens' in the body and in order to be able to feel it, it is necessary to work through the body-mind dissociation, to achieve a better integration of the ego. I was gradually able to understand that her massive projection occupied both her body and mine (in that I only served her as a depositary), with no discrimination between the areas of the body and the external world (my body); the two formed an undivided syncytium occupied by her massive projection. In contrast, a marked mind-body dissociation is maintained in which the mind is her more integrated ego (in an obsessional hyper-adaptation) that rigidly controls the depositary (her body and mine, undivided), in which the more immature part of the personality is projected (the agglutinated nucleus). This mind-body dissociation does not function like a schizoid division between good and bad object, but as a division, separation or fission between two levels of integration of her personality. An accumulation of affective experiences with no discrimination between them, which it would be dangerous to re-introject, are thus controlled in the depositary. We think it important to point out or emphasize that the body-mind dissociation – at least on some levels of the organisation of the personality – is not only this, but a real dissociation between mind and external world, and that the body forms part of the latter, and thus it is totally estranged or alienated.[83] Mind-external world (including the body) is in these cases a separation or fission of two different parts of the personality.[84] On some occasions I found myself feeling guilty for not having made her progress more quickly, after which I realised that this was a consequence of her control, passivity and greed: she made me feel guilty so that I would make an effort – out of guilt – to go on giving her more, while she had no need to be active or to ask for anything, thus avoiding her own guilt for her dependence and greed. I have often found this in symbiotic dependence; the patient passively receives in a disguised (mute) way as if he or she had received nothing and in function of this avoids or hides his or her own guilt for receiving; at the same time these patients try to get the analyst to go on giving more without having to ask for it, as if 'it fell from the sky'; thus she disguises what she is doing so that it will be given to her (she will be mother's favourite).

The alternation of roles was sometimes quite notable: I became blocked when she was more connected, and vice versa: when I understood her better, she became more blocked. Very frequently, especially when psychotic nuclei of the personality were mobilised, I found myself feeling bewildered and sometimes confused about interpreting; in particular, I was unable to differentiate which object and relationship were involved at that moment in the transference. By working repeatedly on this countertransferential reaction, I came to the conclusion that at those times I reacted like her own more mature ego in the psychotic transference to the bringing into play of the more immature parts of her personality, and that my disorientation was due to the quality of the material involved. This was undiscriminated material containing the most divergent and even contradictory and mutually

83 [See p. 11, n. 25.]

84 In various texts, M. Klein (1946, 1957, 1958) indicated the existence of different 'as yet obscure ways in which splitting processes take place' (1958, p. 241), as well as the splitting between parts of the personality, and how the failure of this latter splitting produces a real commotion (1957, p. 192).

Later, I termed this 'fission or separation of two different parts of the personality' systematically as splitting [*clivaje*]. [The Spanish edition of Klein from which Bleger is quoting translates 'splitting' here by *disociación*. Bleger is indicating in this footnote that he decided instead to use *clivaje* for this kind of splitting. See Introduction, p. xlii].

exclusive experiences; but it was contradictory and confused for the more integrated ego (mine or hers), because inside the agglutinated nucleus all this formed a single amalgam, neither confused nor contradictory nor ambivalent. The structure of the agglutinated nucleus corresponds to a polyvalence or ambiguity that I shall discuss later.

It is also necessary to underscore a countertransferential feeling that is very frequent with this type of patients, which is the impression that we are forcing them to connect, to identify and re-introject very segregated parts of themselves; and with this, the feeling that one is breaking a 'pact' and violating the patient. I think that this corresponds to reality, in the sense that to some extent we are forcing the patient and not totally accepting their timing and hence their immobilization. Although there is a limit – very hard to define theoretically – that we must not pass, what we do technically in the analysis of the transference psychosis is no different from what we do in every analysis in regard to handling the timing of the interpretation. However, the countertransferential reaction that I mentioned occurs more specifically in the analysis of the psychotic levels (or of the transference psychosis) because here we are operating with objects that are not discriminated, with an agglutinated nucleus that for a long time can only be mobilised massively or globally; thus, the countertransferential reaction is a consequence of the characteristics of what we are handling or operating. This impression of forcing the analysis is not one of persecuting but rather of overwhelming the patient; this difference also corresponds to the difference between a part-object (persecutory) and the agglutinated nucleus (overwhelming for the ego).

### *(d) Confusion when entering and leaving the sessions*

Entering and leaving sessions are the moments at which there occurs a redistribution of the psychotic part of the personality in relation to the more mature and integrated ego. Ana Maria was very punctual and never missed a session; she generally waited only a few minutes until I invited her to enter. At that moment, she suddenly changed; a real metamorphosis took place: she walked in absently, as if in a hypnotic state, which I progressively identified as a narrowing of the field of her consciousness and as a clouded consciousness. This was even more accentuated when I had heard her laughing and talking vivaciously with another patient whom she had happened to meet. She seemed like an automaton that repeated my movements and did not look at me or the room. She greeted me always after I had done so and in the same way; it always occurred that I was the first to hold out my hand and say hello and she repeated this. It had all the characteristics of a true echolalia and echopraxia. Then, she walked to my desk and dropped her coat, her book or magazine, bag or handbag onto it; she always came with several things in her hands, which she brought in a heap and dropped on the desk without putting them into order there, relieving herself of a burden that weighed her down on all sides and which she held with difficulty between her hands; in this way, she symbolized her depositation in me. Then she would lie down like an automaton, taking care to keep her back turned to me all the while and not look at me, and that my gaze should not meet hers. She did not need to lie down; she would fall, already 'composed', onto the couch, was silent for a few minutes and then would begin to speak in a weak voice, with no vivacity and very slowly. Her narrowed state of consciousness persisted throughout the session, with some alternatives or variations, for many months of her treatment.

Entering the session was the dangerous moment when a re-introjection and massive mobilisation of all her agglutinated nucleus could occur, against which she needed to defend the organisation of her more integrated ego from the danger of psychotic disorganisation. This mobilisation was controlled to a certain extent so as to avoid extreme dangers by avoiding re-introjection with all the ritual I have just described; but all the same, a certain mobilisation of the agglutinated nucleus could not be avoided, with the emergence of disorientation and confusion in the patient; it was a moment when there was a certain fusion between her more integrated ego, the agglutinated nucleus and the depositary, and to some extent the limits were lost between ego and non-ego, between her and me, producing a loss of discrimination and a regression of her whole personality; at such moments, she functioned with primary identification, reproducing within her everything I did, as a part of her own ego, and this is the process or mechanism that forms the basis for the phenomena of echolalia and echopraxia that I described, but that also occurs in other phenomena such as wax-like flexibility, the hypnotic state, mimetism and automatism. In all these cases, the ego is overwhelmed by the re-introjected agglutinated nucleus and it is only possible to function with primary identification, to function as I was doing, with a massive introjective identification with the depositary and not just with the deposited; the introjected depositary is directly made into a nucleus of the ego.[85]

85 Rodrigué, E. (1955b, p. 177n.) says on this subject: 'The peculiar grammatical construction, called "Pronominal Inversal" . . . is obviously related to the underlying confusion between "me" and "not-me". Echolalia in an autistic child . . . could also be seen to represent this confusion and the defence against it: by repeating the word, he was the other person (confusion), but by being the other person's echo, he was reflecting the word outside without assimilating it'.

Freud, in 'Group Psychology and the Analysis of the Ego', referring to hypnosis and falling in love, says that in both processes the hypnotist and the loved person respectively take the place of the subject's ego ideal.

As she walked toward my desk, a re-distribution was already taking place; in the first place, the mere fact of walking involved a certain order in which I was outside and she was separate from me; another important moment was when she 'dumped' her things onto my desk as a massive surrender (re-projection) of a whole part of herself, of which I was to take charge. From there on, her rigid control began to try to avoid fresh mobilisation of this order that she had achieved when she entered. I have observed this averting of the eyes from the therapist in other cases as a fear of being hypnotised or influenced, that is, to be invaded again by the therapist's ego, which would wipe out the patient's own personality. This tallied with a persistent impression I had when Ana Maria came in and I greeted her; that I put her inside of me, inside my things, in a world that was strange, feared and unknown to her. The relative balance she then found was obtained at the price of a great narrowing of her ego, which persisted throughout the session, with rigid control both of the projected and the depositary. Thus, she needed to avoid two dangerous re-introjections: of the projected and of the depositary.

A long time afterwards, when there had been some strengthening of her ego and some working through and discrimination of her agglutinated nucleus in her relation with me, and therefore a lessening of the danger of massive and overwhelming projection and re-introjection, she was able to come in and take her coat off inside the room, greet me at the same time as I did, without waiting for me to do so first and without repeating the same greeting as me; she stopped coming with 'things' in her hands and only brought a small handbag that she always left on my desk. This was also noticeable in the course of the session, since she took me more into consideration as a person: when she told me something, she would for example add, 'I don't know if I'm being clear enough', or 'I don't know whether you understand me.'

At the end of the session, the same operation was repeated. Minutes beforehand, she was already getting ready to leave, she 'composed herself' in order to be able to separate from me; she repeated the same gestures and words I used to say goodbye, gathered all her things haphazardly from my desk and left without looking at me, sometimes quite dizzy or walking hesitantly, or confusing the hand she needed to hold her things with the hand for shaking hands. In the first months of analysis I was often left with a headache, feeling tense or tired or with a feeling of liberation.

A long time afterwards, when her projections were no longer so massive, I no longer had countertransferential reactions of this kind – global and exhausting feelings – but a much more defined impression, and the projective counter-identification was with a very specific role. This happened, for example, on one occasion when I ended the session ten minutes early in the belief that it was actually time to do so, with which I enacted a claustrophobic reaction of hers.

### *(e) The symptom*

A symptom that she had already 'told' me about in the first interview, and which appeared only infrequently in her material, was her abandonment of her university studies, her doubts about taking them up again and the difficulties she faced when she was willing to study or return to the university. This symptom was a true 'magma', a condensation of very heterogeneous things with the function, the structure and validity of a true psychotic restitution. She could never persist for very long in analysing it; it was quickly dissociated; whenever she mentioned it, it was more a way to remind me that she had given it to me and was waiting for me to give her the solution. If I tried to go on interpreting this symptom, her blockage increased together with her tension and silences.

The abandonment of her studies and her difficulty with studying were, evidently, disturbances of sublimation. I believe that many inhibitions due to a deficit of sublimation are related to blockage of the psychotic part of the personality (agglutinated nucleus) and the projection of the latter into the depositary (in this case, the university or her studies), which is then handled evasively (phobically). The disturbance in assimilating knowledge has the same character as the disturbance in the transference relation for assimilating the interpretation: in both cases, the danger is that of massive re-introjection; she thereby becomes the target of her own greed and envy, which are included or involved in the re-introjection.

In this symptom were condensed the restrictions of her ego, the undiscriminated part of her personality, involving a very complex oedipal situation. She could not tolerate it when I made the connection for her between this symptom and her relationship with her parents and siblings. These were the very few times when she could protest a bit more openly, saying that I 'put' her parents into it, or that she already knew 'that' or had already said it on another occasion.

Studying medicine was a highly complex agglutinated nucleus. Her mother had wanted her older brother to study for this degree and she had chosen it in order to realise her mother's wish, thus putting herself in her brother's place. Her mother however did not want her to study medicine, so that doing it was rebellion, a possibility to break the dependence with her. When she was pregnant with her first child, she abandoned her studies in order to retain her mother, but in staying at home she is like her father and feels shut up in her condition as a woman-man subjected to her mother's needs. Her studies meant rivalry with men, but she felt very guilty about studying since her brother failed the same degree. She could not differentiate very well between the mummy-woman who had children and the mummy-man who went out to earn a living; the same situation existed in relation to her father-man and her father-woman who stayed at home doing the housekeeping. This coincides with a deficit in her personification and the concomitant lack of discrimination between feminine and masculine; she did not know, in the oedipal situation, whether she was a boy with her mother-woman or a woman with her mother-man and, respectively, the same situation with her father. At the same time, there was guilt for throwing her mother out and keeping her children, and guilt for her father whom she perceived as weak, submissive and castrated. She did not know whether to be a man she had to be like her father or like her mother, and the same in the case of being a woman. She had not had defined and consistent guidelines for identification, since roles and characters were highly ambiguous. Her siblings were hers and her father's, or hers and her mother-father's, and alternatively in all the variants of these roles. In order to be successful and secure, she had to be like her mother and not like her failed father, but in this case, she became her mother's rival and lost or destroyed her, or else she had to risk her revenge. Her father came up very little in the analysis; he was instead melted into the figure of the mother. All this was contained in her agglutinated nucleus, in the psychotic part of the personality, but as undiscriminated experiences or nuclei, both between her father and mother and between them and her. If I insisted on analysing these situations, her defence was a melancholic organisation in which her superego was the possessive, active, controlling, domineering mother and her ego the weak, phobic, passive and castrated father.

In Ana Maria the very frequent moves that occurred until she was 17 years old have also influenced this deficit in personification, because these continuous changes forced her into a constant mobilisation of anxieties and objects, repeatedly forcing re-introjection, with a consequent and further massive re-projection.[86] With the frequent moves and such a complex oedipal situation, studying was the most permanent factor; she did not change schools even when they moved from one neighbourhood to another, even though she had to walk many blocks. Since studying was the most stable element, it became the most reliable depositary of the psychotic, dissociated part of the personality.

### *(f) Ambiguity, polyvalence and polarisation of the agglutinated nucleus*

We can now progress in our understanding of the structure of the agglutinated nucleus, identifying it as an undiscriminated part of the personality

86 Kanner pointed out in early infantile autism an 'anxiously obsessive desire for the maintenance of sameness' (Kanner, 1972 [1935], p. 718) and the overwhelming effect of changes of routine and residence. E. Pichon Rivière has also pointed out, in his lectures, the triggering role of house removals in Kanner's autism. Routine in the same house is what allows maintenance of the projection and dissociation of the psychotic part of the personality, and by virtue of this dissociation the ego is able to achieve a growing degree

developmentally linked to all the ambiguous experiences that have not produced well-defined norms in the organisation of the personality, because no discrimination has been fundamentally established at the deepest levels of the oedipal situation (between the father-mother objects and the patient's own ego). An observation by M. Klein also provides us with some grounding. She says: 'In very ill individuals, the inability to disentangle the relation to the father from the one to the mother, because of their being inextricably interlinked in the patient's mind, plays an important *rôle* in severe states of confusion.' (Klein, 1957, p. 198). In the psychotic part of the personality a very primitive oedipal situation persists, in which discrimination of the combined couple has not occurred, nor a discrimination between the oedipal objects and the patient's ego. In the agglutinated nucleus, for the same reasons, there is also no discrimination between what in the neurotic constitutes the ego, the superego, the ego ideal and the ideal ego.

A significant fact for understanding the dynamic of the agglutinated nucleus is that, since there is no discrimination between its elements, the psychotic part of the personality is quite ambiguous, in the sense that it may function alternatively in very divergent, different ways depending on the circumstantial predominance of some of its different components or elements. In other words, the psychotic part of the personality (agglutinated nucleus) is capable of extreme functional polarization, and is thus able to polarise itself into some of the nuclei of identification, functioning as an ego, superego, ideal ego or ego ideal. Ambiguity and extreme polarisation support the emergence of the phenomena described above, such as mimetism, metamorphosis, echolalia, echopraxia, imitation, hypnosis, etc. This polarisation is produced as a defence against ambiguity or confusion, and may be extremely labile, changing easily, or may persist as a relatively stable organisation of the personality, but which may alternate, for example, between extreme rigidity and extreme submission.[87]

Therefore, it is its polyvalence that characterises the psychotic part of the personality (agglutinated nucleus), lending it that ambiguous quality as well as a potential for quite varied polarisations; one of these may be the melancholic organisation that we have seen at some moments in our patient Ana Maria.

of integration, by maintaining a very overwhelming part segregated from itself. In our patient, this role of stable depositary was taken not by the house but by her studies.

87 Although it is not my purpose at this time to expand specifically on this theme, I wish to point out that this is precisely what occurs in the authoritarian personality described and studied by Adorno and Frenkel-Brunswick (Adorno et al., 1950); I therefore consider that this is actually an ambiguous personality (with intense psychotic nuclei). I also think that what is actually ambiguity with extreme polarisations is frequently described as ambivalence.

Developmentally, the agglutinated nucleus is the result of an agglomeration of multiple, indiscriminate and non-stratified primary identifications. I think that this probably occurs normally in the development of the earliest stages of the Oedipus complex. M. Klein makes a suggestion that we may now relate to the formation of the agglutinated nucleus; she says that the earliest stages of the Oedipus complex 'are characterised by swift fluctuations between different objects and aims, with corresponding fluctuations in the nature of the defences' (Klein, 1945, p. 407). However, we must also assume that if this situation subsists in a good part of the personality, we need to add a weakness of the ego that would permit multiple introjections that are very easy, without selection and without stratification. We believe that the topic we are developing here is closely related to some descriptions we find, among others, in the works of P. Heimann and M. Klein. The former author says, for example: 'A child who is "too good" indiscriminately absorbs his objects; he remains a shell of impersonations and imitations and does not develop into a "character". He lacks "personality"'. (Heimann, 1952, p. 129). As I have already described, Ana Maria behaves in this way, like 'a too-good child', and her only way to defend herself from this and from ambiguity is with her rigidity of character. In *Envy and Gratitude*, M. Klein also considers that a weak ego is characterised by being exposed to identification with a variety of objects in an indiscriminate way, and that 'Doubts in the possession of the good object and the corresponding uncertainty about one's own good feelings also contribute to greedy and indiscriminate identifications; such people are easily influenced because they cannot trust their own judgement.' (Klein, 1957, p. 187). H. Rosenfeld (1962) also pointed out that the development of a normal superego and ego resolves the possibility of making selective identifications.

In the transference relation, I was often an idealised mother:[88] perfect, demanding and persecutory, who made her submit and took away her personality, and she felt humiliated like her father. Rivalry and envy were constantly operating and, though very far from any possibility of insight, could function by completely rotating our roles: I was rigidly controlled and made to submit – like her castrated father – to her, while she behaved like her mother. Ana Maria behaved passively with me, but at the same time she submitted me to her control, timing and needs; she was active by being passive, and I was always at risk of being passive even when I was being manifestly active.

With no other patient did I have, so clearly and consistently, the experience I had with Ana Maria; that during the analysis she learned and that this was not only a question of bringing to consciousness what already existed,

88 In this way, we may infer the hypothesis that the idealised object is also a consequence of one of the possible polarisations of the agglutinated nucleus and therefore a manifestation of the psychotic part of the personality.

but of discriminating something she had never attained until that moment. This discrimination was always achieved first in material referring to situations outside the analysis and only later in the transference relation. I had to act as a good depositary that allowed her this displacement and I had to help her in the external situation; when I referred it to the transference relation, my interpretation was followed by a silence that blocked her and me, from which I had to recover with great effort. One of the first times she came near to seeing her envy and rivalry was when she was telling me that she had read that a new, recently appointed government minister was her own age. Then she fell silent in an atmosphere of hopelessness and sadness. I said to her that she had compared herself to what other people had at the same age as herself. After a pause she answered me by lamenting that she was never able to have or do anything. Then I said to her that she was comparing herself to me and to what I had. Now she followed with a very heavy and prolonged silence. When I pointed out her reaction, she answered, 'I don't see anything that has to do with you' and resumed her silence.[89] Denial, idealisation in the transference and the projection of her omnipotence into me were operating as a defence against a dangerous situation of fusion with me.[90] Therefore, we can say that the symbiotic relation (the psychotic part of the personality) is the management, within the depositary, of the undiscriminated roles of the oedipal situation. The resolution or working through of this link requires separation and recognition (discrimination) of the very different experiences of which it is composed.

I will now present a series of sessions and fragments of session, with corresponding comments, with which I will try to illustrate some of the aspects I have developed above.

### *(g) Session A*

This is a Monday session that took place over a year ago; in the previous session, I acted by returning what she had projected into me, pointing out her silences and her way of denying, annulling and controlling me. Her reactions were systematically to isolate me with her silence, change the subject and go on as if I had not spoken and did not exist. Although all this

89 'One of the difficulties of bringing about steps in integration arises when the patient says: "I can understand what you are telling me but I do not feel it." We are aware that we are in fact referring to a part of the personality which, to all intents and purposes, is not sufficiently accessible either to the patient or to the analyst at that time.' (Klein, 1957, p. 226).

90 However, there are experiences in which the essence could be the search for fusion with the psychotic part of the personality. This is possibly what occurs in mysticism as well as in sexual intercourse.

had happened before, in the session transcribed below I could tell that she had reached a certain degree of re-introjection and dispersion of the agglutinated nucleus in the preceding session.

In this session, she arrives very punctually as always, with all the characteristics of her entering the room as I have already described. She lies down and speaks in a slow, cold, distant way, in a weak and monotonous voice with many pauses and silences.

> On Friday I had a very good day (pause). Well, it suddenly seems as if . . . everything was losing importance . . . And I myself cannot believe that I could feel that way . . . I had prepared to make a dessert on Friday . . . after I left my students in the afternoon I started to make it . . . I have, well . . . very little practice with desserts . . . I think they're going to turn out badly . . . Well, on Friday the pastry would not hold together . . . luckily, the maid was not there at the time . . . she had already left . . . I was alone in the kitchen . . . somehow I had to get the pastry to hold together . . . I put it into the cake tin . . . I started out with my hands because with the rolling pin it had become completely broken. In the end, it turned out to be a great dessert . . . a bit burnt, but it tasted good. (Long pause) Well. That dessert is always hard for me to make. It takes me a long time . . . The last time it turned out a bit raw, this time it turned out a bit burnt . . . maybe the next time it will turn out just the way it should. (Long pause) My husband had arrived late that night and asked me if I wanted to go somewhere . . . and I told him that I had wanted to go to Emma's house . . . that if I had known he was going to arrive so late, I would have left before . . . so he took me . . . but with Friday my way of feeling well was over . . . on Saturday I didn't want to go anywhere in the evening . . . I was sleepy . . . and yesterday I also went to bed early . . . Really Friday seems like a miracle to me . . . it seems I was less heavy . . . that I was lighter. (Pause)

The interpretation was that I had left her all in pieces, like the pastry, after her last session, and that she had to manage by herself, to put herself together and hold herself together alone, leaving me outside.

The patient begins her session with an indirect reference to the previous session which, even made in this way, is an exceptional occurrence. It already indicates a certain degree of learning and identification with me (introjection of the depositary), since for a long time, whenever I could get past the blockage, it was I who put the material of one session together with that of the previous one, or the material before and after a pause or silence following an interpretation of mine. Another detail of this learning is indicated in this material by the elements it provides, since for a long time she would only give a narrative of events.

In her way of speaking, we should also note the pauses that break up the material; how after each pause she does not repeat or take up the phrase or the noun of the phrase again, which obliges the listener to make a greater effort of attention and synthesis.

She describes a real metamorphosis that was produced when she 'put herself together' after the previous session, in which I acted by forcing the re-introjection (of the projected and of the depositary), by which she felt dispersed. She also forced the re-projection of what had been introjected and was thus able to put be at one with herself on her own, without me (the servant who wasn't there, and without the rolling pin); the maidservant and the rolling pin are two aspects of herself and of her parents, that disturb her more integrated ego (the maid as superego and the rolling pin as the masculine part), and these two parts of herself are the ones she leaves outside (re-projected into me). In this way, she integrates or re-forms her ego, which has been attacked and dispersed by the re-introjection, by means of a re-agglutination and re-projection of what was introjected.[91] All this occurs because at a certain level of the oedipal situation (the one included in the psychotic part of the personality) there is no discrimination between father and mother and from the nuclei of the ego of identification with them. This agglutinated nucleus, thus formed by parts of her ego and her superego and aspects of the mother and father, is what she needs to keep projected in me, because her more integrated ego is disturbed by their re-introjection and is unable to proceed to their repression.[92]

Her husband's return implies the return of a depositary and with it the return of the agglutinated nucleus and the danger of a rupture in the dissociation; thus she falls into a state of sleep that protects her more integrated ego from another dispersion similar to the one that was produced on Friday during the session when she felt that I was forcing the re-introjection. I want to point out that this is the type of re-introjection that is disturbing to the ego, until its components are discriminated so that re-introjection may take place in a more gradual rather than a massive way. This separation between the ego and the agglutinated (psychotic) nucleus is not a dissociation such as that which occurs, for example, in the schizoid division between good and bad object. For this reason we could assign it a more specific term such as splitting, which is then the same thing as the dissociation that divides or separates the neurotic from the psychotic parts of the personality.

91 In an article that I consider of fundamental importance, Bion says, referring to the psychotic personality, that '[the patient] cannot synthesize his objects: he can only agglomerate and compress them. Further, whether he feels he has had something put into him, or whether he feels he has introjected it, he feels the ingress as an assault, and a retaliation by the object for his violent intrusion into it.' (Bion, 1956, pp. 40–41).

92 Bizarre objects, as termed by Bion are described as 'objects which are ordinarily the furniture of dreams. These objects, primitive yet complex, partake of qualities which in the non-psychotic are peculiar to matter, anal objects, senses, ideas, superego, and the remaining qualities of personality.' (Bion, 1956, p. 40).

This interpretation, which we have already used as an example, is an unsplit formulation, in the sense that I include myself in an undivided way with what is projected, while indicating an outside that is related to what is happening inside her and outside the session. As I indicated earlier, such interpretations are 'feeders' for the split interpretations, but they also have the property of indicating the existence of an external world. By virtue of the latter, unsplit interpretations facilitate re-projection or depositation, a movement that the analyst also needs to aid and receive, because through these multiple movements of projection-introjection the ego becomes more integrated and the agglutinated nucleus is progressively and gradually fragmented and discriminated.

A long silence follows my interpretation and then she says:

> Yesterday we were at a barbecue . . . with my parents . . . and with my husband's cousin and his wife . . . Well . . . I was determined to have a good time . . . Well . . . it would seem I don't have anything else to tell you . . . That is . . . what I had that was most important . . . I've already said it and everything ended there . . . I'm still rejecting my father . . . it upset me a lot when he started eating before the others did . . . It didn't matter to him at all . . .

I tell her she is showing me that she was determined to have a good time today with me by avoiding a repetition of what happened on Friday, but when she stays aloof from me, she feels as if I were the one who is being aloof and as if I didn't care about what she says.

In my interpretations at that time I always needed to include that my interpretation derived from what she said (you show me, you point out to me, you tell me, etc.), thereby showing the connection between what I say and what she says, because if I did not do it in this way the interpretation would appear dissociated in her reply and she would mistake it for an opinion of mine, whose origin she did not see, and also generally as a reproach.

In the material just quoted there is an attempt to focus what has been dissociated on the father, salvaging from the parental couple her relation with her mother or with her more accepted or needed aspects; in other words, it is the need for a new depositary. It is interesting to observe that when the first interpretation is not split, which is to say that it does not use or point out to her the internal objects projected into me, she replies to my interpretation by talking to me precisely about what I did not include in the interpretation (her internal objects). Just as she dissociates the latter, she also dissociates me into one part in which I am rejected and dangerous and she needs to keep me at a distance and controlled, and another part in which she needs me and holds onto the relation with me to 'have a good time'. But this double attitude toward me is not sufficiently discriminated, any more than are the internal objects among themselves and from parts of her own ego projected into me, that have both maternal superego aspects (the maid-servant) and masculine aspects (the rolling pin).

This last interpretation is again followed by a long silence after which she says:

> Well . . . on Friday I went to the university . . . I had to ask for the certification of the courses . . . that I had passed . . . Well . . . They told me the name of a member of staff to look for . . . to do the processing faster . . . but I wrote it down in a notebook that I didn't have with me . . . I phoned . . . to see whether the maid could give me the name by phone . . . I explained it to her . . . she found the notebook . . . but she couldn't find the name, but it didn't matter . . . Afterwards I found out that this member of staff wasn't the one that I was looking for . . . They treated me very well anyway . . . I think that this started to make me happy . . .

I interpret to her that now she is showing me that today, in part, she is seeking the relationship with me and that in any case, even though she keeps her distance from me, she feels well-treated by me.

Although the patient has to avoid the re-introjection, which would be disturbing for her, there is an optimal distance at which, without this happening, she has to stay at the same time connected to me and keeping hold of me, and I must continue to take care of her. The patient returns to a long silence and then says:

> All this week I hadn't talked to Elena . . . And I had decided not to call her and she called me on Friday . . . Everything was working out for me . . . And neither of us commented on why we hadn't talked for so many days.

I tell her that it makes her happy when I talk to her, but she is asking me to be silent with her about certain things, not to talk to her about these things and to leave them out. She continues:

> A few days ago . . . my husband told me that . . . that my brother had asked for money from the same man that lends to him and that my husband was upset because he didn't tell him, because he is my brother's guarantor . . . so I told him that he had to tell my brother if he was upset by this situation . . . He said yes, that he was going to tell him . . . But I felt directly attacked . . . I told him that in any case, my family wasn't like his . . . that they pay their debts and that my brother answered for the money he borrowed even though it wasn't directly for him . . . Why would I have answered him in such an aggressive way?. . . Well . . . because a brother of his asked him for money years ago . . . he never returned it and now he's asked him again . . . I thought that my way of answering was going to result in quite a lot of anger . . . I had really been very aggressive . . .

I interpret that she is warning me that, since her direct answers to me may be aggressive, that is why she answers me indirectly.

With the interpretation that both of us need to keep silent about some things, the patient felt doubly affected and she takes out her anger displaced on to her husband. On the one hand she felt the danger of re-introjection (if I refused the 'arrangement') and on the other, she felt reproached for inducing me to continue to take care of her, both of us concealing what she is asking for, without acknowledging what she receives from me and also without recognising that it is she who asks (like her brother). With this, the patient's melancholic structure, which had earlier manifested as deprecation and self-reproach during the entire period of analysis of the neurotic levels, has been mobilised, and now emerges transformed into an accusation, projecting her superego into me. I consider this last step a bit of progress, because any modification of a stereotypy must always begin by re-establishing the potential for using mechanisms of projection and introjection, which are the only ones that can lead progressively to rectification.

After the last interpretation she is silent and then says:

> It strikes me that my husband did not react the same way as other times . . . At other times, he would have become much angrier with me . . . And now I am trying to remember other times when I answered him in that way . . . in a way as if I were attacking him . . . Yesterday, when we were returning home, we saw Pedro's station wagon . . . and . . . Well . . . Elisa greeted me and I said what was that about not coming to Buenos Aires . . . I wanted to catch her in a lie . . . because she once told me when talking by phone that they haven't been coming to Buenos Aires lately . . . I wanted to catch her in a lie . . . how could she tell me that they didn't come to Buenos Aires when they were in Buenos Aires . . . Well . . . afterwards, I reflected on what my intention of reproaching her had been . . . I wanted to catch her in a lie . . .

I tell her that she felt reproached by me and now she is trying to find something in order to get back at me and reproach me for something.

The patient controls and feels her way with her aggression; a reproach is something less than a direct aggression and makes her feel less guilty. As long as I continue to interpret, as I had done in the previous session – in regard to the dissociation, with the psychotic nucleus unsplit from the depositary – the patient goes from a passive autistic defence to a more active paranoid defence in which she attempts a circle of mutual accusations, just like the one she habitually had with her mother when she felt invaded and controlled by her; this mutual reproach that the patient is now seeking keeps the dependence and the relationship less dangerous, and for this she feels guilty and deceitful for hiding, behind the reproach, her good connection with me, which she wants to keep and preserve; she tells me that it is a lie that she doesn't get near me (come to Buenos Aires), in spite of her anger. It is the affection that is not discriminated from her aggression and this constitutes part of the agglutinated nucleus that she still needs to control on the outside. She adds: '... It seems that I don't want to touch on any subject ...'

I tell her that although she doesn't want to touch on any subject, she is at the same time holding onto the couch very tightly; that she is afraid to go too far away from me, to fall off or leave the couch, and that is why she is clinging tightly to me.

Here is where the mind-body division occurs quite clearly,[93] corresponding respectively to the autism-symbiosis organisation (autism: mind, distance; symbiosis: body, contact), and it is also possible for me to show this to the patient. In this way, I point out the distance, but also the contact that she maintains with me on the bodily level, and I break the stereotyping of mutual reproaches with her mother, which was partly repeated in the transference situation as a way of defending herself from dependence, but also retaining the dependence in a less dangerous way (with the reproach). This allows her to continue by referring explicitly to situations in the previous session that disturbed her:

> Well . . . I remember the last session . . . That bit about putting together the parts . . . Since I started the treatment I began to hear about the parts . . . Well . . . I think that deep down I am not persuaded that this exists . . . No . . . It is not a direct attack on you . . . because you make that interpretation or because you base it on that theory . . . but no . . . there is no acceptance on my part of that theory of the parts . . . and although you show it to me . . . I believe that still I can't believe in that . . . Well . . . although I say to myself that this is closing my eyes to reality . . . and not wanting to see something you show to me . . . Well . . . but that's the way it is . . . Because I wanted to think about this to see how I understood it . . . but it went completely out of my head . . . at least from the conscious field . . . There is that . . . and there is that about not wanting to be a woman or rejecting being a woman . . . or rejecting it in part . . . Well . . . in something it surprised me . . . quite a lot . . . because . . . I don't know what it looks like from the outside, but inside I see myself as more of a woman . . . I know it's hard for me to accept everything . . . and that is most of it . . . then one day maybe I'll be more open to accepting . . . more open to do anything . . . that's an abortion . . . And now I remember what I wanted to tell you, that I had been very aggressive with my husband. Yesterday before leaving the house . . . there was an argument about the dog . . . that he wanted to

93 I have explained earlier that the dissociation is not between mind and body, but between mind, on the one hand, and body and external world, on the other hand; the latter two in an undivided and indiscriminate way. [see p. 102].

> take it . . . and I told him not to take it . . . Then I told him that he showed much more affection towards the dog . . . that I had never seen him show towards the children . . . I thought he was going to eat me alive at that moment . . .

I interpreted that she is telling me not to push her by telling her things that she can neither understand nor accept, and that when she forces herself to accept things, she has to abort them. That she cannot show her affection towards me directly and that I shouldn't push her to do so either.

Autistic retraction and active rejection keep her body divided from her mind, and in her body, far away from her, are kept her feelings, which she cannot accept or show directly.[94] After a brief pause, she says:

> His first reaction was violent but he calmed down right away . . . I thought that I must have ruined his day.

I interpret that now she is protecting me and her relationship with me; she is afraid she may have ruined my day. She continues:

> The question is why I have to be so caustic . . . I wanted to tell him that, but in a different way . . . because I had observed him . . . I noticed that he picked up the dog and petted him . . . He is not as demonstrative with his children as he is with the dog . . .

This is the first time that she can deal with the subject of affection explicitly without blocking or annulling it totally, as had occurred systematically until now. The repeated re-introjection had succeeded, to some extent, in breaking the mind-body division and with it, in the same measure, the autism-symbiosis dichotomy, allowing her to receive and experience affection, although she felt that this re-introjection was forced by me; or else that she made me feel that. The patient continues by saying:

> It's not hard for me to give my children affection . . . I do it . . . Then my husband says that I cuddle them too much . . . But I feel that need to cuddle them . . . But at that moment it seems that . . . that I did understand that it is easier for him to demonstrate his affection for a dog . . . a dog is

94 Apart from those I pointed out as causes of the difficulty in accepting affect, I think that the re-introjection of affect is overwhelming in itself, because affect and emotion are by nature inherently indiscriminate in their structure as object relations, that function on a magical level and for the same reason always lead to the danger of a loss of boundaries between the ego and reality (dissolution of identity). To this we must add the enormous greed for affection that burdens its re-introjection. In this respect, Sartre's study on emotion is quite suggestive.

not a child. (She remains silent.) Perhaps because I also wanted him to cuddle me.

I told her that now she wishes that I would cuddle her and give her affection, because in this way I would show her that I am not angry; that criticising is her way of asking for affection.

The insight into her need and her direct request for affection are exceptional in all the time she has been in analysis until this session. All affection is felt by this patient as an infantile need and for this reason she only allows it in herself in relation to her children, as dissociated parts of herself; her need for affection stays blocked in her body, while she has imposed on herself a reactive and demanding independence in the area of the mind, struggling against the affection that sweeps her into infantile dependence. Receiving affection without asking for it, or giving it while she actively or aggressively rejects it, maintains this dissociation between dependence and a relative reactive independence. When I interpret all these aspects, I help her to discriminate among her feelings, to discriminate between receiving, asking and giving, as well as the fact that she is asking it from me.

After a long silence, she says,

> Well . . . again in my mind I see my father and my brother; because yesterday my brother also came over . . . After I married, I didn't usually kiss my brothers when we met. My sister-in-law comes from a home where when she enters and leaves, she kisses everyone there and when she began to come to our home after she married, she kissed my brothers and kisses my parents. And I said, hey, if she kisses my brother, why don't I kiss him. So I got into the habit of kissing my brothers when I meet them. I think my brother likes it and just because he likes it, I used to be mean with it towards him . . . The relation with this need for physical affection that I feel and maybe he also feels . . . My mother used to cuddle us . . . I'm wondering whether what we lack is cuddles from my father . . . It's true that my father is not very demonstrative . . . (Pause) The previous Sunday we had gone to have lunch at my parents' house. There are no servants and my father helps my mother to clear the table and dry the dishes. But he has to do it right away, he can't wait. We were going to leave anyway but he has his scheme and has to carry it through to the letter and he was irritated because somebody had thrown something onto the floor or something like that. On the one hand I was a bit amused by the way my father is and that I had imagined he might change and on the other hand it shocks me that he should be that way . . . Then, the comparison with what I have of him in me . . . it's the same . . .

I interpret that she finds in me things like those of her father's: the need to say things right away, and that I can't postpone them.

When the affection appears, not only has it been discriminated from the aggression, but other problems appear in connection with the oldest levels of affective life, in the sense of whether the affection is connected with or directed to the mother or to the father, or which of them expects it. If I give her affection, she learns from me as she does from her sister-in-law, but this separates her from being like her father and from being a man; learning to demonstrate affection means separating from her father, from me and from the masculine role. This problem is basically burdened by confusion on certain levels of the oedipal situation, in the sense that the roles of father and mother are not well configured or discriminated: her mother was the one who left the house to work while her father was the one who stayed at home and did all the feminine work. To this is added her own maternal role with her brothers in her mother's absence, plus the problems of guilt for the affection (she captured all her mother's affection, in preference over her brothers; she stayed at home with the father, and even with her mother's children as if they were her own). To this lack of clear discrimination of roles (feminine-masculine; maternal-paternal; daughter-wife, etc.) we attribute great importance in the oedipal situation, because it makes for a deficit in personification and identity. All this is stirred up when she feels her feelings as her own.

At the beginning of this same material, she shows that affection is linked to conflictive situations of change; kissing the family when entering and leaving, related to the mother's coming and going when she used to go to work, and with moving house and the coming into and going out of the session. That is, the affection is only felt and expressed at moments of change and confusion of change, thereby putting further weight on the conflictive character of her feelings.

After the previous interpretation, she is again silent and then says:

> Well, although I mean to accept my father the way he is . . . I find so many repellent things about him . . .

I tell her that this is her difficulty in accepting herself.

What is repellent (or what she rejects) in her father is a fragment of the agglutinated nucleus of the oedipal situation, which is also what she has deposited in me and in some measure is now mobilised together with the affect. The interpretation was now a split interpretation, of parts of herself in conflict within her. After a silence, she goes on:

> Well . . . but I am thinking about my father that he is one person and I am another . . . and although an attitude of his is like that for me . . . at certain times so repellent . . . I immediately think, but it's not me that's doing it . . . it's him . . . and he is already like that. He's not going to change . . . But this outweighs everything else for me . . . I can't incorporate it . . . I cannot

> accept . . . Do you know that I felt my father's affection today? (With stifled weeping) . . . But I think that he must feel my rejection . . .

I interpret that on the one hand she now feels her own feelings inside her and on the other hand, she rejects them and doesn't allow them.

The superimposition (agglutination) of the depositary, the internal object and the self[95] is one of the most serious technical problems that we face in the psychotic part of the personality: the lack of splitting and discrimination prevents the re-introjection of the projected internal object and the self, blocking the enrichment of the internal world as long as there is no progress in discrimination, which is a slow and gradual process.[96] Now the patient feels she is a different person from her father and me, but her own affection and rejection are still not experienced as internal events or experiences but continue to be projected into her father.

This has brought us to another technical detail, which we think needs to be taken into account at certain moments in the analysis of the psychotic part of the personality, in the direction of not formulating the interpretation in terms of internal perception or experience, as for example, 'You feel . . .' or 'You think . . .' because for a long time, the patient really has not thought or felt what we are interpreting. We encounter a deficit in the formation of the area of the mind,[97] with a consequent deficit in symbolisation, and in everything that is beyond the rationalisations and intellectualisations already assimilated into the mind and dissociated from the body. In these patients a large part of the affective experiences and experiences of communication with the external world occur in the areas of the body and the external world, without any corresponding representation in the area of the mind, *i.e.* through symbolisation. The session continues after a silence:

> Okay . . . but I have got rid of them. I have given more importance to everything that was repellent to me (silence). As I was speaking about my father, saying that he didn't give us cuddles, I felt my father's warmth.

95 [The English word 'self' is used in the original.]

96 As Bion proposes that 'The dominance of projective identification confuses the distinction between the self and the external object' (Bion, 1962, p. 113); also between these and the internal object. We now have the right to ask ourselves whether the process is not the other way round, in the sense that the projective identification does not explain the fusion, but is explained precisely by the nature of the object involved (agglutinated nucleus).

97 Leaving this theme aside for discussion at another time, I do however wish to note that genetically, the first area to function or appear is the area of the body, in second place that of the external world and in the third and last, the area of the mind. Speaking in terms of phenomenal areas – as we are doing now - for a phenomenon to be psychological it is not necessary that it have first been mental. [For discussion of these three 'areas' see the Introduction, p. xxxiii, n. 13.]

At this point I interrupt the session because we have come to the end of the hour. In this session we achieved a partial rupture of the body-mind dissociation and a certain degree of re-introjection and recognition of her feelings and of the affective tie with me in the transference relation, against which she always defended herself with a rejecting attitude or a reproachful relationship or, more generally, with isolation. Now she was able to communicate with a part of herself that she had always kept segregated as being dangerous and overwhelming.

### *(h) Session B*

In the following session she proposes to talk about the subject of her studies. For a long time after that, whenever it was possible to achieve some re-introjection and analysis of her oedipal situation, the theme of her studies emerged afterwards, something that had practically not appeared in nearly all the period of the analysis of the neurotic levels of the personality. The sequence was generally the following: (1) a certain degree of re-introjection was provoked; (2) the theme of her studies emerged as a new depositary; (3) then, together with the theme of studying, her family relations, especially with her parents, appeared more; (4) this made her feel very uncomfortable; sometimes she protested openly when she felt that I was making a connection between her parents and her inhibition on studying; (5) she would become blocked again and my attempts to provoke re-introjection began to fail again, at least for a while.

Studying was a symptom that condensed her conflictive family relations, which were still undiscriminated and kept segregated from the more adapted central ego by means of splitting and very strict control. The interpretation had to 'break up' the symptom and the family relations, discriminating each of their components.

In the session that followed the one transcribed above, she tells me that she would like to talk about her difficulty in studying, and she goes on:

> On Monday night I didn't have to go to school. Well . . . I thought I could take advantage of this to study . . . Well . . . somehow I occupied my time and I didn't . . . and I didn't devote it to studying . . . Last night I could also have stayed up studying . . . but they were changing my friend Emma's plaster cast and I felt like going to see her . . . and then I waited until my husband came to pick me up . . . but by then it had become too late . . . afterwards too . . . Well . . . I think I always leave the last hours of the day for studying. And I'm already tired at that time . . . I should aim for the first hours of the day . . . In the end, it's . . . it isn't that I don't have time, I could make myself time . . . but I always spend it on something else . . . Since Saturday I've been thinking that I have to do some things that way . . . to

look at something . . . at least I have . . . the idea of sitting down with a book and . . . meditating . . . just sit like that . . . shut inside that world, for a while . . . And I can't find the moment . . . I still haven't found one to do it . . . Well, that's what I wanted to see . . . why?. . . am I escaping from it?. . . (She falls silent.)

After her previous session, it is she who has changed her cast, that is, her control and bodily rigidity that serves as a control. She describes her claustrophobic reaction to studying (feeling shut inside that world), and my impression is that she has come to the session with a fresh cast (a new arrangement in a different depositary); she gives me the theme that she wants to see and then waits for me to show her, to take charge of working through the theme for her, and she will attend as a spectator of what I show her and the fate of what she is giving me now will depend on what she sees.[98] When she did this, she expected a magical solution: that I would give everything back to her completely resolved. In this situation she gives me the phobogenic object (in this case the agglutinated nucleus), and she makes me feel shut inside with it, immobilised, not knowing what to do, not being able to 'open the package' and see what it contains. As she falls into an expectant silence, I wait a few minutes and I return the 'package' to her by saying: 'Since studying makes you feel shut in, you give me the theme so that I can give it back to you resolved.'

Well, what I realise is that I escape from it . . . that I go to look for something else to do . . . or go out . . . or waste my time . . . Why do I do this?. . . I have to study, there's no other way . . . things are not going to fall from the sky . . .

She has taken up the theme and she understands that she has to open it and work it through ("things are not going to fall from the sky"). The patient continues:

But some . . . somehow I escape . . . because if . . . if not I fall asleep . . . and I sit down for a few minutes and I go to sleep . . . I fall asleep, and if I don't . . . I don't find the moment to sit down with a book. I can't imagine it's a lack of ability either . . . Why can't I put my mind to it?. . . Well, before also . . . I used to think at night, when I could do it . . . it would occur to my husband to go out or something like that . . . I can't now either . . . all that has been eliminated . . . I mean I've already eliminated it. . . . that is, it isn't my husband . . . or lack of time.

98 In a previous paper I accepted the term manicheism for the attitude in which the patient situates himself as an observer of the course of his projected conflicts, which he sees as being foreign to him (Chapter 2).

If she accepts her responsibility for the theme of studies, she feels shut in and falls asleep; but now she has not fallen asleep, but she is confused ('I can't say I like it or that I don't like it . . . I like it . . .'), and this is due to the impact of studying (agglutinated nucleus) on her more integrated or more mature ego. She is bewildered (in the sentence just quoted), which is due to the same mechanism, but the bewilderment acts as some defence against the confusion. Evidently, she uses the insight acquired in previous sessions, when she attributed her not being able to study to her husband or other external causes. But now I learn that when I was repeatedly analysing these mechanisms and she was answering me with silence, leaving my interpretations isolated, she took advantage of them and assimilated them anyway. She brings in the conclusions as her own, with no reference to our joint work, and this is due to her fear of forming a couple with me as well as her envy of my ability to interpret things. Several months will pass before I am able to show her the envy and rivalry. Up to now, whenever I included envy and rivalry in my interpretations, my impression was that she didn't see it, that she was still very far from being able to see and experience all that. I believe that in symbiotic dependence this always occurs: the patient does not recognise her envy and rivalry until she has reached a certain degree of separation or independence, that is, established a certain distance between herself and the depositary and between the deposited and the depositary, having to some extent re-introjected what was deposited or projected.

I do not intervene and the patient continues:

> I think that I do not allow myself to study . . . (Silence) Well . . . I can think that I come from a home where . . . studying was not a habit . . . perhaps that's why it's so hard for me to contract[99] this habit . . . But at this stage in life, I think that this is already . . . It can't happen.

She continues to use interpretations that have been given to her in previous sessions and expects me to confirm them. She attempts a denial, with the wish that I should take responsibility for these explanations and try to demonstrate to her that they are true. I do not do this because on other occasions when I inadvertently did so, the reasons became arguments that I suddenly found myself 'offering' to her. Then she as a spectator could deny them, bring forward contrary arguments or simply leave me boxed-in with my arguments.

We also observe that she uses a particular turn of phrase, when she says: 'perhaps that's why it's so hard for me to *contract* this habit'. (This session, like the previous one, had been tape-recorded.) To contract a habit is something

99 [The Spanish is *contraerme* – see the next paragraph but one. The patient has made a slip, saying *contraerme* (meaning 'to grow smaller'), instead of *contraer* (meaning 'to acquire'). The ambiguity of the Spanish is only approximately preserved in the English word 'contract'.]

like contracting an illness, but she also says 'contract' in the reflexive form, that is, studying means to contract herself, to reduce or diminish herself, losing her parents in an immature and symbiotic relation, without having them well incorporated as internal objects yet, an interpretation that we now deduce also from material that appears later.

After this last phrase she remains silent and I do too. Then she continues to speak:

> If I go back to my brothers . . . Well . . . two of them are not studying, but the other one is . . . Well . . . I believe that all this . . . if I . . . if I study I take something away from someone . . . I feel as if [it is] something that were already got over.[100] No, that can't be the reason . . . and if it's not been got over at least it's been seen . . . But what am I going to say now, about why I don't study . . . ? (Silence)

She continues to use interpretations that I formulated on other occasions, and although it is true that there is not sufficient insight in it, it is no less true that it is a kind of deferred echolalia, a certain degree of identification with me, in which she introjected my interpretations and parts of me with them; which is not yet integrated in her ego but is already partly 'deposited' within her and under review[101] to see whether she will finally incorporate it or not into her more integrated or more adapted ego.

She refers to her brother who, as I said above, had abandoned his studies years ago, but shortly after my patient began her treatment, her brother took up his studies again and later graduated as a physician and immediately got a very well paid job.

I also wish to point out how the patient lists explanations or arguments for not studying and expects me to take responsibility for them. But afterwards she herself denies the validity of these explanations ('No, that can't be the reason . . .'), and what she does to herself is what she would have done to me if I had taken responsibility for her attempt to re-project the encysted interpretations. With this, communication would have been cut off and she would have left me 'hanging'. I think that, up to now, my silence was much more valuable than any interpretation. The other type of objection she made to herself ('and if it's not been got over at least it's been seen . . .'), is the one that she directed to me on another occasion when I took that role. It was a kind of disillusionment of magical hope: something had been seen and she expected it would thereby be resolved, and strictly speaking this is a consequence of the omnipotence of her intellect: when it failed she was quite bewildered, as she is now when she adds: 'But what am I going to say now, about why I don't study . . . ?' At other times, she got irritated when she

100 [. . . *como que algo que ya estuviera superado.*]

101 [*en revisión* – which also connotes 'revising' as part of studying]

found that her mind did not control everything that happened in her. The patient continued after a pause:

> Well, I was just thinking that tonight I slept well, I slept seven hours straight through . . . and yet I get up as if I needed to sleep more . . . Well, that is one of the things that . . . that accompany me when I have to study. Sleep . . . Sleep knocks me over . . . And it can be in the morning too. Yesterday I had a morning class . . . I had started out quite well . . . and after an hour . . . I couldn't hold out any longer . . . I was falling asleep . . . And it wasn't at night . . . or in the afternoon . . . or at siesta time . . . It was in the morning, when I could be quite fresh . . .

Her voice has gradually become weaker and her pronunciation of the words less clear; she has gone into a state of clouded consciousness, because the agglutinated nucleus (studying) has finally invaded her central ego. When her difficulty was limited to studying she could still defend herself from invasion by the agglutinated nucleus, but when she associates and expands, showing that she not only falls asleep when she studies but that she already wakes up 'as if I needed to sleep more . . .', and that this occurs not only when she is with her books but also in a class, this finally expands and overwhelms her ego. It is also happening to her right now in the session, which began at eight in the morning. At this point I think that the interpretation can no longer be postponed and I tell her that feeling shut in and knocked over by her studies also happens to her when she gets up and is in class, and is also happening to her now, and she is asking me to help her because otherwise the matter is finally going to knock her over and put her completely to sleep.

> Well, on the one hand I make an effort to get close and to listen . . . and to pay attention, and on the other, there is this force . . . that puts me to sleep . . . and in class I'm perfectly conscious that this is happening to me . . . I try to . . . well, I don't know what to do . . . but at least I try to . . . to be receptive, to be able to go on . . . Well, I think that for my part I make the effort[102] . . . But it's not enough . . .

I tell her she's showing me that she's doing everything she can on her part and that she is struggling to clear up the problem, but that it's not enough and she needs me to intervene more actively.

When the agglutinated nucleus has been re-introjected, she gets closer to me much more directly and can ask me for help.

The session continues and I am already participating more actively by interpreting, but there comes a moment when she gets irritated by this

102 [The Spanish for 'effort' here is *esfuerzo*, the same word as she has just used for the 'force' that puts her to sleep.]

active participation of mine. Then I point out that she's doing with me what she does with dad and with mum: she asks for help but when she feels helped she feels invaded, ordered around and demanded of and she does not tolerate this situation. The shutting in that she feels in her studies is this same shutting in with daddy and mummy that she now feels with me. She is silent and then tells me:

> It's not that I don't think about it, because things do cross my mind . . . but they don't come out of my mouth . . . And I can't get used to this, to the running dialogue . . . I mean, that I make all the effort necessary to answer you . . . or to . . . (Silence)

I interpret that she doesn't know what things are going to come out through her mouth and she's afraid, just as she's afraid of the things that I am going to put into her mouth.

> (Silence) Well, it often happens to me that . . . after the session . . . I think . . . Well . . . why can't I answer right away?. . .

I tell her that she gets afraid of being very demanding with me and of me being demanding with her.

> (Silence) Well . . . it's a fear of asking for . . . (Silence) Well . . . now why did you mention my parents?

I interpret that it is not only the fear of asking for something. It is also the fear of receiving what she asks for. She asked me for help but when I give it to her she feels that I get in however I want to, that I get into her things and inside her and that I invade her and betray her by bringing in her parents, and that by doing this I confuse her.

> (Silence) Yes, why does one always have to go back to them and the brothers and sisters?. . .

I intervene by pointing out that this is not 'going back'.

And she answers:

> Well, then this is what is hard for me to accept . . . That this family relation . . . is what is so heavy . . . (Stifled weeping) It's true that I don't want to think about that.

I interpret that she doesn't want to think about that because it bewilders and confuses her, and to avoid it she goes to sleep and distances herself.

> (Silence) Well, I believe . . . that doing a thing, a different activity to what one's parents have done . . . has to be very difficult . . . That's why it's very difficult for me to be different from my parents. What is easiest for me to do is what my mother does . . .

I tell her that doing something different from her parents means losing me and letting go of her parents.

Studying condenses the conflict of the oedipal situation and the dependence on her parents. Up to now I have managed to bring in what is globally in the symptom, but it still remains to break up and discriminate this agglutinated nucleus, to differentiate what it is that her dad does and what it is that her mum does, what belongs to each of them and what belongs to her, and who she is in relation to her parents. After the last interpretation, the patient remains silent and I interrupt the session because we have come to the end of the hour.

### *(i) Session C*

In the following session, she begins to cast around to find a theme to choose to talk about and immediately tells me that when she was with a pupil she couldn't resolve an exercise and that this never used to happen to her, and that she also noticed that she says one word instead of another and this makes her feel very insecure, and somewhat indirectly she suggests that she feels disillusioned because she had thought that she would feel better after the previous session. I point out that she is ashamed to see and show her difficulties and that if I am sure of what we are doing, why is she afraid that she is getting worse. She continues by saying that she is bewildered and doesn't know what to do or where to go when she goes out with her husband; that she feels strange, and she goes on to speak about a female friend who blamed her husband for not being able to travel but that now her friend recognises that it is she who has the difficulties and she herself is the problem. I interpret that she now feels that she has problems and can no longer attribute them to her husband or to me. However, she again re-projects into her husband, saying that he has difficulty in exchanging their car for a better one and this is because it's painful for him to do things like that, since his siblings are in such a bad economic situation. I again interpret that she is afraid to change if her siblings don't change at the same time and that she feels very guilty for receiving things from me that her mother gave to her but not to her brothers when she was a girl. Then she refers to a number of things she did yesterday, in contrast to her usual inactivity or slowness, and that the day she can do everything she needs or wants to do, it seems she will have lost something. I relate this loss to the loss of her family if she changes. Then she refers to an argument between two of her children because the second one also wants to have a key to the closet. I interpret this, pointing out that she also wants to have her own key to manage her things by herself and for me not to be the only one managing them and knowing what it is that is happening to her. She then speaks of how she notices that her children have changed and then of her fear of being pregnant. Here I interpret that she is trying to condense and control the changes by putting them all together in one place and in the body, in a pregnancy. She continues by saying that this is happening for being trusting and letting her husband 'come inside' and that in any case she's going to think about an abortion, which means that she feels that way for having let me get inside her affairs and inside her and now she needs to abort (re-project).

ψ

These three consecutive sessions that I have presented outline part of the course that this patient's analysis has run, whose steps I have summarised above. In each of these periods, however, a certain modification was produced, since when she 'aborted me' and thereby also 'aborted' the agglutinated nucleus, nevertheless, some modification and some learning had been produced, which increased and progressed until some time later it gradually became quite evident, to her as well as to me.

Gradually, with this rhythm the agglutinated nucleus was analysed through her studies, discriminating within it the different nuclei of primary identification, separating the self from the object and discriminating between the different complex situations of the oedipal situation. With this, a greater degree of personification and more mature, non-reactive independence was slowly achieved.

In the identification with her parents we could thus discriminate very different and disparate elements: the relation with her father as a father, her relation with her father as a mother who cooked the food, cleaned the house and gave her affection, the relation with her mother as such and the relation with her as a father who worked outside the house in a masculine role, the relation with the mother who gave affection and the relation with the severe and critical mother, with the admired or idealised mother and the deprecated father and, inversely, with the envied and rejected mother; hate for her father and pity for him; phantasies of being her mother's husband or the wife of her phallic mother, her father's wife or the husband of her father-mother; together with this, avoidance of forming a couple in any of the possible variants and envy of the parental couple. This whole picture formed a situation of undifferentiation of the separate father and mother roles, as well as an implicit deficit in personification and in her own identity. To this was added the existence of the more well known and usual alternatives of the oedipal situation on the neurotic level of the personality. Symbiotic dependence on her parents resided in the existence of this indiscriminate relation that impeded separation and the consequent mourning.[103] It was this dependence that she constantly tried to re-establish in the transference. We may infer that in these symbiotic patients there is a constitutional deficit in the ego's possibility of discriminating and that when this latter function (as a barrier) does not exist, at least in the optimal quantity, the individual easily introjects and diverse equivalent identifications are produced. This level of (agglutinated) oedipal conflict exists normally, but an exaggerated remnant is responsible for intense symbiosis; we could in this respect quote P. Heimann who says that

> The introjection of the parents is a selective process, certain aspects of the parents being excluded. The ego 'samples' the objects of the external world, introjects certain of their aspects and projects others, and it follows this fundamental pattern also with regard to the parents at the Oedipus stage.
>
> (Heimann, 1952, p. 132)

This author provides other references equally valuable for our theme, as for example, when she speaks of the beginning of the Oedipus complex as of 'a chaotic, overlapping, criss-cross pattern' (p. 163) or as 'a chaotic and polymorphous situation'.[104] All these most primitive levels (of chaotic and polymorphous organisation, without a boundary) are what constitutes the agglutinated nucleus or the psychotic part of the personality.

### *(j) Other vicissitudes of the agglutinated nucleus*

All the most primitive links with her parents (primary identification) were condensed in the agglutinated nucleus, which she kept massively projected into me, and when I achieved the re-introjection (splitting between the depositary and the deposited), it was displaced onto and condensed in her studies (a new depositary), by means of a fresh re-projection. Studying was being like the mother, that is, doing men's things, but if she stayed at home she was a wife like her father. Both situations provoked confusion, and therefore this conflict was kept dissociated and segregated. Studying was

103 We may suppose that in any pathological mourning there intervenes an agglutinated nucleus (deficit in schizoid division) which blocks entry into the depressive position and its consequent working through.

104 [This last quotation does not correspond exactly to the English original, so we have translated it directly from the Spanish. Heimann wrote: '. . . the infant's instinctual impulses are "polymorphously perverse". Oral, urethral, anal and genital stirrings co-exist and form a chaotic, overlapping, criss-cross pattern. . . .' (Heimann, 1952, p. 163).]

also the consummation of the theft from her brothers of all her mother's preference and affection. To be like her phallic mother, she had to study, but her mother did not support her studies and in this regard the patient once told me:

> I don't know why my mother was against medicine. She wanted the second one to study, the one who never even finished secondary school and was always the most intelligent of all. My mother wanted me to lead a different life from hers.

Ana Maria didn't know, actually, whether studying was leading a life that was the same as or different from her mother's, whether with that she was complying or was rebelling against her mother's wishes. Much later in her treatment the memory emerged that she had wanted to be a boy and used to play with the boys like a boy, while her mother, because Ana Maria was a girl (the only girl child), demanded that she help her take care of the house and the children; she rebelled by studying, and also by not doing anything, which allowed her in phantasy to be a boy. As we see, there are too many unranked, non-stratified, conjoint terms or variables to allow all this to form a conflict that the more mature ego might confront successfully. Every time this agglutinated nucleus approached the ego, the latter was invaded or shut in and defended itself by narrowing itself and with clouded consciousness, sleepiness or depersonalisation. Another type of defence was the use of the body, especially the phantasy of pregnancy followed by an abortion; immobilising or condensing the agglutinated nucleus in a pregnancy was the way to gain some control over it and keep it halfway between total introjection and total projection. In this way, pregnancy may be compared dynamically to a hypochondria (fixation of the agglutinated nucleus in the body), and abortion to an epileptic expulsion.

When the work of discrimination of the agglutinated nucleus had advanced in her treatment, a need arose in her to move out of the house where they lived and into an apartment, a need that she imposed on her husband, and she achieved her goal. The house move was also a kind of use of her body and of the external world in order to cast around and try out the change, in a spatially controlled way, before its total assimilation into the ego. In the period of several months that were taken up by the project of moving house, until the move actually occurred, phobic symptoms also appeared (agoraphobia) but they were displaced and experienced through her children, in fears about them crossing the street or going to school by themselves, or travelling by bus alone. The house move imposed itself as an imperative and unavoidable need; it was a question of very traumatic situations (the moves of her childhood) needing to be acted out and re-experienced in reality: since they are so traumatic their symbolisation in the area of the mind has remained disturbed and they can therefore not be faced or worked through symbolically in the analysis, but only reproduced in reality.[105]

Much later in her analysis, it emerged for the first time that her abandonment of her studies coincided with her pregnancy with her first child, a moment in which the oedipal situation became acute. During this first pregnancy they moved out of her parents' house where they lived, to a house they occupied by themselves. When she moved out of her parents' house and because she was pregnant, her studies lost their value as a source of identification and rebellion against her mother. The pregnancy, on the other hand, allowed her to define her role as a woman better, to be like her mother-wife. After she moved out of her apartment – during the analysis – she had a long menstrual delay that she thought was a pregnancy (as I also did). The learning thus has to take place directly through action and cannot be accomplished symbolically.

When she achieved a certain degree of dispersion and re-introjection of her agglutinated nucleus, in the following session she withdrew even further from me, and on other occasions she totally forgot the material of the previous session: at other times, she came with material whose latent content was the attempt to re-agglutinate, as occurred in Session A ('get the pastry to hold together'), a phenomenon that we differentiated from integration in the depressive position. In another session, this phenomenon appeared in the following material:

> Today the alarm clock surprised me as if it were the middle of the night. I was dreaming something and it interrupted me: I was cutting pieces of cloth and putting them in piles. (Pause) Yesterday I was at Beatriz's in the afternoon. She's calmed down now. She's still in bed.

I interpreted that she is calming herself by piling up all the things that got scattered here in yesterday's session.

> Beatriz is a very good friend of Mrs. Peralta's. They used to go to the same analyst. Mrs. Peralta said that she was going to leave her treatment as a trial to see whether she's cured and this affected Beatriz very much. That Beatriz's friend was leaving didn't get to me at all. But when Beatriz said, it's as if I . . .

I told her that she is frightened of her own wish to leave the analysis to see if she is already cured, to see if she can live without me.

105 In working through symbiosis there is a necessary and unavoidable passage through both hypochondriac manifestations and episodes of psychopathic acting. The process of genesis of the area of the mind has to be produced; for this, the acting is previous to and necessary for symbolization.

Leaving the treatment and fancying that she was cured was something permanent in her sessions during this period, or was at least quite frequent. We need to observe that in this material she already does not make the pauses and the silences that she used to, she does not isolate the interpretation from her response and does not use the 'Well' that was her magical formula or ritual of isolation and annulment of the interpretation. Just when she is feeling more connected to me, her phantasy that we would separate increased, for fear of a symbiotic fusion and of never being able to separate from me. As a cure, she needs to act as in the case of the house move, because if she does not act, she cannot account for the facts symbolically. This is what I have pointed out as the psychopathic phase in the treatment of symbiosis. The session continues in the following way:

> I don't know why it affected me so much. Yesterday I was thinking . . . that we always wait for next year to see what happens and I feel that each time it's worse, especially in the economic arena. Fear is getting into me.

I relate her idea of leaving the treatment with her now feeling worse and that she feels her things are scattered about and that's why she's feeling afraid.

> All this week, ads have come out for the sale of the house and nobody has come. Yesterday in the morning I went out to do the shopping, I went into a shop and it was all empty, there were no people.

Again, I tell her that her fear is therefore that the treatment might empty her of everything that is hers.

This reaction, in which the patient feels empty when she risks being left without the agglutinated nucleus as such, is frequent. This is because when she loses it – due to its dispersion and discrimination – she also loses the dependent relation with her parents. She replies:

> After the last session I had a *café au lait* and went to the children's school. I waited for half an hour and I was freezing cold. I always discuss the fees, but that day I wasn't up to it and they raised me by five hundred pesos but I said absolutely nothing. We were talking about many things, about new ways to teach a language. It was the first time I felt so well received at the school. I felt gratitude. And in spite of that, a depression came over me immediately afterwards.

The dispersion of the agglutinated nucleus makes her feel that I empty her, because I separate her from her parents in her immature dependence. She is grateful to me because she feels well received by me, but this attention, because of its consequences, produces her depression. She recovers the agglutinated nucleus, filling up that emptiness (piling up pieces of cloth).

She also feels that she is losing me and empties me and proposes an increase in my fees, which she is not going to argue about.

She and I appear now as more differentiated persons (personified), which later gradually allows the emergence and analysis of greed, envy and rivalry, as well as gratitude, depression and fear.[106] For the appearance of all the phenomena that I have enumerated, some advance in the working through of the symbiosis is required and therefore a certain degree of separation and personification. Until the latter takes place, interpretation in terms of greed or envy has not the slightest experiential repercussion. If the patient is to perceive and experience them, there has to be an ego with a certain degree of integration.

In the period to which this last session belongs, she applies for her university identification card, which also indicates some development of personification and of her sense of identity.

When she returned to her studies, for a long time it was on an irregular basis, with the variation that she began to take dentistry courses as a medical student but without having a university identification card for either faculty. She alternated between one and the other with very complicated paperwork and I was often unable to understand entirely what it was all about. While she was doing all this, her doubts continued: to study or not and in case she did, for which degree: she could finish medicine or she could continue dentistry regularly, having already transferred credit from several courses as valid for the dentistry degree. Ana Maria needed to constantly be worried about something or about several things at the same time; this was another way to keep depositaries of her agglutinated nucleus projected and controlled or immobilised. This is a need for persecutors, to perpetually convert the fright of re-introjection into fear of external things, as in Freud's (1920) definition of fear as a defence against fright.

In relation to all this, another factor in the agglutination appeared, unknown to me until that time: because her mother went out to work, a maternal aunt and her daughter came to live in their house for several years, so that her aunt could take charge of the housekeeping. But soon she too went out to work, and so the patient had to take care, not only of her brothers, but also her cousin. Her phantasies in this regard were quite complex and unclear, because they were superimposed. One of these, for example, was that she had had two mothers (two faculties) or that her mother and her mother's sister were, respectively, father and mother, while her father was another sibling, namely, another child of this mother-aunt marriage. All of this reinforced the oedipal situation on the psychotic levels of the personality (the agglutinated nucleus).

106 'Many primitive affects are already compounded and fused before they are experienced as depressions, elations, envies, jealousies, etc., and the simplest anger affect is not so simple as it feels.' (Glover, 1943, p. 9).

Together with the two Faculties, she was always doing complicated paperwork in the two schools where she taught: changes of subjects, schedules, shifts, schools, etc. All this was also linked to the very many changes of residence that had also contributed to a deficit in her personification and identity.

Another way in which she tried to get or actually obtained re-agglutination of the dispersion of her agglutinated nucleus, achieved in a previous session to some extent, was to centre everything on her mother, using her as a depositary of all the elements of the dispersion. Thus, in one session she speaks of her fear of a revolution (a projection of her internal revolution) and asks me, in the latent content of her material, to take precautions, but immediately starts to talk about her mother. She doesn't trust my control of the revolution and re-agglutinates herself in her mother, who has just returned from a vacation and phoned her: 'my father doesn't call me; if my mother phoned that's enough.' With this, it is she who now communicates with her mother while the latter contains her father. Similar material appears in relation to her brothers. Once she has agglutinated everything in the mother and the mother within me, she draws away from me again in the course of the session; in her manifest material, her struggle emerges against her domineering and absorbing mother who demands things of her; she demands that she clean her house in an exaggerated way, with which she uses an active, paranoid rejection in order to avoid re-introjection of the agglutinated nucleus; but this active rejection is also a very solid tie of dependence. Of that session she says that her father never intervenes between her and her mother, indicating that she is expecting me to be the strong father who will help her to confront her mother. However, if I were to intervene in this way, she would join forces with her mother against me or be rivalrous with me and castrate me.

At other times, when dispersion of the agglutinated nucleus was provoked, this phenomenon could be handled or controlled not by re-agglutination but by projection of each fragment into different persons around her. There would then be mentioned in the session a very large number of persons with different roles, each representing a part of her own immature ego. This is the phenomenon that in Chapter 2 I termed diversification of links, which I consider a very positive step in discrimination and in gradual or discriminated re-introjection. It was particularly through her children that she really learned and modified her own standards regarding her parents; she compared herself to her children: what they were like and how she had been at their ages or how her children's behaviour modified her fears and apprehensions or certain distorted roles and standards.

When the ego is more integrated or when re-introjection of fragments of the agglutinated nucleus has not been massive, there is no re-agglutination, as seen in the fragments of previous sessions, but the patient feels full of things that are neither entirely discriminated nor agglutinated, and yet are not totally incorporated into the ego. The fragment of a session that I present below is taken from a period when the relationships with her husband, her children and her mother were less conflictive, she was much more emotionally connected in the transference relationship, she became depressed more easily and more frequently because economic insecurity always persisted, with the consequent insecurity about being able to continue the treatment, together with difficulties in selling her house when she had already purchased an apartment and had serious problems paying for it. Also, a girlfriend, her best friend, had moved to another country with her family. She felt abandoned by her husband and by her mother because the symbiotic relationship no longer existed with its former intensity. She also felt that the sessions were too frequent so that their rhythm was too fast. She told me that all her difficulties had come together and that she never had to go through so many difficulties or had so many debts that she didn't know how to repay. In this period there was a very particular situation: before starting her treatment, she would feel anxious when there was nobody with her or when she wasn't busy doing something, whereas now she feels loneliness and abandonment when her husband is at home or with her and it's the same with her mother. This is due to re-introjection of the agglutinated nucleus, because now the abandonment and loneliness appear precisely when the depositary is present (an 'empty' depositary); since it is either no longer a depositary (at least to the extent it was before) or is not a secure or trustworthy depositary. There is more guarantee or security when the agglutinated nucleus is introjected. When these situations are interpreted, she replies that previously she felt economically backed by the property and now she doesn't, since it seems that the house they want to sell is no longer worth anything. The house is another depositary that she can no longer support herself with, or depend on securely. She can't depend on me either, because she doesn't know how long she can hold on to me. When she talks about the property, now at the end of the session, she pauses and says:

> I am afraid that with the property the same thing will happen that happened with the stock market, where everything went down and down. (Another pause) Yesterday my mother came to visit me. Afterwards, my father spoke to her on the phone. She comes at least once a week to visit me and my father contents himself with that. It's enough.

She leaves this session looking at me directly, her face placid or calm.

Parents-husband-analyst are not support enough now, we are not secure depositaries; she has re-introjected what was projected into us: fragments of her agglutinated nucleus. There is, in any case, mourning for the depositaries, but not yet for the internal objects that have been re-introjected. When she is alone (without depositaries) she feels accompanied, whereas when she is with the depositaries she feels alone and abandoned. In the following session, she says:

> My eyes are red from sleepiness. I'm so sleepy. I was just working out how many hours I've been asleep. Yesterday I spoke by phone with a lady that K. recommended to find out whether I can go to work there. It's the second time I've spoken to her and she says that they have many difficulties and she couldn't complete her personnel.[107] (Pause) Yesterday we stayed at home and I wanted somebody to come over or for us to go to somebody's house. I remembered a couple who were friends years ago. I called them and they agreed to come. (Pause) How many people we know and how little we get together with them. Today I woke up an hour earlier. I dreamed that I was trying on dresses. I put one on and it wasn't finished. The room where I was trying them on was all filled up with furniture. It was the house of the dressmaker who lives on the ground floor of Elena's house (the name of the friend who emigrated). But it wasn't this dressmaker who was fitting me but another one I know. And I was thinking, what a lot of furniture this woman put in here. (Pause) I had to go in a few days to the dressmaker's to try on an overcoat. She told me she got a letter from Elena and how sorry she was that Elena had left.

I interpret that she is quite afraid that I too might go away, she is afraid of losing me too and that I might leave her full of unfinished things inside and with her personality incomplete.

> (She sighs) Now I remember that before, I used to dream about big, empty, immense houses, and now everything was in one room. . . . I can see that physically I have changed but inside I don't see myself as any different. It's more difficult.

The session continues with the things she wants to do or achieve and cannot; then, she begins to complain that it is useless, that she is not going to get anywhere, that everything is a failure and at that point she says:

> Although this has nothing to do with it (with what she was saying), when those friends were going to come over, I told the children to go to bed. They made an effort to help me and fought over where to put things; I was grateful for their cooperation. (She falls silent.)

I interpret that, so that she won't be left alone and abandoned she is carrying a burden of hopelessness and is hoping that I will do what the children did: make an effort to help her.

107 [*completar su personal*, *i.e.* fill her vacancies]

(After a pause): I was thinking that it had nothing to do with that. It was like having a compensation, something that would raise my spirits. I'm sure that I cannot let someone else do the walking for me and that nothing is going to fall from the sky for free. But I can't get started . . . It's also not true that I can't, but yet I don't do it, and there must be a reason why I don't do it. (Pause) A question occurred to me yesterday: "What does it mean to break away from one's parents: to be equal to them, or different?

I tell her that these are the different dresses she is trying on in the dream as ways of trying on what she has to do, which solution she will choose.

It always occurs to me to think that if I had been a boy I would have been even more of a failure, as if being a woman covered up failure. I'm not so much. But then I think that here in Argentina I'm not so much. Elsewhere I would also be a failure as a working woman. Now I think that it's more difficult to be different than to be the same as one's parents. But it can't be only that, breaking away and being equal or being different. I think that one has to be able to support oneself alone . . . and then I thought that when I got married I lived in my parents' house. I didn't have to think about the shopping or the food. Deep down it must be something like that: that I don't want to provide for myself. (The session ends.)

In this session, which is the first of the month, she arrives in a state of worry about her debt to me ('I was just working out how many hours I've been asleep'), and immediately tells me about another difficulty, which is completing her personality ('. . . she couldn't complete her personnel'), or achieving her full identity. Her search for people to be with contains an attempt to seek new depositaries to replace those that are no longer fully available to her (her friend Elena, her mother, father, husband and analyst). The attempt is unsuccessful, and she dreams about trying on dresses: that is, trying to take different roles or identifications belonging to re-introjected fragments. However, the analysis is not finished and she does not take a role with a finished degree of identification because these roles that are included in each fragment of the agglutinated nucleus are not yet totally discriminated. I am the dressmaker who has filled her up with furniture: that is, I have forced her to re-introject the fragments of her agglutinated nucleus. Now we see the fear that I might leave her unfinished for failing to pay for the analysis, just as her friend Elena left her.

After my interpretation she tells me that before, she felt empty and now she feels full of many things, but that this change has occurred in her body and not in her mind (which is from the dynamic perspective the most important change that we needed to introduce in her body and in her mind-body dissociation). If she had re-introjected the totality of the agglutinate nucleus without fragmentation, there would have ensued a hypochondria or a psychosomatic illness, as I have described in Chapter 2 [see p. 51]. The re-introjection here has been of fragments of the agglutinated nucleus, in the body, but it has not yet extended to the mind. The latter could be achieved with greater discrimination and subsequent integration into the ego; as we have seen (in the dreams) this process is not yet entirely completed,[108] and so there is a danger of invasion of the ego by these not entirely discriminated fragments retained in the body, and it is for this reason that she seeks new depositaries. The way in which she seeks them is by trying to fill me with anxiety and preoccupation concerning her paralysis, to which she has to return in order to defend the integrity of her ego. When I interpret to her that she again wants me to take on the role of depositary, a possible solution arises as a transaction: being not different from but equal to her parents, she was able to let go of them, and thereby not to lose them at all, but to retain them as depositaries and protectors inside herself. Faced with the danger or risk of losing the depositaries, she re-introjected them. When I interpret to her that she is trying to decide whether to keep her personality the same as or different from her parents, she keeps hold of the discrimination between male and female, but gives up and wants to continue being a dependent child 'who doesn't want to provide for herself'.

To summarise: I wanted to show two different alternatives for the re-introjection of the agglutinated nucleus, or rather of its fragments. In one of these there is a re-agglutination and in the other a re-projection of the fragments into new depositaries.

This further fills out our knowledge of the vicissitudes of re-introjection of the agglutinated nucleus, which I studied in a previous work (hypochondria, psychosomatic illness, the phenomenon of the double, etc.).

What I have added here also confirms the important role played by the body in the re-introjection of the agglutinated nucleus or its fragments, whereby it serves as a 'buffer' to protect the central ego from disorganisation or invasion (which would lead to psychotic disintegration).

### *(k) Fusion, confusion and discrimination*

M. Klein considers that some states of confusion arise normally at different periods of development (Klein, 1957, p. 220) and that this confusion may occur between love and hate, good and bad objects, between oral, anal and genital impulses and phantasies, between depressive and persecutory anxieties, confusion of the parents by intensification of the combined figure,

108 Lily S. Bleger has suggested that there is learning in dreams and that this may be the bridge between body and mind; and that dreams may indicate the beginning of the establishment of symbolization.

confusion between individual and object and between the internal and external worlds. Excessive envy, strong paranoid-schizoid traits and projective and introjective identification are factors impeding the normal and necessary differentiation and dissociation. According to this author, any confusion is based on a disturbed early relation with the mother's breast (Klein, 1957, p. 184), 'when the fundamental normal splitting into love and hate and into the good and the bad object is not successful'. (Klein, 1957, p. 216)

For H. Rosenfeld, 'Feelings of confusion are part of normal development and they are a common feature in many pathological conditions'. (Rosenfeld, 1950, p. 52). This author explains in a note I consider very significant:

> We may assume that in earliest infancy the baby lives in a state of unintegration (Winnicott, 1945), where perception is incomplete and where external and internal stimuli, external and internal objects and parts of the body can often not be differentiated. *This confusion due to unintegration is normal and gradually disappears during development.* We also have to keep in mind here that any developmental progress may lead temporarily to some confusion until a new adjustment is made.
>
> (Rosenfeld, 1950, p. 52. n. 2) (My emphasis)

In studying symbiosis and other associated phenomena, I postulated the normal existence, in the earliest stages of development, of this situation that H. Rosenfeld clearly and explicitly postulates. The difference, however, is that instead of primitive confusion I think there is fusion, and that instead of describing this state as non-integration, I consider it much more precise to describe it as non-discrimination. To this I have added the systematic examination of this primitive organisation under the name: glischro-caric position. The mechanisms of dissociation act by discriminating this primitive syncretic world, and with this dissociation and discrimination the transition to the paranoid-schizoid position is brought about; the transition may be interfered with by excessive envy and intense mechanisms of projective and introjective identification. These latter factors are involved in the psychotic levels of the personality, which are characterised by the persistence of non-discrimination (fusion), and which being dissociated from the central ego form the agglutinated nucleus.

Confusion is produced by regression from the neurotic levels of the personality to the psychotic levels (regression to the glischro-caric position) due to loss of the discrimination of the paranoid-schizoid position, that is, due to re-establishment of primitive fusion, which is normal in the initial stages of development. But confusion may also be produced by the persistence of psychotic (undiscriminated) nuclei in what I have termed the agglutinated nucleus, when these nuclei invade the more mature or more integrated ego of the personality. This is what occurs when the agglutinated nucleus (or fragments of it) is re-introjected in such a way that there is no immediate re-projection, producing an impact on the central ego with danger of its psychotic dissolution. Other phenomena attributable to the same mechanism are perplexity, indecision, suspense, disorientation, drowsiness, clouding, etc.

Thus, my hypotheses agree with and extend the fundamental postulates of M. Klein and H. Rosenfeld and I believe they constitute a broadening and deepening of their studies rather than a correction of them.

In the material that I present below, I shall try to examine and demonstrate the presentation of confusion in relation to mobilisation of the agglutinated nucleus, the defences to which the patient has recourse and the close relation between confusion and agglutinated nucleus with the *undiscriminated oedipal situation*, a remnant of psychotic levels of the Oedipus complex, which is unresolved or arrested in its development, even though part of it may have reached neurotic levels and a higher degree of development and integration, these levels constituting the genital and pre-genital organisations of the Oedipus complex. The material of these sessions refers to a period, which was very difficult for the patient, when they had bought an apartment under construction that was very nearly finished, but they had not yet sold the house where they lived and for that reason found themselves in serious economic difficulties.

In her treatment, we had progressed to some extent in the integration of the ego, which allowed mobilisation of the processes of projection and introjection that no longer occurred so massively; and, among other things, she could feel the anxiety when she came into the session without falling into the state of clouded consciousness that I described earlier.

In this session, which I will label (a), she tells me that she has a bad pain in her back, that she went to a meeting of the owners of the apartment where heavy financial demands were made. She immediately says she is going to put up a wall to divide a room into two parts. I interpret that with what I said to her in the previous session she feels I have made heavy demands on her as if I had given her a beating and this is why she is going to build a wall between us to defend herself. She replies that she is happy with the change of house, but that the increase in outlays and the aristocratic neighbourhood make her feel nauseous.

In this fragment we find the results of introjection, the new encounter with her greed, and this is what produces nausea; the wall separates her from her greed which produces feelings of demands from the outside and invasion from the inside. She goes on to say that when she thinks about the costs she gets depressed and that she prefers to have back pain rather than depression. I interpret that she is telling me that today I should not touch on her back pain, since she prefers to have things that worry her in her body but not on her mind. She answers that having the pain in her back has the advantage that she has a clear head and that she was comparing two worlds: the cost of the apartment and the paucity of her earning, as if they were two different worlds. I interpret again that now, having the pain in her back, her head is not free of problems either, and that she has to decide between staying in the world of the apartment and the analysis or in the world of her parents. Now she says, displacing on to her husband, how much it must cost him to move, since his family comes from an economic level lower than hers, and that she tried, out of jealousy, to get rid of a woman who is going to go into partnership with her husband. I interpret, then, showing her the jealousy she feels towards her husband's relationship with his analyst, and that since she cannot show and see the affection that she has for me, they appear in the form of jealousy toward her husband's affection for his analyst. She takes up the theme directly and talks about her envy of women who have a degree, which I interpret as envy of having to share me with my wife. Then she continues to associate:

> Although it seems a little . . . I think that I envied my mother . . . That I envied my fa . . . my mother . . . for the affection that she showed . . . my father . . . and the need to have someone who would show affection for me like he showed her. In public, she did not react well. My dad still says to her, 'What a pretty young lady, you look 18.' I don't remember that my mother ever answered, at least not with words. As if to say, 'He's always like that!'

I interpret that she didn't know in whose place she was, in her father's or her mother's, and now she doesn't know whether to put herself in my place or my wife's. Then she asks:

> You mean I don't know where I am?

I answer yes, and she asks again:

> Why, because of that remark about a pretty young lady? It occurred to me like maybe . . . that I might envy my fa . . . my mother . . . because of the things my father said to her and still says to her. And what else could I envy?

I interpret that she envies my relationship with my wife and my wife's with me.

The patient now moves her feet (restless) and says that she met a girlfriend and unexpectedly found herself talking about selling the house and about her envy, and that the friend told her that envy is something ugly and she answered that now it doesn't frighten her any more. I interpret that she is telling me that we can go on with this because now the envy doesn't frighten her as much as it did before. She answers that today, when she was coming to the session, she began to think about the apartment and that she had warned herself: 'You're preparing the session already' and she came in without an agenda. I told her that she is explaining that she has contributed to this by relinquishing control. She leaves this session smiling and looking at me when she says goodbye.

In this session (a) I believe that it is fundamentally important to emphasise that the division the patient establishes with the theme of putting up a wall to separate a room in two parts does not refer to a schizoid division between good and bad object, but to a mind-body dissociation or, what is the same as this, a division between the neurotic and psychotic levels of her personality. The back pain is the hypochondriac symptom resulting from re-introjection into the body of the agglutinated nucleus,[109] and by virtue of this depositation in the body she is able to keep her head clear (free of confusion). When I show her that in her clear head she also has problems to decide on (choosing between the apartment and her parents), there occurs a (discriminated) displacement of the problem onto the husband and jealousy arises in connection with a woman associated with her husband, then immediately envy of my wife. In this displacement of the problem onto her husband, there is projection of her more integrated ego (the neurotic level with a discriminated problem), which she salvages in order to take responsibility for the psychotic level of her personality (the agglutinated nucleus), which appeared first as a hypochondriac symptom.

This psychotic level of the personality (agglutinated nucleus) is what keeps her greed and envy encapsulated and to some extent controlled, and these are closely linked to the most primitive levels of the Oedipus complex (that of the fused, undifferentiated couple), and concomitantly undiscriminated parts of her ego. The *confusion* that emerges when she mentions her father and mother, when she mistakes one for the other, is actually the emergence of a primitive *fusion* of the parental couple and of parts of her ego, which may now be actualised and brought into the transference situation as a function of the existence now of a more integrated ego able to tolerate re-introjection of these psychotic levels; and this is what the patient makes clear to me at the end of the session, when she emphasizes

109 Although I do not propose to discuss this theme here, I wish to observe that hypochondria corresponds to the pathology of the agglutinated (undiscriminated) nucleus, while conversion hysteria is the somatisation of a (discriminated) part-object. The former corresponds to the glischro-caric position; the latter to the paranoid-schizoid position. I want to recall here that M. Abadi (1961) finds the existence in hypochondria of a bad-good object, dual and ambivalent, with which I agree to some extent, although I believe that it is not dual and ambivalent but ambiguous and polyvalent. On another occasion, during the discussion of the paper by G. Royer (1963b), I also suggested that psychosomatic illness is a somatisation of the agglutinated nucleus directly in the body, while hypochondria is a disorder of the body schema.

her active participation, unlike before, when she found herself forced into re-introjection by me.

Envy corresponds to the analysis of psychotic levels of the personality, for which sufficient and previous integration of the ego is necessary for confronting these levels of analysis. 'To enable the patient to face primary envy and hate only becomes possible after long and painstaking work . . .', in the words of M. Klein (1957, p. 221), this author adding: 'The resistance we find in both male and female cases in analysing their Oedipus jealousy and hostility, though very strong, is not as intense as that which we encounter in analysing the envy and hate of the breast.' I believe that envy pertains to the psychotic levels of the personality and is strongly split off from the rest of the personality, while jealousy corresponds to the neurotic levels of the personality and is more tolerable, since in the latter the objects are better discriminated and the depositaries are more diversified than in envy. In this session (a), that we are now discussing, the patient speaks of her jealousy, but when I interpret it, she talks about her envy, which implies a shift from the neurotic to the psychotic level of the personality. Jealousy is the result of a discrimination within envy. In this regard, I again draw on concepts of M. Klein:

> If envy is not excessive, jealousy in the Oedipus situation becomes a means of working it through. When jealousy is experienced, hostile feelings are directed not so much against the primal object but rather against the rivals—father or siblings—which brings in an element of distribution.
>
> (Klein, 1957, p. 198)

To this we add that distribution favours discrimination. The patient recognised her jealousy in the material but returns to the analysis of the remnant of her envy in the psychotic levels. In the next session (b), for the first time she takes off her coat inside the room, and after lying down she tells me she has an upset stomach (she describes the discomfort). I point out that today she took off her coat inside and today she is not afraid of me because she holds the dangerous things in her stomach, having put them there in the previous session. (Being able to take her coat off inside the room implies less massive projections.) She then tells me that her mother wanted to give her a present because it was her birthday and she asked her for a suspender belt, but they couldn't find one she liked, and when her mother got irritated Ana Maria asked her to buy her an umbrella. Her mother bought it for her, but afterwards she had a bad diarrhoea.

In this session (b) we analyse that she does not know yet whether what she incorporated in the former session are women's things or men's things (lack of discrimination), and how she now eliminates these things that she receives through the intestine. Then her fear of feeling that she is a thief emerges, as does the way in which she disguises her state of mind when she is happy and connected with me for fear of being envied by her mother and her husband, and how if she is happy, neither her mother nor I will take care of her any more. In the following session (c) the subject of her birthday comes up, and that her father had said to her if only he were 20 years younger, and that she notices her mother is more tired. With this, we go on analysing the oedipal situation with her consequent envy, greed and guilt. In this session, her fear of the analysis (of her greed) returns, that is, her fear of exhausting and emptying me, leaving me all worn out or dead (like her parents).

In the following session (d) she says that today the way her husband was driving frightened her and she tells me about the case of a girlfriend who disappeared and she was told that she had separated from her parents and then she found out that she had attempted to kill herself. I show her the fear that analysis may go too fast, that I may separate her from her parents and that because of her sadness she might not be able to stand it and would die. Here, there is a return to neurotic levels, and the theme of her conflicts in changing her house for an apartment in a much better neighbourhood, and her guilt toward her brothers; that she took all the best for herself, that in her house she always had the best on the pretext that she was a woman. She narrates an episode with her children when she felt embittered, and I tell her that she is embittered because she feels that everything she has she sucks and takes in with guilt.

In the following session (e) many fears of analysis come up with strong resistance to changes, indirectly demanding to know why she has to go on with the treatment; this is connected with her great fear of detaching herself from her parents but remaining strongly attached to me forever. In sessions (d) and (e) she again sets up the 'wall' between the neurotic and psychotic parts of her personality.

In the session that follows, (f), she talks to me about her anger toward her pupils; when I show her that it is the anger she took with her from the previous session because of what I told her, she falls silent and tells me that her husband is very annoyed and that she could relieve the situation by talking to him, but she doesn't feel like doing it. Then I point out the displacement and how she needs her husband to continue being angry in order not to recognise that it is she who is angry with me. She assimilates this latter interpretation as a reproach, in an attempt to see me as angry like her husband. In fact, at that moment, I did feel irritated and immediately saw that this was also the mechanism that she used with her husband to induce him to take responsibility for her anger.[110] She answers that she feels

110 Rosenfeld, in his study of the superego in schizophrenia, referring to the case when the patient takes the interpretation as a reproach, says that 'This is a very common occurrence in treating psychotic or even pre-psychotic patients. I think that it implies that the

that the whole relationship with her husband is shaky and she has to wait until her anger against her husband goes away; in the meantime, she feels lonely and very immobilised. With this she is signifying her fear of re-introjecting her aggression and with it her destroyed internal objects deposited in the exterior. When I interpret her fear of feeling her anger inside herself because she is afraid that this will make everything she has inside shaky, she falls silent and then says:

> I dreamed about stained teeth and that I was brushing and brushing. I knew that the stain wasn't going to go away. (Pause) This thing about the teeth I'm sure was one part. Another part was about the apartment and cleaning . . . In some way housework attracts me too much . . . and I think I would like to do it, and if I don't do it, it is because I reason that I could do more important things. Then I do neither one nor the other, nor what I like.

I interpret that she feels shaky with the fury with which she would bite me and this is why she is afraid that she might not be cured by the analysis.

> I think so . . . that I must feel guilty because I always act in a defensive way.

She goes on to narrate how a city council inspector scolded her for throwing things on the street and that she thought that with what the city charged her, they could very well clean up; I interpret that with what I charge I could very well clean up her aggression and her guilt.

> (She moves, uncomfortable) That is an explanation that I find quite satisfying.

I answer that she finds it quite satisfying but it makes her very angry, just as in the previous session.

interpretation has been taken concretely' and that 'when projective identification is reinforced the patient loses some of his capacity to understand symbols and therefore words, and he takes interpretations very concretely' (Rosenfeld, 1952a, p. 121). That is, there is not enough splitting between the analyst and the role projected into him (lack of sense of reality).

In connection with this, there is a very specific indicator which allows us to recognise that at a given moment we are working with material on the psychotic level. This is when the patient doesn't understand the separation between manifest and latent content, and takes what we interpret, not as latent content but as our reflection or opinion, which he can then apply to the manifest material that has just been unfolding. In this case there is also a deficit in symbolisation, or more precisely a symbolisation that has not yet been acquired by that part of the personality

(Puzzled) Now I would have to make an effort to remember the previous session. Still, I felt fine afterwards.

I point out that she reacted with surprise because she does not recognise that *her* fury is in her husband.

Now I understand less . . . If I left with anger or was angry in the previous session, why did I feel better afterwards?

I interpret that it is for the same reason as when she tells me that she receives what I give her with satisfaction, but at the same time she moves around uncomfortably with the anger in her body.

(Silence) Well. I was thinking that we went to the cinema with the children. Conditions were right for the day to be happy, but it wasn't like that. I ruin it all.

I interpret that she is telling me that I ruin a session for her that could have been happy.

Session (f) mobilises the affects *en bloc*: for fear of separating from her parents because of the treatment and when her anger emerges the patient does not recognise it as such or as her own. She is learning through her projection and displacement. The anger appears as such only to me, but if I try to show it to her she becomes confused, because for her anger does not exist in a form that is discriminated from her other feelings, and it appears together with affection, with sadistic oral greed (stains on her teeth) and guilt. She also tried to use the projection of her anger with me, to make me angry like her husband, and when I countertransferentially detached myself from this role, she tried, after reproaching herself, to make me feel guilty for having made her feel that way.

In the next session (g), she greets me in a connected way but very seriously. She tells me that some friends have already moved apartments and that they have done it so fast; then, that her husband arrived last night and gave her chocolate and she thought what kind of way was that to get closer, and that they are going to the cinema a lot.

In the previous session (f), there has been a re-introjection of different components of the agglutinated nucleus, and consequently she begins by saying that she feels she has changed rapidly and that she now needs more positive things (chocolate) from me, in order to thwart the agglutination of such different (not well discriminated) things inside her;[111] therefore, I

111 What H. Rosenfeld describes has occurred: 'However, when aggressive impulses become temporarily predominant, the reparative process may be interfered with in a particular way. The libidinal impulses succeed in bringing the pieces of the objects and the ego

interpret that she now feels that something has changed rapidly inside herself, that this disorients her, and that it seems to her that she is coming to the sessions too often and that I should keep hold of her the way her husband does by giving her chocolate. She answers that yes, the treatment is very long for her and she goes on to say that yesterday she sat down to study and fell asleep over the book. I again point out that she is telling me that the treatment is getting too long for her and that in spite of this her studying hasn't yet been sorted out.[112] She answers that it is not only her studying but the way she feels, and that when she goes into the classroom in the Faculty, she gets confused. I tell her that in coming to her session here today, she again leaves with me all the things from her previous session, and this is why she feels confused and is afraid of falling asleep as she did over the book.

> Well. I don't like to come into the session. (Pause.) Today I brought my knitting in the car and was knitting on the way. I never do that and now I discovered I can take advantage of the time.

I tell her this is a way of coming in accompanied by something from her home, to feel calmer.[113]

> Today my mother has to come to my house (she moves her feet and pauses). Today I remembered that Mrs. K.'s mother is very ill. Why did I put them together? I put it together because it seems to me that it is very difficult for her to separate from her mother. I think that I too feel very mixed up with my mother.

I interpret that she feels mixed up with me, because she has me, destroyed, inside her and she is afraid for this reason that she will never be able to separate from me.[114]

> Well . . . The . . . Everything we talked about regarding her here in the session . . . I never feel inclined to go to my mother's house. If she doesn't

together, nevertheless the aggressive impulses prevent the pieces from being sorted out and put together correctly. In the worst instance, the objects and the ego become pieced together but in a completely mixed up and faulty way. The result is a state of confusion . . .' (Rosenfeld, 1950, p. 62). I think that what Rosenfeld is describing is what I term re-agglutination.

112 Falling asleep over the book is a phobic situation, a consequence of re-projection (onto the book) of the agglutinated nucleus introjected in the previous session.

113 I regard this phobic re-dissociation as a step forward in the large-scale handling of the agglutinated nucleus.

114 The re-dissociation fails due to lack of discrimination between the patient's ego, her mother and the analyst, between the dangerous and the protective objects. A regression from the paranoid-schizoid position to the glischro-caric position occurs.

> come to my house, weeks could go by without my going, and they do. It is she who comes. Just now I remembered that yesterday at noon, during lunch, Juan (the elder son) said he had to tell me something and he told me that I demand that he come straight home from school and that the boys make fun of him. It wasn't the content that moved me but the fact that he was able to bring up a problem. It seems very important to me that he could do it.

I interpret that on the one hand she feels I make demands on her and that I chase after her as her mother does; but on the other hand she is very moved because she has been able to bring up her problems here, and it is because of this feeling mixed with my demands that today she was afraid to come here to the session.

> (Pause) Again I'm thinking about my mother . . . and . . . I often think when I'm on the tram . . . the other day I almost didn't realise that I had to get off.

I tell her that it is her fear of putting me so far inside that she won't ever be able to separate from me.

> In any case I'm much less afraid than before. In that sense, I think that I've improved a bit.

I tell her again that this is what moves her, and that when she is moved she gets confused.

> (Uncomfortable) I don't believe I was moved because of anything I did but because of what little Juan did.

She goes on to refer to how her son is able to tell a story with sexual content in her presence, and that it would never have occurred to her to do that in front of her mother; that this confuses her and she doesn't know whether it's good or bad, or whether it's better or not that way.

I interpret that she doesn't know what to do, whether to bring her sexuality into the session, whether this is going to be better or worse. She is then uncomfortable and changes the place of her head on the pillow. I point out the movement and say that now she wanted to change the ideas inside her head. From this, her dissociation and the dissociation with which she views her mother and me, as being without sex, is analysed.

The next session (h), begins this way:

> I'm always cold . . . Yesterday I had to take part in an examination board in the afternoon. We gave the exam to the children who had been ill. It was a surprise to arrive at the school and have to give examinations. Of two,

> one came. It was very cold, the room had a tile floor and I said: I'm going to freeze here, this is like a cemetery, and I went to ask for coffee. The other teacher said, 'But madam, you're always cold . . .' Well, yes. I'm not cold everywhere. Where there's heating I'm not cold.

I interpret that she is asking me to treat her affectionately, to feel her feelings, because otherwise she feels that her cold part is a cemetery full of destroyed things.

> Well. I want to tell you something that happened to me. After the session I met my husband and we went to have something to drink. We were talking about giving and receiving in relation to my being constipated, and he said that this is because I don't know how to give or receive. The conversation turned a bit sour and then I went home. On the way home I was carrying a full bag. At the shop, when they counted the things, they counted six things, and when I got home I counted five things. I took a piece of paper and did the sum and a packet of rice was missing. It cost 35 pesos and I returned to the shop to see if I had left it. I went and I hadn't. So the owner told me: 'Take another packet and pay me half'. Well. I returned home and I hadn't bought rice and had the six things. How had I managed to add up five things . . . ? How did I do the sum so it came out exact? I counted wrongly, I added up wrongly. I went to ask for a packet of rice that I hadn't bought. I really felt quite badly after that.

The patient comes to the session expressing her surprise at having found herself in the previous session examining the unwell part of herself, which is a cemetery, and is the part that she needs to keep blocked. She was left quite confused at finding one more part of herself that she wasn't counting on finding; that to keep it immobile she can neither give nor receive in relation to me because in her feelings she does not know how to distinguish between affection and rage. However, I am like the shopkeeper she keeps asking from as if things were missing, paying little or half of what she must assume are my fees. As long as she goes on receiving from me, I am an internal object that she destroys with her greed, and to counteract the destruction she has to go on asking me for affection in a vicious circle that feeds my destruction inside her. This division between affection and destruction indicates the existence, now, inside of her, of a certain difference or discrimination between her living part, which can be moved and have feelings, and the other paralysed, immobile part, a cemetery, formed by parts of herself and of the objects destroyed by her greed. This now enables us to open up the problem of giving and/or introjecting. Her relationship with me is different from that of some time ago, because there is now a certain discrimination between my affection and her affection and between me – a real, external being – and me as an internal object of hers that she sucks on and kills, or me that demands, sucks and kills. This dissociation was installed after the confusion of the previous session, a confusion that was directly acted out (evacuated) after the session, because it could not be retained in the area of the mind. Here, the phantasy of losing an object is equivalent to the diarrhoea in session (b).

However, I do not believe that this yet constitutes a good discrimination, which is to say a sufficiently stable one. In the previous session she felt she was re-introjecting very diverse things (parts of her ego and of the mother-analyst objects with different roles: protection, reparation, making demands, affection, destruction, rage, sexuality). Because of this re-introjection she left the session full of things, like her bag, and full of two persons in the session with different parts of herself. She felt when leaving that she had everything inside her ('Of two students only one came'), and she had to act as a re-inforced dissociation, trying to free herself of the re-agglutination that was threatening her from inside. This reinforcement of the dissociation makes her feel her ego is poorer, and therefore she needs to return to the shop to ask for more, as if they hadn't already given her everything. In spite of it all, this acted out dissociation is a step in her testing that may lead to more stable discrimination, and then enable her to differentiate between one part of her that is alive with warmth and another that is cold and dead. Thus, we need to recognise that confusion, alternating with agglutination and dissociation, with projection and introjection, is a necessary step in the process of development and learning, because it permits progressive expansion of the patient's psychological world through the mobilisation of blocked and segregated parts of her personality (the psychotic part or levels); these can only be assimilated into the personality when it is followed by the discrimination of the elements of which it is composed.

In the material that I have transcribed I interpret to her that among the things that she incorporated in the previous session there were many that confused her and that she had to lose them on the way home. She continues as if she hadn't heard me and, very frightened, asks me repeatedly and in different ways how that lack of control could have happened and what other things she might do if she lost control that way. The session continues around this fear that the analysis might lead her to greater lack of control, and later in the same session, she reflects on how she could go to ask for things that didn't belong to her. 'I went to ask for things that they took away from me that I had actually taken away.' With this, the analysis turns to her confusion with me between the phantasies of stealing and of being robbed, and how she covers up her guilt for robbery by always asking for more and concealing what she receives. She then tries to see what we talked about in the previous session, and I interpret that she wants to locate the dangerous theme in order to control it better so that it doesn't come up without her control. She then remembers what I interpreted at the end: that she viewed her mother and me as being without sex.

The theme of sexuality has not emerged until now in her analysis, and its inclusion in session (g) confused her, as one more element, a component of the oedipal situation that is yet to be discriminated. This is another characteristic of the psychotic levels of the analysis: when a fragment of the agglutinated nucleus is re-introjected, it is dispersed and a large number of its components appear without offering a possibility of persisting much in the analysis of any one of them separately, since the elements again re-agglutinate and repeatedly appear and disappear.

Other moments of confusion that I have already described are those which occur on entering and leaving the sessions, when I described clouded consciousness as a minimal degree of confusion due to a defensive regression of the ego in the face of massive invasion by the re-introjected agglutinated nucleus.

In the descriptions of her dreams she quite often confuses waking and sleeping or does not discriminate between them, as for example, when she says in one session: 'This morning I was dreaming . . .', in another: 'Today, when I woke up . . . I dreamed something so strange . . .'; or she comes into a session, lies down and says: 'Well. I was dreaming that . . .'. On another occasion, also at the beginning of the session: 'Well. I got up with . . . Trying to remember the dream . . . I dreamed that . . .'.

An important period of confusion occurred when they had sold the house, which meant they had to move to the new apartment immediately. At the same time, her menstruation was overdue to the point that both she and I assumed that it was a pregnancy, a delay of two weeks. She was very confused about the decision to make about this pregnancy, whether to allow or discontinue it. The menstrual delay was connected with re-experiencing the move from her parents' house to her own house, a period when she was pregnant with her first child and also the period when she stopped studying. I have already observed that since some situations cannot be worked through symbolically this has to be done through facts (through acting it); and this was what made Ana Maria need to move house. The pregnancy was the equivalent of a hypochondriac condensation, a localisation and controlling in the body of all the changes in order to avoid confusion. In turn, the change was experienced as her own re-birth or separating from her mother; and so she began to remember her impressions when she used to come to the first sessions of the analysis and had a dream:

> in which I had to go up a very tall staircase and then I had to go through a passageway and I was afraid that it was too narrow and I called my husband and I woke up . . . Sometimes it happens that I'm afraid of not being able to get through.

In regard to the problem of confusion in all its manifestations (clouded consciousness, disorientation, dizzy spells, etc.), in this material I wanted to point out its relation with the re-introjection of the agglutinated nucleus or fragments of it that appear to be fused, that is, material of undifferentiated experiences, and that during the analysis we need to discriminate, to mark the limits of its components; in a prominent place among these we find the fusion of the oedipal couple and envy, which I believe is characteristic of the psychotic levels of the personality. I also showed that discrimination is a gradual process alternating with re-agglutination and re-projection. In it, before the installation of the schizoid division (well established discrimination), extreme or reinforced dissociations (as Rosenfeld calls them) frequently intervene, sometimes organised by a very precarious or very inconsistent phobic control. *Discrimination transforms the psychotic levels into neurotic levels* (passage from the glischro-caric position to the paranoid-schizoid position) and with this, *the fusion and confusion are transformed into contradiction and the ambiguity into conflict.*

In his works on phobia J. Mom describes, as we do, splitting between the ego and what is projected and a concomitant dissociation of the latter; if this dissociation is lost, the ego is invaded by confusional anxiety. The same is found in the work by Garbarino (1965 [1962]) on the analysis of a phobia. I consider that loss of the dissociation (a dissociation that allows phobic control to act) implies re-agglutination of good and bad objects with a wholesale loss of discrimination between them and between the parts of the ego and the depositary related to one or the other type of object.

It is my opinion that the psychology and psychopathology of confusion (clinically and dynamically considered) is a chapter that is sure to attract growing interest (theoretical and technical) in psychoanalytic work.

### *(l) Permeability between the neurotic and psychotic levels*

Between the cycles or periods of mobilisation I have described, there were periods during which neither new re-introjection of the agglutinated nucleus (a new transition) nor its dispersion was possible; therefore, the patient segregated and immobilised the analysis of the psychotic levels; in these periods she needed to consolidate her more integrated ego, incorporating new elements into it from the analysis ( the discrimination) of the psychotic part of the personality. In other words, the analysis returned to neurotic levels, which have remained quite dissociated from the psychotic levels. In order to show the difference I want now to present a brief example from a more recent period, when there is already more permeability between the neurotic and psychotic levels of the personality; this session takes place shortly before she returns to her studies by taking and passing an exam. The session begins thus:

> It was hard for me to get up early. All day today I've been going around as if I had slept too little. I know that I dreamed, but I can't remember what; the sensation it left me with is like something that is collapsing or falling to pieces. Then I remembered a previous dream where *on my glasses the frame was separating from the lenses*. But today's dream I don't remember.

The psychotic levels of the personality (going around asleep, the collapse) are segregated or dissociated from the more integrated ego ('. . . on my glasses the frame was separating from the lenses'. This dissociation can also be seen in the forgetting of the dream.) Without my having interpreted, the patient continues:

> On Saturday night we went to the cinema. We went separately, I arrived first and then my husband. On the way back, we took the bus and I recognised a lady who had been a classmate in medical school. We were classmates until we got angry with each other. I got on, I saw her and I felt very happy, but I remembered I was angry at her. She did something to me that I didn't like. But she also did other things for me and thanks to her I passed many exams. All day yesterday, I was going around and around on this theme.

The psychotic part of the personality being segregated, the neurotic levels show well discriminated elements: good and bad objects, affection and anger. At this point I interpret that she can recognise inside her that she is angry with me but she also has affection for me and appreciation of me. The patient answers: 'I think that if this were to happen to me now, I wouldn't get angry. At that time, it was enough to ruin a friendship.' I tell her that she is reassuring herself and me that the same thing is not going to happen now and that our relationship is going to continue. And she answers: 'That positive part was maybe the one I wasn't taking into consideration.'

When I identify a division in the personality, with the consequent segregation of the psychotic part, I have two fundamental alternatives on which to centre the interpretation: in one of them I can interpret this division of the personality (between the more integrated ego and the agglutinated nucleus), attempting a re-introjection of the latter. In this case, my first interpretation in this session could have been, for example: 'on the one hand you recognise the affection and the anger that you have for me, but this is leaving aside something that collapses and makes you feel you're asleep'.

The other alternative is to centre the interpretation on the schizoid division in the neurotic levels of the personality, ignoring and segregating the psychotic part as the patient does, and this is what I did in the interpretation at the beginning of the session.

These two ways of centring the interpretation correspond to what may be called interpretation on psychotic levels and on neurotic levels of the personality respectively. Also, both examples of interpretations used here correspond to the type I classified above as split interpretation.

Just as split interpretation promotes re-introjection and unsplit interpretation promotes re-projection, interpretation on psychotic levels mobilises the latter, while interpretation on the neurotic levels maintains or follows the timing and the splitting of the personality; however, precisely because of this, it tends to integrate the more mature ego, resolving the schizoid division. In the case of the session I am discussing, I opted for this latter type of interpretation because we had gone through a cycle of dispersion of the agglutinated nucleus, and again precisely because of this it was necessary now to bring about a better integration of the ego, with that obtained by discrimination of parts of the agglutinated nucleus, in order subsequently to return to a new cycle of dispersion and re-introjection of the psychotic part. Taking care with timing, between interpretations centred on the neurotic and the psychotic levels of the personality is, as I have pointed out, one of the fundamental technical problems in symbiosis.

After what the patient said, if we had continued with interpretations centring on the neurotic levels, guilt for feeling better would probably have appeared, with some difficulty in recognising her improvement out of guilt toward her siblings and parents, because of being able to live better than they, as well as depression for feeling her improvement as a separation from her parents, and the problem of the passing of time, the death of her parents and becoming an adult, with the problem of her own inescapable death.

In the session, however, I returned to the analysis of the psychotic part and formulated an interpretation centred on the division between the central ego and the agglutinated nucleus: I told her that now she is trying not to consider the part of the dream that collapses and makes her go around asleep during the day.

> I feel heavy and fat. It makes me angry and I'm still gaining weight. It's hard for me to move. On Mondays I have to come into the city centre twice and that tires me. Up to now I could keep my weight down, but now I weigh more and more. (Pause) And I think that being calmer and although I may eat less, the calmness is what makes me get fat. The time I lost a lot of weight was with the commotion with my husband. Of course I wouldn't want to go through that again. But I wonder if I have to be anxious in order to get my weight down. (Pause) Well, I'm going to change the subject.

When I interpret the part that collapses, and with this I confront her central ego with the psychotic part (agglutinated nucleus), it is evident that she is not as blocked as before, nor does she block me, as she did in the sessions that I presented earlier; she does not isolate the interpretation but associates to its contents. Re-introjection does occur, but in the body, which serves as a mediator or 'buffer'. As well as the improved permeability between the different parts of the personality, there is also greater insight, in the sense that to resolve the fatness (to mobilise the agglutinated nucleus immobilised in the body), she recognises that she will have to go through anxieties and a 'commotion' with me, as she did before with her husband (she is referring to the project of the divorce for which she started her analysis). Afterwards, she explicitly proposes that we change the subject; now it is no longer a question of annulment and rejection in order to immobilise the psychotic part, but of the time she needs to preserve her ego and her relationship with me. I ignore the proposal to change the subject and go on interpreting the psychotic levels, telling her that she is quite afraid that if I pick on her body and on what collapses, she's going to get into a commotion with me as she did with her husband. She answers:

> It was in the last session that I told you that my gums hurt. The pain lessened after that session.

I interpret that she trusts that the change in her body can now take place without getting into a commotion, just as the problem with her gums got fixed.

After this interpretation, the patient continues to talk about her planned change of house and how previously moving made her anxious but now she feels like experiencing this change, and about her hopes as well as her fear of being disillusioned.

In this material I wanted to show the joint manifestations of the psychotic and neurotic parts of the personality and the use of the interpretations on each of the two levels, as well as the increased permeability or porosity at that moment between the two. I consider it an indicator of a favourable development, since this permeability can only appear with a more integrated ego that no longer suffers – at that moment – from re-introjection as an overwhelming and disintegrating invasion.

## Summary and conclusions

(1) Symbiosis is a close interdependence between two or more persons who complement each other in order to keep the needs of the most immature parts of the personality controlled, *immobilised and to some extent satisfied.*

(2) In adults, these parts make up the psychotic part of the personality, which I have identified and termed the agglutinated nucleus.

(3) The psychotic part of the personality remains strongly segregated from the neurotic part of the personality and its more integrated levels.

(4) The psychotic part of the personality is the remnant of a primitive organisation, previous to the paranoid-schizoid position, which I have termed the glischro-caric position.

(5) The agglutinated nucleus (the psychotic part of the personality) is formed of the most primitive identifications in which there has not yet been established even a discrimination between ego and non-ego, and on the other hand it is the most primitive organisation of the Oedipus complex, which is characterised by fusion (lack of discrimination) in the parental couple and between the latter and the patient's ego.

(6) The agglutinated nucleus may undergo modifications in its extent due to regression from the paranoid-schizoid position, or progression toward it.

(7) The agglutinated nucleus is not characterised by confusion but by fusion of its component elements. Confusion appears when the agglutinated nucleus has invaded the more integrated ego.

(8) The agglutinated nucleus *is ambiguous and polyvalent*, being capable of undergoing extreme polarisations, as a result of which it may appear functionally as an ego, an object or a superego.

(9) The schizoid division discriminates the components of the agglutinated nucleus and makes possible the transition from the glischro-caric position to the paranoid-schizoid position. *Schizoid division transforms confusion into contradiction and ambiguity into conflict.*

(10) The mind-body division corresponds to the division between the neurotic and the psychotic parts of the personality, there existing at the same time in the psychotic part a lack of discrimination or a fusion between the body and the external world.

(11) Repression predominates in the neurotic part of the personality, while projection predominates in the psychotic part. In symbiosis there is fusion between what is projected and the depositary, with massive projective identification.

(12) Schizoid division is characteristic of the neurotic levels of the personality, and enables the action of the defence mechanisms: hysteric, phobic, obsessional and paranoid.

(13) In the psychotic part of the personality, fusion or lack of discrimination causes the agglutinated nucleus to mobilise itself massively, giving rise to different defensive phenomena: hypochondria, psychosomatic illness, psychopathy. Autism is also a defence: an omnipotent denial of symbiotic dependence.

(14) Envy pertains to the psychotic levels of the personality, while jealousy corresponds to the neurotic part.

(15) The clinical presentation of three types of patients is postulated, depending on the degree of control and splitting between the neurotic and psychotic parts of the personality.

(16) In patients with clinical symbiosis, the latent autistic nuclei need to be investigated and analysed, while in clinical autism the latent symbiotic nuclei need to be investigated and analysed.

(17) Entering and leaving sessions, as well as any change, mobilises the psychotic part of the personality.

(18) In the psychotic part of the personality – when it is predominant – there is extreme facility or permeability for indiscriminate introjection and identification, which explains dynamically some phenomena such as echolalia, echopraxia and mimetism.

(19) Narrowed and clouded consciousness characterises the presence and activity of the psychotic part of the personality.

(20) The working through of symbiosis sometimes makes it necessary for the patient to learn through action because of a deficit in symbolisation (psychopathic phase).

(21) The transference of the psychotic part of the personality is a psychotic transference, characteristically massive, invasive, sudden, tenacious and labile; totally equivalent to transference symbiosis.

(22) Psychotic (symbiotic) transference is based on massive projective identification that merges the depositary with the projected, which structures its lack of sense of reality.

(23) This massive projective identification is a consequence of the nature of what is projected (the agglutinated nucleus, which is mobilised globally and massively).

(24) The countertransference reaction to the acting of the psychotic levels is generally to feel overwhelmed and to have crushing global feelings, which yield to better discriminated impressions and reactions insofar as there occurs a transition from the psychotic part to the neurotic levels of the personality.

(25) Guilt in the countertransference is a very frequent phenomenon through which the patient tends to succeed in getting the analyst to continue giving by inducing guilt without having to ask for anything and therefore without having to mobilise the psychotic part of the personality.

(26) Countertransferentially, it is quite frequent to feel that we are forcing the patient's timing and overwhelming or crushing the patient by mobilising the psychotic part.

(27) As a matter of technique, it is necessary to go on to discover the psychotic part of the personality in all neurosis.

(28) It is necessary as a matter of technique to tend towards a discrimination in the agglutinated nucleus by the more integrated ego; in other words, towards the establishment of the schizoid division in the psychotic part of the personality.

(29) With this, the psychotic part of the personality becomes a neurotic part.

(30) We identify two types of interpretations: split and unsplit, which make it possible to handle the timing and mobilisation of the psychotic part of the personality.
(31) The handling of timing is fundamental for analysing first, to some extent, the neurotic levels that enable better integration of the ego, so that it is able to face the work of discriminating the agglutinated nucleus without succumbing to its massive invasion.
(32) The mobilisation of the agglutinated nucleus is an indispensable step in its working-through (discrimination).
(33) Repeated introjections-projections, re-introjections and re-projections produce a certain fragmentation of the agglutinated nucleus, as a necessary transition on the way to discrimination.
(34) The emergence of confusion in any of its manifestations (dizziness, clouding of consciousness, suspense or perplexity) is an 'index of re-introjection'. It is the equivalent, on the psychotic levels, of the alarm signal on the neurotic levels.
(35) The analyst constantly needs to split, for himself, his own role from the role the patient projects into him, thus constantly preserving a discrimination of his identity.
(36) Interpretation on the neurotic levels tends to integrate the dissociations and bring about the transition to the depressive position; on the psychotic levels, interpretation tends to discriminate and bring about the transition to the paranoid-schizoid position.
(37) Interpretation of the psychotic levels lands on the line of the split separating these from the neurotic part of the personality.
(38) The interpretations of the psychotic levels are, for a long time, apparently ineffective, but an explosive or cyclical insight may result subsequently.
(39) Technical efforts should not be centred on getting into the patient's autism but rather on breaking out of the symbiosis. By working this way, we mobilise the patient's entire narcissistic organisation (including the autism).
(40) The analyst must act by discriminating, as an auxiliary ego for the patient; through this activity the patient learns to discriminate.
(41) In the psychotic part of the personality one should not interpret in terms that imply attributions of the existence of feelings or thoughts, since affects and symbolic activity emerge from discrimination. Affects expressed by the body must be pointed out first as bodily events.
(42) When the analysis has made some progress, it is necessary to avoid confusing the schizoid division of the neurotic levels with splitting between the neurotic and psychotic parts of the personality. Equally, it is necessary not to confuse re-agglutination with the integration of the depressive position.

# PART TWO

# On Ambiguity

# 5

# Ambiguity in psychoanalytic clinical work

> . . . we take for granted the synthetic nature of the processes of the ego. But we are clearly at fault in this. The synthetic function of the ego, though it is of such extraordinary importance, is subject to particular conditions and is liable to a whole number of disturbances.
>
> (Freud, 1940b, p. 276)

## Introduction

An early scheme by K. Abraham in 1921 considered that in the course of development there are four fundamental stages, three in relation to different illnesses: the first stage was the one from narcissism to autoerotism; the second was that of object love with a sadistic-anal organisation; the third was that of object love with a genital organization; the fourth corresponded to normality: object love with genital organisation, control of organic innervation and the capacity to deal with psychic stimuli. (Abraham, 1921, p. 325).

This scheme is considerably modified in his longer paper of 1924: he divided the oral, anal and genital stages into primary and secondary, and he included together with these stages of libidinal organization the characteristics of the development of object love; and in the latter there was a *pre-ambivalent* stage (objectless, narcissistic, auto-erotic) and at the other extreme, the *post-ambivalent* object relation; between these two poles, that is, between the first oral stage (of sucking) and the final genital stage, he included *ambivalence.*[115]

115 Abraham's scheme was completed by E. Pichon Rivière, including a pre-natal (fetal) stage; more recently it was revisited by M. Langer in relation to the Kleinian theory and conceptions. D. Liberman also worked on it, including the basic anxieties in function of the theory of communication and the differentiation of 'a spectrum of emotions'.

What is most evident is that with Melanie Klein's contribution the pre-ambivalent (or objectless) object relation postulated by Abraham disappeared, narcissism and auto-eroticism were also put in question, the concept of the stage became enriched by the concept of the position, and the partial object relation, previous to ambivalence, was introduced into the course of development. At the same time, however, much of what Abraham considered 'partial love', within ambivalence, was left in the paranoid-schizoid position, or as what we could call *divalence*, a term introduced by E. Pichon Rivière.

Investigations and contributions by different authors and by myself regarding the problem of symbiosis lead me to state that Abraham's scheme is correct to some extent: not in the sense that the object relation begins in the ambivalent stage (which nowadays, strictly speaking, would correspond to the divalence of Melanie Klein's paranoid-schizoid position), but in the sense of an organization prior to the paranoid-schizoid position, which I now wish to relate to the problem of ambiguity. Summarising, we could say that the *pre-ambivalent* in Abraham's scheme is, strictly speaking, *pre-divalent* or *pre-paranoid-schizoid* and that, of course, the latter is not *objectless* but neither is it object-related in the usual sense of the term 'object'.

For Melanie Klein, ambivalence corresponds to the depressive position, while divalence (the relation to a part-object) pertains to the paranoid-schizoid position described by Fairbairn-Melanie Klein. However, ambiguity corresponds to a very specific (pre-paranoid-schizoid) organisation that I have termed the glischro-caric position.

I believe that in clinical work and in the consideration of psychological mechanisms we very often confuse *ambivalence and contradiction*, on the one hand, and *divalence and dissociation with ambiguity*, on the other. In the same way, when we do not recognise ambiguity for what it is, we consider it confusion. I believe that we need to re-consider these problems which seem to me of fundamental importance, not only from the clinical viewpoint but also from the perspective of psychoanalytic technique and theory; in this chapter I discuss some of these aspects.

I have tried to identify ambiguity in the course of psychoanalytic work and to differentiate it from contradiction as well as from ambivalence, dissociation and confusion. In this way, I was able to detect a type of personality that we could term *ambiguous personality*, as well as certain ambiguous personality traits that appear clinically; but it also brought me to the relation between ambiguity and the most primitive psychological organisation (of the glischro-caric position), and from there I was able to relate

A. Rascovsky contributed the theory of the fetal psyche, previous to the oral stage, which he describes as a fetal or autistic position.

Another important study is Rickman's (1926–27), elaborating on Abraham's scheme in a very thorough way: its relations with the evolution of the ego, the defence mechanisms, relations between the ego and the superego, etc.

the latter to the ambiguous personality and to ambiguous personality traits. I also learned to identify nuclei of ambiguity that are concealed in various psychopathological manifestations. In previous papers, I coined the term 'agglutinated nucleus' for what is nothing other than the persistence of nuclei of ambiguity (persistence of the primitive undifferentiated psychological organization), quite split off from the personality after the latter has reached a variable degree of integration of the ego. In other words, symbiosis is coincident with the persistence of an ambiguous structure, which enables us to understand more clearly the different modalities of symbiosis as well as the clinical picture of ambiguity. With this study, I now pass from the psychology and psychopathology of ambiguity which has been reduced to a split-off nucleus of the ego, to the examination of cases in which the *ego itself is ambiguous*. Although these two studies are closely related, we need to recall their differences.

## Discrimination of the concept of ambiguity

Let us begin by attempting to define ambiguity. The *Diccionario de la Lengua Española* [*Dictionary of the Spanish Language*] of the Royal Academy (Real Academia Española, 1956) defines ambiguity as 'what may be understood in several ways or admits different interpretations and consequently motivates doubts, uncertainty or confusion'. Definitions in other dictionaries, for example, of philosophy,[116] are similar to the one quoted above: they all define ambiguity from the observer's perspective (or we could say from the viewpoint of the countertransference), from which we say that someone is ambiguous (their behaviour, character or personality) when they can be understood 'in several ways' or their behaviour admits 'different interpretations, and consequently motivates doubts, uncertainty or confusion'. However, for the person who experiences or manifests the ambiguity, it is neither doubt nor uncertainty nor confusion. It is *undifferentiation*, which means *a deficit in discrimination and identity, or a deficit in differentiation between ego and not-ego. I believe that the most frequent error resides in attributing countertransference confusion directly to the structure of the phenomenon that produces it.*

Perhaps the definition is further clarified if we recall that both ambivalence and divalence are contradictions that are lived or 'experienced' by the individual; in ambivalence, a confluence of two antinomic, contradictory terms concerns the same object at the same time, while in divalence (schizoid division), the contradictory terms are separated and kept separate by neurotic (hysteric, phobic, obsessional and paranoid) techniques. In ambiguity, no delimitation or discrimination of different terms, or of antinomic or contradictory terms, has been reached; in both subject and

116 Lalande (1953); Abbagnano (1963). It does not appear in Hinsie and Campbell (1960).

situation, terms, attitudes or behaviours co-exist *without contradiction or conflict for the individual,* and they are *different* (not necessarily antinomic) but *not mutually exclusive* , sometimes *co-existing* and in other cases *alternating* in their appearance.

It may be that our psychological structure or organisation is able to tolerate contradictions of no more than two terms, while in reality there could exist without conflict (at other levels of organisation of the ego) more than two contradictory or different terms, and that this is why, what for the observer appears in the ambiguity as unresolvable contradictions of many terms or different behaviours (provoking confusion), for the ambiguous subject presents no such confusion or contradiction . Hence, I wish to underscore that *ambiguity is not confusion*, but the persistence of or regression to a state of primitive fusion or undifferentiation, which characterises the earliest adumbrations of psychological organisation (glischro-caric position). In other words, ambiguous subjects have not yet reached the stage of giving shape to contradictions. Equally, *they have not yet been able to discriminate different terms*, which for them are comparable, equivalent or co-existent. This is the basic characteristic of ambiguity and of the glischro-caric position or position of primitive undifferentiation (syncretism), and of ambiguity due to the persistence of the glischro-caric position or regression to it.

ψ

Psychoanalytic literature concerning the clinical aspects of ambiguity is sparse, practically nonexistent. The author who has come closest to the topic is Madeleine Baranger in various works. In 'Mala fe, identidad y omnipotencia' ['Bad faith, identity and omnipotence'], she studied bad faith as a phenomenon in which the patient 'remains in an ambiguous position, as expressed by the lack of authenticity in the material'. She gives examples for the study of bad faith, in which 'the patient uses his right to dissociate, but he does not actually dissociate'. (Baranger, 1963, p. 183).

In one of her examples, she says:

> Yet in the second example, the supposedly dissociated positive and negative aspects of the transference are both actually present, one conditioning the other, belonging to a more complex structure that has its own goal and mechanisms ... *Therefore, bad faith is opposed both to dissociation and to ambivalence.*
>
> (Baranger, 1963, p. 184)

I believe that bad faith, as a phenomenon of ambiguity, is not strictly speaking opposed to dissociation or ambivalence but is instead a different phenomenon, just as this author tells us: it is 'a more complex structure' with its own properties.

The starting-point of her study of bad faith is the rupture of the psychoanalytic setting, and I agree on this in relation to the ambiguous personality, but this rupture of the setting is not the individual's aim or goal: it is what results when we study it with a different structure that is imposed on us as a norm. This point is taken up in the next chapter.

An important aspect of her paper is that she correctly, as I see it, related bad faith with an *identity disorder*. However, I would add that this is not simply about an identity disorder but about *a different* identity whose own structure needs to be understood. In bad faith the ego is 'a multiplicity of contemporary and contradictory identifications that have not settled down'. (Baranger, 1963, pp. 186–187). I consider this typical of ambiguity in general, not only of bad faith, which is a particular case of ambiguity.[117] I will now try to discuss this theme with the aid of some examples which, of course, are at best only of value as illustrations.

When I refer below to the authoritarian personality, I shall also mention other papers on ambiguity, but which are not strictly psychoanalytic. Finally, I shall discuss some studies that I consider relevant to ambiguity.

Summarising what has been said so far, we could say that ambiguity is defined by: (a) a specific type of identity or ego organisation, characterised by the co-existence of a multiplicity of nuclei that have not integrated and consequently may co-exist and alternate without involving confusion or contradiction for the subject; (b) each nucleus of this 'granular ego' is characterised in itself by a lack of ego/non-ego discrimination or, in positive terms, by a syncretic organisation. We can synthesize these two characteristics as belonging to a very primitive or very regressive ego (or identity).

ψ

In Chapter One, in the discussion of 'Re-introjection and the body as a buffer', *in material (3)*, the patient narrates a dream in which she sees a man die and says: 'It's the first time I've seen a man die'. The formulation is presented as if she had talked about an event in waking life, the same occurring at the start of the narration when she says: 'I lay down to sleep and suddenly I saw . . .'

Both instances were treated in the first chapter, at the time it was written, as a confusion between waking and sleeping, but I am now inclined to consider them as a lack of discrimination between waking and sleeping, that is, as a phenomenon of ambiguity: the actualisation of a primitive ego organization that has not yet discriminated between waking and sleeping.

In the session in Chapter Four, we find a different example when the patient says, in reference to her studies: 'perhaps that's why it's so hard for me to contract this habit'.[118] I pointed out that the use of the word 'contract'

117 All the emphases in the quoted material are mine.

118 [See Chapter 4, p. 123, n. 99]

means equally contracting an illness and also shrinking, becoming smaller and losing her parents. She avoids studying because to incorporate it means to her incorporating a disturbing part,'the psychotic part of the personality'. This coincides with loss of the undifferentiated image of her parents, which is presented all together as a loss or contraction of her more adapted ego. In this case, the ambiguity resides in the fact that different meanings are contained in the same word, but that these do not contradict each other.

In session A of the same chapter, in the study of 'Fusion, confusion and discrimination', the patient says:

> Although it seems a little . . . I think that I envied my mother . . . That I envied my fa . . . my mother . . . for the affection she showed . . . my father . . . and the need to have someone who would show affection for me like he showed her . . . ;

and in subsequent material:

> It occurred to me like maybe . . . that I might envy my fa . . . my mother . . . because of the things my father said to her and still says to her. . . .

About this fragment I stated that:

> The *confusion* that emerges when she mentions her father and her mother, when she mistakes one for the other, is actually the emergence of a primitive *fusion* of the parental couple and parts of her ego, which may now be actualised and brought into the transference situation as a function of the existence now of a more integrated ego able to tolerate the re-introjection of these psychotic levels ...

ψ

I now present another example, that is a bit different and to some extent more complex.

> *Example A*: The patient talks, during the session, about 'how badly his wife behaved toward him over the weekend' and I show him what he did that made her 'behave badly' and how, for him, it was I who was behaving badly by leaving him alone over the weekend
>
> He immediately says yes, it's true, and adds details that confirm it (but only in reference to his wife) and then, without awareness, talks about 'how badly his children behaved all weekend'.

This example very clearly highlights the fact that the patient does not differentiate between talking about himself, his wife and his children. When he talks about them he is talking about himself. A structure is functioning, in which the ego and the objects are not discriminated, so that nothing keeps him from accepting with conviction what I say, while at the same time he continues to affirm what he was saying before. The total situation that results is definitely unauthentic, but we need to use the term ambiguous rather than unauthentic, because the former corresponds to the structure of the phenomenon while the latter is the countertransference reaction (which may be different for a different observer). As I said, this failure to clarify the two perspectives obscures our understanding of ambiguity.

If we continue to analyse the example, we deduce that there is no relation between him and me as two different persons, but rather a syncretic relation, in which nothing prevents him from immediately incorporating or adopting what I say as his own. Also, there is a striking lack of contradiction, but this has a specific feature: the different terms are both 'active' at the same moment and in the same situation. In other words, the different terms are neither mutually exclusive nor contradictory for the patient. This may also occur partially in the paranoid-schizoid position, with the difference that in the latter the terms are contradictory and mutually exclusive. If they co-exist, they do so as a conflict or by resorting to defence mechanisms (neurotic techniques: hysterical, obsessional, phobic and paranoid), which are absent in this example. The explanation for the non-contradiction resides in what M. Baranger describes for the phenomenon of bad faith: the ego consists of 'a multiplicity of contemporary and contradictory identifications that have not settled down'.

In other words, in ambiguity the different nuclei of the ego are not integrated. They form what could be described as a 'granular' ego, since it appears with different nuclei or segments, between which *there is no need to interpose defence techniques*. We may add that each nucleus of this 'granular' ego has a syncretic or undifferentiated structure. In the paranoid-schizoid position, however, the object and the ego are dissociated, but an integrated ego exists or is preserved, which 'bears' the conflict or resorts to defence techniques or sets them into motion. Ego/non-ego syncretism is also absent.

All the different types of ambiguous personality may be included within the term proposed by E. Pichon Rivière (in a paper by S. Resnik, 1955) as '*dispersonalisation*'.[119]

The ambiguous personality characteristically does not assume responsibility, but avoids or does not commit to or take responsibility for a situation, its meaning, motivations or consequences. However, all this results not from denial but from lack of discrimination: nothing is affirmed, nor is it totally denied. Its behaviour is *furtive*, unlike the *futility* characterising the schizoid. To this we add the permeability or mimetism that enable the acceptance

119 [Resnik's paper was originally titled 'Síndrome de Cotard y dispersonalización' ['Cotard's syndrome and dispersonalisation'] (Resnik, 1955), but the term 'dispersonalisation' (*dispersonnalisation*) is absent from the subsequent French and English versions (Resnik, 1970, 1978, 2001), where the title refers instead to 'depersonalization' (*dépersonnalisation*).]

or incorporation of different types of behaviour, that is also due to the characteristics of the ego that 'functions' in this way (though not always, as we shall see).

> *Example B*: L.L is a patient who recently underwent very traumatic situations, the deaths of members of his family and the loss of his economic position, as a result of which he 'coincidentally' began his analysis. The analysis has been characterised by his extreme dependence on the analyst and total submission to and undisputed acceptance of everything that is said or interpreted to him, although the sessions always transpire with intense ambiguity, since although he accepts everything that is interpreted to him, on the other hand, and at the same time, the characteristics of behaviour that brought him to analysis persist.
>
> In one session he announces that the following day he will not be able to come because he will have to go on a trip. I interpret his attempt to draw apart from everything that he perceives as disturbing in the relation with me.
>
> The following morning, during the course of his hour, I was reading in a place where I can hear the doorbell, but as I learned afterwards, it was ringing much more softly than usual that day.
>
> He comes to the next session and says that he did not go away and explains the reasons in detail. At one moment, I point out that he is explaining why he did not go away, but is not saying that yesterday he missed his session and that this omission must have some meaning, since although he did not go away as planned, he didn't come to the session either. At that moment, he tells me that he came to the session, rang the bell, waited a few minutes and, since nobody answered the door, returned home.

The ambiguity here is that the session occurred as if none of the above had happened: he had told me that he was not coming, then he did not tell me or inform me by telephone that he was going to come; he did not tell me that he really came, that he was not received and that he had to return home. All this is present, but in a very peculiar way, given the total disconnection in the manifest material between what he is now informing me, that he did not go away, and the concrete reference to his announced absence, and then, his coming and not being received. He knows that he came, but allows me to believe that he missed his session or else assumes that I already know what he knows. Actually, he stopped knowing it. He knows that he came when I take charge of his 'not coming' and this allows him to recognise that he did come.

We can say that this is dissociation, which is evidently true, but it is not the dissociation of contradictory, conflicting terms, or terms that are kept separate by neurotic defences, as in the paranoid-schizoid position. Neither is it a contradiction between coexisting antinomic terms as in the depressive position. This dissociation is present but in a singular way: not as paranoid-schizoid contradiction, nor as depressive (ambivalent) contradiction, but as a potential conflict, present but damped down, or simply as *a non-conflict* in which everything occurs *as if nothing had happened or were happening now* (the furtive behaviour that I mentioned).

> After insisting on the analysis of all these aspects, the patient says, at a certain point, that he feels calm because I realised the importance all these events had for him; then I interpret that he makes himself calm by leaving it up to me to become conscious of these different things, but so that he can go on as if nothing were happening.

Until the moment when I introduce the theme of the session he did not have, the ambiguity is much more serious here than in other cases, because it affects the setting itself, since we are dealing with two superimposed settings that are not the same. My setting includes the assumptions that he did not go away and missed his session. His setting includes that he came and I did not admit him. This ambiguity that extends into the setting undermines the very foundation of analytic work (the setting), a problem I will not discuss at this time.[120]

With this example, I wish to point out again the characteristics of ambiguity, which I believe are different from those of the contradiction of ambivalence and from those of contradiction dissociated into its antinomic terms: the divalence of the paranoid-schizoid position.

In this case, it is not (for him) actually a question of contradictions, but of *different terms* that are all present, without having become mutually contradictory for the patient. For me, the analyst (for my more integrated ego, into which he also projects his own more integrated ego), this situation may seem bewildering, contradictory or confusing, but it is not like that for the patient, who does not experience it as contradiction or confusion, even when it is interpreted to him.

If contradiction is to become established and conflict to appear (either in the depressive or in the paranoid-schizoid position), *a discrimination has to be made* between the terms that are going to act in the contradiction (and a certain concomitant integration of the ego that 'bears' the conflict), and these terms must also correspond or pertain to the same unit, the same order, the same series or class, or the same set (good-bad, empty-full, feminine-masculine, etc.). In ambiguity, elements, behaviours or traits pertaining to different series or sets co-exist; for example: bad, empty, faeces, orality, etc. In other words, there is no discrimination of antinomic terms or of the different sets or series to which these phenomena correspond. The

120 I discussed this in 'Psicoanálisis del encuadre psicoanalítico' ['Psychoanalysis of the psychoanalytic setting'] at the APA Symposium in 1966. It corresponds to the next chapter, which I wrote at the same time as the present chapter.

ego is not discriminated from the non-ego, homosexuality from heterosexuality, body schema from external world, oral or anal from genital zones, etc. (to varying degrees, and in different ways).

Lalande relates ambiguity, amphiboly and equivocation. We will not go into this thesis because it is not very important for our theme but he does provide a definition of equivocation that is significant for us; he refers to two definitions of the word equivocation: (a) 'speaking of words or expressions: that they have various meanings'; (b) 'that can be explained in several different ways; therefore, of an uncertain nature that cannot be placed in any well defined type'.[121] I quote Lalande's definition because I consider that he points out one of the fundamental characteristics of ambiguity, which is the 'uncertain nature', that is, what is still not defined, what has not yet been discriminated, what permits the co-existence of things, situations or attitudes that for a different subject, or for the more developed ego of the same subject, are confused or dubious but are in themselves uncertain, undefined, undiscriminated and not hierarchised in types or sets.[122]

Clinically, the ambiguous subject (or someone with traits of ambiguity) may impress us as being confusing or contradictory, but the fact that this subject is able to provoke confusion or contradictory feelings in the observer does not define the characteristics of ambiguity, since these phenomena (contradiction and confusion) appear when the ambiguity is perceived by the more mature ego (the observer's or the subject's own). A variable sector of the personality of every individual remains split off from the more mature ego and constitutes the psychotic part of the personality, which is fundamentally ambiguous.[123] However, in ambiguous personalities, life has been organised around this primitive undifferentiation, while the more mature individual keeps it split off (as an agglutinated nucleus).

From the clinical perspective, we may summarise the different possibilities and identify:

121 The emphasis is mine. [The reference is to Lalande, 1953 [1946], p. 296]. Definition (a) is of the linguistic order and I therefore leave it aside. The interested reader may consult the book by S. Ullmann on this topic. (Ullmann, 1962).

122 In her study, Simone de Beauvoir says that in ambiguity 'the meaning is not fixed' (Beauvoir, 1947, p. 186). But although this author differentiates ambiguity from absurdity, she confuses ambiguity with ambivalence and with contradiction. Although they are tempting, I leave aside the studies by Sartre and Merleau-Ponty, since I wish to focus on clinical work and the hypotheses that may be derived from it, and also because it would require elaboration and a philosophical erudition that I am not sure I possess.

123 I have repeatedly pointed out the differences between splitting and schizoid division or dissociation (as I use these terms).

(1) The structure of the most primitive psychological organisation, which corresponds to primitive undifferentiation;[124]
(2) The predominant durability of this primitive structure *in the ambiguous personality* (which, as we shall see, may be organised into different types);
(3) The persistence of ambiguity in certain *personality traits*;
(4) Phenomena of ambiguity due to reactivation or regression produced in periods of social change or other kinds of change;
(5) The extreme polarisation of ambiguity: *the authoritarian personality*;
(6) The persistence of a certain amount of the primitive (ambiguous) organisation, strongly split off from a personality that has reached other levels of organisation and integration. (I have called this split-off part the agglutinated nucleus);
(7) Pathological phenomena deriving from two facts:
    (a) from the maintenance of this splitting: symbiosis, emotional blockage, negative therapeutic reaction, 'monosymptomatic' neuroses,[125] etc.;
    (b) from the breakdown or danger of breakdown of the splitting: in this pathology I include confusion, epilepsy, melancholia, mania, psychopathy, perversions and hypochondria; they may become stabilised or may be stereotyped as a regular form – for some individuals – as ego defences;
(8) Ambiguity coming to the fore due to breakdown of the splitting, which normally occurs (in our culture) in certain stages of development, typically in *adolescence*;
(9) The emergence of ambiguity in other normal phenomena, such as dreams, paradoxes, certain symptomatic acts in the field of aesthetics, etc.

Since points (6) and (7) have already been discussed in the studies on symbiosis under the headings of 'agglutinated nucleus' or 'psychotic part of the personality', I will now turn to the others listed, leaving aside points (8) and (9) for the time being.

124 This statement has been arrived at hypothetically, but various direct studies in children also seem to confirm it (Wallon: syncretism; Piaget: a-dualism), etc. In psychoanalytic works, other authors also describe this primitive undifferentiation. It would be convenient to have opinions on this from child psychoanalysts who have direct experience with infants.

125 E. Rolla (1963, 1966) studied a male patient in whom he described what he termed 'systematised phobia'. I believe that the four techniques of the paranoid-schizoid position may establish themselves as defences between the ego and the agglutinated nucleus, as I have described in my paper, 'Symbiosis: study of the psychotic part of the personality' [which forms chapter 4 of the present book], as 'monosymptomatic neuroses'. I now believe that it is preferable to adopt Rolla's terminology, but not only for the phobias, and to accept the existence of 'systematised neuroses', which must lead us to assume the existence of strong psychotic nuclei in the personality.

## Ambiguity and other phenomena

The phenomenon of syncretism, which has drawn my attention in virtue of experience gained in the psychoanalysis of psychotics, constitutes nothing other than narcissistic transference. Only the study of symbiosis and ambiguity has enabled me to re-consider and re-assess this experience and thereby better to situate and understand all these phenomena in a unified way.

Although I have defined, as one of the specific features of ambiguity, persistence or regression to an organisation characterised by syncretism, there are differences between ambiguity and participation or the syncretism of primitive undifferentiation. In the same way, I wish to describe in closer detail the difference between ambiguity, ambivalence and divalence.

As a point of departure, I will offer the example of a patient with simple schizophrenia.

> *Example C*: This young man often fights with his parents, especially his mother, whom he attacks physically. For a long time in his analysis, we worked on the problem of his fantasy of murdering his father.
>
> One morning he left the house in a great hurry, angry because the breakfast his mother had served him was cold; on these occasions, without saying a word, he would attack his mother physically, but this time he rushed out of the house. When he arrived at the bus stop, without saying a word, he hit another person who was standing in line in front of him waiting for the bus. The other person looked at him, terrified, and ran away.

In this manner, the phenomenon of syncretism appears clearly in this patient, in the sense that he hits someone who, for him, *is* his mother; in other words, there is a failure of discrimination in which different persons are, as a function of his anger, the same person, and he makes no distinction between them.

In this case we cannot strictly speak of ambiguity, but rather of syncretism or participation, since the person he attacks *is* his mother, and both this person and his mother are at the same time parts of *his* world. For us, they are two different persons, but for him they are the same person. This clearly differentiates the syncretism of the psychotic from the ambiguous personality, since in the latter different terms that are not discriminated from each other co-exist psychologically (although the syncretism subsists in the structure of each nucleus of the ego), while in the psychotic in Example C, the ego with which he operates at a given moment does not co-exist with other segments of the ego. Structurally, we have to accept a very important difference between the syncretism of the psychotic and the ambiguous personality, which is that in the latter the ego is a non-integrated ego in the sense that it exists as a 'granular' ego (fragments of the ego with different identifications that do not come into contradiction with one another), while in the psychotic the ego that is acting at a given moment without differentiating one person from another *represents the totality of the personality at that moment.* As we have seen in practice, nothing prevents that person from moving from ambiguous behaviour into psychotic behaviour, but it is also important to remember the difference between the two, not only from the phenomenological point of view but fundamentally from the perspective of the ego structure that is acting at the moment. We shall see below that syncretism is not always psychotic.

Another important difference that we need to clarify is the distinction between the ambiguous personality and the psychopathic personality, particularly given that I consider the nucleus of psychopathic acting to be an ambiguous nucleus. The difference between these two is not the same as that between the ambiguous personality and the syncretism of the psychotic, since in the psychopathic personality there is a more integrated ego that establishes and maintains a splitting from the ambiguous nucleus of the personality, that is, a splitting from the syncretic ego, so that the psychopath gets rid of this syncretic (psychotic) part of the personality with a total lack of insight into what he is doing. We need to recall the basic fact that in the psychopath splitting is not established between different segments of the same ego structure, as happens in the ambiguous personality, since in the latter the different nuclei of the ego *all have the same level of organisation (the same syncretic structure)*; in the psychopath splitting operates between two parts of the personality or two egos at *different* levels of organisation or of different structures.

The difference between ambiguity and ambivalence is rooted in the fact that although the splitting (in ambiguity) and the schizoid division (in ambivalence) operate on the same ego structure in both cases, the totality of this structure is different in each case. This is what happens, for example, in a patient who is about to enter into a marriage although he has great doubts about the stability of his future tie and who therefore decides to get married in Montevideo, so that the eventual possibility of a divorce will be an easier legal procedure.[126] The patient is facing a contradiction in such a way that, for his psychological structure, the conflict between marrying and not marrying is 'resolved' by a situation in which he makes a decision such that he retains the possibility of annulling what he does, as a function of his own doubts about contracting matrimony. That is, in ambivalence the antinomy is between discriminated terms that correspond to an ego with a greater degree of integration and a greater sense of reality than in the case of ambiguity. The difference therefore lies in the quality or the structure of the ego that intervenes. (In this example, it does not mean that the patient's 'solution' has resolved his ambivalence.)

126 [Divorce was possible in Uruguay but not in Argentina at this time.]

The similarity resides in that different behaviours or attitudes in both cases operate on the same level of ego organisation, which differentiates them from psychopathy and psychosis. However, the difference (between ambivalence and ambiguity) also lies in the difference between the ego structures involved, since in ambiguity the subjects do not recognise some behaviours as their own, whereas they do in the case of ambivalence. In other words, the degree of integration and sense of reality of the ego is totally different in ambiguity in contrast to ambivalence, as is the differentiation between the diverse terms involved.

In divalence the conflict is also played out (as in ambiguity and ambivalence) on the same level of ego structuring, but in divalence the ego is more akin to the ego of ambivalence than to the ego of ambiguity. Also, in the case of divalence, neurotic defence techniques (hysteric, phobic, obsessional, paranoid) come into play between the contradictory terms (which pertain to the same structure or level of ego organisation). Another important difference is that two terms are involved in ambivalence and divalence, while in ambiguity there may be many more.

Turning now to the analytic situation and the characteristics of the transference, we must first make clear that neurotic transference is frequently considered 'as if', meaning that the patient perceives the analyst 'as if' the analyst were the patient's mother or father or other internal objects, while also *knowing* that the analyst is none of these but is, in addition and fundamentally, a distinct person, an analyst.[127]

Because in the countertransference ambiguity may sometimes appear as fiction, the 'as if' of the analytic situation is sometimes mapped onto the phenomenon of ambiguity. Hence, M. Baranger, in her paper, 'Regresión y temporalidad en el tratamiento analítico' ['Regression and temporality in analytic treatment'] says:

> In the analytic situation the patient's adult and regressive parts must be present together, which permits the simultaneous presence of the phantasied aspects of the analyst and of his real role. We understand by ambiguity this unstable and fluid mixture of simultaneous meanings and contents that allows the mobilisation of the analytic situation.
>
> (Baranger, 1960, our translation)

Although the psychoanalytic situation may be defined as an 'as if', it is not basically an ambiguous situation, since 'the patient's adult and regressive parts' are present together; the two different terms that are in activity correspond to different levels of ego integration: an adult ego and a different

127 [This is a reference to Baranger & Baranger (1961–62), for whom 'as if' is a quality of the analytic field generally, rather than to Deutsch's (1942) concept of the 'as-if' personality which is discussed later (pp. 218ff).]

regressive ego, while in ambiguity these two terms correspond or pertain to the same structure or to the same level of ego integration.

The situation is further complicated since the 'as if' of the analytic situation may be lost, but in that case we are directly faced with a psychotic transference. However, the patient may also handle the 'as if' of the analytic situation with ambiguity, moving from one nucleus of the ego to another, in such a way that when we interpret something the patient is doing the patient answers us with another part of the ego that we are not interpreting, or vice versa. In these cases we are faced with a psychopathic use rather than with ambiguity. The differences between these latter two have been described above and will be examined again later.

We still need to clarify the 'as if' in the relation between ambiguity and hysteria, since 'as if' is a peculiar or inherent characteristic of the hysterical personality; but in hysteria, the 'as if' or the impression of a performance or fiction pertains to the nature of the phenomenon itself, while in ambiguity, the 'as if' and the fiction or performance may be a countertransference reaction but they do not belong to the nature of the phenomenon. In hysteria, the 'as if' is due to the action of two contradictory attitudes on the same level of ego organisation or structure, one of which is explicit but hints at the repressed, antinomic attitude or situation, the phenomenon itself assuming the appearance of a performance or fiction. We could say that in hysteria the performance or fiction occurs 'as if something were happening', while in ambiguity it is anyway 'as if nothing were happening'; that is, the 'as if' does not appear as a fiction but as non-commitment or evasion of commitment (furtive behaviour). The similarity is that the antinomic phenomena, both in hysteria and ambiguity, occur on the same level of ego structuring. However, the ego structure in ambiguity differs from the ego structure in hysteria, as we made clear in reference to the phenomenon of divalence in general. Also, in ambiguity either the two terms or several different terms co-exist while in hysteria one of them is repressed, indicating that a successful schizoid division must have acted previously.

## The clinical picture and structure of ambiguity

Ambiguity, as I have said, is characterised fundamentally by lack of discrimination and the co-existence of terms or attitudes or traits that are not mutually differentiated, but are not necessarily contradictory. Hence, there is no contradiction for the subject, since this has not yet come into play; that is, the schizoid division has not yet been established (or has been lost through regression). We could say that in ambiguity, the schizoid division 'chooses' the contradictory terms between and within all the different co-existing ego nuclei, arranged in series or sets.

The *ambiguous personality* is constituted by the persistence of the structure of primitive syncretic organisation, with lack of discrimination between ego and non-ego (and therefore also a lack of discrimination within the non-ego), but in a manner that configures an individuality with characteristics that are *different* from the ego of a mature subject, and which for this reason (because it is *different* rather than *missing*), I propose to call the 'syncretic ego'. This would seem to be a contradiction, since I have established, as a fundamental point, that in ambiguity (and in the glischro-caric position) there is no discrimination between ego and non-ego. However, when we express it in these terms, we are studying a particular structure in function of another that we take as the norm, so that this ego–non-ego undifferentiation constitutes *a different* type of organisation of *the personality and of reality*. I maintain that we need to study scientifically each structure of behaviour or of the personality, not only in terms of relations or opposition, taking as a measuring stick or normative term the more mature ego that has configured the sense of reality, but that we should study each structure in itself and its own organisation.[128]

Thus, the ambiguous personality is not actually lacking an ego and a sense of reality, but instead has a *different* type of ego and a *different* sense of reality. We may deduce from this that the omnipotence (for example) which characterises the ambiguous personality and primitive syncretic organisation is not a lack of sense of reality (in the conventional sense), but configures a different relation and a different handling of reality, which may even be 'successful' for the subject. In this sense, the omnipotence of primitive ambiguity is not a defence against reality as an escape from it, but a different way of structuring and handling it,[129] which does not rule out its use as a defence through regression.

The ego of the ambiguous personality shifts constantly and is *not interio-*

128 My methodological attitude has been influenced by phenomenology and some anthropological studies (Lévi-Strauss, Leenhardt, etc.). I may cite the work by Ferenczi, 'Estadios en el desarrollo del sentido de la realidad' ['Stages in the development of the sense of reality'] (Ferenczi, 1913) as an approximate antecedent. On this subject, see also the book by H. Werner (1940). When I describe the different forms of self-organisation of the ambiguous personality *I am describing a typology and not necessarily a pathology*; for these reasons I do not include here some disturbances that are closely related to ambiguity, such as schizophrenia, schizoidia and borderline disorder. For the same reason I do not give prominence to identity deficit in the study of ambiguity, although I am interested in studying it in its own right with its own vicissitudes and pathology.

129 I believe that in this sense we can understand the problem formulated by Arnaldo Rascovsky in some scientific meetings, of how the psychopath (to whom we attribute an important lack of sense of reality) is able to get along, sometimes successfully. There is no one type of identity or one type of sense of reality, to which we may add that each individual 'constructs' his own reality (it would be better to say his own 'Umwelt', to

*rised* as a defined or 'crystallised' ego. It is 'superimposed', fused (with the objects) and the ambiguous subject may assent to and rapidly appropriate the different ideas or attitudes of diverse objects, without either contradiction or confusion emerging for the subject. In any case, what is interiorised is not an ego but a fusion of ego and non-ego.

> *Example D*: A patient with great ambiguity said in a session, when shown the different nuclei of identity he used, that this reminded him of the story of the drunk who is embracing a lamppost. When a policeman comes along and asks him what he's doing, the drunk says that many houses are passing by in front of him and he is holding onto the lamppost and waiting for his house to come by so he can go in.

By this he means that he is like the drunk, who goes through life taking different roles (different houses), waiting for *his house, his identity* to arrive at last so that he can move into it. However, since this identity depends on pure contingency[130] it is not a project that the subject is able to elaborate and finish by himself.

In ambiguity individuals exist without really being;[131] in other words, we could say that they [have] *existence* but do not *experience*;[132] they are 'in themselves' but not 'for themselves';[133] that is, they exist as pure contingency in the sense that they see themselves, in everything they are and everything they have, as a result of 'luck', 'chance' or 'happenstance' and feel that they have done nothing for themselves. They are missing authentic satisfaction for what they are or have; but 'remaining' in something is 'to lose freedom', which does make them feel the contingency (very frequent complaints and fears come up about this in the course of the analysis). Not feeling that their achievements are their own corresponds to their reality, to their

use a term by V. Uexküll). What we accept as the sense of reality – which we take as a standard or norm is, after all, only another 'Umwelt', culturally conditioned and more accepted as normal, standard or ideal, but as relative as the others (which are also culturally conditioned). For this reason, the more integrated ego 'with a sense of reality' I call the *conventional ego*.

130 Contingency refers to something that may or may not occur; but whether it occurs or not depends not on the subject but on other factors that are not the subject. 'Metaphysically, the contingent entity has been considered an entity that is not in itself but in another' (Ferrater Mora). What I consider important to underscore in my use of this term is that the attributes of being are subordinated to the non-subject, but in this case the non-subject is not discriminated from the subject. [The citation is from Ferrater Mora (1941, p. 349).]

131 [*. . . se existe y no se es . . .*]

132 [*vivencia*: the Spanish word invented by Ortega y Gasset to translate the German *Erlebnis*]

133 [*. . . se es 'en sí' y no 'para sí' . . .* : the contrast made by Sartre between *être-en-soi* and *être-pour-soi*. See following footnote.]

psychological organisation, since it is – as M. Baranger says – 'a kaleidoscope of characters'.

They also have a deficiency in the use of repression and anxiety as alarm signals, and they react directly with panic. It may be considered a deficiency of identity compared to the identity of the mature or conventional ego, but it is actually *a different type* of identity. The ambiguous personality is as empty of interiority as it is of exteriority (or has a different kind of interiority and exteriority); they give us the impression (and this addresses countertransference experiences) of furtive behaviour, inauthenticity, lack of autonomy, naivety, vagueness, disorientation, oscillation, inconclusiveness, inconsistency, changeability, and sometimes of being indecisive and vacillating. We could say that ambiguity has a real *polyvalence* or *proteiform character.*

Ambiguous subjects are perfect partners for psychopaths, since they function with primary identification and quickly assume the role that the psychopath has them take; they have an absence of contradiction, great permeability or mimetism, they switch easily in taking roles or in expressing behaviour; their identity is fundamentally a group identity rather than individual, they have a strong dependence on objects and events, which may change or alternate; we could say that they themselves are objects or events like any other; another trait that I describe below is their *mentalisation* rather than thought. There is a facile transition or oscillation in the roles they assume or in their behaviour, and hence we could define it with the formula that in them 'anything can be anything'. We could also say that the mature identity (or conventional ego) is characterised by the organisation of projects, while the identity of ambiguous subjects is characterised by their absence, by pure contingency or by 'fictitiousness',[134] that is, great permeability for taking different roles, which produces the impression of dispersion, temporariness or an indefinite postponement of decisions. What they do, have and are does not correspond to or belong to them. They seem to live with indefinite and eternal time ahead of them.

*Example E:* This patient talks about his intention to get cured and finish his analysis and he expands on this theme; at another moment he tells me that

134 As I mentioned, I do not wish to discuss the Sartrian conception of ambiguity and 'in itself' and 'for itself', but I do at least want to point out that the translation of the term *facticité* used or employed by Sartre was questioned (in a personal discussion) by W. Baranger, who considers that it should not be translated as 'factic' [*fáctico*] but as 'fictitious' [*ficticidad*]. In any case, what I am interested in pointing out is that my terminology pertains to clinical issues rather than to the Sartrian conception. [Further complications arise in translating *fáctico*, and *facticidad* into English. To preserve the author's intended connotation of pure contingency we translate these terms as 'factic' and 'facticity' respectively, in contrast with *ficticidad* which we translate as 'fictitiousness'.]

> he is thinking of applying for a scholarship to go to Spain to study at the end of the year, since he is related to the consul, and he explains this family connection to me. Then he tells me about his engagement and his desire to get married before leaving and to have children soon. Then he begins to say that he is not sure that he loves his fiancée and that he should break off with her.
>
> When he is shown the incompatibility of all these aspirations, he says yes, that he recognises that they are incompatible, but that he wants it all.

His engagement, his analysis, his work and his entire life are permeated by the same ambiguity: he has and doesn't have a fiancée, he's going to marry her and he's going to leave her, etc., but he does not experience this as contradictory, although he can recognise that they are incompatible when this is interpreted. But for him, this incompatibility is also pure contingency.

I wish to add that this patient is in no way clinically psychotic; in spite of his age (32), he seems to have the dispersion of an adolescent (and psychologically that is what he is). Together with a (reactive) independence, he continues to be quite attached to his parents; he has severe sexual taboos but also periods of sexual promiscuity. He can be tyrannical and also very submissive. All this he experiences without contradiction and without the anxiety of contradiction. The anxiety arises when he sometimes wants something 'more decidedly' (that is, without ambiguity) and does not get it (because of his own ambiguity). The absence of contradiction is possible because each attitude or intention is a *function of a different segment of the ego.* We observe what seems to be dissociation, but it is not this in the sense of the dissociation of the paranoid-schizoid position. In the latter, aside from other differences already described, a defence is installed between the dissociated terms because they are contradictory for the subject, and the loss of this defence mechanism produces anxiety, none of which occurs in ambiguity. This also differentiates (in some of the cases cited) ambiguity from repression (for example), since in the latter, what is dissociated is not conscious and when it is interpreted correctly, anxiety is produced because the contradiction is experienced. As we may easily see, it is also different from obsessional undoing.

> *Example F:* This patient very often makes appointments with different persons for the same hour on the same day and if, at some point, both persons come to fetch her, she lets 'chance' resolve it and takes no responsibility for the situation. ('Chance' as contingency).

As we see, here it is not a question of two appointments (behaviours or attitudes) being contradictory, but rather essentially exclusive or incompatible in time.[135] However, since the patient has not yet discriminated between them, they are not mutually exclusive for her.

In this patient's sessions there also appear incompatible behaviours, *explicit and co-existing*, whereas in repression (in which the terms are *antinomic or contradictory* terms, and not different or discriminated, as in ambiguity), one of the terms of the contradiction *is not explicit but latent* or unconscious, just as in displacement or projection. Neurotic techniques (hysteric, phobic, obsessional, paranoid) and their corresponding mechanisms (conversion, displacement, undoing, projection) can only act on opposite or contradictory terms, *discriminated* by the dissociation of the paranoid-schizoid position.[136]

ψ

There are here in the syncretic personality some highly important problems which, however, I cannot dwell on in detail, but only indicate.

One is the problem of the management of time, which I mentioned, as well as the management of space. In both cases we observe that there is a lack of abstraction of them and a management of time and space in themselves,[137] disconnected from things, events, functions and phenomena, so that when they refer to time and space they need to refer to and orient themselves through these other factors. Although the theoretical grounding is different, J. Mom describes this condition in his contribution to the Symposium on the work of Melanie Klein, in a patient who used 'indirect means' to enable her to identify herself and orient herself in time and space. He offers the following fragment as an example, which is also valid for what I am interested in pointing out at the moment. The patient said, 'Oh, yes, now I remember, because Mr X was talking to Mrs Y and Mrs. Y was sitting in that place, etc. Yes, yes! I must have been there!'[138]

The other important problem connected to all this and characteristic of the syncretic ego is the problem that these persons seem unable to recognise individualised entities but only functions; and functions in which the same subject recognises neither himself nor others as an entity. This could be exemplified succinctly by a patient whose treatment I supervised (the patient in Chapter 6 who [we shall see later] addressed his analyst in the

135 One of the characteristics of participation (syncretism) is undifferentiation of time, at least as assimilated by the 'conventional ego'. If the *entire* personality is in the glischro-caric position, it is a case of simple schizophrenia.

136 Except in the case of 'systematised neuroses' in which these techniques keep the agglutinated nucleus split off from the ego.

137 [. . . *del tiempo y del espacio en sí mismos* . . . : the Spanish expressions are the same as those standardly used to translate Kant's notions of objective space and time, *Raum an sich* and *Zeit an sich*.]

138 [Mom, J (1962), p. 32]

familiar form). When the treatment had advanced much further, in a situation when the analyst had to give a series of lectures in a place this patient frequented, the analyst was countertransferentially worried whether the patient knew about it or not, since it did not appear in the material he contributed. At one point the analyst introduced the subject and the patient reacted very violently, feeling invaded and not respected in the still poor organisation of his identity and interiority. However, after this initial situation has been sufficiently analysed, the patient later points out that he cannot bear to think that his analyst could speak anywhere except in the session, and about things that had nothing to do with him, and that he had decided not to attend that course since

> I know you when you are speaking about me and if I make an effort to think that you can speak outside, I have the idea that you are also going to talk about me, you're going to talk about me. Besides, it's very hard for me that you can be my teacher or professor. You are not going to stop being my analyst.

He later added that he couldn't conceive of or accept that he might hear his analyst speak in a situation where he wouldn't be paying to hear him speak, as occurs in his sessions.

Here, I believe that we see clearly how analyst and patient are not two differentiated entities. Instead, identity is given by a structure based fundamentally on functions and relations and not on entities that establish these relations or functions. Genetically, in development, we know that the appearance of identity of functions is prior to identity of entities, of subjects or, in general, of objects; anthropology has also contributed elements that improve our knowledge of this particular structure of identity, time and space.

Without much commentary, since it is eloquent in itself, I reproduce a graphic representation by Leenhardt.

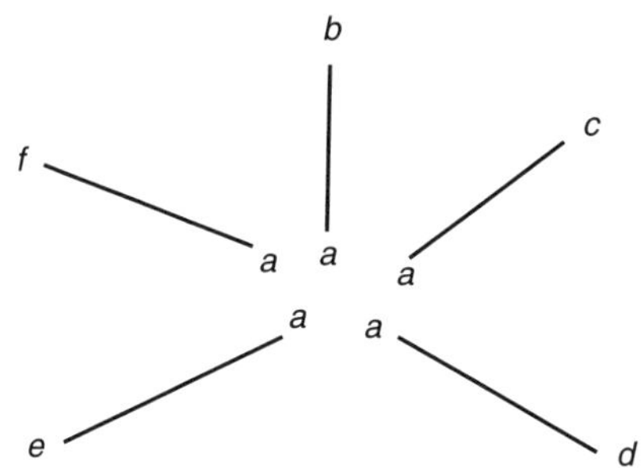


Reproduced by permission from Maurice Leenhardt (1979 [1947]), *Do kamo: person and myth in the Melanesian world*. Chicago: University of Chicago Press. © 1979 by The University of Chicago

This is Leenhardt's representation of the structure of the person in the Melanesian world. He says that the Melanesian

> is unaware of his body, which is only his support. He knows himself only by the relationships he maintains with others. He exists only insofar as he acts his role in the course of his relationships. He is situated only with respect to them. If we try to draw this, we cannot use a dot marked 'self' (*ego*), but must make a number of lines to mark relationships: *ab*, *ac*, *ad*, *ae*, *af*, and so forth. The lines correspond to him and his father, him and his uncle, him and his wife, him and his cross-cousin, him and his clan, and so forth. In the midst of these rays, an empty space is circumscribed by the *a*'s denoting the points of departure for relationships. These *a*'s are replicas of his body. The empty space is him, and this is what is named.
>
> (Leenhardt, 1979 [1947], p. 153)

This graph by Leenhardt is totally applicable to the syncretic ego. I leave aside other similarities and explanations related to anthropological contributions, mainly since I wish to focus on clinical issues and secondarily, because I plan to develop that subject more extensively in another publication.

## The omnipotence of the 'syncretic ego'

Omnipotence is a feature of all the clinical manifestations of ambiguity; however, it is not omnipotent *control* of reality, but rather it pertains to the syncretic organization as one of its qualities or characteristics. In the ambiguous personality, omnipotence is a way of living and of structuring the world, and not, basically, a way of avoiding it. It is in itself a specific organisation of the ego-world. The 'controlling' character of omnipotence derives, again, from privileging the conventional sense of reality and judging omnipotence in relation to it. Omnipotence (which is always a property of ambiguity) may certainly appear as a consequence of regression to the glischro-caric position, as a defence against a highly persecutory reality. However, I am here discussing not regression but rather the persistence of ambiguity. Nonetheless, even in regression, it is a question of the installation of a *different* structure of the ego and reality; and in this way *the* 'sense of reality' may also be categorised as control of reality, by the same principle of regarding control as a function of omnipotence.

Also, and in this way, omnipotence (in the ambiguous personality) is not the result of a denial of reality nor is denial of reality a result of omnipotence. Denial of reality does not exist where undifferentiation has persisted. I consider that in this chapter and others, we have committed a kind of 'adultomorphism' or 'normalmorphism'. I repeat: ambiguity is not *essentially* a deficit of identity;

it is a *different* identity and a *different* sense of reality (which may or may not be judged to be deficient with respect to *the* identity).[139]

M. Baranger says, in her article, 'Bad faith, identity and omnipotence':

> It should not surprise us, then, that the analysands who have bad faith as a life style are so difficult to apprehend. They are as slippery as Proteus in Greek mythology. According to legend this seagod, in charge of Poseidon's herds of seals (his ambiguity is already present in his being a shepherd of amphibious creatures), enjoyed omnipotent knowledge of the future, but was unwilling to utter prophecies. To avoid being questioned, he assumed different shapes and transformed himself into any animal or element, such as water or fire. The legend does not account for Proteus' flight. One may conclude that through his metamorphosis he is protecting his omnipotence.
>
> (Baranger, 1963, p. 196)

Omnipotence is maintained precisely by 'fictitiousness': by the potential for 'jumping' from one role to another, that is, by means of metamorphosis, which is what keeps the subject from acquiring a *different* organisation of the ego and reality. It is very much like the violinist in a certain story, who always carried his violin inside its case wherever he went and was considered and considered himself a great violinist, but never played the instrument. In other words, *he is* a great violinist (he preserves his omnipotent, narcissistic image), as long as he does not confront a different reality: as long as he does not play the violin.

This situation or behaviour, which we observe quite frequently in our patients and in everyday life, makes the subject feel capable of a certain action or role as long as it is never taken. An example is a similar situation occupied by those politicians who, while in opposition, always appear to be and present themselves as being omnipotent to solve economic and social problems but who actually wish they will never be in a position to really have to face them, and who if they do get into that position fail spectacularly.

ψ

139 Studies by Lévi-Strauss show that the primitive person is in no way 'a-logical', but has *a different* logic; and among its other qualities, it implies no failure in mastering reality. Clinical work confirms these facts, since, for example, psychopaths and children are not absurd or unintelligent: they have *different* thinking, a different logic and a different intelligence. In this sense, I wonder whether we should not re-consider the 'properties' of the unconscious: a-logical, a-temporal, etc. Hartmann stated that there are many ways to adapt to reality, and we need to study and separate the different modes of adaptation. (Hartmann, 1958 [1939], pp. 22–37).

M. Baranger, referring also to Proteus, says: 'Thus, as in the Proteus myth, he cannot simply refuse to answer his interlocutor and has to dodge him by metamorphosis. If the interlocutor is not discouraged and keeps on asking, Proteus has to give in and answer.' (Baranger, 1963, p. 198).

I think that what actually occurs, both in the myth of Proteus and in the ambiguous personality, is that the metamorphosis (the transition to a different ego nucleus) is not used to avoid or not answer, but because he is really unable to answer; he is able neither to give a reply nor to face a different reality that will show him that he has no omnipotence and that he has no omnipotent possibility of knowing the future, as in the case of Proteus.

This author also says: 'bad faith precludes the intrusion of . . . reality . . .' (Baranger, 1963, p. 199). In the case of ambiguity, intrusion of *the* reality is prevented because they already have a reality that is organised at the level of what they are capable of.[140]

The omnipotence of the 'syncretic ego' is, briefly, a quality that derives from the ego-world structure itself: in which there is a basic non-discrimination between ego and non-ego and between ego and superego. This is not, at first, a way to avoid reality but a way to organise it and a way to contact it. Neither 'fictitiousness' nor metamorphosis creates the omnipotence: they only preserve it.

*Example G:* A patient has reached what is for him a very important goal and he comes to the session and tells me about it; but in the telling, a moment arrives when he says he feels strangely quite burdened and disgusted. Then I interpret that this burdened feeling arises because he feels his achievement is a destructive triumph over others and, at this moment, over me; then he associates that he thought that having achieved this success he had come to the termination of his analysis and that he had to separate from me and that, although he does not believe it, he had fantasised it.

After that, he refers to the political situation in the country and says that many important things may occur; I tell him that what he is referring to is

140 We have grounds for thinking that at each level of ego organisation or structure the reality principle and the pleasure principle function *at the same time*. For Hartmann, 'The requirements for the survival of the species can take a form, in the mental development of man, which may be independent from the pleasure principle – and from a reality principle that is secondarily derived from it – and can even regulate the possibilities of pleasure gain.' He immediately adds that: 'We have before us a relationship to the external world which, as an independent factor, regulates certain prerequisites of the application of the pleasure principle. Thus we arrive at a conception in which relations to reality are determined by a *reality principle in the broader* and a *reality principle in the narrower sense*. . . . The reality principle in the broader sense would historically precede and hierarchically outrank the pleasure principle.' (Hartmann, 1958 [1939], pp. 43–44).

that if he orients himself with a greater sense of reality and with a more real image of himself and of me, many important things may happen that would burden him greatly.

The session continues with the analysis of the fact that what he feels is the most burdensome situation produced by his triumph is that he has to leave behind his omnipotence, his self-idealised image and an idealised image of me, which means that this is destroyed and he needs to position himself in a reality that weighs him down when he loses his idealised world.

He then says that he had opportunities in the last few days to establish relationships with many very pretty women who were very accessible from the sexual angle, but that he does not know why he did not do so, that he thought that they must smell bad and associated that until recently he had never wanted to look at a woman's genitals because he felt disgusted.

I tell him that what disgusts him is his penetration of reality and that reality may penetrate him, and that this disgust is produced because of having to incorporate a different reality that breaks with the idealisation he had of himself and of me; that now he is quite afraid to put himself to the test and to fail in something that he has wanted and that means so much to him.

In this example I want to point out that what he experiences as a step forward and as a triumph *is converted into destruction of his omnipotent world* (his syncretism), and that this destruction results from incorporating or being penetrated by the external world, which is to him sickening, indigestible or unabsorbable, because there is in him a fusion between orality, the external world, genitals, the contents of the intestines, and the primal scene.

ψ

If we accept primary undifferentiation, the statement that the first psychological mechanism is projection (as postulated by Melanie Klein) is also placed in doubt, and the same applies to projective-introjective identification. It is a question of primary identification (Fairbairn);[141] both projection-introjection,

141 Fairbairn says in this regard: 'I employ the term "primary identification" here to signify the cathexis of an object which has not yet been differentiated (or has been only partly differentiated) from himself by the cathecting subject. This process differs, of course, from the process ordinarily described as "identification", *viz.* an emotionally determined tendency to treat a differentiated (or partly differentiated) object as if it were not differentiated, when it is cathected. The latter process should properly be described as "secondary identification".' (Fairbairn, 1952, p. 145. n.).

More than a few authors have had difficulty in accepting the existence of introjection-projection in the earliest phases, when there is still no difference or discrimination between what is internal and external (S. H. Foulkes; E. Jacobson; R. Freeman.). Thus,

and massive projective-introjective identification appear as phenomena of a more integrated ego (although still in its earliest forms) which uses them to 'manage' ambiguity by keeping it split. Whether projection-introjection leads to identification depends not on the mechanism in itself but on what is projected-introjected; whenever identification appears, what is projected-introjected is ambiguous (not discriminated).

For all these reasons, as I have already said, in order to define the ambiguous personality in terms not of what it is lacking but of what it is, I propose the term 'syncretic ego'.

The 'syncretic ego' is characterised by lack of discrimination; in it, there has been no introjective-projective identification, as I illustrated briefly in example C; however, syncretism is not always a question of a psychosis. For example, a patient begins his first session of analysis and the relation established from the first moment corresponds to a narcissistic transference. The patient had been treated for several years by a female psychoanalyst, and when he changes to a male psychoanalyst the patient totally superimposes this change of analyst onto a very intense emotional situation he experienced when his parents, separated in his infancy, and years later (during which he did not see his father) began to live together again, were reconciled, and for several weeks he was waiting for the moment when he would meet his father. This is neither projection nor projective identification, since on the basis of a feature common to both situations (the meeting with an unknown father-analyst arranged in both cases by the mother-analyst), the patient's ego begins to function on a level lacking in discrimination between past and present.

The phenomenon of participation does not inevitably require the hypothesis of projective-introjective identification; instead, participation consists in the mobilisation and actualisation of levels of the personality that function directly with that structure. Having to accept, as we are in the habit of doing, the existence of projective-introjective identification in all cases, requires that we consider each subject a 'closed system' that communicates with other human beings through diverse channels; whereas, accepting participation as an originary phenomenon implies the hypothesis that human beings begin or start out from an organisation that is an 'open system',

Freeman says that primary identification is not based on introjection, since it is a 'developmental phase antedating the ego and the boundary separating the self from objects.' (Freeman, 1959, p. 205).

Greenacre recalls that for Hartmann, Kris and Lowenstein, the ego and the id emerge from a state of undifferentiation and not, as Freud postulated, that the ego is differentiated out of the id. Greenacre also differentiates the primary identification pertaining to a state of incomplete undifferentiation between the ego and the object, as quite different from identification 'as we understand it after the establishment of the ego'. (Greenacre, 1952, p. 582).

gradually becoming individualised and personified. In this example,[142] there is a mobilisation and actualisation of the levels of participation.

This does not discount the existence of projective-introjective identification, but these are 'mechanisms' at the service of the more integrated ego for handling the psychotic part of the personality, whereas in this example, as in many other cases, it is immediately a question of the coming into play – in the first place – of a different level of organisation, which corresponds to what I term the 'syncretic ego'.

In order to show the difference more clearly, I offer two examples of identification: one projective and the other introjective.

> *Example H:* A patient says that his girlfriend is ill, has a fever, and has cystitis. He goes on associating and realises that the date of her menstruation this month has passed and he begins to fear that his girlfriend might be pregnant and that the cystitis might be a symptom of this pregnancy.
>
> I interpret at that moment that he is very upset and under a lot of pressure, because although on the one hand he is worried about the pregnancy, on the other hand he is afraid that his girlfriend might have to have an abortion and he feels under a lot of pressure about facing both a pregnancy and an abortion.
>
> The patient confirms that he has thought with terror about the possibility of an abortion; then he is silent a moment and says that he has a very urgent need to urinate that is becoming unbearable, that he is wanting the analytic hour to end so that he can leave and urinate.
>
> The introjective identification is in his feeling that his girlfriend's pregnancy and cystitis (polyuria and urination urgency) are his own.

This patient has a very passive personality, whose docility was repeatedly analysed and interpreted as concealing his greed; he is docile in order to induce others to give him advice, a way of taking something in a passive way, which allows him to receive without feeling guilty (since they 'give it to him' and it is not he who is stealing or sucking it).

One day he says that his girlfriend is very good and docile, and that once he realised that, he started to reject her and cannot bear her, and he fantasises or plans to break off the relationship with her.

In this case, it is projective identification: the patient's ego knows nothing of his own docility and also rejects it in the girlfriend because of what this docility means and contains; the patient's more integrated ego establishes a split from the levels of participation. In this example, the syncretic ego (the levels of participation) does not come into play in the first place but has been split off, while the more integrated ego has used projective identification to 'free itself' of them.

142 [*i.e.* the patient discussed in the preceding paragraph]

I simply make a note of this problem, which obviously requires deeper discussion. I wish to add only that the syncretism of a psychotic differs from that of a non-psychotic only in the easy reversibility of the latter. In themselves, considering each on its own, there is no difference between them.

## Transitional phenomena

When this 'syncretic ego' (or its 'fictitiousness') begins to change in the direction of a different degree of identity or personification, transitional phenomena emerge, such as the experience of emptiness ('spleen' or 'huff'), doubt and desperate anxiety for an object 'to fill them' and 'give meaning to their existence'. What they are actually seeking is a stable or 'good' symbiotic (syncretic) relationship that will allow them to develop their personality.[143]

The expression 'what do I know'[144] is frequent, as occurs in the following example, in which a first outline of 'self' or interiorisation appears, but as a void or lack *of* . . .

*Example I:* This is an interview by a student and the interviewee is a young woman 23 years old. The interview was clearly established as such, but at the outset, the interviewee is *puzzled* because she thought she would be tested. Then she says:

'I took the wrong street . . . I was walking . . . and I saw a street that had a number. You had said November 12th Street and I saw something similar . . . *what do I know* . . . it was a different number in a different month . . . yes . . . February 3rd . . . *I believe* . . . The question is, I couldn't find the exact number but I went into the one I thought looked most like it . . . I went up to the second floor, I rang the bell. A fat old lady, a German, opened the door and gave me an odd look. Who knows what she was thinking to herself. I asked her for A. and she answered, "There's no A. living here", and she closed the door on me. She consulted somebody inside, *I don't know*. Isn't that amazing! Afterwards I looked at the street better and realised that I was mistaken. *Not bad, huh?*'

She takes a cigarette from a pack on the desk (belonging to the interviewer) saying: 'Excuse me'. She smokes in silence. She points to a

143 This emptiness and the consequent anguished search for objects may lead to sexual promiscuity, in which case the genitals are used to fill a void that is never filled and the promiscuity is compulsive (like masturbation). Other times, instead of sexual promiscuity, there may be bulimia or other phenomena with an equivalent meaning.

144 ['*Qué se yo*' is a typical idiom of the *porteños*, the European immigrants in Buenos Aires and Montevideo.]

round, tall ashtray and says, 'It makes you want to fill it up . . . Yeah? Well, what's this about? It's different having to talk about my things, not like tests . . . I don't know . . . it's not the same . . . Well, you see everything with them too, right?. . . but you know what you're saying.'

Then she speaks about being unable to study or take exams. In an [oral] exam, 'if the professor thinks that something I say is wrong, well, I know that after that I'm going to say all the rest wrong . . . That always happens to me.'

Then she talks about her family, that 'they don't understand her' and her wish to break away.

'Besides, it doesn't matter to them if I leave them. What does it matter to them for me to leave? They don't need me; they can carry on just the same. But I without them, what can I do? I don't know, I have the feeling that with me gone nothing will happen to them, but without them I can't exist.' 'I haven't got anything. What will I do without them? I don't know, without them *I could die*. It's as if *I had nothing*. I depend on them for everything. Besides, I can't do anything. Sometimes I argue, but only to *take the opposite view*. I don't know, when I speak, for example, with Communists, well I give my opinion, I say something, but deep down nothing matters to me; it's as if it doesn't reach me. I can be against someone, or not agree with them . . . or the same with rightism (she adds immediately), well, no, with rightism not so much, that bothers me more . . . Well, but the question is that I can be against it just to be contrary . . . I don't know if you understand me: *to take the opposite view and not to be in favour of it*, do you see? The same happens to me with my problems. Sometimes I wonder whether they are problems or not. Before, I knew what problems I had, what they were like, what was happening to me. But now I don't, now I don't know, well, whether they are or aren't problems, what a problem is, what my problems are like, what problems they are. And it's much worse because I think I'm getting used to it, do you see? I think that at least *before I knew, but now I'm in doubt* . . . and I believe it must be because I'm getting used to it. What do you think? Tell me if you think I have problems, if they're serious . . . *what should I do?*' Without waiting for an answer, she goes on:

'Well, first the one about *activity*. The one about doing things, doing something. I feel that nothing interests me. Absolutely. *As if I couldn't move*. I would like to do something for the pleasure of doing it . . . something like a vocation for doing something. But nothing matters to me. Not even going out . . . That is, it's not only doing things, but also going out: recreation, don't you see?, doesn't matter to me either. I never feel like moving from where I am. When I'm at home I don't want to move, I want to stay there, and when I go out I don't want to return. *I always want to stay where I am. Not to change*. I can't change. When I wake up in the morning I want to go on sleeping. (Silence) I don't know; I would like something that would let me think, when I wake up, that I feel like doing it; but nothing. *I can never be firm about anything. Everything is always the same to me.'*

ψ

At first, we notice that the interviewee agrees to the interview but still thinks that it is a test, so that when she has to face the interview, puzzlement appears; we see a typical ambiguity: she knows that it is an interview, but she came for a test.

Then she becomes disoriented, she heard the name of the street as 'November 12$^{th}$', but in reality she did not hear it, because for her it is not differentiated from a different number and a different street; there is spatial disorientation and a lack of discrimination, which is also an expression of her ambiguity.

She shows us that only *after acting* can she recognise that she made a mistake, rectify her behaviour and remember correctly.[145]

Another aspect of her ambiguity appears in the frequent 'I don't know' and in phrases that end with the expression: 'Not bad, huh?'

When she sees the ashtray and says: 'It makes you want to fill it up ... right?', she is talking about herself: that she is as empty as the ashtray and is expressing her wish to be filled up with contents and with feelings: with herself. Her need is to be filled up by others, and this is why she prefers the test: in order not to find out what she will say and what is happening to her. She is seeking to be filled up and needs someone else to tell her the meaning of what she does, but at the same time she avoids being active herself (she prefers a test) or taking responsibility for what she wants (because she also does not want it).

When she talks about the exam and her attitude toward the professor, she is describing her mimicry: the rapid installation of syncretism with a depositary from whom she is not differentiated at that moment.

When she refers to her family and says that they do not understand her, she is expressing her own feeling of not understanding herself. In all the references to her family, she shows a dependence and a tendency to break it off externally; she proposes to solve her psychological problem through actions, and she tries to solve her psychological dependence by leaving, but cannot because she has a group identity. She clearly feels that if she separated from her family and left, she would destroy herself ('without them I could die'). Then, when she speaks about the attitudes that she assumes in her arguments, we see how '*being against' is being someone* and in this way also she resists or opposes her syncretism. It is the typical adolescent attitude, which

145 Lily S. Bleger has pointed out that acting and perversion are not only 'discharges' but also lead to the possibility of learning.

may be defined as the 'identity of being against it'.[146] Experience does not reach them: is not internalised or interiorised as the meaning of their actions. However, through action they may sometimes rectify it (after having taken the wrong street). Then, we see her ambiguity and the rupture of her precarious former identity (her group identity) when she says that she does not know whether what she has now are or are not problems, or what her problems are like and what problems they are, and that she used to know but now she has doubts.

Her dependence is also evident when she ends the next sentence by addressing the interviewer and saying, 'What should I do?'.

Afterwards, she says that she feels as if she couldn't move, that is, that if she 'moves' (psychologically) her ambiguity re-emerges: when she says that she wants to change but does not want to change. This is because in order to change she would have to go through confusion and contradictions that she can neither tolerate nor bear. For this reason, she waits for everything to come from contingency.

There is a lack of identity; but not only a lack, it is also the 'existence of . . .', the existence of a syncretic identity (or ego) that is now in crisis'. But this is a blocked crisis, which does not erupt completely since this would provoke disorganisation, confusion and contradiction. In order to resolve this symbiotic situation and its ambiguity, she needs the backing of a secure symbiotic relationship: that is to say, a frame to give her the security to face (with a supplementary ego) the confusion and contradictions that would appear if she tried to resolve her ambiguity, her symbiosis. As I said on several occasions, in order to resolve the symbiosis there is a need, paradoxically, for a good symbiotic relationship; in other words, the symbiosis can only be resolved within a satisfactory symbiotic relationship that provides security, and not within a symbiotic relationship that offers insecurity, either because it is precarious or absent, or because it is asphyxiating or claustrophobic.

ψ

Another typical transitional phenomenon (at the outset or with the setting-in of a period of rupture of ambiguity) is what we could call the '*phenomenon of manicheism*', which consists in the extreme polarisation that individuals sometimes suffer in the form of an unsolvable dilemma in which they struggle with very distressing reactions. Of course, these transitional phenomena, as we termed them in the sub-title of this section, may not be transitory and may instead become installed permanently or re-appear for very long periods.

146 A student leader, as soon as he arrived at meetings, used to 'joke' by saying: 'I don't know what the issue is, but I'm against it', and in so doing he acquired an identity, overcoming his ambiguity. Here, I touch on a problem that I have mentioned but have decided not to examine here: the relation between jokes and ambiguity [see p. 250].

> *Example J:* As an example of manicheism, we recall a patient who keeps up two simultaneous and stable relationships as 'flirtations' and cannot decide for either of the two. Thus, he says that A. doesn't like to dress well and he therefore sees her as a wretch; but he sees B., who likes to dress very well, like a 'queen'; that A. isn't sporty and can't bear the sun or the outdoors and this 'makes him angry', but B., who is quite the opposite of A. in this sense, also irritates him because she impresses him as being a narcissist.

What interests me in this brief example is to illustrate the phenomenon of manicheism, since the ambiguity is polarised in two mutually exclusive extremes. However, it is not a contradiction or opposition of two antinomic terms, as occurs in schizoid division, but the opposition of two aspects *with which he is in conflict, in - or inside – each separately*. He tries to distribute his ambiguity among depositaries because he cannot tolerate his ambiguity or the discrimination of this ambiguity inside himself. Therefore, the manicheism resides in an opposition that does not counterpose two antinomic terms that form parts of a single unit but rather *different terms* containing undiscriminated contradictory terms *in each of them*.

## Conflict and dilemma

K. Lewin described three types of conflict. One is 'approach-approach' or 'positive-positive'; in it, the subject is 'between two positive valences of approximately equal strength'; it is a 'Buridan's ass' conflict. Although Lewin states that its solution is relatively easy, he says that in some cases it may lead to 'an oscillation between two attractions'. The second basic type of conflict 'occurs when the individual finds himself between two approximately equal negative valences'. The third type of conflict arises 'when both positive and negative valences are in the same place'. (Lewin, 1935, p. 123).

The 'approach-avoidance' conflict is the one that has been most studied in the psychoanalytic literature since Freud. However, we include the other two types of conflict in it, in spite of essential differences that we need to clarify, which is now my intention.

The cases that K. Lewin describes as 'positive-positive' and 'negative-negative' conflicts are actually phenomena of manicheism but which appear as conflicts even though they are not, strictly speaking. In the 'positive-positive' case, the subject wants two mutually exclusive things, but he thereby maintains ambiguity since on closer examination we find that he has conflicts of approach and avoidance with each of the two mutually exclusive things that he desires. The same is true of the 'avoidance-avoidance' conflict. It is the case, for example, of the student who for years could not decide whether to study medicine or engineering, which seems to be a conflict of 'approach-approach', in K. Lewin's terms. However, when we investigate it more closely we see that he has the same amount of conflict with studying medicine as he does with studying engineering, is afraid to fail and makes no decision for either of the two: in other words, there is no decision in favour of one or the other, taken separately. Here, what appears to be a conflict actually conceals a situation of ambiguity towards each one of the two objects, which appears to be exclusively one of approach ... In the case of 'avoidance-avoidance' conflict, the subject needs to decide between two things that he is avoiding, but if we look more deeply we also observe that there is approach and avoidance in relation to each of them, but maintained as an ambiguity that cannot be resolved because the terms are not defined but instead polarised manicheistically.

Manicheism is the situation posed by *dilemmas*, which conceal situations of deep ambiguity, unlike the conflict in which two contradictory, antinomic tendencies confront each other *at the same time and in relation to the same object* (schizoid division derives from the latter).

We described these transitional phenomena in the former case as the 'phenomenon of emptiness' and in the latter as the 'phenomenon of manicheism'. They are not always pathological situation in themselves, but may be transitional phenomena through which ambiguity may be resolved or may progress: it may discriminate, moving from syncretism and the glischro-caric position into the paranoid-schizoid position. In any case, the pathology resides or could reside in the persistence or stereotyping of manicheism (dilemma) with no true solution of the ambiguity that is managed or controlled in these attitudes or behaviours.

We may now add (in passing) that when there is a shift from one nucleus of identity to another in the fictitious ego (or in the factic ego), there may appear the phenomenon of the patient's mind going 'blank' or his resorting to embololalia. The oscillation may be a transitional phenomenon, but it is also ambiguous in itself.

ψ

## 'Factic ego' and psychopathic personality

As I said, the ambiguous personality may persist as such, and I have described it in these terms. However, this primitive ambiguity (its persistence in the ambiguous personality) may be organised in other ways. Two of them are typical, and I would like to summarise these briefly: the 'syncretic ego' may be organised as a psychopathic personality or as a 'factic ego'. The shifts from one to the other (progressive and regressive) give rise to the 'transitional phenomena' that I have just described.

In the 'factic ego' the subjects 'adhere' to or are immobilised in some nuclei of their ambiguity and they thereby limit and 'fix' it. I believe that this forms the basis of certain types of *characteropathy*, especially obsessional characteropathy. The fluctuation or 'fictitiousness' of the 'syncretic ego' no longer exists, and they 'organise' by *attaching themselves* to an institution, a group, a job, things, persons and/or events from which they have not yet discriminated themselves. The ego is not yet interiorised and exists as a 'factic ego': the subject *is* in the action, in the relationships, in the job, in the group, etc. Action and activity predominate, there is no interiority or 'self' and when they speak (in psychoanalytic treatment or outside of it), they speak about events, things, persons and activities, because this is the way they talk about themselves; because they *are this*. Relationships with other people are also established by 'doing something'. To them we could apply Handelsman's expression: they have a 'people addiction'. (Handelsman, 1965, p. 374).

ψ

*Example K:* This interview was held by a student in a hospital with a person who went there to visit a patient. The physician on the ward introduces the student, who immediately reacts with rejection and bewilderment as he thinks, 'What is this good lady going to be able to say to me?'

The interviewee is a person approximately forty-five years old who agrees to the interview and keeps looking at the interviewer's eyes the entire time, quite concerned about the effect her words may have on him; she often ends her sentences in the interrogative form, with expressions such as: 'don't you think?'

The interviewee begins to speak and says with a smile that she came to visit a sick person and didn't find him there, because he had gone out to purchase something, but she doesn't know how they could have allowed him to go out, 'poor man', she says, 'who knows what they might do to that man alone on the street.' She expresses her pity and compassion for the patients.

In a moment of silence, the interviewer says that he would be interested to hear something about her: what she does, how she feels and what she thinks.

The interviewee answers, 'Talk about myself? You want to know something about me? Well, well . . . What can I say about myself? Work, going to Mass, visiting the sick and the little orphans. Because, it's true that I've never been one of those people who like dances and parties. And so, what else can I tell you?'

The interviewer asks her what work she does and she answers:

'I do housework. I'm very good at that. Since I was a girl. I'm from the country. My employers took me from Córdoba to Santa Fe, I did the housework, everything a young girl can do, helping in the kitchen, cleaning, all that. Then when the children were born I started to take care of them, so I was a nanny. When my employer decided to come to Buenos

Aires they asked me if I wanted to go and said that I should ask permission from my parents. They said yes, so I came. I used to write to them, because I know how to read and write since I was eight; with letters and all those things I don't have any problems. I stayed on with them here in Buenos Aires. I took care of the first child. Then they had another one, and I also took care of him. Now, later on the younger one got sick in the chest, he was very jealous of the older one, and since he was very sick the doctor told him that the climate in Buenos Aires wasn't good for him; they decided to go back to Córdoba. Sure, they had a house there. They asked me if I wanted to go with them. In the end, I stayed here and went on working as a nanny, I was in many houses; I took care of many children. Then, I was fatter. I started to get thin and especially in the chest. My doctor told me it was because of holding children in my arms so much. Then I stopped working as a nanny. I just did housework. Now I take care of the house of some people who are almost always in Europe. They trust me a lot, they leave me the keys. I go in, I clean, I look after the house, every day. I go at whatever time I want to. I also clean a doctor's office. I live in a different part of town; I have my house, where I live on my own. I had many employers; when I was a nanny I only used to leave because the children were grown up and they didn't need me anymore. I always visit all my employers, they love me very much. I never had problems in the houses where I was, they always trusted me; I was like one of the family.'

At that point, the interviewer wrote that he feels overwhelmed and that as time passed he began to feel bad, upset, and above all, very sad. This feeling of sadness and sorrow grew throughout the interview.

The interviewee leaves a short silence and then continues:

'Besides, my child, I always liked to work. I don't know what I would do without work; it's a thing that always brought me satisfactions, happiness.' (She stops talking.)

The interviewer says, 'And what about besides working?' She answers:

'Well, I already told you, I visit the sick, I like to do good deeds, help people, the little orphans and the old people in the Home. I have a friend who is a very good friend of mine. With her and her husband, they don't have any children, we always collect clothing for the old people, toys for the children. Besides, all my ladies always give me money for these charities, and then, once we have collected a lot of things, we go for example to the Old People's Home in Cáceres and we take things to the old people. I always, when I can, I do it. I also go to the Children's Hospital, in short, everything that is charity work. Because I believe that we have to do good for those who are suffering, don't you think?' (She goes on talking.) 'I believe that it must be that way. I always think that I have to help others and I don't ask others to help me. Thank God I'm very well. I always ask God for me to always have faith as I've had it all my life. And besides, I always ask three things of Divine Providence: health, work and resignation.'

The interviewer asks, 'Why those three things?'

Interviewee: 'Because if I have health, which is the main thing, I'm fine, and then I can work. And resignation, well, resignation, because . . . well, that way I can accept what He wants me to do. I'm very thankful to God because life has been very good. There are two things I appreciate, above all, that I've achieved through my life and my work. One is the trust that all the people have always had for me and the other is all the relationships it has created for me. I've always had employers from the best society, they were the best people, whether it was a doctor a lawyer, or ranchers; others, factory owners; for example, one was the owner of X. X, you know, that very large factory, and all like that. And well, my child, what can I tell you, they have always treated my very well. In all the houses they've always left everything in my charge, they've given me the keys, even when the employers travelled abroad. And they all had big houses, I always made friends, with the cook, the maid, the chauffeur, in short, they all loved me very much, and I still see them. Sometimes I'm walking down the street, and one of the children I took care of passes by, and a honk, a greeting, they take me where I'm going , they bring me back. They call me the Cordobesita, because I've always been very much a Córdoba person.'

The interview continues because the interviewer asks about what her family in Córdoba was like, and then she recalls facts about her siblings, her parents, and later, when there is another silence, the interviewee asks whether he wants to ask her anything else, and then the interviewer reminds her that she had said that she didn't like parties, and she answers:

'No, I never liked them. I always used to go out with my employers. They would take me for tea at Harrods,[147] at The Paris. I would dress up and go with them. We always went to very fine places: I would take care of the children, for example, and have tea. Even now, for example, one of the ladies calls me and says: come, Carmen, let's go to the country house. Then I go to the house. I help her to prepare the things for tea, and we all go in the car to the country house. There, I help them, because even though there are caretakers and other personnel, one has more experience. And sometimes I spend the weekend there. Sometimes, instead of going in the car, I go beforehand to the cemetery at . . . to see one of my employers who is there. I always go to see my employers who died, to take them flowers, to visit them. I have one in Chacarita, another in Recoleta,[148] and so on. I always visit them. I also pray for them.'

The interview continues about religion and the charitable work she does, etc.

147 [*i.e.* the Buenos Aires branch of the London department store]

148 [Chacarita and Recoleta are cemeteries in Buenos Aires]

In this interview, we see the dependence of the interviewee, who stares at the interviewer and often ends her phrases with 'don't you think?' Later, her own helpless situation is expressed in the pity with which she treats the poor and the old people and, before this, a paranoid or persecutory situation of 'who knows what they might do to that poor man alone on the street'. She overwhelms the interviewer with her manner of speaking, but this overwhelming is due to her narcissistic organisation. The facticity appears here in that *she is what she does*, she takes on with ease the roles assigned to her and she identifies with the families with whom she lives or for whom she has worked; for example, she says: 'I was like one of the family'. And later she mentions 'my ladies' as if they were her ladies and not her employers.

The situation of dependence and submission in the formula: 'health, work and resignation' and then her identification with her employers: her entire personality is based on participation, as if everything her employers have or had belonged to her: 'I've always had employers from the best society ... we always went to fine places ...' Her facticity is also in the fact that all the past continues to be present: she goes to the cemetery to 'see' her employers who died, to visit them and take them flowers. And then she says '*I have* one in Chacarita, another in Recoleta and so I always *visit* them'.

ψ

They maintain extreme dependence on their work, or on a group or other persons (with a stable organisation or identity), but because of the character of this dependence, regarding events and actions they superficially appear to be subjects with great independence, which is however actually reactive. In other words, we could say that it is a 'flight into reality'. There is very frequently a real 'flight into health', and the patient and the analyst do not quite know why they need to start or continue the analysis. Sometimes they feel pressured, confined, pushed or persecuted by events, things or persons and there is a deficit in their perception or insight into the meaning of their own action: they feel they are victims of it rather than protagonists. They always feel they are doing 'what others want'. This facticity makes them feel sometimes confined and pressured, as if time were 'hurrying' them; time is 'hurrying them' but they feel stopped or paralysed, which is unlike the detention of time in clinical symbiosis that I described elsewhere.[149] Strictly speaking, they *are* the actions they carry out; this *is* their identity and not simply a support for it, and they are 'condemned' to carry on in action, because otherwise they are 'nothing'.[150] Identity derives from, is maintained

149 [See p. 54]

150 I believe that this puts into question the existence of the superego in the ego organisation at this level; here, the superego would be the description of a phenomenon: of the behaviour, character or personality of the individual, insofar as this individual is obliged or 'condemned' to go on being subject to certain actions; the question remains whether

by and resides in doing, since there is a lack of discrimination between the ego and the objects of the external world. To the 'phantom object' (an object that exists psychologically for the subject only as long as it is emotionally present), there has to be added the 'phantom ego':[151] an ego that exists only as long as there is action.

They live in pure 'facticity' rather than – as in the previous case – in the 'fictitiousness' of alternating and changing roles' (in which case there is a deficit of 'stable identity' or , to put it in a better way, the existence of an 'unstable identity: there are no persons, only characters').

ψ

A patient said in his first interview and repeated frequently in the initial period of his treatment that he felt he had 'a skeleton outside, like some bugs that have a shell but no skeleton'. He was always very tired and was constantly looking for a place to sit down or lean against. Another patient, after several years of analysis, said that a girlfriend of hers had described how she felt that people were like shells, and that she answered that she didn't feel that way; that she 'feels that she isn't empty but that she was never inside her body'; that she 'feels as if her body is always just in front of her and she can never catch up to get inside it'. Later on in the same session she said that she was trying on dresses and that she felt as if she were trying on shells. At the end of this session, she said that she couldn't breathe, that she had dyspnoea, and that when this used to happen to her when she was little, her mother would lift up her arms repeatedly to help her catch her breath.

The first case, the patient who felt he had no skeleton or that it was on the outside like a shell, is describing a characteristic of the personality with a 'factic ego'; the same occurs in the second case, but in this one it is easier to see that not being inside her body and never being able to get into it corresponds to her experience that her body is still her mother's body, and her mother needs to effect the movements that allow her to her breathe. It is precisely with these two examples that I want to illustrate some characteristics of the identity that I have described for the 'factic ego'.

ψ

In the 'factic ego' we are dealing with a subject of 'action', a personality that is in activity, in permanent 'contact' with events, persons or activities, from which it does not discriminate itself as a distinct subject. We observe an evident narrowing of the ego, which is the basic condition for transformation of the 'syncretic ego' into a 'factic ego'. In other words, it is a personality

we can accept in the case of the 'factic ego' a superego as a psychic agency or as a substructure of the ego.

151 [The Spanish expressions are *objeto fantasma* and *yo fantasma,* by analogy with *miembro fantasma,* or 'phantom limb'; see Chapter 6.]

whose 'type' is configured in area three, with minimal development in areas one and two which implies, among other things, a lack of insight and non-configuration of the body schema apart from the body as it is involved in its activity and limited by it.[152]

This deficit in the organisation of the body schema more readily shows itself as a deficit in the organisation and handling of space: they easily become disoriented, bumping into objects or dropping them, etc. Thus, a patient was incapable of orienting herself if the light of her room was turned off: she would 'forget' the positions of the furniture.

> *Example L:* A patient with a very rigid personality, the only function of whose analysis for years was to show her – or induce her to acquire insight into - her limitations and lack of interiority. Deep down this was a person with great ambiguity, organised quite rigidly as 'facticity'.
>
> She always spoke about others and about her activity (very restricted, stereotyped or limited). Moreover, she never spoke with anger, jealousy, love or other feelings.
>
> In one session she says that, over a certain period of time, whenever she was invited to a party she always gave an expensive book (always the same one) to the host or hostess, until at one point her boyfriend pointed this out to her: that she always bought the same book as a present. Then she realised that actually she wanted to buy and have this book herself. It is interpreted to her that she is afraid to realise that she wants a book, because she wants so many things; that she is afraid to discover her greed and envy.

Ever since this patient was little she always took the role that she wanted nothing and needed nothing, with an attitude of great independence, which was totally reactive and defensive.

In this case, we cannot say that the origin or motivation of giving the book is her greed and envy, but rather that, inversely, she gives the book and

152 The concept of areas of behaviour that I use here was introduced by E. Pichon Rivière, to which I have added the 'principle of equivalence of the areas'; among other things, this implies that genetically a psychological phenomenon does not begin by being mental and that – in a totally inverse manner to what is generally accepted – the last area to develop and organize is the mind. Many clarifications concerning omnipotence or the 'flight into reality' derive from this inversion: from not privileging the area of the mind; thus, to be psychological a phenomenon does not necessarily have to first be mental. This implies a fundamental inversion of assumptions: the child's psychological organization does not start out as a 'closed system' that gradually opens up, but as an 'open system' that gradually closes up.

The classical conception or model of assuming genetically that the individual is a closed system is what leads authors like M. Mahler, erroneously I believe, to postulate an initial autistic period, from birth to three months, as being previous to a symbiotic period from three months to one or one and a half years.

takes the role of the person who neither wants nor needs anything, precisely to avoid 'discovering' her greed and envy.

> After the interpretation the patient associates that her parents recently gave her money for her birthday and she went out to buy herself something with the money but wanted to buy so many things that in the end she didn't buy anything.

The role of ambiguity is to blunt her envy and greed, but these do not exist (discriminated) as long as she preserves her ambiguity; thus, we cannot say that her ambiguity originates in her envy and greed but that the ambiguity is maintained in order to avoid confronting the highly dangerous situations that ambiguity blurs so that they *do not exist for her.*

> When she was further on in her analysis, in one session, somewhat moved and sad, she was recalling part of the course of her life and her analysis as a poor and empty life. This was prompted by the fact that when she was speaking – as always – about her children, husband (she had married by then), other persons and activities, a friend had asked her whether she permitted herself any pleasures. This question greatly confused her, but afterwards she thought that she gave herself many pleasures: she likes going for walks, going shopping, going out with the children, and working. I interpret that she derives pleasure from doing things and that her confusion is generated when she discovers that there is something more, which is herself, and there arises for her the problem or discovery that pleasure in doing things is different from allowing oneself some pleasures.
>
> She began the next session by saying that she is moved because she had a 'lovely' experience with her son: he discovered words and how they are formed; before, he only knew how to copy his name and his mother's, and by putting together letters from each of their names he brought her a new word written down. I tell her that it is she who has discovered how she has put her life together and that, like the child, she has not only put together letters or parts of her life but has put together or found herself as a person.
>
> After this, there is a very long silence (usual for her).
>
> Then, she again talks about people and how worried she is by what is happening to N. Then I interpret that she got very frightened when I showed her that now she could think and have things inside herself.
>
> This is followed by analysis of her fear of the changes that may now occur in her life, precisely because of the possibility that her greed and envy at the primal scene might make an appearance.

In the last example, some 'interiority' and 'thinking' emerge, which take shape starting from the 'factic ego'; and this is why we may call this new organisation an 'interiorised ego'.

I now wish to add – as in the case of omnipotence for the 'syncretic ego' – that it is not a question in these patients of obsessional control or of a flight into reality, because strictly speaking, it is an organisation belonging to the ego, primitively fused with reality, from which it is not discriminated. And this clarification corresponds to the same methodological principle discussed above: of characterising each structure by what it is and not by what it is 'lacking'. Obsessional control functions between the more mature ego and the factic or ambiguous ego and is a modality of the 'monosymptomatic neuroses' or 'systematised neuroses', which must always point to a strong psychotic (or ambiguous) nucleus. Could we say, perhaps, that it is an obsessional *organisation* rather than obsessional *defences*?

The second type of organisation or stabilisation of the 'fictitiousness' (of the ambiguity of the 'syncretic ego') is the case of the psychopathic personality. Although there may be others, I am now interested in considering this case, since I wish to differentiate between *action* (of the 'factic ego') and the *acting* of psychopathy or the psychopathic personality.

The 'factic ego' has a potential for learning and adaptation and even intelligent activity. In short, the factic ego is (because of the limitation of the facticity) an attempt to establish or consolidate a symbiosis in which ambiguity will be controlled and immobilised.

In psychopathic acting, ambiguity forms a nucleus (ambiguous nucleus), strongly split off from an ego that has reached a degree of greater integration. The nucleus of ambiguity uses external reality as a depositary, with very destructive impulses. In short, in the psychopath, there is a more integrated ego that defends itself from ambiguity, while *in the 'factic ego' the subject 'accepts' the ambiguity and organises the personality around it.* The 'factic ego' behaves as if it did what others wish it to do; the psychopath behaves towards the other according to his own needs.

The difference between doing and acting has not gone unnoticed for many authors. R. Serebriany establishes a difference between

> *acting*, in psychopathy, and *doing*, by which I understand useful and productive movement, both physical and psychological, which implies growth, learning, enrichment, progress and which has a reparatory aim. *Acting* will be the typical movement of the paranoid-schizoid position, *doing* that of the depressive position.
>
> (Serebriany, 1962 p. 33.n.)

This author quotes D. Liberman, who establishes a similar difference between *acting* and *realisation*.

I agree with the differences between *acting* and *doing* and between *acting* and *action* and I also consider that the former is found in psychopathy. However, I disagree that acting is typical of the paranoid-schizoid position, since I believe that in acting, the ego with a higher level of integration is freed (by establishing a split) from an ambiguous part of the personality. The case history presented by Dr. Serebriany could easily be understood in terms of the way I am postulating this difference here.

In the 'factic ego', and in the psychopathic personality, the patient 'existences'[153] events that have meaning, but they have no interiorised meaning; nor do they perceive or experience the affects that on the move in what they are doing.

*Example M:* A youth eighteen years old says, during a psychoanalytic session, that he had agreed to go to the cinema with his mother and went to fetch her at the home of some friends of the family, but the mother had left with another person. Then he goes out to the street and 'at that moment, if someone had followed me I would have paid attention, I needed for someone to "pick me up" or for me to pick someone up. Afterwards I called Norma and went out with her'. When the therapist interprets his frustration about what his mother had promised him, to go to the cinema with him, then going with someone else, he says no, that he doesn't care what his mother does and that he felt nothing, that it makes no difference to him what his mother does.

Then, he continues the session by saying that Norma (his girlfriend) 'has a bad smell, a smell like shit . . .'

The therapist interprets that it is the mother inside him that got filled up with shit because she abandoned him, and then he answers:

'But it's true that Norma does smell badly, it's true what I say.'

In this case we see how he is unable to separate or discriminate what he is talking about from its meaning (the meaning of this reality). Since the facticity persists, he doesn't discriminate himself either as 'himself', nor as the meaning of the signifier.

Later he says that on the bus, when a person closed a window, he grazed his arm; he turned around, very angry, and told him that he could at least have apologised, and added: 'in my country we do it that way, we say "Excuse me"'.

'His country' is his narcissistic world, his ego to which everyone must yield.

This is a patient who, in all situations of frustration, even minimal, reacts by seeking company.[154] He has a serious deficit of stable maternal and

153 [*existencia*; see also p. 177]

154 These are patients who react, precisely, to minimal frustrations – preferably – but who are unable to react to very intense frustrations (paradoxical or ultra-paradoxical reaction), precisely because the latter would totally disorganise their weak ego. Another complication or characteristic is that their reaction or response may not be immediate but instead deferred or postponed. This low threshold for minimal stimuli co-exists with a very high threshold for intense stimuli; it was described by one patient with a 'factic ego' as

paternal identifications; in him, ambiguity appears as the capacity or potential to set different kinds of behaviour into action; thus, for him it's all the same whether he finds a male or a female partner, young or old, and just as randomly, heterosexual or homosexual, active or passive; he may also practise masturbatory, phallic or anal acts, fellatio or cunnilingus. That is, all possibilities are potentially present in him, which are not 'chosen' from or discriminated. His behaviour is not stabilised around a central organiser; instead, all his behaviour is equipotential or completely equivalent. His behaviour depends much more on chance (contingent) circumstances, since all possibilities co-exist potentially in him, due precisely to his ambiguity; he may organise himself as a factic ego or as a psychopath. This alternation between fictitiousness, psychopathy and characteropathy (factic ego) may co-exist quite frequently.[155]

Thus, ambiguity may have diverse types of 'organisation' that may also in some cases alternate and co-exist. The 'factic ego' is the 'best organisation' that ambiguity is able to achieve before it moves on to discrimination.

The ambiguous personality, as I said, may become the partner of the psychopath (because of great 'permeability' or 'fictitiousness'), but psychopaths may make a partner of any person in whom, they are able to mobilise or actualise the ambiguous nuclei of the personality, which in any case exist in everyone.

Psychopaths may also 'mutate', transforming their ambiguity (their 'agglutinated nucleus') into a central ego and thereby becoming the partner of another psychopath. The phenomenon of 'metamorphosis' is based precisely on this mutation, which may occur not only in psychopaths.

Another phenomenon observed in clinical work is the psychopath who is able to 'crystallise' in a task or relationship and transform himself into a 'factic ego'. (The 'cures' of the psychopath.)

Thus, in clinical practice we find that even one and the same basic structure (ambiguity) offers a variety of organisations of the personality, as also occurs with character traits.

In all these cases, we are discussing only some of the 'vicissitudes' of symbiosis.

*Example N:* This patient has a 'factic ego' with manifest lack of insight and strong homosexual tendencies, acted out through his wife's frequent extramarital relations, which he always eventually discovered. After one of his wife's recent extramarital affairs, and following a small argument

having 'a musician's ear and a schizophrenic's memory' [*oído de tísico y memoria de esquizofrénico* – literally 'the hearing of a consumptive and the memory of a schizophrenic'. The first expression is widely used to mean someone with acute hearing].

155 This could be related to the perverse-polymorphous stage described by Paula Heimann.

between them, the next day he buys her a necklace and give it to her 'to consolidate the reconciliation'.

What is interpreted and shown to this patient is how he induces confusion in his wife when he gives her the necklace; that for him, from the conscious viewpoint, for him, it is a question of 'consolidating the reconciliation', but that for her it is like a prize for her extramarital relation and a kind of stimulus for her to go on doing it. And this confusion and psychopathic acting which he induces in her is his own ambiguity between homo- and heterosexuality, which he himself is unable to manage very well within himself.

In effect, during their prolonged engagement, this patient had relations with his fiancée as well as homosexual relations, both active and passive; that is, up to that time, he accepted his ambiguity until later when there was a polarisation within the ambiguity, which he now handles psychopathically, or rather by inducing psychopathy in his wife.

## The ambiguity of acting out

I do not intend to discuss the problem of acting out at any length here but, in connection with psychopathy, I do want to give a brief example that shows its relation with ambiguity.

*Example O:* This is the patient in a treatment that I supervised. He begins his session by asking whether the analyst is going to work the following day (a holiday) or not. Continuing with the analysis, we see that he does not know whether he himself is going to work tomorrow or not, but he doesn't know that he doesn't know either; that is, he is not indecisive but is trying to escape from a situation of ambiguity whose terms are undefined. After analysing this problem throughout the session, at the end, when he says goodbye at the door, he asks the analyst if he is going to work tomorrow.

This patient started his analysis with a diagnosis of psychopathy and in the course of the treatment this was replaced by a 'factic ego'. In the present organisation of his personality, he is quite afraid of falling into fictitiousness or total ambiguity. Thus, he continues to look for signs in the session which will show him whether the analyst is going to work or not the following day, so that he can make a 'decision' for his own problem, which he doesn't present to himself but 'hands over' for the analyst to present and solve.

His fear of ambiguity is great and he tries to occupy an oppositionist position; if he were given an answer, he would feel pressured or obliged to do as his analyst does, thus raising protests and fantasies of being violated and 'that his personality is not being respected'. On the other hand, if he is not given an answer, he is quite frustrated and his ambiguity is hidden behind a persecutory situation. If he decides for himself what he is going to do, before the analyst tells him his own decision, he is afraid that he will be frustrated by a position that is the opposite of that of his analyst; if his attitude coincides with the analyst's he experiences this as an idealised and omnipotent situation.

> *Example P:* A patient talks throughout the session about his conflicts between his political ideology and his way of life. When he gets up to say goodbye and leave, already at the door, he asks me whether he needs to come to his session the next day (the next day a general strike has been announced by the General Confederation of Labour).

This is evidently an acting out, but in this case we see that the dissociation he manifested in the course of the entire session between his political ideology and his economic situation was not actually a schizoid division or a real contradiction and conflict, but a polarisation of his ambiguity, and the acting out at the end of the session is the use of his contradiction to 'put on me' the ambiguity that he can neither tolerate nor resolve. During the session he made no effort to resolve his contradiction, preserving it in an ambiguous form, and when he says goodbye, he 'hands it over' to me for me to resolve or simply to keep. In the case of true schizoid division (good object–bad object), he would have tried in any case to project one of the antinomic terms into me and not the totality as he does here.

I think that the phenomenon of 'bad faith' studied by M. Baranger (with whose work I opened this discussion) is not in itself ambiguity but a psychopathic organisation or utilisation of ambiguity.

## Thought

In reference to thought there is, in all these cases, a serious deficit in area one.[156] Although there is general consensus that it is due to its destruction, I am inclined to consider that in many cases it indicates a lack of development and organisation. However, if we examine it more closely, we also observe that they frequently do not lack intelligence (especially in the 'factic ego': 'practical' persons): they think 'in a different way'. It is possible that thinking may not be exclusive to the area of the mind; just as there is bodily memory and learning, in action there may also be a process of thinking that is not only mental.

In this sense, I also wish to establish a difference between 'thinking' (which requires high development and organisation of area one) and

156 [See Introduction, p. xxxiii, n. 13]

'mentation' in which the world and objects may have a representation in the area of the mind, but in which the representation has no independence of action (from the objects). What is characteristic in the ambiguous personality is mentation, but this does not mean that they do not think and cannot be intelligent, but that they do and they are *in a different way*, with a different organisation. In thinking, an 'interiorised ego' is formed that is able to function with some autonomy from the external world.[157] In mentation, there is no interiority independent of experience (or of objects); there is a maintenance in area one of syncretism or undifferentiation between ego and object and between the ego and the symbol symbolised.

This problem is still difficult to clarify. Mentation may possibly be a symbolic equation, while thinking is an operation with symbols. Thus, the symbolic equation is not confusion between the symbol and the symbolised, but the internalisation of a syncretic nucleus in which the object and its abstract (mental) representation still co-exist, but are not yet totally discriminated. Mentalisation is genetically previous to thought, and in it there is no discrimination between the word and the thought.

In the ambiguous personality and its different forms of organisation, we observe the phenomenon of a 'deferral of thought': they are unable to think at a given moment, but may do it later, when they are out of or far from the situation. They frequently use the answer, 'We'll see', or something similar that gives them time for 'deferred thinking'.

We also observe that the ambiguous personality and the personality with a 'factic ego' live with what we could call a clouded consciousness, which is not confusion[158] but the lack of awareness of the self, as different from awareness of the world; it is what I defined before as 'being in itself' rather than 'being for itself'.[159] The affects are not experienced, not because they are blocked, but *because they have not formed* as experiences, and are expressed or revealed directly in conduct or in action.

An indicator of the degree of a person's maturation may be the ego's capability to accept, tolerate and work through ambiguity. When ambiguity breaks into the ego, confusion or disintegration results, and working through depends on the ego's capacity to tolerate confusional anxieties and proceed to the discrimination of ambiguity. (This phenomenon is found normally in adolescence.)

157 This problem must be far more complex. G. Ferschtut and R. Serebriany described the 'pseudo-symbol', which may be found between the symbolic equation and the symbol proper (Ferschtut and Serebriany, 1964).

158 I repeat that in my opinion ambiguity is not confusion, and that the latter only appears in the more integrated ego, when it is invaded by ambiguity.

159 [see p. 177]

## The authoritarian personality

The ambiguous personality may persist as a 'syncretic ego' unable to organise itself as a 'factic ego'. In this case another alternative for organising in a more stable manner is *extreme polarisation*: the entire personality is configured on the basis of one of the nuclei of ambiguity. What emerges has been described by social psychology as the 'authoritarian personality': extreme rigidity as a reaction formation in order to avoid any return to ambiguity.[160]

The polarisation 'fixes' the personality on one of the terms of the ambiguity, and maintains itself in a stereotyped way in order to avoid returning to it. Polarisation must not be mistaken for contradiction: in the latter there is schizoid division; in the former there is dichotomy and splitting. The authoritarian personality fears the unexpected and any external change and shows great intolerance for anything imprecise or ambiguous. It is a stabilisation or 'resolution' of what I previously termed 'manicheism', although in the latter the polarised terms co-exist, while in the authoritarian personality the personality is centred on only one of them.

I will not further examine the characteristics studied by Frenkel-Brunswick and by Adorno & co-workers. I only intended to locate the authoritarian or prejudiced personality within the vast panorama of ambiguity.

## Synthesis

Ambiguity appears clinically (apart from those cases where it exists in the form of an agglutinated nucleus split off from a more integrated ego) in four typical ways:

(a) Directly as ambiguity, with 'fictitiousness', the expression of a 'syncretic ego', with great dependence and volubility, and one that may turn into the partner of a psychopath;
(b) With some organisation of the ambiguity in a 'factic ego' that is directly fused with objects and events;

160 Ambiguity as a social phenomenon is observed clinically in: cohesion groups, marginal communities, political parties, prejudices, action groups, etc. In contemporary society, the basic problem is no longer that of dissociation but rather that of ambiguity; sociologists describe our period as a 'formless society', an 'amorphous society', a 'formless world', 'uncertainty'; the contradictions remain unstructured; the world and the subject become 'homogenised'. This social phenomenon, I believe, is the reason we no longer find the traditional clinical pictures of psychiatric pathology, but more and more frequently meet with different and often more polymorphous pictures. The study of ambiguity may contribute some clarity to this new pathology.

(c) In the psychopathic personality;
(d) With extreme polarisation: in manicheism and the authoritarian personality.

We also need to bear in mind that I am presenting extreme situations or 'pure' pictures that dynamically co-exist in diverse proportions and may 'mutate' into each other. We are also omitting the cases of regression in which an integrated and interiorised ego may become a 'factic ego'. Also, I do not want to discuss here in detail the 'mutation' of the psychopath, who may totally accept his ambiguity and then turn himself into the partner of a psychopath, or the return to the full ambiguity from the authoritarian personality, or *vice versa*.

## Why does ambiguity persist?

Up until my most recent work on the theme of symbiosis, I studied its persistence (as dependence) in subjects who had reached a more integrated ego, in whom these nuclei of symbiotic dependence were managed by maintaining a strong splitting from the more integrated ego. In this way I studied the agglutinated nucleus and the glischro-caric position. I want to suggest that in these cases the symbiosis persists *as a nucleus* and to some extent also this exists in every human being, because of deficient discrimination in the split-off part of the more integrated ego. In these studies I identified the eminently ambiguous character of this agglutinated nucleus. What I want to do now is to examine the inverse situation, in which the more integrated ego is only a minimal part of the personality and the latter functions totally or predominantly with an organisation that keeps the symbiosis to the fore. This requires me to study ambiguity *per se*, as it presents in different personality types or traits, unlike the earlier studies in which I studied the dynamics of the agglutinated nucleus in its different manifestations (hypochondria, epilepsy, mania, melancholia, etc.). Strictly speaking, these latter manifestations depend on the defence of the more integrated ego against the possibility of invasion by the agglutinated nucleus.

In ambiguous personalities (which constitute or structure themselves in four basic types as described above), there is a lack of solid and integrated persistence of nuclei of identification, and a lack of internalisation of a discriminated ego. All this is combined with deficient or nonexistent discrimination between ego and objects, the body schema and the external world, homo- and heterosexuality, etc. I relate these four types of ambiguous personality to the lack, in the earliest infancy, of 'trustworthy' depositaries, who should have fulfilled two fundamental roles: first, to serve as a depositary for the psychotic (ambiguous) part of the personality and second, as a function of the former, to enable interiorisation by discriminating the experience of objects and of nuclei of the ego; that is, the depositary's ego has not been efficient as a supplementary ego to restore 'sense' or 'meaning' and to permit stable identifications by keeping the ambiguity 'fixed'.

Although on the one hand we may recognise in the ambiguous personality this lack of a 'trustworthy' depositary (with its consequences), on the other hand, in close relation to this, we observe in their history that they were 'very good' children who never complained and at the same time were very greedy. It may be not simply a question of increased greed but that the absence of a trustworthy depositary results in difficulty or impediment in confronting this greed or envy, which may be intense in relation to the ego's lack of integration. This is a strange situation, since greed does not exist as long as the subject's ego is not organised and integrated. When it acquires some organisation, regression occurs in the face of the intolerable greed that its organisation provokes. For this reason, I do not consider greed and envy to be causes of ambiguity, although they certainly intervene.

Sometimes it is not only a question of the lack of a 'trustworthy' depositary, but of frequent changes of the persons taking care of the child, in which case there is no *one* trustworthy and lasting person (depositary). In this case the problem of affective deficiency has a specific meaning, since although affection and caregiving may not be lacking, there may be a lack of a continuing or sustained experience with one person (a sole depositary).

Often, we also find very serious traumatic situations in the history: abandonment, death of siblings or parents, psychosis of a member of the family, etc.

In all cases of ambiguity, interiorisation and discrimination of the ego and objects has not been achieved in a stable manner, because if discrimination and interiorisation had been reached, they would have had to face highly persecutory and therefore very destructive experiences. Children need a secure symbiosis that permits them to count on a depositary or 'supplementary ego' so that they may face their greed and destructive envy. The function of psychoanalytic treatment is to provide a symbiosis that was lacking or distorted. This function is fulfilled fundamentally by the setting, which undoubtedly includes the role of the analyst. Ambiguity and its persistence 'blunt' the persecutory situations (arising basically from greed and envy) by not discriminating them and not recognising them (paralysing entry into the paranoid-schizoid position). From this results a great restriction of the ego and a clouded consciousness (which is not confusion).

*Example Q:* In this treatment (which I supervised), a patient age 29, a passive homosexual with an ambiguous personality, very immature and highly dependent, manages to make considerable advances in several years of treatment and establishes a heterosexual relationship with very paranoid and unstable characteristics. His panic breaks out when his girlfriend begins to have orgasms and he begins to feel subject to tremendous demands, his greed having been projected into his girlfriend and into the therapist.

During this period, he has a nightmare in which someone wants to kill him and he was hanging onto his girlfriend, in the dream, in order to calm down.

The therapist interpreted that he hangs onto his feminine part and to the therapist when he feels he's in danger because he is afraid that it will be killed from within by his own demands and greed.

He answers that when he was small whenever one of his two elder brothers would beat him, he would hold onto him to make him stop.

The therapist interprets that this is the function of his homosexuality: to hold onto his feminine part in order to avoid being destroyed by his aggressive and destructive greed.

The patient associates with the fantasy of having cancer of the throat. It was interpreted to him that what he is controlling in his homosexuality is, in phantasy, as destructive as cancer.

He answers that all this depresses him very deeply and the therapist interpreted that he prefers to be depressed instead of frightened by how destructive he looks inside.

At this moment the patient says that he very fleetingly fancied that the therapist introduced his penis into his anus.

It was interpreted that now he tried to do exactly what he did with his brothers to defend himself because he felt attacked; the patient answers that he feels confused and that he now does not know whether he is depressed or frightened.

In this patient's homosexuality he tries to control very destructive tendencies connected to his voracity or greed. However, what I wish to highlight basically is the meaning and role of the symbiosis: a way to remain attached to the depositary so that the destructivity resulting from his greed will not appear.

The symbiosis (with its characteristic ambiguity) is not in itself a defence against what is dangerous, but he can resort to it as a defence through regression. *What is dangerous appears if they separate, and that is why they cannot separate.*

The ambiguity here is that he holds on, but to avoid being destroyed, to blunt the destructivity of his greed.

Although ambiguity may appear by regression as a defence against persecution, we must not assume that this is also the dynamic of the primitive ambiguity pertaining to primary symbiosis. There are other dangers in the symbiotic relationship itself from which the subject flees, as in the following example:

*Example R:* He says that he feels very irritable with his children and reacts violently; I interpret that he is irritated because in relation to a trip he will take very soon, he feels that his children demand that he be a father and that they demand that he stay, feelings that are very difficult for him to tolerate, since his own father also subjected him to frequent frustrations and absences.

The patient then associated that he had to go into a shop that sold women's things and that he entered while smoking a pipe so that they would realise he isn't a woman, as if affirming his manliness. I remind him that what happens now is like the period when he was a boy and was frequently alone with his mother; his mother would take him to a club and into the women's locker room, where he would see many naked women, and that now, feeling that his children demand that he be a father, this demand irritates him because he suddenly feels absorbed and put inside his own mother.

He rejects the interpretation and then speaks of his satisfaction now in doing small things, hobbies of different kinds, and describes the recreational activities he now has at home, but suddenly interrupts to say that he feels quite burdened, that he has been feeling increasingly burdened.

I interpret that when he puts aside external demands, he feels burdened from the inside by his mother who pressures him to be a woman, to be with women and also to take his father's place and get excited with her.

This is a patient organised with a factic ego, with very frequent psychopathic acting so that he always feels pressured and working. When he wants to demonstrate the contrary (that now he no longer makes demands on himself nor feels subject to demands), he begins to feel burdened, that is, he becomes absorbed by his mother, by the asphyxiating relationship with her, and by all the consequent dangers of losing his father permanently and replacing him, and by the guilt and the consequences of replacing him.

This would make us think that facticity, at least, or ambiguity in general, is related to an unending escape from a very absorbing and dangerous symbiotic relationship that becomes a burden: if he stopped escaping he would be totally invalidated and burdened inside the mother. But the absorbing and dangerous relationship does not explain the ambiguity; it does explain its persistence or non-solution.[161]

The paradox is that, in order to solve the symbiosis, he must have a good symbiotic relation that satisfies this need. When the symbiotic relationship has been deficient, distorted or excessive (as in this case), there is a premature escape from this very exhausting symbiosis, with the result that the symbiosis is not resolved or satisfied: ambiguity is then organised as 'fictitiousness', as a 'factic ego' or as psychopathic acting, or as the other types of organisation

161 M. Abadi (1962) highlighted an image of the 'terrifying mother' prior to the oral stage associated with the fantasy of captivity.

of ambiguity that we have discussed, which are other ways of preserving symbiosis in the most acceptable, least destructive and most protective form possible.

The diversification of links is important for the resolution of symbiosis and in this regard we need to consider the intervention of the father and siblings. In a good mother-child symbiotic relation, the father's intervention helps to resolve it, but in the bad mother-child symbiotic relation, the diversification of links not only does not help to work it through but deepens or strengthens it, making it assume in any case a different structure.

The oedipal structure found in these cases is always quite complex: mother containing the father, a fused couple and fusion of the subject with the mother's body. In my opinion, it is not basically a question of links of a sexual character, but of complex interpersonal links in which primitive fusion and lack of discrimination are dominant. A relative 'solution' or distance in this fusion is introduced by the discrimination that a body zone may attain, which then serves as a control, however relative, of this primitive fusion. The precocious genitalisation sometimes observed in these patients is not the cause or co-cause of the non-resolution of the primitive, fused oedipal situation, but the opposite: an attempt to discriminate a bodily zone and use it against primitive fusion.

In her paper, 'Homosexuality and confusion', M. Baranger (1959) describes some characteristics that I consider also quite typical of symbiotic persistence (in symbiosis or in clinical ambiguity): absent father and over-protective mother, frequent changes of residence, limitation of the child's social relations, a situation in which the child is kept 'cloistered' inside the mother, lacking in initiative and subjected to the mother's impositions through rigid and stereotyped rules with no place for spontaneous manifestations; the mother's attitude is complemented by a lack of emotional relationship and of direct, personal, bodily contact with the mother.

The father's absence may be real in the sense that the father is not there or he may be only sporadically in contact with the child. However, in other cases this lack of father may stem from his non-intervention and leaving the child totally in relation with and dependence on the mother.

The child does not find sufficient support or identification in the father to be able to separate or leave the enclosure inside the mother's body.

If this situation of enclosure inside the mother continues, the child may establish certain relations and a certain development of the ego beyond the contact with the mother while maintaining a strong symbiotic nucleus that may later appear as a psychopathic, perverse, hypochondriac, etc. nucleus. If this child tries to flee and permanently does flee enclosure inside the mother, the result is constant fluctuation of sporadic contacts without the organisation of stable nuclei of identification, in which case there results the ambiguous personality or ambiguous personality traits whose different forms I have described.

However, from the psychological viewpoint, of fundamental importance seems to be the particular character of the primal scene or the formation or structure of the Oedipus complex. There is a failure in the establishment of the triangular situation, a failure in the inclusion of the father between the mother and the child, which appears as a deficit in discrimination between the two parents and of both of them in relation to the subject. The very singular oedipal constellation prevents these children from distributing their conflicts between their parents, that is, from establishing the paranoid-schizoid position and the possibility of counter-balancing one with the other, establishing the contradiction or the antinomic terms of a conflict; thus, the conflict (paranoid-schizoid position) does not appear or take shape and the oedipal situation emerges as a constellation that is without discrimination between the subject and the mother, between the child's body and the mother's. Therefore, I assign great importance to the achievement of the triangular oedipal situation in the progress to the paranoid-schizoid position.

*Example S:* One of the cases I supervised was a homosexual who until age nine had slept in his parents' bed between them. He remembers that on some nights his parents would tell him to sleep on one side of the bed and not in the middle, which for him made it obvious that his parents were going to have sexual relations that night. On other occasions, it was he who asked his parents whether that night he had to sleep on one side of the bed or in the middle, as an attempt to control the sexual relation between his parents.

Besides presenting compulsive homosexual activity this patient had a very underdeveloped, infantile personality, with hysteric and manic traits, but fundamentally and essentially ambiguous. In this case the two characteristics, in some ways different, that we have identified for symbiosis and for the ambiguous personality, could coincide, since the persistence of an undiscriminated primal scene appears in his own homosexual relation as a split off part of his personality. However, on the other hand, the ambiguity persisted not only in this homosexual nucleus split off from his personality but also in the entire structure of his personality by means of a certain control of the primal scene and a permanent flight from it.

This patient experienced all his homosexual episodes in a compulsive but ego-dystonic way: one of the complaints he expressed in his first interview and the sessions at the beginning of the treatment was always that he had to define himself. By this he meant that if he were a homosexual he would like to experience his homosexuality with pleasure and total acceptance rather than the suffering it caused him. He came to analysis in search of a definition: either to give himself up totally to his homosexuality or to configure his heterosexuality.

The lack of a father or his absence is also surely what leads a mother to take a cold, distant and imperative attitude with her son, since through this attitude she reactively tries to control her tendency to physical intimacy with the child as a replacement for her own husband, since if a father is lacking for the child we may infer that a real husband for the mother is also missing.

The symbiotic subject and the ambiguous personality do not succeed in structuring the Oedipus complex in its triangular form: they have been unable to separate the combined parental couple and to include the third party, which has also prevented the subject and his mother from establishing a relationship between two persons. Thus the subject, as well as the father, appears always to be fused with the mother, 'swallowed up' or included within the body or interior of the mother. When the father is included, this does not resemble for the child the inclusion of a third in a relation of two, but the discrimination of two persons, and of himself, from a primitive fusion with the mother.

Subjects with extreme ambiguity try to reproduce these situations compulsively, always failing in this resolve: they try to reproduce them, certainly to solve them, finally discriminating them, but the way they reproduce them also determines the failure of discrimination of the ambiguous primitive situation.

Returning to the clinical history studied by M. Baranger, which is quite similar to the case of homosexuality that I supervised, the aim of the homosexual compulsion may not be the homosexual act in itself but the preliminaries to the act. For this reason the fantasies are interrupted and the homosexual coitus is either interrupted or totally unpleasurable. Patient number three studied by M. Baranger, at a certain moment cuts off the fantasy and starts again, changing the details, and does this many times:

> 'One thing that excites me quite a lot is when the situation has an ambiguous character. Of course I know I am fooling myself, but it is more exciting when it is not defined. That's probably why I don't have fantasies in which it (the homosexual act) goes through; the situation loses its attraction . . .'
>
> (Baranger, 1959)

The patient in Example S. was in a similar situation: the primal scene, its undiscriminated character, was also reproduced by his own body in a situation of extreme ambiguity: he masturbated by putting his own penis between his legs and took both roles, female and male: the role of the mother and the father together, preserving the ambiguous character of the relation in which he was at once the father and the mother, not differentiated from each other. However, more basically, he was not himself: he was both the father and the mother without ever being able to be himself, because of this syncretism of the primal scene.

M. Baranger treats her clinical material as a confusional situation. In this regard I have repeatedly clarified my view that it is incorrect to speak in terms of confusion in these cases, whereas it would be appropriate to speak of ambiguity, which is also how the patient presented by this author effectively describes it.

In the ambiguous personality, we regularly observe a lack of experiencing, of feeling that they inhabit their own body, because they really live inside the mother's body, but with no discrimination of their own or the other's body. An ever-present fantasy in Example S., when walking down the street and often searching with his glance for a man he liked, was to imagine himself inside that man's body and try to feel what that man might feel, in an attempt to structure the experience of his own body and be able to inhabit his body instead of his mother's body.

In her paper 'Homosexuality and confusion', M. Baranger says:

> the confusional situation, although it is not structured as a 'position' in Melanie Klein's sense, could be considered a series of intermediate states between the paranoid-schizoid position and the depressive position. These states seem to correspond to the phase of instinctive development described by Paula Heimann as a perverse polymorphous phase.
>
> (Baranger, 1959)

Confusional situations are due to the invasion of the ego by a psychotic nucleus of the personality, while the perverse-polymorphous phase corresponds, in my opinion, to the re-installation of ambiguity. For this reason, I consider the perverse-polymorphous phase as regression to or persistence of the position that I have termed the glischro-caric position. The same occurs normally in adolescence.

## The 'blunting' function of ambiguity in regression

We also see the 'blunting' function of ambiguity in regression to the glischro-caric position in the course of psychoanalytic sessions: when highly persecutory situations arise, which the patients cannot face because they would become totally disorganised or would have a psychotic breakdown, they blunt the contradiction or the persecution they are experiencing, regressing to ambiguity.

Although in regression ambiguity is the mobilisation of a primitive level of organisation (corresponding to the 'syncretic ego') in the face of very intense persecutory situations, I believe that we cannot extend this scheme to the genesis and persistence of ambiguity itself, since ambiguity and its persistence reflect a deficit of discrimination. Any discrimination would force the appearance and internalisation of greed, envy and a highly persecutory and disorganising situation, while in regression the discrimination already acquired (for this sector of the ego and reality) is lost defensively.

Here we see two different situations that we need to clarify: in the first, facing increased confusion and danger of confusion, subjects try to shake off the confusion by means of a persecutory situation or by choosing or configuring a persecutory object in the external world. When Freud studies anxiety in his *Introductory Lectures on Psychoanalysis*, he says that 'a person protects himself from fright by anxiety' (Freud, 1916–17, p. 395). Here we could say that he defends himself from fright and anxiety by fear (by persecution). A different situation occurs when the persecutory situation is very intense, in which case individuals tend to defend themselves with ambiguity. Although this sounds contradictory, in the first case we are describing how a more integrated ego defends itself against confusion when it may be or is the object of the invasion and disorganisation that is provoked when the agglutinated (ambiguous) nucleus breaks into it. In the second case, a very precarious ego tries to defend itself with ambiguity from the persecutory situation that would be highly disorganising; in other words the persecution is blunted. Clinical experience offers us many examples of 'blunting' by the use of ambiguity in persecutory situations. One example is the attempt to 'keep up appearances', which consists in behaving 'as if nothing were happening'. We observe another type of blunting phenomenon when the subject is experiencing a very persecutory situation in the present, but refers to it in the past tense. We see a third example of blunting, again due to regression to the glischro-caric position, when the subject resorts to self-reproaches and self-deprecation. This appears clearly in a female patient whose father has just fallen gravely ill: in the following sessions her self-reproaches, self-deprecation and emphasising of her guilt are an attempt to bring about a situation of ambiguity when faced with an immensely persecutory oedipal situation.[162]

A fourth example of this regression and use of ambiguity to blunt the persecutory situation is quite frequent: when a patient enters the consulting room she finds another person about whom she had been talking for a long time in her sessions very fearfully. As was to be expected, this meeting was very persecutory. However, the patient mentions it in passing and then says that hundreds of ideas occur to her and she doesn't know which to start with. The 'hundreds of ideas' tend towards a dispersion and the introduction of ambiguity, precisely to avoid facing the highly persecutory situation.

Ambiguity may serve to absorb the shock of insight and to avoid having to take it on board. Thus, when a patient brought in anguishing material she

162 The phenomenon of melancholia has been discussed in earlier chapters as an ambiguous (agglutinated) nucleus.

would joke about herself (she would 'load' herself,[163] as she once said), and in another session she remembered how she once told about an event jokingly and was amused by it, and that now (owing to the analysis of this ambiguity), when she narrated the same material, she was anguished and weeping.

Another use of regression to ambiguity is the case of a patient who has always gone through life with a strong feeling of falsity while impressing people favourably. He spends a good part of his time impressing them well, but all the while he feels deeply bad and despicable and useless; he then uses dissociation to preserve ambiguity, so that when one thing is interpreted to him he shows the other, and resorts to the former when shown the latter.

If both things are interpreted together, he goes on to a third, and so on. The countertransferential feeling is that he is ungraspable, since he functions with a high degree of fictitiousness. He always has another ego nucleus to escape into, to preserve the ambiguity and avoid any contradiction.

In clinical work, we frequently encounter patients who *use* contradiction and dissociation. Some use it constantly and others sporadically.

Another type of 'shock-absorption' through ambiguity is found in a special use of words; one patient now acknowledges that his father's illness when the patient was an adolescent was a psychosis, but he does not use this word. He says, for example: 'When my dad was *ill* ...' Another patient referred to his wedding saying, 'When I changed my marital status ...'

In all these cases, the shock-absorbing or defensive function of ambiguity impedes the development or appearance of potentially disintegrative tendencies or 'blunts' very persecutory and dangerous situations and affects. In some cases individuals attempt to avoid the *appearance or formation* of the danger while in others, since it already exists, the ambiguity blunts it. In the first case, it is important to underscore that the danger does not exist psychologically for the subject as long as he remains in ambiguity; it only *appears or is generated* with the attempt to move out of it. (In Chapter 4 I showed that when the depositary is held at a distance, envy emerges and the difference and discrimination appear between ego and object and between internal object and depositary.)

This 'blunting' always involves a restriction or limitation of the ego and the external world and the existence of a 'clouded consciousness' in all or part of the ego.

Ambiguity always involves maintaining or transforming events, objects and the ego, into an abstractionism in which the abstract is not discriminated from the concrete.[164] It is a variant of the problem of the symbolic equation.

163 [ .... *se 'cargaba' a sí misma* ... Literally, she 'loaded' herself, but the Spanish also figuratively means that she made fun of herself.]

164 In the Appendix to Volume I of the *Psychological Works of G. Politzer,* I differentiated abstractionism from abstraction. The former is always ambiguous and blunted or

## Comments on the literature related to ambiguity

H. Deutsch described in 1942 a type of emotional disturbance in which the relation with the external world and with one's own ego appears to be impoverished or absent, and she says that it is manifested in diverse forms. She termed this type of personality 'as if' and justified it by the observer's impression that the entire relational life of these persons seems to be somewhat lacking in genuineness; although they seem normal, have no behaviour disturbances, preserve their intellectual capacity and have well ordered and appropriate emotional expressions, they present something 'intangible and undefined' that invariably leads us to ask: 'what is wrong with them'. To the analyst it becomes clear that all the relationships of this type of personality lack warmth, that their emotional expressions are formal and that all internal experience is completely excluded. They simulate, as in the performance of a technically well trained actor, but who lacks something of real life. (Deutsch, 1942).

She also describes how in the 'as if' personality there is no repression, but instead there is a lack of object cathexis; their apparently normal relationship corresponds to the imitations of children and is the expression of an identification with their surroundings: a mimetism that results in a good adaptation to the world of reality despite the absence of object cathexes. The author adds that their attitude toward their environment is completely passive and they have great plasticity for fitting into others' behaviour, which renders them capable of great fidelity, any object serving as an object of identification. Women with this personality appear to be the quintessence of feminine devotion, a characteristic stemming particularly from their passivity and their rapidity of identification. However, the absence of a real emotional relationship suffuses the emotional atmosphere with emptiness, which soon leads the relationship to break up. When this occurs, the abandoned person has an affective explosion that is also 'as if', with a definite absence of affectivity. At the first opportunity the object is replaced by a new one and the process is repeated.

The same emptiness and lack of individuality that is so evident in emotional life also appears in their moral structure; they appear to be lacking in principles of their own, and their ideals or convictions are simple reflections of those of other persons, whether good or bad. They readily adhere to ethical, social or religious groups in order to furnish their reality and their internal emptiness with some content and to establish some value for their existence through identification.

Deutsch also points out that adhesion to one philosophy may be rapidly and completely replaced by another, even a contradictory one, without any

blunting (of the abstract and the concrete), while abstraction is discriminated from what is concrete. (Politzer, 1965–66).

sign of a real internal transformation but only as the simple result of accidental regrouping.

A second characteristic of these patients is their great suggestibility, which is easy to derive and understand on the basis of everything described up to now. Many criminal acts attributed to an erotic connection are due to this passive speed of being influenced. Another characteristic of this personality is that the aggressive tendencies are completely hidden by the passivity, which leads these persons to a negative goodness that may easily become damaging.

She describes a number of cases from which she deduces a common factor: a deep disturbance of the process of sublimation resulting in a failure to synthesise diverse infantile identifications into a unique and integrated personality and in an imperfect, totally one-sided intellectual sublimation of their instinctive impulses. While their critical judgment and intellectual organisation may be excellent, they lack the emotional and moral part. Deutsch relates the aetiology of these conditions first to a depreciation of the object that provides a model for the development of the child's personality. This depreciation may be based on reality or, for example, on the shock of discovering parental coitus in a developmental period when the child is fighting against masturbation. Another cause of this emotional disturbance is insufficient stimulation of the sublimation of the emotions.

She differentiates the 'as if' personality from hysteria because the objects of identification in hysteria are heavily charged with libidinal cathexes and repression of the affects frees them from anxiety and conflict. In the 'as if' patient, a primitive deficit in emotional development reduces internal conflict and leads to a total impoverishment of the personality. This does not occur in hysteria.

Narcissism and poor object relations, characteristics of the 'as if' personality, bring into consideration its relation with the defects of psychosis. However, the preservation of the sense of reality sets them apart from the condition of psychosis. The objects of the 'as if' personality continue to be external, and all conflicts are acted out in relation to them.

However, the author notes her impression that the schizophrenic process has gone through an 'as if' phase before the delusional forms are constructed.

She quotes 'The Ego and the Id', where Freud discusses a 'multiple personality' resulting from a process in which the many identifications provoke a disruption of the ego. This may lead to a manifestly psychopathological picture or alternatively the conflicts between the different identifications may take a form that we do not necessarily have to consider as pathological.

Khan, in a paper presented at the XXI International Congress of Psychoanalysis (Khan, 1960), proposes to present a new type of patient and to give them clinical status in their own right and specificity. He related this new 'model patient' to the description of the schizoid personality contributed by Fairbairn, to the 'as if' personality described by Deutsch in 1942, and to a type of personality with a 'false self' described by Winnicott in 1956 in his article, 'On transference' (Winnicott, 1956) and to contributions by Erikson, Anna Freud and Greenson.

His contribution refers basically to the study of the most significant behaviour of these patients in the analytic situation, their transference, their needs and demands of the analyst. He describes the following characteristics:

(1) instead of transference, they tend to provoke or seduce the analyst;
(2) instead of communication, they manifest an exhibition of psychic contents;
(3) all the affects are presented with an urgent need of discharge and as described by Stone, Greenacre and Winnicott, they have a need for new objects and experiences in order to be able to experience themselves as persons;
(4) their narcissism has a patent quality of deficit and is defensively concealed by self-compensatory pseudo-aggressive techniques;
(5) instead of taking an initiative, they rely on the help of others, which they are always successful in mobilising;
(6) from the outset, they have great urgency to exteriorise and act out their past experiences and tensions in the analytic situation;[165]
(7) they exploit partial regressions of the ego and the id as well as the superego, with great skill, which lends a psychotic quality to some of their behaviour. Any attempt to reduce this type of management causes them to panic;
(8) they need control and limitation by the analyst. They only have pieces of a variety of incomplete experiences of all the stages of development and they induce the analyst to feel their fear, anger and needs, desperation, love, etc.;
(9) lack of capacity to tolerate anxiety, trying to transform it into psychic pain and being addicted to this pain. A second technique for management of this anxiety is to transform it into a state of diffuse, excessive tension;
(10) they use defence mechanisms randomly, in the sense that there is no consistent specificity in them. The most prominent defences used are: splitting, depreciation of objects and their emotional experiences, projective identifications and idealisation. This author advises us to evaluate their mechanisms and to discriminate the defensive function from the communicative aspects;

165 [This appears to be Bleger's direct translation of Khan, who writes: 'From the very start these patients seem to be in a great urgency to exteriorize and "act out" all their past experiences and current tensions in the analytic situation' (Khan, 1960, p. 433). In this case, Khan's 'act out' (in quotes) was rendered in Spanish by *actuar.*]

(11) in relation to idealisation as a defence, Khan observes that their ego is highly organised, that this psychic formation tends to deal with frustration in relation to the primary object, and that it is a means of establishing a defensive psychic structure against the emotional reality of the interpersonal relationship.

He wonders whether we have in our theoretical conceptions and in our clinical setting the means for dealing with the needs of these patients. He regards as important the contributions in the last two decades resulting from investigation which has supplemented or filled-out the classical theory, basically in three dimensions:

(1) the knowledge that, in the development of the child, the ego and the id emerge from an undifferentiated matrix;
(2) this has changed our emphasis on the conflictive dynamic of the primitive processes, especially with the contributions of Hartmann and Winnicott;
(3) the emergence of the ego and the id from an undifferentiated matrix has broadened our conception of the role and function of the environment in the crystallisation of the first feelings of the ego; by environment he means the total sum of the maternal caretaking of feeding and affective relation toward the child.

J. Weiss summarises a panel of the American Psychoanalytic Association (Weiss, 1965) dedicated to the clinical picture and theoretical aspects of the 'as if' character. In this panel, S. Atkin reviews the article by Deutsch, and says that these 'as if' personalities present: (a) a primitive stage of object relations without object constancy; (b) poor development of the superego with predominant objective anxiety; (c) prevalence of the primary processes of identification; (d) lack of a sense of identity; (e) emotional superficiality and general poverty of affects; (f) lack of insight. The last point is an aspect of these patients' narcissism, but their sense of reality is well enough preserved to differentiate them from the psychotics. Nonetheless, P. Greenacre is of the opinion that the sense of reality in the 'as if' character is defective.

Atkin also quotes M. Gitelson who, when expounding on the problem of character pathology, introduces a new dimension when he takes into account the notable stability and adaptability of the 'as if' character. He maintains that this character formation, rather than manifesting a defect or weakness of the ego, is an expression of incomplete development resulting from a lack of stable relationships and compatible identifications. For this author, the ego is immature but is intact on *its* level of development.

In the same panel, H. Tartakoff questions whether the 'as if' phenomenon may not have its genesis in Mahler's phase of separation-individuation. He also differentiates primary identification, which refers to imitation and mimetism or the following of a leader's behaviour, and which does not involve internalisation, from secondary identification, which refers to identifications of the ego and superego that lead to structural change. He considers that in the 'as if' personality the identifications seem to belong to the primary type.

N. Ross maintains that 'as if' personalities have undergone a loss of object cathexes and their behaviour is simple mimetism based on very primitive identification; the ease of identification is such that their behaviour acquires kaleidoscopic characteristics that reflect the personalities of the individuals with whom they come into contact. Consequently, these patients do not develop or move beyond the period of imitation, the precursor of identification, and into a stage of true identification. They do not acquire the ability to internalise and they fail to form the superego. In 'as if' personalities all the objects are preserved externally. This author holds that 'as if' phases may be observed in schizophrenia and puberty.

In his synthesis, Ross makes two points: (1) that it would be useful not to isolate the 'as if' personality as a clearly differentiated syndrome, but to consider a spectrum of 'as if' states; (2) that the lack of affect in the 'as if' personality may result from the persistence of a primitive barrier against overstimulation.

R. R. Greenson proposes to recognise a variety of 'as if' states. Many character types present 'as if' phenomena and it is possible to speak of 'as if' symptoms, 'as if' mechanisms and 'as if' character traits, all these states having in common a lack of genuineness, a transience and variability. These patients regress to a condition in which they cannot differentiate representations of the object from representations of the self, and in which self and object are partially fused and confused; they confuse identifications with object relations and also with identities (entities). As a result of this poor individuation, Greenson affirms that 'as if' patients suffer from a defect of self-observation, although their sense of reality may be adequate. He maintains that the fixation of these patients occurs at around one and a half years of age, in the period when the child separates from the mother, and that the central feature in the different forms of 'as if' is the mechanism of denial.

In this panel, H. Deutsch maintains that 'as if' is a modality of ego functioning that appears in various normal and pathological situations. She differentiates a transitory psychological 'as if' phenomenon, which is extremely common and nearly universal, from 'as if' referring to the structure of the personality or to a well-defined type that is rarely encountered. She adds that from 1932, in 33 years of practice, she found only one case of personality that she could consider as of the 'as if' type. As for the etiological factors, she considers that these patients present emotional deprivation in the earliest period of infancy, a disturbance in the balance of gratification and frustration in primitive periods of ego development with consequent limitations and defects of the ego, and that the result of these defects is the persistence of primitive identifications in which dependence is expressed by imitation as a method of adaptation.

She also insists on differentiating the 'as if' personality from other manifestations in which 'as if' is used in a broader sense. She agrees on this point with Katan, but considers that the term 'pseudo as if' does not solve the problem.

At the close of the panel, Atkin suggests that the conception of 'as if' should be used in such a way that it preserves a defined and separate entity, as presented by H. Deutsch in her original work.

ψ

The lack or deficit of identity mentioned is correct, I consider, if it is analysed from the perspective of identity or of the 'conventional' sense of reality; or, in other words, taking ourselves as a normative model. For this reason I choose to describe it, not as a lack of identity, but as a particular identity of the syncretic personality and as an equally particular identity, in this case of the group, which I have termed the factic personality.

In the panel of the American Psychoanalytic Association, Gitelson's position, quoted by Atkin in his presentation, is very striking. He states that instead of considering it a defect or weakness of the ego, this particular formation of the character is an expression of its incomplete development, but that the ego, however immature, keeps itself intact at *its* level of development. I wish to highlight this statement because it is one of the aspects that I have insisted on repeatedly: we need to describe a typology, and not necessarily a pathology, and moreover these are not semantic but methodological differences that I believe are very important. H. Deutsch says the same in her original article, quoting Freud in his article, 'The Ego and the Id'.

The absence of contradiction and the lack of internal transformation in these patients, emphasized by H. Deutsch, also seem very important to me, as well as their passivity and reactive goodness. The lack of a synthesis of infantile identifications is underscored by many authors on this panel, as it has been in our part of the world by M. Baranger.

In the panel the emphasis placed on the concept of *object constancy* is very important, but I am pointing out that this phenomenon is specifically lacking in the syncretic personality and not in the factic personality.

Our work with the concept of ambiguity enables us to characterise, in my view, many phenomena in a unitary way. It allows us to recognise different types of organisation of the personality based on different types of organisation of ambiguity and, I believe, constitutes an advance on the terms in use such as the 'as if' personality or Winnicott's 'false self', since it is a question of 'as if' or 'false self' only for the countertransferential reaction. The characteristics of the phenomenon, considered in itself, are by no means false or 'as if'. They are genuine phenomena in their own right that need to be characterised by their own qualities. Also, working with the concept of ambiguity permits us to recognise this phenomenon both in the personality as a whole, and in character traits and in different normal and pathological phenomena, a problem that becomes very complicated if we are working with the concept of the 'as if' personality. By contrast, the problem is made very clear in the contribution, among others, of Ross, when he proposes that we not isolate the 'as if' personality as a clearly differentiated syndrome, but consider a spectrum of 'as if' states. The same occurs when Greenson, in this panel, studies a variety of 'as if' states.

The emphasis placed by some authors (Greenson) on fusion or lack of discrimination between object representation and self representations, and on the fact that self and object are partially fused and confused, and the fact that these patients confuse identifications with object relations and also with identities, seem to confirm my views on the study of ambiguity.

The statement by H. Deutsch in this panel that 'as if' is a form of ego functioning that appears in varied normal and pathological situations seems to me a highly important statement, although I do not agree with this author on the scarcity she assigns to the types defined as an 'as if' personality. I do agree with H. Deutsch in not accepting Katan's concept of 'pseudo as if', since this does not solve the problem and even complicates it, something that also occurs with the concept of 'false self' (Winnicott) and even now with the term 'as if' personality proposed by H. Deutsch herself. Similarly, I consider Atkin's final position incorrect when, at the close of the panel, he suggests that the conception of 'as if' must be used in a way that preserves it as a defined and separate identity. For we cannot and should not continue to work in psychology and dynamic psychiatry with the concept of illness as an entity, but as organisations or structures of behaviour and personality, dynamically interrelated to each other, mobile and changing; otherwise, we would be going back to Kraepelin's conception, one of whose fundamental defects is precisely this conception of nosological 'entities'.

ψ

Khan's paper on the subject presents still more problematic complications when he superimposes, as corresponding to the same 'model patient', Fairbairn's description of the schizoid personality, Deutsch's 'as if' personality, Winnicott's 'false self' and the studies by Greenson.

In particular, I believe that the schizoid personality described by Fairbairn cannot be superimposed on the 'as if' personality described by Deutsch, since the former is characterised by three fundamental or salient features, which are: an omnipotent attitude, isolation and detachment and preoccupation with internal reality. These characteristics do not appear in the 'as if' personality, since it is completely contrary to isolation and detachment, and internal reality has not been structured.

If from the clinical point of view, to which I have just referred, there are differences which do not allow the superposition of these different pictures, the same is also true from the point of view of the structure of each of these personalities, since the former is characterised by schizoid division and the latter by ambiguity. However, it may be that the schizoid personality results from splitting in the ambiguous personality and that the schizoidia as well as schizoid traits are an attempt at schizoid division on entering the paranoid-schizoid position from ambiguity, but that this transition has not taken place completely or in a stable way.

Here we encounter still further problems, at least one of which is unavoidable. I refer to the use of the concepts of schizoidia and autism, which are frequently superimposed and confused in practice.

In my opinion, schizoidia and autism are not synonymous, since the former is an intense and not easily reversible form of the phenomenon that Jung called introversion, characterised precisely by isolation, detachment and preoccupation with, or overvaluation of, the internal world at the expense of the external world. On the other hand, the autistic is not necessarily an introvert nor schizoid and, in this regard, we need to return to the original definitions by Bleuler, who introduced the latter term.

Bleuler says in his book: 'This detachment from reality, together with the relative and absolute predominance of the inner life, we term autism' (Bleuler, 1911, p. 63); he adds that 'autism nearly coincides with what Freud has termed auto-erotism' and that

> [I]n essence the term, autism, designates in a positive way the same concept that P. Janet formulated negatively as 'the loss of the sense of reality'. However, we cannot accept Janet's term without discussion because he understands this symptom in a far too general sense. The sense of reality is not entirely lacking in the schizophrenic. It fails only in relation to matters threatening to contradict his complexes.
>
> (Bleuler, 1911, p. 63, n. 19)

From this we deduce that for Bleuler autism and schizoidia are synonymous, since in both there is detachment from reality and a predominance of internal life. However, many doubts arise in this respect, which are particularly clarified by E. Minkowski in his book, *Schizophrenia*, in which he postulates the existence of primitively autistic activity and states that because this has been neglected 'we have been inclined to identify autism with interiorisation, passive states of daydreaming and absorption of the personality in an internal life made of complexes and imaginary factors'. (Minkowski, 1953, p. 177). I agree with this last author in not identifying autism with interiorisation, since autism may exist with or without interiorisation, or rather, with or without introversion or without detachment. Many autistic activities are not associated with detachment from external reality or with introversion. The external world is totally organised in an autistic way without this involving, in my view, interiorisation in the sense of detachment from external reality and a projection of internal life. In autism reality is organised in a particular way and the autistic subject may be an active subject, as appears in some examples presented by Minkowski and in some of those provided by Bleuler.

Minkowski is completely correct when he says that 'reality' is far from always being synonymous with 'external world'. Consequently, it seems erroneous to try, at whatever cost, to assimilate the loss of contact with reality to interiorisation; this author adds that a chapter on *autistic activity* is required, in the sense that activity does not exclude autism, just as it does not exclude introversion.[166] What especially characterises autism is, I believe, a loss of the sense of reality, which may appear either with behaviours of introversion, isolation or detachment, or with behaviour that reaches an intense level of activity.

In this sense, autism characterises both Fairbairn's 'schizoid personality'[167] and Deutsch's 'as if' personality, as well as what I describe as the ambiguous personality.

The problem is further complicated when, as we have now done, we recognise that the schizoid or schizophrenic, even when presenting an exaggerated degree of introversion, detachment and isolation, also presents an intense transference with very specific characteristics, which I have termed symbiotic transference. As I pointed out in the previous chapter, schizophrenia and schizoidism always coincide with a symbiosis, to the extent that the latter is also always an autistic organisation. In this sense, schizoidia would be a deep splitting in the personality as a defence against the symbiosis, both symbiosis and schizoidia being autistic or narcissistic phenomena.

Hence, I must correct my description of autism in a previous chapter as a polar phenomenon with respect to symbiosis, since the polar phenomenon of symbiosis is actually schizoidia, while autism is a phenomenon common to both. I could ultimately define or characterise autism by a lack of differentiation or discrimination between ego and non-ego and between internal and external world.

Thus, we may re-consider the formulation in Chapter I[168] that both the autistic and the symbiotic relationship are narcissistic relations, replacing it with the statement that both the schizoid and the symbiotic relationship are narcissistic relations, and formulating the concepts of narcissistic relation and autism as equivalent.

ψ

In view of all the above, I believe that the clinical concept of ambiguity and its detailed study clarify and place on a more specific basis the characteristics of personality and behaviour studied by the different authors quoted.

166 [The reference is to Minkowski (1953), pp. 166, 176.]

167 [Translated here in Spanish as *esquizoidia*, although *personalidad esquizoide* is also used.]

168 [See p. 12]

The 'as if' personality described by H. Deutsch coincides, almost point for point, with what I described above in the study of ambiguity in regard to both the syncretic personality and the factic personality. The lack of genuineness that appears in this type of personality corresponds to what M. Baranger studied as inauthenticity. I have already mentioned this, showing that the descriptions correspond to countertransferential aspects. Moreover, since they include an element of value-judgement, I proposed that it is more appropriate to describe the phenomenon itself than the countertransferential reaction, since the inauthenticity or lack of genuineness is promoted by the phenomenon of ambiguity. The same is the case for other characteristics emphasised by Helene Deutsch and by M. Baranger, in reference to facile identification or, as we could also put it, to a great permeability for identifications, together with a lack of persistence in certain nuclei of this identification, that could provide a continued, preserved or persistent identity to the personality. I agree that this facile identification is manifested in the phenomena of facile suggestibility, to which I added echolalia, echopraxia, echomimia, etc., in the course of my study.

The facile change of object described by H. Deutsch refers more to the syncretic personality than to the factic personality, for which the case is exactly the opposite. However, in both cases, they are not true objects but depositaries.

The lack or deficit in identity is correct if analysed from the perspective of identity or adaptation or in the sense of 'conventional' reality: in other words, if we take ourselves as a normative model. In this regard, I chose to describe it not as a lack or loss of identity but rather as a specific identity in the syncretic personality and also as a particular identity, but in this case a group identity, in the factic personality.

# 6

# Psychoanalysis of the psychoanalytic setting[169]

Winnicott defines the '*setting*' as 'the summation of all the details of management' (Winnicott, 1956, p. 297).[170] For reasons that will be discussed as we develop this theme, I propose that we adopt the term *psychoanalytic situation* for the totality of the phenomena included *in the therapeutic relationship* between analyst and patient. This situation encompasses phenomena that constitute a *process*, which is what we study, analyse and interpret. However, it also includes a *setting*,[171] in other words a 'non-process' in the sense that these are the constants within the framework of which the process takes place.[172]

The analytic situation may thus be studied from the perspective of the methodology that it represents, the setting corresponding to the *constants* of a phenomenon, a method or a technique, and the process to the set of *variables*. However, we shall here put to one side this methodological aspect and mention it only for the purpose of making clear that a process can only be investigated while these constants (the setting) are maintained. Thus, within the psychoanalytic setting we include the role of the analyst, the combination of spatial factors (the surroundings), temporal factors and part

169 [This is the chapter previously published in English in the *International Journal of Psychoanalysis* as 'Psycho-analysis of the psycho-analytic frame' (Bleger, 1967a). See Introduction, p. xvii, and concerning the translation of *encuadre* as 'setting' instead of 'frame' see pp. xli–xlii.]

170 [In this instance Bleger has translated 'management' into Spanish as *técnica* instead of *manejo*.]

171 [When quoting Winnicott at the start of this paragraph, Bleger uses the English word 'setting' in quotation marks; here he uses the Spanish *encuadre*.]

172 We could compare this terminology with that used respectively by D. Liberman and E. Rodrigué.

of the technique[173] (including the establishment and maintenance of session times, fees, regular breaks, etc.).

For now, my concern is with the psychoanalysis of the psychoanalytic setting and there is a considerable literature on the need to maintain it and on the disruptions and distortions that the patient provokes in it in the course of any analysis (of various kinds and degrees, from exaggerated obsessional compliance to repression, acting out or psychotic disintegration). My work with the psychoanalysis of psychotics has taught me clearly the importance of maintaining and defending those fragments or elements of the setting that may have survived, which is sometimes achieved only with hospitalisation.

However, I will not focus just now on the problem of 'disruption' or 'attacks' on the setting. I wish to examine what is involved in the maintenance of an *ideally normal setting.*[174]

Stated in these terms, such a study would seem to be impossible, since this ideal analysis does not exist. I agree with this opinion. The fact is that, sometimes permanently and at other times sporadically, the setting is transformed from the background of a *Gestalt* into a figure, that is, into a process. However, even in these cases, it is not the same as the process of the analytic situation itself, because in relation to the 'failures' of the setting, our interpretation *always tends* to maintain or re-establish it: which is an important difference from our attitude in the analysis of the process itself. In this sense, I am interested in examining the psychoanalytic meaning of the setting *when it is not a problem*, in an 'ideal' analysis (or in the moments or periods when it is being that). I mean that I am proposing the psychoanalysis of the setting when it is being maintained and not when it is broken; when it continues being a set of constants and not when it has turned into variables. The problem that I wish to examine is the problem of those analyses in which the setting is not a problem. And I want to do this precisely to show that it is a problem. This will necessarily take up a good part of my available time, since it is not possible to analyse a problem that has not been clearly stated and is not yet recognised as a problem.

ψ

173 The setting corresponds more to a strategy than to a technique. Part of the setting includes 'the analytic contract', which 'is an agreement between two persons, with two formal elements of reciprocal exchange: time and money'. (Liberman et al., 1961, p. 86).

174 The problem as I present it is similar to what physicists call a thought experiment: a problem that does not occur totally or precisely in the form in which it is defined or presented, but which is of great usefulness (theoretical and practical). Perhaps this ideal analysis or problem was what E. Rodrigué once referred to as the case history of the patient that nobody wrote or could ever write. [The reference is to what in German is called a *Gedankenexperiment*, the Spanish for which is *experiencia ideal*, literally 'ideal experiment', which then gives rise by analogy to the notion of 'ideal analysis', the ideally normally maintained setting, etc.]

A relationship that lasts for years with the maintenance of a set of norms and attitudes is precisely the definition of an *institution*. The setting is therefore an institution within whose framework, or in the midst of which, phenomena occur that we call behaviour.[175]

What became evident to me is that each institution is a part of the individual's personality, and this is of such importance that identity is always – wholly or partially – group or institutional, in the sense that always at least a part of one's identity is configured by belonging to a group, an institution, an ideology, a party, etc. Fenichel wrote: 'Unquestionably, the individual structures created by institutions help to preserve these institutions'. (Fenichel, 1946, p. 447). However, in addition to this interaction between individuals and institutions, institutions always function (in varying degrees) as boundaries of the body schema and as the fundamental nucleus of identity.

The setting is maintained and tends to be maintained (actively by the psychoanalyst) as invariable. As long as it exists in this way, it seem to be nonexistent or not to count, like institutions or relationships that we only take notice of precisely when they are missing or obstructed or come to an end. (Someone said about love and children that you only know they exist when they cry.) What is the meaning of the setting while it is being maintained (when it 'doesn't cry')? In every instance this is the problem of symbiosis, which is 'silent' and which only manifests itself when it is broken or on the point of being broken. It is the same as what happens with the body schema, the study of which began with pathology, which is what revealed its existence in the first place. Just as we speak of the 'phantom limb' we need to recognize that institutions and the setting are *always* constituted in a 'phantom world': the world of the most primitive and undifferentiated organisation. What is always there remains unperceived unless it is missing. We could apply to the setting Wallon's term 'ultra-things' (Wallon, 1934, p 713): that is, everything that is experienced as vague, undetermined, without any conception or knowledge of what it is. What organizes the ego are not just stable relationships with objects and institutions but also the ulterior frustrations and gratifications that are due to them. There is no perception of what is always there. The perception of the missing object and of the gratifying object comes later; at first there is only the perception of an 'incompleteness'. What exists in the *subject's perception* is whatever experience has shown him might be missing. By contrast, stable or immobilised relationships (non-absences) organize and maintain the non-ego and form the *basis* for structuring the ego as a function of frustrating and gratifying experiences. The fact that the non-ego is not perceived does not mean that it does not exist psychologically for the organisation of the personality. The

175 I have arrived at this study, in part, precisely as a result of a series of seminars on institutional psychology and of my experience in this field (although this is still rather limited).

knowledge of something arises only in the absence of that something, until it is organised as an internal object. But that which we do not perceive also exists. This 'phantom world' exists deposited in the setting even though the setting has not been broken, or precisely because of that.

ψ

I want to digress again briefly and thereby, I hope, provide more elements for the investigation that I am undertaking. Until quite recently, we were very comfortable working in science, language, logic, etc., without realizing that all these phenomena or behaviours (I am interested in all of them as behaviours, that is, as human phenomena) occur in a context of assumptions that we ignored or treated as nonexistent or invariable. However, we now know that communication includes a meta-communication, science a meta-science, theory a meta-theory, language a meta-language, logic a meta-logic, etc. If the 'meta . . .' varies the content varies radically.[176] Thus the setting, being constant, is decisive for the phenomena of the *process* of behaviour. In other words, the setting is a *meta-behaviour* and the phenomena that we will identify as behaviour depend on it. It is what is implicit, but what is explicit depends on it.

The *meta-behaviour* functions as what M. and W. Baranger call 'the bastion': an aspect that the patient, by avoiding the fundamental rule, tries not to put at risk (Baranger and Baranger, 1961–62). But in the meta-behaviour that I am interested in analysing *the fundamental rule is being observed*,[177] and what interests me is precisely the examination of this observance. I agree with these authors in considering the analytic relation as a symbiotic relation. But in cases where the setting is being respected, the problem is that the setting itself is the depositary of the symbiosis and the latter is not present in the analytic *process* proper. Symbiosis with the mother (the immobilisation of the non-ego) allows the child to develop his ego. The function of the setting is the same: it is a support and a framework, but it can only be seen – for now – when it changes or is broken. The most persistent, tenacious and unnoticeable 'bastion' is the one deposited in the setting.

ψ

I now wish to illustrate this description of the setting with the brief example of a patient (A.A.) who has a phobic character and intense dependence

176 This variation of the 'meta . . .', or variation of fixed or constant assumptions, is the starting-point of non-Euclidean geometry and of Boolean algebra (Lieber, 1960). In psychotherapy, each technique has its assumptions (its setting) and therefore also its specific 'contents' or processes.

177 [The Spanish is *se cumple con la regla fundamental*, and later in the same sentence we render *cumplimiento* as 'observance', while in the next sentence but one we translate *en que se cumple con el encuadre* by 'where the setting is being respected'. In each case something more voluntary than mere compliance is implied.]

concealed beneath a reactive independence. For a long time he vacillated, wishing and fearing to buy an apartment, a purchase that never materialised. At a certain moment, he accidentally learned that I had bought an apartment some time previously in a building that was still under construction, and at that point a period of anxiety and of various kinds of acting began.

One day he told me what he had learned and I interpreted his attitude: the way he told me about it included a reproach that I had not told him about my purchase, even though I knew that this was a fundamental problem for him. He tried to ignore or forget the episode, offering strong resistance every time I insisted on connecting this fact with his acting, until strong feelings of hate, envy and frustration began to appear, with violent verbal attacks, followed by an atmosphere of withdrawal and despair. As we continued the analysis of these situations, the 'background' of his infantile experience gradually began to emerge, which I was able to re-construct through his narration of different memories: at home his parents would do nothing, absolutely nothing, without informing and consulting him so that he knew every detail of the course of family life. After the appearance and reiterated interpretation of these memories (which had to overcome strong resistance), he started on the accusation that everything between us had been broken and he could no longer trust me. Frequent fantasies of suicide, disorientation and confusion and hypochondriacal symptoms appeared.[178]

For the patient, 'something' was broken which *was so* and which *had to be* as it had always been, and he could not conceive of it being otherwise. He demanded the repetition of what he had experienced, of what was 'always that way' for him. It was a demand or condition that he was able to maintain throughout his life by means of a restriction or limitation of his ego in social relationships and by always keeping hold of the management of those relationships, and by demanding a strong dependence from his objects.

In this example I wish to point out how the 'non-repetition', by respecting the setting, brought to light a very important part of his personality: the most fixed and stable part of his personality, his 'phantom world', the delusional transference (Little, 1958) or the psychotic part of his personality: a non-ego that formed the framework of his ego and identity. Only with the 'non-observance' of his 'phantom world' could he see that 'my' setting was not the same as his, and that his was already present as a 'phantom world' before the 'non-observance'. But I want to emphasise that the maintenance of the setting is what allowed the analysis of the psychotic part of the

178 As Little (1958) describes in regard to delusional transference, there appeared associations referring to his body, from very early experiences: that he felt immobilised, and he associated that when he was a baby he was wrapped in a swaddling cloth that kept him completely immobile. The non-ego of the setting includes the body, and if the setting is broken the boundaries of the ego formed by the non-ego have to be recovered at the bodily level.

personality. What I am trying to bring out is not how many of these phenomena appear because of frustration or a collision with reality (the setting) but – more importantly – the question: how much of it does *not* appear and may therefore possibly never be analysable? I have no answer to this question. What concerns me at present is to make clear (to discriminate) what the problem is. It is similar to what happens with the character trait that has to be transformed into symptoms in order to be analysed; that is, it has to cease to be ego-syntonic. And should we not do with the setting as we do in character-analysis? The problem is different and even more difficult, since not only is the setting not ego-syntonic but it is the framework on which the subject's ego and identity are constructed, and it gets strongly split off from the analytic process, and from the ego that configures the neurotic transference. Although we assume that in the case of A.A. this material would somehow have come up anyway, since it was already present, the problem remains unsolved in terms of the psychoanalytic meaning of the setting.

ψ

Summarising, we could say that the setting (thus defined as a problem) constitutes the most perfect repetition compulsion[179] and that there are actually *two settings*: one which is proposed and maintained by the psychoanalyst, and accepted consciously by the patient, and another, that of the 'phantom world', into which the patient projects.[180] The latter is such a perfect repetition compulsion, because it is the most complete, the least recognised and the most unnoticed.[181] Something that has always surprised and fascinated me, in the analysis of psychotics, is the co-existence of total denial of the analyst with an exaggerated sensitivity concerning the infringement of any detail of what the patient is 'used to' (in the setting), and how the patient may become disorganised or violent, for example, if there is a difference of a few minutes at the start or end of the session. Now I understand this better: what becomes disorganised is the 'meta-ego', which to a large extent is *all the patient has.*[182] In the psychotic transference, it is not affect that is

179 This repetition compulsion is not only 'a way of remembering' (Freud) but a way of living or the *condition for living.*

180 Wender (1965) wrote in his paper that there are two patients and two analysts, to which I now add that there are also two settings. [A handwritten note by the author, in his copy of the Spanish original, elaborates the phrase '... into which the patient projects', so that it reads '... into which the patient projects his own phantom world'.]

181 Rodrigué (1965) describes a 'suspended transference' and writes that the 'difficulty stems from speaking about a phenomenon that, if it existed in a pure form, would have to be silent by definition'. [See Rodrigué, and Rodrigué, 1966, p. 225].

182 I believe that it is rash to speak always in terms of an 'attack' on the setting when the patient does not comply with it. The patient brings 'what he has' and this is not always an 'attack' but the patient's own organisation (even though it is disorganised).

transferred but instead 'a total situation, the totality of a development' (Lagache, 1952);[183] it would be better to say the totality of a 'non-development'. For Melanie Klein, the transference repeats the primitive object relations, but I believe that something even more primitive (the undifferentiation) is repeated in the setting.[184]

E. Jacques says that institutions are unconsciously used as defence mechanisms against psychotic anxieties, but I think it would be better to say that they are depositaries of the psychotic part of the personality, that is, of the undifferentiated and unresolved part of primitive symbiotic relationships. Psychotic anxieties are played out within the institution and, in the case of the psychoanalytic situation, within what we have characterised as the *process* (that which is 'in motion', as opposed to that which isn't: the setting).[185]

The development of the ego (in analysis, in the family, or in any institution) depends on the immobilisation of the non-ego. This term 'non-ego' induces us to think of it as something non-existent, but its existence is real: so much so that it is this 'meta-ego' on which the possibility of the formation and maintenance of the ego itself, and thus the ego's very existence, depends. On this basis we were able to say that identity depends on the way in which the non-ego is maintained or handled. If the meta-behaviour varies, the entire ego is modified (possibly to equivalent degrees in terms of quantity and quality).[186] The non-ego is the background or framework of the organised ego: they are the 'ground' and 'figure' of a single *Gestalt*. Between ego and non-ego (or between the neurotic and the psychotic parts

183 [The phrase 'total situation' is a quotation by Lagache of M. Klein's paper given at the Amsterdam Congress of 1951 and published the following year (Klein, 1952b, p. 55).]

184 The ambiguity of the 'as if' of the analytic situation, studied by W. and M. Baranger, does not cover 'all aspects of the analytic field', as these authors say (Baranger and Baranger, 1961–62, p. 800), but only the process. The setting does not admit ambiguity: either in the psychoanalyst's technique or in the patient. Each setting is what it is and does not admit ambiguity. Equally, I consider that the phenomenon of participation (Lévy Bruhl) or syncretism, which they accept for the analytic situation, applies only to the setting.

185 Reider describes different types of transference to the institution instead of to the therapist: psychoanalysis as an institution seems to be a way to recover lost omnipotence by participating in the prestige of a great institution. I believe that what is important here is to consider the psychoanalytic situation as an institution in itself, especially the setting.

186 G. Reinoso has remarked that although, as Freud pointed out, the ego is a body ego, *the non-ego is too* (García Reinoso, 1956a, 1956b). We could add something more: the non-ego is a different ego, with different qualities. This also means that there is not *one* sense of reality or lack of it: there are different structures of the ego and of the sense of reality. [In the previously published translation of this chapter in the *International Journal of Psychoanalysis*, this footnote was incorporated into the text, and the following clause appended to the second sentence: '. . . and I suggest (Bleger, 1967) calling it a *syncretic ego*'. (Bleger, 1967a, p. 514). The reference was to Chapter 5 of the present book.]

of the personality) there is no dissociation but instead a splitting, in the sense that I have used this term in a previous text.[187]

N.N. was a very rigid and limited patient who always lived with her parents in hotels in different countries. The only thing that she always took with her was a small picture. Her poor relationship with her parents and the incessant moves made this picture her 'surroundings', her non-ego: her meta-behaviour, which gave her 'non-change' for her identity.

The setting *'is'* the most primitive part of the personality, the ego-body-world fusion on whose *immobilisation* depend the formation, existence and discrimination (of the ego, the object, the body schema, the body, the mind, etc.). Patients with 'acting in' or psychotics also bring 'their own setting': *the institution of their primitive symbiotic relation*. But *all* patients also bring this.

Thus, we are better able now to acknowledge the catastrophic situation that the analyst's disruption of the setting (holidays, or cancelled, missed or incomplete sessions, etc.) *always* entails to a variable degree, since in these disruptions (disruptions that are part of the setting) a 'crack' is created through which reality is introduced, which is catastrophic for the patient. 'His' setting and his 'phantom world' lose their depositary and it becomes evident that 'his' setting is not the psychoanalytic setting, as occurred with A.A. Now I want to offer an example of a 'crack' that the patient tolerated until he felt the need to recover his omnipotence and 'his' setting.

Z., the only son in a family that in his childhood was very wealthy, socially quite prominent and very close-knit, lived in an enormous and luxurious mansion with his parents and grandparents, for whom he was the centre of attention and lavish care.

For political reasons many of their possessions were expropriated, which resulted in a considerable economic decline. For a time, the entire family made an effort to keep up appearances as rich people, hiding the disaster and poverty, but his parents ultimately moved into a small apartment and accepted employment (his grandparents had died in the meantime). While the family faced and accepted the change, he continued to 'keep up appearances'. He separated from his parents and earned a living from his profession as an architect, while covering up his great insecurity and economic instability. So much so that everyone believed he was wealthy, while he lived and kept alive his phantasy that 'nothing had happened', thus preserving the secure and idealised world of his childhood (his 'phantom world'). This was also the impression that he produced in me in the treatment: a 'person of good standing', from a superior social and economic class, who without any '*nouveau riche*' ostentation preserved an air of security, dignity and superiority, of being outside and above the 'penuries' and 'pettiness' of life, which included money.

187 [This probably refers to Chapter 5.]

The setting was well maintained, he paid regularly and punctually. When his attitude and his duality (the split in his personality), his way of moving in two worlds, of maintaining a fiction, were analysed more and more closely, he began to owe me money and to be late, as well as to speak (with great difficulty) about his lack of money, which made him feel 'humiliated'.

Here, the disruption of the setting meant a certain disruption in his omnipotent organisation: the emergence of a 'breach' that became the route for penetration 'against' his omnipotence (the stable and secure world of his childhood).

His respecting the setting was here the depositation of his magical omnipotent world, infantile dependence and psychotic transference: his deepest phantasy was that the analysis would consolidate this omnipotence and give completely back to him 'his' 'phantom world'. The disruption of the setting meant the disruption of a splitting and the emergence of a 'breach' where reality broke through.

'Living' in the past was not his unconscious phantasy; it was the immediate, basic organisation of his existence. I shall transcribe parts of a session at a moment when his parents suddenly had an accident and were gravely ill. In the previous session he paid part of his debt and began that session by telling me that today he brought me this many pesos, that this many remain and that this debt feels 'like a breach', like something that's missing'. (Pause) He goes on: 'Yesterday I had sexual relations with my wife and at the beginning I was impotent and this frightened me very much.' (He had been impotent at the beginning of his marriage.)

I interpret that now that he is going through a difficult situation because of his parents' accident, he wishes to return to the security he had in his childhood, to the parents and grandparents inside him, and that the relationship with his wife, with me and with today's reality leaves him impotent in relation to that; that he needs to close the breach by paying me everything, so that the money will disappear from between us, so that I will disappear along with everything that now makes him suffer.

He answers that yesterday he had the thought that he only needs his wife in order not to be alone, and that she was a mere add-on to his life.

I interpret that he also wishes that I would satisfy his needs in reality so that they might disappear and thus allow him to return to the security of his childhood and his phantasy of reunion with his grandparents, father and mother, just as everything was in childhood.

(Silence) After this he says that when he heard the word fantasy, it seemed strange that I would talk about fantasies and that he was afraid of going mad.

I tell him that he needs me to give him back all the security of his childhood that he tries to hold inside himself in order to confront the difficult situation, and that he also feels that I, and reality with its requirements and pains, get into the breach that money, his debt, puts between us.

He ends the session by talking about a transvestite. I interpret that he feels like a transvestite: sometimes like a rich and only child, sometimes like the father, sometimes like the mother, at times like the grandfather, and as each of them, he feels both rich and poor.

ψ

Any variation of the setting throws the non-ego into crisis, 'disavows' the fusion, renders 'problematic' the ego and forces re-introjection, a fresh working-through of the ego or activation of the defences in order to immobilise or re-project the psychotic part of the personality. This patient (Z.) was able to accept the analysis of 'his' setting until he needed to recover it defensively, and what is interesting to emphasise is that his 'phantom world' appears and is put in question by 'faults' in the setting (his debt) and that the recovery of his 'phantom world' was connected with 'respecting' 'my' setting, precisely in order to ignore me or cancel me out. The phenomenon of the reactivation of symptoms described at the end of psychoanalytic treatment is also due to the mobilisation and regression of the ego through mobilisation of the meta-ego. The background of the *Gestalt* becomes the figure.[188]

The setting may thus be considered an 'addiction'. If it is not analysed systematically it may become a stabilised organisation, the basis of the organisation of the personality, and the subject may obtain an 'adapted' ego as a function of an external moulding by institutions. This is the basis, I believe, for what Álvarez de Toledo, Grinberg and M. Langer (1964) have called the 'psychoanalytic personality', which the Existentialists call a 'factic' existence, and which we could identify as a truly 'factic ego'.

This 'factic ego' is an 'ego of belonging': it is constituted and maintained by the subject's inclusion in an institution (which may be the therapeutic relationship, the Psychoanalytical Society, a study group or any other institution): there is no 'interiorised ego' to provide the subject with internal stability. We could say, in other words, that the entire personality is made up of 'characters', that is, of roles, or else that the whole personality is a façade. I am now describing the 'extreme case', but we need to take the quantitative variation into account, since there is no way in which this 'factic ego' can stop existing entirely (nor do I consider it necessary that it should).

The negative therapeutic reaction or 'pact' is the perfect installation of the patient's non-ego in the setting and its non-recognition and acceptance by the psychoanalyst. We could also say that the negative therapeutic reaction is a real perversion of the transference-countertransference relation. The 'therapeutic alliance' is, on the other hand, an alliance with the patient's healthiest

188 This must be what has led some authors (Christoffel, 1952) to use the disruption of the setting as a technique (abandoning the use of the couch and interviewing face to face); I do not agree with this opinion.

part (Greenacre, 1959). This is true for the process but not for the setting. In the latter, the alliance is with the psychotic (or symbiotic) part of the patient's personality (with the corresponding part in the analyst? I do not know yet.).[189]

Winnicott says that:

> For the neurotic the couch and warmth and comfort can be *symbolical* of the mother's love; for the psychotic it would be more true to say that these things *are* the analyst's physical expression of love. The couch *is* the analyst's lap or womb, and the warmth *is* the live warmth of the analyst's body.
>
> (Winnicott, 1949, p. 72)

With regard to the setting, this is always the most regressive, psychotic part of the patient (for every type of patient).

The setting is what is most present, as the parents are for the child. Without them there is no development of the ego, but its maintenance beyond what is necessary or the lack any modification of the relationship (either with the setting or with the parents) may indicate a negative factor, a paralysis of development.[190] In every analysis, even with an ideally maintained setting, the setting anyway needs to become an object of analysis. This does not mean that this is not being done in practice, but I wish to emphasise the interpretation or the meaning of what is being done or not being done, and its importance. The de-symbiotisation of the analyst-patient relation is attained only by the systematic analysis of the setting at the right moment. With this, we meet with the most tenacious resistance, because it is not something repressed but something split off which has never been discriminated. Its analysis is an upheaval for the ego and for the more mature identity reached by the patient. We do not interpret the repressed, but instead we create the secondary process. We are not interpreting gaps in memory but something that was never a part of memory. Nor is it a projective identification, but the manifestation of the patient's syncretism or 'participation'.

The setting forms part of the patient's body schema. It *is* the body schema in the part where this has not yet been structured and discriminated. This means that it is something different from the body schema in the narrow

189 I do not believe that this psychotic split transference deposited in the setting is a consequence of repression or infantile amnesia.

190 E. Rodrigué, in 'The context of the transference' (1965), compares the analytic process with evolution. It has been emphasised that the child's ego is organized according to the mobility of the environment that creates and satisfies the child's needs. The rest of the environment that does not promote needs is not discriminated and remains as such (as background) in the structure of personality. The significance of this fact has not yet been fully recognised.

sense of the term: it is the undifferentiation of body and space, and of body and environment. For this reason, the interpretation of gestures or physical positions is often quite persecutory, because we are not 'moving' the patient's ego but his 'meta-ego'.

*ψ*

I now wish to give another example that also has the peculiarity which is precisely that I cannot describe the 'muteness' of the setting but only the moment at which it is revealed, when it ceases to be mute. I have already compared this to the body schema, which we began to study precisely because of its disturbances. But in this case, the psychoanalyst's setting itself was also vitiated.

A colleague brings to supervision the analysis of a patient whose transference neurosis he has been interpreting for several years, but chronicity and therapeutic inefficacy have set in, for which reason he decides to bring the case to supervision. The patient 'respected' the requirements of the setting and in this sense 'there were no problems': the patient associated well, there was no acting out and the analyst interpreted well (concerning the part he worked on). But the *patient and the therapist spoke to each other using the familiar form of address*[191] because the patient had proposed this at the beginning of his analysis (and this had been accepted by the therapist). It took many months to analyse the therapist's countertransference until he 'found the courage' to rectify the familiar form of address by interpreting to the patient what was happening, and what was hidden inside it. The cancelling of the familiar form, through its systematic analysis, made manifest the narcissistic relation and omnipotent control and the annihilation of the person and role of the therapist, which had become immobilised in the familiar form of address.

In using the familiar form of address, the patient superimposed his 'own setting' on that of the analyst, but in reality he was annihilating the latter. The colleague was faced with work that demanded very great effort in the session with his patient (and in his countertransference) and this led to an intense change in the analytic process and to disruption of the patient's ego, which was being maintained in precarious conditions, with a very limited 'spectrum' of interests and with intense and widespread inhibitions. The change in the form of address through analysis led the analyst to see that it was a question not of phobic character but of a simple schizophrenia with a phobic-obsessional 'façade'.

I do not believe that it would have been feasible to modify the familiar form of address from the outset, since the candidate was not technically equipped to handle a patient with a highly narcissistic organisation.

191 [... *paciente y terapeuta se tuteaban* ... that is, they addressed each other as *tú* (familiar) instead of *usted* (formal).]

I do know that the analyst should not use the familiar form of address to the patient, although he may accept it from the patient and analyse it at the appropriate moment (which I cannot identify retrospectively). The analyst needs to accept the setting brought by the patient (which is the patient's 'meta-ego'), because within it will be found in summary form the primitive unresolved symbiosis. However, we need to state at the same time that accepting the patient's meta-ego (his setting) does not mean giving up the therapist's own, as a function of which it is possible to analyse the process and the setting itself when this has been transformed into process. Any interpretation of the (unaltered) setting mobilises the psychotic part of the personality. It constitutes what I have called a split interpretation.[192] But the analyst-patient relation outside the rigorous setting (as in this example), as well as in 'extra-analytic' relations, makes possible a covering up of the psychotic transference and allows a 'cultivation' of the 'psychoanalytic character'.

ψ

Another patient (B.C.) always kept to the setting, but as her pregnancy advanced, she stopped greeting me as she entered and left (from the beginning of the treatment she had never shaken hands with me). My inclusion of her interrupted greeting in an interpretation was hugely resisted, but in that one could see the mobilisation of her symbiotic relationship with her mother, with some very persecutory characteristics, which had been brought about by her pregnancy.

She still does not shake my hand as she enters or leaves, and this is where a large part of 'her setting' resides, which is different from mine. I believe that the situation is even more complex, because not shaking hands is not a *detail* that is missing to complete the setting. It is an indicator that she has a *different* setting, a different *Gestalt* that is not mine (that of the psychoanalytic treatment), in which she keeps her idealised relationship with her mother split off.

The more we deal with the psychotic part of the personality, the more we need to bear in mind that a detail is not a detail, but instead the sign of a *Gestalt*, that is, of the entirety of a particular organisation or structure.

ψ

In sum, we may say that the patient's setting is his most primitive fusion with the mother's body and that the psychoanalyst's setting must serve to re-establish the original symbiosis, but only in order to change it. Both the disruption of the setting and its idal or normal maintenance are technical and theoretical problems, but what fundamentally disturbs the possibility of thoroughgoing treatment is the disruption introduced or accepted by the

192 [See p. 91]

psychoanalyst in the setting. *The setting can only be analysed within the setting*; in other words, the patient's dependence and most primitive psychological organisation can only be analysed within the analyst's setting, which should be neither ambiguous nor changing, nor altered.

## Summary

It is proposed to consider the *analytic situation* as the totality of the phenomena included in the therapeutic relationship between the analyst and the patient. This situation encompasses phenomena that constitute a *process*, which is what we study, analyse and interpret; but it also includes a *setting*, which is a 'non-process' in the sense that it provides the constants within whose framework the process takes place.

The relations between the two are studied and the setting is defined as the set of constants within which the process (the variables) occurs. The basic aim is to study, not the disruption of the setting, but its psychoanalytic meaning when it is being maintained under 'ideally normal' conditions.

Thus, the setting is studied as an *institution* within whose framework phenomena occur that we call behaviour. In this sense, the setting is 'mute' yet not non-existent; it forms the patient's non-ego on the basis of which the ego is configured. This non-ego is the patient's 'phantom world', which is deposited precisely in the setting, and represents a 'meta-behaviour'.

The role of the setting is illustrated with several clinical examples showing the depositation of the patient's most primitive 'family institution' into the setting. This is a most perfect repetition compulsion, which actualises the primitive undifferentiation of the initial stages of personality organisation.

The setting as an institution is the depositary of the psychotic part of the personality, which is the undifferentiated and unresolved part of the primitive symbiotic links.

The psychoanalytic meaning of the setting thus defined is studied, as well as the repercussions of these considerations for clinical work and psychoanalytic technique.

PART THREE

# Appendix

7

# Ambivalence and ambiguity: the background literature[193]

## Bleuler

E. Bleuler introduced the term ambivalence to characterise one of the fundamental symptoms of schizophrenia. Since then, it has been readily adopted by psychiatry,[194] psychology and psychoanalysis. However, in spite of the time elapsed since then, the term was not completely clarified in the literature, and studies aimed at clearing up its meaning and scope are infrequent.

In *The History of Psychiatry*, Alexander and Selesnick note the precedents in Spinoza's *Ethics*, in which this philosopher presents the details of the phenomenon that 'two hundred years later, Bleuler called ambivalence' (Alexander and Selesnick, 1966, p. 99). Thus, in *Proposition XVII* [Part III] he says:

> If we conceive that a thing, which is wont to affect us painfully, has any point of resemblance with another thing which is wont to affect us with an equally strong emotion of pleasure, we shall hate the first-named thing, and at the same time we shall love it.[195]
>
> (Spinoza, 1677, pp. 54–55)

Spinoza calls this mixture of two opposing emotions '*vacillation*; it stands to the emotions in the same relation as doubt does to the imagination . . .;

193 I shall refer only to the psychoanalytic literature and more especially to the works of Freud.

194 After reviewing the *Reports* of the Second International Congress of Psychiatry (Stoll, ed., 1959) dedicated to the theme of schizophrenia, I now doubt this statement, since it is very difficult to find the use of this term in them.

195 [Quotations in the original are from the Spanish translation by C. G. Bardé. We have substituted the English translation by Elwes.]

vacillation and doubt do not differ one from the other except as greater differs from less.' (p. 74). He ends the *Note* to this *Proposition*: 'Hence we can easily conceive, that one and the same object may be the cause of many and conflicting emotions'. (p. 74).

However, it is undoubtedly Bleuler who introduced the term, identifying three types of ambivalence: affective, volitional and intellectual.

Of the first he said that 'The very same concept can be accompanied simultaneously by pleasant and unpleasant feelings (*affective ambivalence*): the husband both loves and hates his wife' (Bleuler, 1911, p. 53); for ambivalence of will or ambitendency, he gives the example that: 'the patient wishes to eat and does not wish to eat' (p. 53). and for intellectual ambivalence, the example of a patient who said, 'I am Dr. H.; I am not Dr. H.' (p. 54).

Bleuler himself points out that: 'one can easily demonstrate that the patients do not note contradictions when we take their negative answers for positive ones' (p. 54) and: 'Ambivalence shows every gradation down to negativism, particularly in the form of "Ambitendenz"' (p. 55). We shall see below that this is important in the structure of delusional ideas.

The proposition becomes clearer when Bleuler returns, later in his book, to the problem of ambivalence, saying that:

> Even for the healthy everything has its two sides. The rose has its thorns. But in ninety-nine out of a hundred instances, the normal person compares the two aspects, subtracts the negative from the positive values. He appreciates the rose despite its thorns. The schizophrenic, with his weakened associative linkings does not necessarily bring the different aspects of a problem together. He loves the rose because of its beauty and hates it because of its thorns. Thus many simple as well as complicated concepts and, above all, many complexes have for him both affective signs, the plus and the minus, which appear side by side, or alternatingly, one after the other. Certainly even under normal conditions, synthesis may be omitted.
>
> (Bleuler, 1911, pp. 374–375)

Further on, Bleuler offers another example and says that:

> Children often present us with very clear examples of this attitude. Many of them use the phrase, 'Close the door', when they actually want the door to be opened. After all, the common factor is the movement of the door; in comparison, the antithesis of opening and closing becomes so unimportant that the child does not hesitate to use the expression with which it is more familiar, for both.
>
> (Bleuler, 1911, p. 376)

On the same page, Bleuler says:

> In the dreams of healthy persons, affective as well as intellectual ambivalence is a common phenomenon. In such dreams, therefore, many ideas are almost always expressed by their opposites; thus, a 'secret' may be represented by the appearance of a crowd of people.
>
> (Bleuler, 1911, p. 376)

If we consider today the development of knowledge since the period when Bleuler's book was written (over fifty years ago), we see that the concept of ambivalence as presented in his works includes very diverse phenomena: one of them is undifferentiation or lack of discrimination, as in the example of children who use the same phrase for their wish to get the door either opened or closed. In this case, it is not ambivalence strictly speaking, but a lack of discrimination or the remnants of primitive syncretism and as I have already explained this is related to ambiguity. In the latter case, we also include those who (in Bleuler's words) 'do not notice contradictions' (p. 54) or '[do] not necessarily bring the different aspects of a problem together' (p. 374).

The term ambivalence must be reserved for cases in which two antinomic behaviours coincide in relation to the same object at the same time: they may be two opposite attitudes, affects, ideas or tendencies, as long as they have not arrived at a synthesis or working-through of the conflict. When, as in the case of schizophrenics, they do not necessarily bring together 'the different aspects of a problem', as Bleuler puts it, then we cannot use the concept of ambivalence but only that of *divalence*. This phenomenon may present not only in pathology for, as Bleuler notes, 'even under normal conditions, synthesis may be omitted.' (p. 375). This divalence is developmentally prior to ambivalence. The latter is, then, inevitably characterised by the simultaneous or joint presence (in relation to the same object at the same time) of two contradictory terms. If the presentation alternates (in time) it is divalence. The same occurs when they are directed at the same object, although for the subject they are different objects whose antinomic qualities have not yet been integrated. When this integration, synthesis or working-through has been reached, we still cannot designate it as ambivalent. In short, ambivalence always means conflict, whether it is conscious or unconscious ambivalence.

In Bleuler's example of dreams that represent a secret by its opposite, a crowd of people, it is in any case a reaction-formation rather than ambivalence.[196]

196 I wish to explain that, in my opinion, it is not strictly a reaction-formation, since this concept derives from prioritising the waking ego organisation. However, reaction-formation is also a case of the polarisation of ambiguity.

In brief, we could say that Bleuler included in ambivalence what we can now identify as divalence, ambiguity and reaction-formation, concepts that we must now differentiate and clarify, while also recognising the connections between all these phenomena.

Freud repeatedly used the concept of ambivalence and did not make the distinctions that we draw nowadays. These distinctions actually came in with the Kleinian conception, which limits the concept of ambivalence to the depressive position; this is characterised by the recognition of a total object with prevalence of integration, depressive anxiety and guilt. The Kleinian school did not create any specific term corresponding to the paranoid-schizoid position, which is characterised by the prevalence of dissociation and the partial object relation. Pichon Rivière did do so, however, with the term *divalence*, which denotes all the feelings, tendencies or attitudes that are dissociated and directed toward different depositaries or objects when originally or subsequently these relate to a single object. We must therefore speak of divalence whenever schizoid division intervenes or, in other words, whenever a defence mechanism is interposed between two contradictory terms which nevertheless belong to the same order or to the same group. Divalence always indicates potential or avoided conflict, although clinically it may also be a source of conflicts. I now want to review the use made by Freud of these three types of phenomena, and how he understood them.

## Ambiguity in the works of Freud

In *The Interpretation of Dreams* (1900, p. 340)[197] Freud observes the use of words which, by virtue of their ambiguity, are able to express more than one thought or give expression to more than one latent idea. In the same paragraph he points out that since words are points of convergence of multiple

197 I have translated Freud's texts from the English and do not follow the Spanish translation by López y Ballesteros, except where indicated. I use the English edition in order to avoid errors of translation in the Spanish edition (Freud, 1952–56), since the former uses the word 'ambiguity' [*ambigüedad*], whereas the translator López y Ballesteros generally translates it as 'equivocal' [*equívoco*]. The English edition will be abbreviated hereafter as *SE.* and this Spanish edition as *OC.* The subsequent numbers indicate the volume and page.

All references to the German edition of Freud's works have been taken from the *Gesammelte Schriften.* (Freud, 1925) and I gratefully acknowledge this valuable collaboration by Dr. Susana Lustig de Ferrer. [*N.B.* For this English edition of *Symbiosis and Ambiguity*, the quotations by Freud are taken from the *Standard Edition* (Strachey, ed., 1953–74), the references have been converted to author-date format, references to the Spanish edition have been omitted except where specific details of the Spanish translation are mentioned, and references to the *Gesammelte Schriften* (Freud, 1925) have been converted into references to the *Gesammelte Werke* (Freud, 1991).]

representations, they must be considered as predestined to ambiguity. He adds that the neuroses, no less than dreams, use this advantage provided by words for the purposes of condensation and disguise.[198]

Quoting H. Sachs, he says,

> If, for instance, the expression that is to be represented is an ambiguous one, the dream-work may exploit the fact by using the ambiguity as a switch-point: where one of the meanings of the word is present in the dream-thoughts the other one can be introduced into the manifest dream.
>
> (Freud, 1900, p. 410)

In German he used, not ambiguity, but the word *Zweideutigkeit* the first time, while the second time he used the word *Doppelsinn*. The former could be translated as double meaning or double interpretation and the latter as double sense.

In the same volume, when he studies absurd dreams (p. 431), Freud says that dreams of dead people whom the dreamer has loved raise problems that cannot always be satisfactorily solved; this is due particularly to the marked emotional ambivalence dominating the dreamer's relation to that person. It commonly occurs in these dreams that the dead person is treated at first as if he were alive, but then he suddenly appears dead. This has a confusing effect. This alternation between life and death occurs as if there was an attempt to 'represent *indifference* on the part of the dreamer'. ('It's all the same to me whether he's alive or dead.'). According to Freud, this indifference is of course, not real. The dreamer uses it to try to repudiate the ambivalence toward the dead person, that is, the 'contradictory emotional attitude'.[199]

The term ambiguity also appears in *The Psychopathology of Everyday Life*, when he analyses the forgetting of names and series of words, pointing out that an inhibited name has necessarily touched on a personal complex.

> The relation of the name to myself is one that I should not have expected and is usually arrived at through superficial associations (such as verbal

198 ['. . . a form of words which owing to its ambiguity is able to give expression to more than one of the dream-thoughts. . . . Words, since they are the nodal points of numerous ideas, may be regarded as predestined to ambiguity; and the neuroses (e.g. in framing obsessions and phobias), no less than dreams, make unashamed use of the advantages thus offered by words for purposes of condensation and disguise.' Freud (1900), pp. 340–341.]

199 The paragraph in which Freud speaks of *indifference* and of *ambivalence* was added as a *Note* to the 1911 edition of *The Interpretation of Dreams*, as Strachey points out, and incorporated into the text in the 1930 edition. These two words are italicised in the text.

> ambiguity or similarity in sound); it can be characterized quite generally as an oblique relation.
>
> (Freud, 1901, p. 22)

The word *ambiguity* figures in the English edition (p. 22), but not in the Spanish edition, where it was translated as the 'double meaning of the word'.[200] In the original German we find the word *Wortzweideutigkeit* (double meaning of the word).

Thus, when in example (2) Freud denies the existence of a third inn in a summer resort, its name is quite similar to that of a Viennese physician who also practised Freud's specialism. The name itself has two meanings or senses, and this is what is being referred to as ambiguity. Thus, the latter has the function of 'blunting' a conflict and Freud speaks of the 'predatory activities of the "family complex".' (Freud, 1901, p. 23).

Further on, Freud says:

> A name which has more than one meaning and consequently belongs to more than one group of thoughts (complexes) is frequently interfered with in its connection with one train of thought owing to its participation in another, stronger complex.
>
> (Freud, 1901, p. 40)

I wish to point out here that this *plurality of meanings* of a name or a word corresponds, in my opinion, to the phenomenon of ambiguity.

In Dora's first dream, in 'Fragment of an Analysis of a Case of Hysteria', he emphasises the fact that the patient said that 'something might happen in the night so that it might be necessary to leave the room.' (Freud, 1905a, p. 65). And he puts these words in italics because they constitute an equivoque. The English edition says in a footnote that they have an aura of ambiguity,[201] since they may also refer to certain physical necessities and adds that in a line of associations the ambiguous words act like points at a railway junction. In German he uses *zweideutig* (double meaning).

In this work, (p. 82), when he examines the word 'catarrh', he refers to it as a 'switch word,' since this term refers equally to the patient's discharge, her mother's analogous illness and her father's cough (catarrh).

*Jokes and Their Relation to the Unconscious* (1905c) is particularly rich in the study of the use and function of ambiguity in jokes, considered by Freud a use of the technique of double meaning. This book would require a study by itself.

In *Delusions and Dreams in Jensen's Gradiva* (1907), Freud says: 'Anyone who reads *Gradiva* must be struck by the frequency with which the author

200 [In Spanish: *doble sentido de la palabra*. (*OC*, I, p. 27)]

201 [*Un halo ambiguo*. The English edition has: 'They seemed to have an ambiguous ring about them'; Freud wrote: *Sie klingen mir zweideutig* (*GW*, V, p. 226)]

puts ambiguous remarks into the mouths of his two principal characters.' (Freud, 1907, p. 84). In English the word *ambiguous* is used instead of *phrases with double meaning*[202] used in the Spanish edition. In German he uses *zweideutig* (double meaning). The English translation goes on to say, 'In Hanold's case these remarks are intended by him unambiguously and it is only the heroine, Gradiva, who is struck by their second meaning.'

On the same page, Freud says:

> Zoe's speech in which she explains the situation to her friend and at the same time succeeds in getting rid of the interrupter is full of ambiguities of this kind. It is in reality a speech made by the author and aimed more at the reader than at Zoe's newly-married 'colleague'.
>
> (Freud, 1907, p. 84)

In the English edition he says that Zoe's phrases are full of ambiguities.

Freud wonders (p. 85) why in *Gradiva* there is such a preference for 'ambiguous speeches', while the Spanish edition has 'preference for phrases with a double meaning.'[203] Freud points out that this is not accidental, since these words signify a compromise between the conscious and the unconscious and that 'it is simply that this double origin is more easily noticed in speeches than, for instance, in actions.' (p. 85). He adds the observation that this ambiguous language is also observed in psychotherapeutic treatment.

ψ

From this point on, we find no more references to ambiguity in Freud's works, and its place is taken instead by the concept of ambivalence, which does not mean that he no longer includes the phenomena that correspond to ambiguity. In any case, in what I have reviewed up to now, Freud's contribution to the study of ambiguity and its psychological meaning is of fundamental importance.

In his studies of dreams, the psychopathology of everyday life, delusions and hysterical phenomena, the investigation of ambiguity stands out in Freud's works. It consists in the fact that a word has various meanings and is used precisely because this characteristic allows the individual using it (whether awake or in dreams) to refer consciously to one of its meanings while also alluding to another of which the individual is unaware. This other meaning is also - at the same time - another psychological phenomenon of which the subject is unaware or which he has not yet made conscious. Freud says explicitly that words, by virtue of their ambiguity, are able to express more than one thought and to give expression to more than one latent idea. Words, he says, are predestined to ambiguity (Freud, 1900, p. 340).

202 [*frases de doble sentido*; (*OC*, III, p. 365)]

203 [*preferencia por las frases de doble sentido*]

It is easy to see in the works of Freud that the different components or meanings converging in an ambiguous word are not necessarily mutually contrary, antinomic or opposite (a condition that is indispensable in the case of ambivalence and divalence): they are different.

Freud also notes the blunting role of ambiguity in the case of dreams of deceased loved ones, in which they appear either as living or dead, as if the dream were trying to 'represent *indifference* on the part of the dreamer'. However, this *indifference* 'is intended to help the dreamer to repudiate his very intense and often contradictory emotional attitudes and it thus becomes a dream-representation of his *ambivalence.*' (p. 431).

Thus we have, deducing now from Freud's writings, two types of ambiguity: (a) when a word is ambiguous because it contains different but not necessarily contradictory meanings and phenomena, which may not belong to the same order, class or group of phenomena. Hence, 'catarrh' applies both to coughing and to vaginal discharge; (b) when the terms of an ambiguous dream are originally opposites and belong to the same series, order or group of phenomena (love-hate for the dead person), the ambiguity intervening by 'blunting' this contradiction or ambivalence. Freud states it very well: ambiguity (indifference in the dream) both repudiates and represents ambivalence and, I would add, is therefore no longer ambiguity.

Both types of ambiguity may be used by dreams or by waking phenomena, and among the latter Freud explicitly singles out slips of the tongue and neuroses. There is a certain difference between these two, since in the first conflict is not yet present, while the second conflicting terms are present (although in a blunted form).

Another observation which we extract from Freud's works is that the subject is unaware of the ambiguity. Hanold (in the *Gradiva*) uses phrases that for him 'are unambiguous' (according to Freud). It is Zoe 'who is struck by their second meaning' (Freud, 1907, p. 84). Zoe acts like the psychoanalyst in the course of a treatment in that she transforms ambiguity into discrimination.

Since for Freud the symptom too is a settlement or compromise of a conflict, we could also consider the symptom as ambiguous. I would like to turn my attention to this issue now, since I think that in his works prior to 1900, the phenomenon most studied by Freud (precisely through the symptom) was what we now call divalence, which he returned to much later, especially in 1938. These works are followed by a period in which he explores ambiguity (up to *Gradiva*, 1907). In a third period he focuses more attention on ambivalence, in close connection particularly with his studies of obsessional neurosis.

Summarising: if we apply current terminology, we may identify three periods in Freud's writing in relation to the present subject of interest:

(1) Study of *divalence* in neurotic symptoms; taken up again in 1938 in 'Splitting of the Ego in the Process of Defence' (Freud, 1940b [1938])

and in *An Outline of Psychoanalysis* (Freud, 1940a [1938]) and earlier in 'Fetishism' (Freud, 1927).

(2) Study of *ambiguity* in dreams, slips of the tongue, delusions and words (whether or not in waking phenomena and whether or not in the neuroses).

(3) *Ambivalence*, in his studies on obsessional neurosis and in the phenomena related to it (totem, taboo, melancholia).

Up to now, I have concentrated only on what I call the second 'period,' but now I would like to return to the first. I repeat: to avoid confusion, although Freud used the term ambivalence, this is not the case with divalence, which never appeared in his works. In relation to ambiguity, although this word appears in the English edition, we have seen that in German he uses *zweideutig* or *Zweideutigkeit*, which do not correspond exactly to ambiguity. However, the phenomena examined do correspond to it.

## Divalence in the works of Freud

In a letter to J. Breuer on June 29th, 1892 (Freud, 1940–41 [1892], p. 147), Freud mentions the theorem 'which lays it down that the contents of different states of consciousness are not associated with one another.' In the study 'On the Theory of Hysterical Attacks' [Section C of 'Sketches for the "Preliminary Communication" of 1893'] (Freud, 1940–41 [1892]), written in collaboration with J. Breuer, they say (p. 151): '. . . we regard it as indispensable for the explanation of hysterical phenomena to assume the presence of a dissociation – a splitting of the content of consciousness.'

In Note III (Freud, 1940–41 [1892], p. 149), Freud formulates the hypothesis according to which 'the content of consciousness easily becomes temporarily dissociated and certain complexes of ideas which are not associatively connected easily fly apart.'

What is dissociated or split off from the content of the conscious are memories that return in the hysterical attack. Thus, in these works of 1892 we already see the fundamental characteristics of what we now know as divalence: the splitting or dissociation of consciousness into different contents that cannot be associated with each other.

This phenomenon is described in detail in 'A Case of Successful Treatment by Hypnotism' (Freud, 1892–93, p. 121). In this work, Freud discusses aims and expectations, as well as of the 'counter-expectation' that 'is itself represented by a collection of ideas to which I shall give the name of "distressing antithetic ideas".'[204] These distressing antithetic ideas arise in the

204 The Spanish translation says: 'painful contrasting representations' [*representaciones contrastantes penosas*] and the translator of the Santiago Rueda Edition of Freud's works

neuroses and appear manifestly, says Freud, in the '*folie de doute*', that is, the obsessional neurosis, although

> [precisely] at this point, the two major neuroses, neurasthenia and hysteria, each behave in a different manner, characteristic of each. In neurasthenia, the pathologically intensified antithetic idea is combined with the volitional idea into a *single* act of consciousness; it subtracts from the volitional idea and brings about the weakness of will which is so striking in neurasthenics and of which they themselves are aware. The process in hysteria differs from this in two respects, or possibly only in one. [Firstly,] in accordance with the tendency to a *dissociation of consciousness* in hysteria, the distressing antithetic idea, which seems to be inhibited, is removed from association with the intention and continues to exist as a disconnected idea, often unconsciously to the patient himself. [Secondly,] it is supremely characteristic of hysteria that, when it comes to the carrying out of the intention, the inhibited antithetic idea can put itself into effect by innervation of the body just as easily as does a volitional idea in normal circumstances. The antithetic idea establishes itself, so to speak, as a '*counter-will*', while the patient is aware with astonishment of having a will which is resolute but powerless.
>
> (Freud, 1892–93, p. 122)

Today, we recognise that obsessional doubt is a characteristic case of ambivalence, while hysteria would be what we now call divalence, since the two antithetic terms remain dissociated and have different vicissitudes. In neurasthenia we will confront the problem of ambiguity.

This discussion is by no means, as I have already said, an attempt to state that Freud used the term divalence, since at that time (1892) even the term ambivalence had not yet been introduced. It is only a question of showing the presence of the phenomenon of divalence in Freud's works, especially as I said in his studies on hysteria. This review of the literature is aimed at clarifying the differences between divalence, ambiguity and ambivalence.

In *Studies on Hysteria* (Breuer and Freud, 1893–95) we find described and examined the phenomenon of splitting or dissociation, which in my view is fundamental to divalence, although we find it superimposed on what I am now calling splitting.[205] Of course the authors (Breuer and Freud) do not use this terminology to describe it.

In Strachey's *Introduction* to the English edition (referring to the first chapter, written by Breuer and Freud and published as the *Preliminary*

considers (Freud, 1952–56, Volume XXII, p. 465) that the correct translation is 'painful antithetic ideas [*ideas antitéticas penosas*].'

205 [In the first half of this sentence the English word 'splitting' is used, apparently in contrast with the Spanish *clivaje* in the second half.]

*Communication* in 1893), he notes that they explain their fundamental hypotheses and the use of what we now term dissociation or splitting. Thus, Strachey says that in hysterical patients:

> The affect remains in a 'strangulated' state, and the memory of the experience to which it is attached is cut off from consciousness. The affective memory is thereafter manifested in hysterical symptoms, which may be regarded as 'mnemic symbols' – that is to say as symbols of the suppressed memory.
>
> (Strachey, 1955, p. xviii)

For me, this description obviously corresponds to dissociation and divalence. The concept of dissociation was used by Freud as early as 1893 in 'Some Points for a Comparative Study of Organic and Hysterical Motor Paralyses' (Freud 1893 [1888–1893]).

The term splitting is used repeatedly, as in the *Preliminary Communication* (Breuer and Freud, 1893–95), where the authors say:

> The longer we have been occupied with these phenomena the more we have become convinced that the splitting of consciousness which is so striking in the well-known classical cases under the form of '*double conscience*' is present to a rudimentary degree in every hysteria, and that a tendency to such a dissociation, and with it the emergence of abnormal states of consciousness (which we shall bring together under the term 'hypnoid') is the basic phenomenon of this neurosis.[206]
>
> (Breuer and Freud, 1893–95, p. 12)

And in such a way in these studies they speak of dissociation in similar terms.

In Breuer's description of the case of Anna O., which is omitted from the Spanish translation (Breuer and Freud, 1893–95, pp. 21–47), he describes his patient as having two entirely different states of consciousness that presented alternately and became increasingly differentiated from one another in the course of the illness. In one of these states she was relatively normal, while in the other state of consciousness she hallucinated.

Strictly speaking, the dissociation of consciousness in cases of '*double conscience*' does not correspond to divalence but to what we now term splitting[207] between the neurotic and the psychotic part of the personality. I reserve the word dissociation for divalence, in which what are dissociated are not two states of consciousness, two parts of the personality or two different egos, but the antinomic terms of the same conflict that the subject

206 [In the *Standard Edition* the last part of this quotation is also in italics.]
207 [*clivaje*]

directs toward different objects that, for the subject, are not integrated into a single one. Thus, Breuer describes his patient as

> split into two personalities of which one was mentally normal and the other insane. The sharp division between the two states in the present patient only exhibits more clearly, in my opinion, what has given rise to a number of unexplained problems in many other hysterical patients.'
>
> (Breuer and Freud, 1893–95, pp. 45–46)

In the case of Lucy R., Freud says that it is a '*sine qua non* for the acquisition of hysteria that an incompatibility should develop between the ego and some idea presented to it.' (Breuer and Freud, 1893–95, p. 122). He adds:

> The actual traumatic moment, then, is the one at which the incompatibility forces itself upon the ego and at which the latter decides on the repudiation of the incompatible idea. That idea is not annihilated by a repudiation of this kind, but merely repressed into the unconscious.
>
> (Breuer and Freud, 1893–95, p. 123)

(The Spanish edition uses *contradiction*[208] while the English term is *incompatible.*)

And at the end of the Lucy R. case, Freud says, 'The therapeutic process in this case consisted in compelling the psychical group that had been split off to unite once more with the ego-consciousness'. (p. 124).

In the *Discussion* of the Katharina case, Freud says, 'The splitting-off of psychical groups may be said to be a normal process in adolescent development; and it is easy to see that their later reception into the ego affords frequent opportunities for psychical disturbances.' (Breuer and Freud, 1893–95, pp. 133–134). In this case it is again more correct to use splitting rather than dissociation.

Dissociation is clearly described in the *Discussion* of the case of Elisabeth von R., where he attributes the hysterical symptom, consisting of intense pain in a certain area of the right thigh, which arose during her father's illness, to a certain moment when her filial duties had come into conflict with her erotic wishes. 'Under the pressure of lively self-reproaches she decided in favour of the former, and in doing so brought about her hysterical pain.' The affect of the erotic representation was transformed by conversion into the hysterical symptom. (Breuer and Freud, 1893–95, p. 164). Here, the description of the dissociation of consciousness as divalence is quite clear: the (ambivalent) conflict arose between filial love and erotic wishes originally directed toward the same object, thereby creating 'an intolerable

208 [*contradicción*]

mental condition' (p. 166) that the patient escaped through dissociation of consciousness at the cost of physical suffering.

In the theoretical section, Breuer dedicates a special part to unconscious ideas and ideas unacceptable to the conscious, and to the splitting of the mind, and he introduces the concept that we cannot continue to refer to dissociation of consciousness, since it is dissociation of the mind.[209]

In the first of the *Five Lectures on Psycho-Analysis* (Freud, 1910a [1909]), when Freud summarises his early discoveries and experiences in the work with Breuer on hysteria, he says that the study of hypnotic phenomena led him to the idea, strange at first, that

> in one and the same individual there can be several mental groupings, which can remain more or less independent of one another, which can 'know nothing' of one another and which can alternate with one another in their hold upon consciousness. Cases of this kind, too, occasionally appear spontaneously, and are then described as examples of '*double conscience*'. If, where a splitting of the personality such as this has occurred, consciousness remains attached regularly to one of the two states, we call it the *conscious* mental state and the other, which is detached from it, the *unconscious* one.'
>
> (Freud, 1910a, p. 19)

The word splitting, used in the English edition of Freud, is no longer for us now really a dissociation corresponding to divalence but a splitting of the personality.

At the beginning of the second of the *Lectures*, in the English edition, the terms dissociation and splitting of consciousness are used as synonyms, while in the Spanish edition they are translated respectively as dissociation and fragmenting of consciousness.[210]

In the same *Lecture* Freud sets out the difference between his conception and Janet's, saying,

> We do not derive the psychical splitting from an innate incapacity for synthesis on the part of the mental apparatus; we explain it dynamically, from the conflict of opposing mental forces and recognize it as the outcome of an active struggling on the part of the two psychical groupings against each other.
>
> (Freud, 1910a, pp. 25–26)

Further on he continues:

209 [Strachey's translation has 'splitting of consciousness' and 'splitting of the mind'. Breuer has *Spaltung des Bewusstseins* and *Spaltung der Psyche*.]

210 [*disociación y desdoblamiento de la conciencia*]

> The reflection cannot be escaped that further determinants must be present if the conflict is to lead to dissociation. I will also readily grant you that the hypothesis of repression leaves us not at the end but at the beginning of a psychological theory.
>
> (Freud, 1910a, p. 26)

Here Freud states absolutely clearly the existence of conflict that for us nowadays is necessarily ambivalent, unlike divalence in which the antinomic terms of the conflict have been dissociated.

At the end of a short work written in 1924, 'Neurosis and Psychosis' (Freud, 1924a), Freud states that the ego may deform itself spontaneously, tolerating encroachments on its unity or even dissociating in some cases. The *Standard Edition* uses the term 'cleavage or division of itself' to refer to a dissociation of the ego. This problem is discussed later in 'Fetishism' (Freud, 1927) and in two unfinished works: 'Splitting of the Ego in the Process of Defence' (Freud, 1940b [1938]) and in chapter VIII of *An Outline of Psycho-Analysis* (Freud, 1940a [1938]). Between 1909 and 1924 he does not use these terms.[211]

In 'Fetishism' (Freud, 1927), Freud discusses the fetishist's double attitude, which involves a dissociation of the ego. Strachey adds a footnote to the effect that the beginning of these ideas on splitting and the dissociation of the ego can be found in a letter to Fliess on January 1, 1896 and in his work, 'The Neuro-Psychoses of Defence' (Freud, 1894).

In the case of fetishism, we would now say that this dissociation of the ego is actually a splitting between a more developed, adult part of the personality that recognises reality and another infantile part that still adheres to a primitive organisation.

In 'Splitting of the Ego in the Process of Defence', Freud points out that 'a rift in the ego' is produced and 'two contrary reactions to the conflict persist as the centre-point of a splitting of the ego.' (Freud, 1940b [1938], p. 276).

In *An Outline of Psycho-Analysis* (Freud, 1940a [1938]), in Chapter VIII, Freud refers to a 'psychical *split*' to explain that

> two psychical attitudes have been formed instead of a single one – one, the normal one, which takes account of reality, and another which under the influence of the instincts detaches the ego from reality. The two exist alongside of each other.
>
> (Freud, 1940a [1938], p. 202)

Then he adds:

211 I venture the hypothesis that Freud abandoned the concept of dissociation and therefore the study of divalence, not only because of Bleuler's introduction of the concept of ambivalence but also in order to differentiate his theories from those of Janet.

> The view which postulates that in all psychoses there is a *splitting of the ego* could not call for so much notice if it did not turn out to apply to other states more like the neuroses and finally, to the neuroses themselves. I first became convinced of this in cases of *fetishism*.
>
> (Freud, 1940a [1938], p. 202)

Then he adds:

> The two attitudes persist side by side throughout their lives without influencing each other. Here is what may rightly be called a splitting of the ego.
>
> (Freud, 1940a [1938], p. 203)

In all these cases, I believe it is a splitting between the neurotic and the psychotic part of the personality, and that we cannot apply to it the concept of dissociation nor that of divalence as in the paranoid-schizoid position.

At the end of Chapter VIII, I believe that Freud incorrectly superimposes the splitting that he is studying up to that moment (between the neurotic and the psychotic part of the ego) onto the dissociation that occurs between the good and the bad object as well as in the ego involved in the conflict, because he says that this ego splitting is not so new or strange and that it corresponds to a general characteristic of the neuroses, except that 'one of these attitudes belongs to the ego and the contrary one, which is repressed, belongs to the id.' (Freud, 1940a [1938], p. 204).

The second of these actually corresponds to divalence and dissociation rather than to splitting. A fundamental difference is that dissociation is a separation of antinomies within the same level of ego structure, while splitting is a separation between two organisations with different structures or between different levels of organisation (maturity and immaturity).

## Ambivalence in the works of Freud

After Bleuler introduced the term ambivalence in 1910, Freud used this concept exclusively even for phenomena that we have seen would correspond to what today we call divalence on the one hand and ambiguity on the other.[212] If we wish to trace chronologically the use of the concept of

212 As I have pointed out he reverts to the use of other terms (dissociation, splitting) in 1924, 1927 and 1940. In this regard, it is appropriate to quote from Ernest Jones's, *Sigmund Freud, Life and Work*, volume 2: 'Most students of Freud have been struck by what has been called his obstinate dualism; had he been a philosopher he certainly would not have been a monist nor would he have felt at home in William James's pluralistic universe. Running all through his work there is what Heinz Hartmann has called

ambivalence in his works, we must bear well in mind that in successive editions of his works prior to 1910, he sometimes made additions to the text that included the concept of ambivalence.

We must also bring out the fact that when Freud examines and recognises the phenomenon of ambivalence and calls it that, it is different from those cases in which he describes the phenomenon of ambivalence without applying this term to them. One example of the former is found in *Three Essays on the Theory of Sexuality*, originally published in 1905, whose subsequent editions include in the text a section directly titled ambivalence (Freud, 1905b).

In 'Notes upon a Case of Obsessional Neurosis' (1909), Freud added a note in 1923 in which he recalls that Bleuler introduced the term ambivalence in 1910 to describe the emotional constellations that he is discussing in the case of obsessional neurosis, the conflict between love and hatred:

> But the *chronic* co-existence of love and hatred, both directed towards the same person and both of the highest degree of intensity, cannot fail to astonish us. . . . And in fact such a protracted survival of two opposites is only possible under quite peculiar psychological conditions and with the co-operation of the state of affairs in the unconscious. The love has not succeeded in extinguishing the hatred but only in driving it down into the unconscious; and in the unconscious the hatred, safe from the danger of being destroyed by the operations of consciousness, is able to persist and even to grow. In such circumstances the conscious love attains as a rule, by way of reaction, an especially high degree of intensity, so as to be strong enough for the perpetual task of keeping its opponent under repression. The necessary condition for the occurrence of such a strange state of affairs in a person's erotic life appears to be that at a very early age, somewhere in the prehistoric period of his infancy, the two opposites should have been split apart and one of them, usually the hatred, have been repressed.
>
> (Freud, 1909, p. 239)

(It is here that Freud adds the footnote dated 1923.) In other words, for Freud

"a very characteristic kind of dialectical thinking that tends to base theories on the interaction of two opposite powers". This was of course more pronounced in his basic classifications: love-hunger; ego-sexuality; auto-erotism–hetero-erotism; Eros-Thanatos; Life-Death, and so on. I remember how alien this seemed to me, having being brought up in a biological school that thought of instincts in the plural. But the same fondness for pairs is to be found again and again: love-hate; exhibitionism-scopophilism; etc. It is as if Freud had a difficulty in contemplating any topic unless he could divide it into two opposites, and never more than two. That there was a fundamental conflict between two opposing forces in the mind was for him a basic fact.' (Jones, 1955, pp. 469–470).

the term ambivalence applies both to the juxtaposed, joint existence of love and hatred 'directed towards the same person' and to the dissociation between love and hatred, even when one of them is conscious and the other unconscious. Thus, Freud uses the same term for both ambivalence and divalence.

In *Three Essays on the Theory of Sexuality*, Freud refers to ambivalence when he examines infantile sexuality and says that 'it is further characterized by the fact that in it the opposing pairs of instincts are developed to an approximately equal extent, a state of affairs described by Bleuler's happily chosen term "ambivalence".' (Freud, 1905b, p. 199).

In 'The Dynamics of Transference' (1912), he says that in psychoneurosis the positive transference co-exists with the negative transference *directed simultaneously to the same person* and adds:

> Bleuler has coined the excellent term ambivalence to describe this phenomenon. Up to a point, ambivalence of feeling of this sort seems to be normal; but a high degree of it is certainly a special peculiarity of neurotic people. In obsessional neurotics an early separation of the 'pairs of opposites' seems to be characteristic of their instinctual life and to be one of their constitutional preconditions. Ambivalence in the emotional trends of neurotics is the best explanation of their ability to enlist their transferences in the service of resistance.
>
> (Freud, 1912b, pp. 106–107)

In the *Note* on page 106 Freud says that Bleuler introduced the term *ambivalence* in 1910 and that Stekel proposed the term *bipolarity* for the same phenomenon. Strachey comments that this is Freud's first mention of the word ambivalence, but that he also uses it occasionally in another sense, to describe the simultaneous presence of active and passive impulses.

In 'Instincts and Their Vicissitudes' (1915) Freud applies the term ambivalence to the existence in each instinctive movement of its opposite. He adds that

> the amount of demonstrable ambivalence varies greatly between individuals, groups and races. Marked instinctual ambivalence in a human being living at the present day may be regarded as an archaic inheritance, for we have reason to suppose that the part played in instinctual life by the active impulses in their unmodified form was greater in primaeval times than it is on an average to-day.
>
> (Freud, 1915, p. 131)

In the English edition of this article Strachey says that the term ambivalence does not seem to have been used by Bleuler in the sense that Freud uses it here. Strachey continues, saying that Bleuler identified three types of ambivalence: (1) emotional, that is, the oscillation between hatred and love;

(2) voluntary, that is, the inability to decide on an action; and (3) intellectual, that is, the belief in contradictory propositions. Strachey says that Freud generally uses the term *in the first of these senses* and that a passage in 'Instincts and Their Vicissitudes' is one of the few cases in which Freud applied the term *ambivalence* to *activity and passivity.*

In the same article, 'Instincts and Their Vicissitudes', when Freud examines the transformation of an instinct into its opposite, he also uses the term ambivalence for the antithesis love-hate and says that '[Since] it is particularly common to find both these *directed simultaneously towards the same object,*[213] their co-existence furnishes the most important example of ambivalence of feeling.' (Freud, 1915, p. 133).

ψ

To summarise: up to now, Freud has used the concept of ambivalence for different phenomena (sometimes in the same article):

(a) Conflict of feelings, between love and hate, in 'A Case of Obsessional Neurosis' and in 'Instincts and Their Vicissitudes'. However, in the former work he uses ambivalence to refer to both the juxtaposition of love and hatred towards the same person and also the dissociation between love and hatred.
(b) Opposed pairs of instincts, in *Three Essays on the Theory of Sexuality* and in 'Instincts and Their Vicissitudes'.
(c) Activity-passivity, in 'Instincts and Their Vicissitudes'.
(d) Positive and negative transference 'directed simultaneously toward the same person' in 'The Dynamics of Transference'.

Today, we may include all these definitions in the term ambivalence, except the love-hate dissociation (that he describes in 'A Case of Obsessional Neurosis' and which strictly corresponds to the divalence of the paranoid-schizoid position). What characterises ambivalence is not precisely its content (which may be very different in each case) but the simultaneous co-existence, in conflict, of antithetic pairs directed to the same object. Freud uses, instead of object, the word person, but today we recognise that it may not be a person but a part of one (what we now call a part-object).

But let us continue with other important texts by Freud.

ψ

In *Totem and Taboo* (1913), Freud dedicates chapter II to the study of taboo and ambivalence of feelings and he gives as an example a typical case of 'touching phobia' in which

213 [The emphasis is Bleger's]

> in very early childhood, the patient shows a strong *desire* to touch, the aim of which is of a far more specialized kind than one would have been inclined to expect. This desire is promptly met by an *external* prohibition against carrying out that particular kind of touching.
>
> (Freud, 1913, pp. 29–30)

This resulted in a repression of the wish to touch in the unconscious. Freud adds:

> The principal characteristic of the psychological constellation which becomes fixed in this way is what might be described as the subject's *ambivalent* attitude towards a single object, or rather towards one act in connection with that object. He is constantly wishing to perform this act (the touching), [and looks on it as his supreme enjoyment, but he must not perform it][214] and detests it as well. The conflict between these two currents cannot be promptly settled because – there is no other way of putting it – they are localized in the subject's mind in such a manner that they cannot come up against each other. The prohibition is noisily conscious, while the persistent desire to touch is unconscious and the subject knows nothing of it. If it were not for this psychological factor, an ambivalence like this could neither last so long nor lead to such consequences.
>
> (Freud, 1913, pp. 29–30)

Here Freud includes in ambivalence the dissolution and repression of one of the terms, to which (thus described) we would now apply the term divalence rather than ambivalence. However, the obsessional acts that appear as compromises

> ... from one point of view ... are evidences of remorse, efforts at expiation, and so on, while on the other hand they are at the same time substitutive acts to compensate the instinct for what has been prohibited.
>
> (Freud, 1913, p. 30)

In this way, in the obsessional neuroses, the obsessional act really is ambivalent and the dissociation cannot be strictly maintained. Symptoms and defence mechanisms represent a compromise rather than a total or successful repression.

After this, Freud says that primitive peoples have adopted an ambivalent attitude towards their taboos.

> In their unconscious there is nothing they would like more than to violate them, but they are afraid to do so; they are afraid precisely because

214 [The square brackets are Strachey's]

> they would like to, and the fear is stronger than the desire. The desire is unconscious, however, in every individual member of the tribe just as it is in neurotics.
>
> (Freud, 1913, p. 31)

Freud indicates (pp. 35–36) the psychological factors in the case of neurosis and says that symptoms, and particularly obsessional acts, defensive measures and obsessional commands, derive from ambivalent impulses, and he proposes to demonstrate that the same occurs in the taboo, adding: '. . . ambivalence, that is, the dominance of opposing trends . . .' (p. 36).

Freud remarks (p. 157),

> I have often had occasion to point out that emotional ambivalence in the proper sense of the term – that is, simultaneous existence of love and hate towards the same object – lies at the root of many important cultural institutions.
>
> (Freud, 1913, p. 157)

Here, Freud defines the strict sense in which he uses the term ambivalence: the *simultaneous* existence toward the same object of two antithetical terms. This definition, I believe, is the correct one and the one that should be reserved for the concept of ambivalence.

Freud comments on the 'Little Hans' case, saying that the child finds relief from the conflict stemming from his double relation with his father, from the ambivalent emotional attitude toward him, by displacing his hostile and fearful feelings onto a substitute for his father.

> The displacement cannot, however, bring the conflict to an end, it cannot effect a clear-cut severance between the affectionate and the hostile feelings. On the contrary, the conflict is resumed in relation to the object on to which the displacement has been made: the ambivalence is extended to *it*.
>
> (Freud, 1913, p. 129)

Here again, our impression is that Freud continues to apply the term ambivalence to the co-existence of contradictory sentiments, at the same time toward the same object, given that when the separation cannot be established between them (what we would nowadays call schizoid division) he considers that the ambivalence continues to persist toward the object replacing the father. However, we have seen that Freud (in the same book) does not exclude the dissociated terms from ambivalence.

In *Introductory Lectures on Psycho-Analysis* Freud defines ambivalence as 'the direction towards the same person of contrary – affectionate and hostile – feelings.' (Freud, 1916–17, p. 428). When he describes the Oedipus complex (p. 332) as the opposition between the child's desire to have his mother for himself and his rejection of the father, he says that the latter may often be obscured by the circumstance that on other occasions the child may simultaneously give evidence of great affection for his father. He adds,

> But contrary – or, as it is better to say, 'ambivalent' - emotional attitudes, which in adults would lead to a conflict, remain compatible with each other for a long time in children, just as later they find a permanent place beside each other in the unconscious.
>
> (Freud, 1916–17, p. 332)

When Freud refers to the Oedipus complex as attraction to the mother and rejection of the father, these contrary attitudes are compatible because, strictly speaking, they are not ambivalent but divalent. If ambivalence persists without promoting conflict, then strictly speaking we are dealing with ambiguity.

In *Group Psychology and the Analysis of the Ego* (1921), in a footnote, Freud writes:

> In young children, for instance, ambivalent emotional attitudes towards those who are nearest to them exist side by side for a long time, without either of them interfering with the expression of the other and opposite one. If eventually a conflict breaks out between the two, it is often settled by the child making a change of object and displacing one of the ambivalent emotions on to a substitute. The history of the development of a neurosis in an adult will also show that a suppressed emotion may frequently persist for a long time in unconscious or even in conscious phantasies, the content of which naturally runs directly counter to some predominant tendency, and yet that this opposition does not result in any proceedings on the part of the ego against what it has repudiated. The phantasy is tolerated for quite a long time, until suddenly one day, usually as a result of an increase in the affective cathexis of the phantasy, a conflict breaks out between it and the ego with all the usual consequences.
>
> (Freud, 1921, p. 79)

Further on he says: 'When this hostility is directed against persons who are otherwise loved, we describe it as an ambivalence of feeling . . .' (Freud, 1921, p. 102).

In *Inhibitions, Symptoms and Anxiety*, Freud repeats the same definition of ambivalence: love and hate directed towards one and the same person. (Freud, 1926, p. 102).

In 'Remarks on the Theory and Practice of Dream-Interpretation' (1923), Freud says:

> It is by no means easy to arrive at general conclusions upon the value of correctly translated dreams. If a conflict due to ambivalence is taking place in a patient, then the emergence in him of a hostile thought certainly does not imply a permanent overcoming of his affectionate impulse – that is to say, a resolution of the conflict: neither does any such implication follow from a *dream* with a similarly hostile content. During a conflict such as this arising from ambivalence, there are often *two dreams every night*,[215] each of them representing an opposite attitude. In that case the progress lies in the fact that a complete isolation of the two contrasted impulses has been achieved and that each of them, with the help of its unconscious reinforcements, can be followed and understood to its extreme limits. And if it sometimes happens that one of the two ambivalent dreams has been forgotten, one must not be deceived into assuming that a decision has been made in favour of the one side. The fact that one of the dreams has been forgotten shows, it is true, that for the moment one tendency is in the ascendant, but that is true only of the one day, and may be changed. The next night may perhaps bring the opposite expression into the foreground. The true state of the conflict can only be determined by taking into account all the other indications, including those of waking life.
>
> (Freud, 1923b [1922], p. 113)

In *Civilization and Its Discontents* (1930), when he studies the sentiment of guilt, he says that it is an 'expression of the conflict due to ambivalence, of the eternal struggle between Eros and the instinct of destruction or death.' (Freud, 1930, p. 132). The term ambivalence is now applied not only to a conflict between two opposing tendencies or to two contradictory emotions, but directly to the conflict between the primal instincts, as he says on page 137.

In 'Dostoevsky and Parricide' (1928), he refers again to ambivalence in the child's relationship with his father and considers ambivalence as the child's hatred that attempts to get rid of the father as a rival, while at the same time having affectionate tendencies towards him.

In 'Female Sexuality' (1931), he says that

> We cannot go so far as to assert that the ambivalence of emotional cathexes is a universally valid law, and that it is absolutely impossible to feel great love for a person without its being accompanied by a hatred that is perhaps equally great, or vice versa. Normal adults do undoubtedly succeed in separating those two attitudes from each other, and do not find themselves obliged to hate their love-objects and to love their enemy as well as hate him. But this seems to be the result of later developments. In the first phases of erotic life, ambivalence is evidently the

215 [The emphasis is Bleger's]

> rule. Many people retain this archaic trait all though their lives. It is characteristic of obsessional neurotics that in their object relationships love and hate counterbalance each other. In primitive races, too, we may say that ambivalence predominates.
>
> (Freud, 1931, p. 235)

In *New Introductory Lectures on Psycho-Analysis* (1933) Freud refers to the subdivision of the oral phase and says that

> In the first sub-stage what is in question is only oral incorporation, there is no ambivalence at all in the relation to the object – the mother's breast. The second stage, characterized by the emergence of the biting activity, may be described as the 'oral-sadistic' one; it exhibits for the first time the phenomena of ambivalence, which become so much clearer afterwards, in the following sadistic-anal phase.
>
> (Freud, 1933, p. 99)

In *An Outline of Psychoanalysis* (1940), Freud says:

> Since the transference reproduces the patient's relation with his parents, it takes over the ambivalence of that relation as well. It almost inevitably happens that one day his positive attitude towards the analyst changes over into the negative, hostile one. This too is as a rule a repetition of the past. His obedience to his father (it is his father that is in question), his courting of his father's favour, had its roots in an erotic wish directed towards him. Some time or other that demand will press its way forward in the transference as well and insist on being satisfied. In the analytic situation it can only meet with frustration. Real sexual relations between patients and analysts are out of the question, and even the subtler methods of satisfaction, such as the giving of preference, intimacy and so on, are only sparingly granted by the analyst. A rejection of this kind is taken as the occasion for the change-over; probably things happened in the same way in the patient's childhood.
>
> (Freud, 1940a [1938], p. 176)

On the previous page, he says that the transference is ambivalent: 'it comprises positive (affectionate) as well as negative (hostile) attitudes towards the analyst, who as a rule is put in the place of one or other of the patient's parents, his father or mother.' (Freud, 1940a [1938], p. 175).

ψ

In summary, we see in these studies by Freud the same propositions that I reviewed earlier. *Totem and Taboo* is the text in which all the modalities and phenomena that Freud includes under the term ambivalence culminate and are worked out. On the other hand, I believe that it confirms the need to separate from this term everything that pertains strictly to divalence and ambiguity.

In this regard, the studies by M. Klein and R. Fairbairn were decisive.

## M. Klein and R. Fairbairn

In *The Psycho-Analysis of Children*, published by Melanie Klein in 1932 she says, in reference to the case of Ruth, that she

> . . . was one of those children whose ambivalence shows itself in an over-strong fixation upon the mother and certain other women, while they dislike others, usually strangers.
>
> (Klein, 1932, p. 26)

Strictly speaking, this is not ambivalence but divalence, since antithetical feelings that are part of the same conflict are dissociated and distributed among different objects that thus, as M. Klein explains in subsequent papers, become part-objects although they are persons.[216]

Further on she superimposes ambivalence and divalence much more, when she studies the forms the ego acquires to overcome anxiety, saying that

> the individual may turn away from it [the object], on account of his fear of it as a source of danger and also in order to shield it from his own sadistic impulses; or he may turn towards it with greater positive feeling. This process of relating to objects is brought about by a splitting up of the mother-imago into a good and a bad one. The existence of this type of ambivalence towards the object indicates a further step in the development of object relations, and also helps to modify the child's fear of the super-ego. This fear is displaced onto the external object and then spread over several objects by means of displacement. As a result certain persons take on the significance of the attacked and therefore threatening object, others – particularly the mother – take on the significance of the kindly and protecting object.
>
> (Klein, 1932, p. 153)

When she examines the development of the girl's attitude towards the father's penis, she says:

216 I will not consider other types of dissociation suggested by M. Klein, H. Rosenfeld and W. Bion.

> In favourable circumstances the girl believes in the existence of a dangerous, introjected penis, as well as of a beneficent and helpful one. As a result of this ambivalent attitude ... her fear of the introjected 'bad' penis is an incentive to her continually introjecting a 'good' one in coitus ...
>
> (Klein, 1932, p. 199)

Therefore, during the period in which Melanie Klein wrote *The Psycho-Analysis of Children* (1932), the term ambivalence included both ambivalence and divalence.

In 'Some theoretical conclusions regarding the emotional life of the infant', M. Klein speaks of the paranoid-schizoid position and refers to ambivalence:

> Synthesis between feelings of love and destructive impulses towards one and the same object—the breast—gives rise to depressive anxiety, guilt and the urge to make reparation to the injured loved object, the good breast.
>
> (Klein, 1952a, p. 65)

For M. Klein, ambivalence is related to whole objects, and dissociation to partial objects. However, her use of these two terms is not completely clear. In this regard, Fairbairn is much clearer and more definite. For Melanie Klein, in dissociation (or schizoid division), each of the antithetical feelings is experienced separately with the breast, and for her, this part of the totality of the mother is what she calls a part-object. In contrast, ambivalence is experienced with a whole person, that is, with the mother and not with her breast. However, in section two of this article, she says that 'ambivalence is at times experienced in relation to a part-object, the mother's breast' (Klein, 1952a, pp. 65–66), and in a footnote on the same page she adds:

> In my paper 'A Contribution to the Psychogenesis of Manic-Depressive States', I suggested that ambivalence is first experienced in relation to the complete object during the depressive position. In keeping with the modification of my view regarding the onset of depressive anxiety (cf. 'On the Theory of Anxiety and Guilt') I now consider that ambivalence, too, is already experienced in relation to part-objects.
>
> (Klein, 1952a, p. 66, n.)

The difference between part-object and whole object is more clearly formulated by Fairbairn, in the sense that the part-object is not only a part of the mother's body or of another person with whom the child or the adult is in some relation, but that fundamentally, part-object refers to the fact that what is experienced with a person (or with a part of the person) is only one of the feelings that are in conflict or of the antinomic terms. Thus, what is important about the concept of the part-object is that it does not refer to the fact that this is a part of the person, but much more fundamentally to the fact that the person is only seen through one of the feelings.

In the same way, the whole object cannot refer fundamentally, in my opinion, to the person as a whole; instead the term should be used to designate an object towards which ambivalence may be directed, whether this object is a person or part of a person.

For Melanie Klein there is no pre-ambivalent state as postulated by Abraham 'in so far as it implies that destructive (oral-sadistic) impulses first arise with the onset of teething.' (Klein, 1952a, p. 68, n.). For her, the aggressive and libidinous drives exist from the outset of orality and in the most primitive states. She adds that

> there is little reason to doubt that in the relation to the first object – the breast – the ego is at times able, by means of splitting, to keep libido apart from aggression.
>
> (Klein, 1952a, p. 68)

There can be no doubt that in the works of Melanie Klein the term ambivalence is used for the depressive position, when contradictory feelings that can be united and integrated are directed towards the same object. However, the point that remains critical or problematic is the fact that this ambivalence may occur both towards a part of the mother's body and also in relation to her as a person.

In my opinion, these latter formulations by M. Klein are correct. However, without undermining her contribution, we do need to introduce the concept of divalence to improve the characterization of the object relations of the paranoid-schizoid position. Also, ambivalence may exist towards a part of the mother's body or towards the whole of her as a person, but when we speak of part-object we do not need to refer to one part of the mother's body but to an object treated as a function of or on the basis of only one of the dissociated antithetical feelings. Again, this object may be a part of the body or the whole person.

In this sense, as I said, it is clearer in Fairbairn, in his 1940 article, 'Schizoid factors in the personality', in which he describes the characteristics of schizoidia[217] and its tendency or orientation towards a part-object relation. He offers examples, referring to the way another person may be treated, not for this person's inherent value, but to satisfy the patient's own requirements through an unsatisfactory emotional relationship, or when other persons are treated as if they were bodily organs. (Fairbairn, 1940). In his 1941 article, 'A revised psychopathology of the psychoses and the

217 [See p. 226, n. 167.]

psychoneuroses,' Fairbairn says that the transitional stage, situated between infantile dependence and mature dependence,

> only begins to dawn when the ambivalence of the late oral phase has already commenced to give way to an attitude based upon dichotomy of the object. Dichotomy of the object may be defined as a process whereby the original object, towards which both love and hate have come to be directed, is replaced by two objects - an accepted object, towards which love is directed, and a rejected object, towards which hate is directed.
>
> (Fairbairn, 1941, p. 257)

Here, the word dichotomy is used in the same way as we have used the term divalence, but we consider it preferable to use the latter, since dichotomy seems more like a synonym of dissociation while divalence characterises the nature of the object relation.

However, the conception of part-object as I am using it is not clearly defined in Fairbairn either, although it is difficult to follow the step-by-step evolution of his thinking, since he, like Melanie Klein and Freud, modifies his points of view. However, let us read one of his followers who presents his teacher's position on this subject. We refer to Guntrip, who writes as follows:

> When the mother begins presently to be experienced as a whole person and the good and bad parts, aspects or phases of her dealing with the infant are brought together, *an ambivalent relationship to the mother arises to replace the earlier 'splitting' of the object into unrelated good and bad objects.* In the earlier position the infant could feel desire towards the good object and terror towards the persecuting bad one, without these two reactions influencing each other. Now that love and hate can be felt towards one and the same changeable object, the anxiety arises that in hating one's object as bad one may destroy it as good.[218]
>
> (Guntrip, 1961, p. 217)

Further on (p. 296) he refers to a modification introduced in 1951 by Fairbairn, in which the latter no longer maintains that the original internalised object was simply a bad object, since in the early pre-ambivalent oral stage good and bad objects have not yet been separated in the mind. It is the pre-ambivalent object that must be internalised first, since it is just as satisfactory as it is unsatisfactory, which creates a need to internalise it in an attempt to make it more satisfactory; in other words, to deal with the problem in the mind, since it cannot be handled in reality. Only when it has been internalised is it dissociated into good and bad objects in the world of

218 [The emphasis has been added by Bleger]

internal phantasy, and *thus the ambivalence arises*: the good object is then desired and the bad object is hated and rejected.

Here, he again confuses ambivalence, which is quite clear in the Kleinian conception, while for Fairbairn ambivalence appears when there is splitting of the pre-ambivalent object into good and bad objects. In short, for M. Klein ambivalence follows the divalence (of the paranoid-schizoid position), while for Fairbairn it follows the pre-ambivalent object. However, strictly speaking, division of the latter does not produce ambivalence (as Fairbairn states), but divalence.

ψ

The development of the Oedipus complex is a clear example of divalence and ambivalence. The Oedipus complex, described traditionally as love towards the parent of the opposite sex and hate towards the parent of the same sex, corresponds to divalence, while the recognition of each parent as a total person with good and bad aspects, both hated and loved, is ambivalence.

ψ

Dissociation is used not only in the paranoid-schizoid position but, as M. Klein describes it in 'Some Theoretical Conclusions Regarding the Emotional Life of the Infant', it may also be used toward the whole object, which is then divided into a living, unhurt object and a damaged object in danger (perhaps dying, or dead): '. . . splitting thus becomes largely a defence against depressive anxiety.' (Klein, 1952a, p. 74). This division or dissociation of the whole object is still, in my opinion, divalence and therefore is no longer ambivalence.

ψ

An important aspect of the description of part-object and whole object is to emphasize the difference between *internal object* and *depositary*, since if we omit this differentiation, frequent misunderstandings and confusions may arise. When we speak of divalence or ambivalence we are referring to internal objects, and the same is true when we speak of part-object or whole object: we are also referring to an internal object. Both the divalent part-object relation and the ambivalent whole object relation (these always being understood as internal objects) may be established with a partial or a whole depositary. I consider this differentiation between internal object and depositary of fundamental importance. I shall return to it later.[219]

To further clarify these aspects, I will briefly review Abraham's position in this regard, and then I will refer to two review studies, one by Sterba and the other by Marie Langer.

219 [See p. 282.]

Abraham, in his 1924 paper, 'A short study of the development of the libido, viewed in the light of mental disorders', does not define the concept of ambivalence, but refers to it frequently as the need (in obsessional neurosis and in melancholia) for an adaptation between emotions of love and hate and between hetero- and homosexual tendencies, as well as between the positive attitude towards an object in order to retain its properties and the negative attitude in order to reject it, as well as between the tendency to destroy the object and the contrary tendency to control it.

In the schema that appears near the end of his article, Abraham seems to refer to 'partial love' as to a part-object, in the sense of what we now consider a partial depositary, and his examples are 'penis, breast, excrements, etc.' However, towards all of these he allows attitudes that are ambivalent, 'that is, he desires and rejects it at the same time.' (Abraham, 1924, p. 497). Strictly speaking, what Abraham describes as ambivalent would actually be ambivalent in relation to impulses and internal objects, but would be directed towards a partial depositary, in the sense of parts of a totality. However, we do not deduce from his study that partial love (as he uses the concept) would imply dissolution, that is, divalence. Although he does not include the process of dissociation and divalence, we could deduce from some fragments of this article that divalence also has a part in his understanding of the development of object love and of libido, since he says, for example, that we assume that the anal-sadistic stage contains within itself two different levels: on one, 'the conserving tendencies of retaining and controlling the object predominate, whereas on the earlier [primary anal] level those hostile to their object – those of destroying and losing it – come to the fore.' (Abraham, 1924, p. 432). The latter description corresponds much more precisely to today's concept of divalence, but does not appear clearly in his final scheme of the stages of libidinal organisation in relation to the stages of object-love.

The panorama offered by Abraham is actually more complex than that which we have described up to now, since the first oral stage is auto-erotic and without an object, while in the second (cannibalistic) oral stage narcissism predominates with total incorporation of the object, although this relation is also ambivalent. However, in the latter we can no longer refer to a part-object, either in the sense of part of a depositary or in today's sense of divalence. This seems to be solved by Abraham when he defines the primary auto-erotic oral stage as pre-ambivalent and the secondary narcissistic oral stage as characterised by total incorporation of the object, as ambivalent. That is, the ambivalent stage of object love includes both part-objects (in the sense of parts of depositaries) and the whole object (also in the sense of a depositary).

When Glover, in his book, *Psycho-Analysis*, discusses the concept of ambivalence, he says that sexual and aggressive tendencies, as well as love and hate, alternate rapidly between each other in relation to each member of the parental couple, but 'this alternation leads to a permanent mixed attitude, a simultaneous loving and hating which is called *ambivalence*. Ambivalence is subdivided in the usual way in accordance with stages - oral, anal, genital, etc.' (Glover, 1949, p. 43).

When Sterba studies the second oral phase, he includes ambivalence. He describes the oral phase of sucking with auto-erotic satisfaction derived from the child's own body, 'but later, after the acquisition of the teeth, instinctual activity demands an outside object.' (Sterba, 1968 [1942], p. 27).

In the same study, Sterba says:

> The fact that two instinctual excitations arising from the same fundamental source can be contradictory, one having an active, the other a passive instinctual aim with regard to the same object, justifies our use of the term ambivalence.
>
> (Sterba, 1968 [1942], p. 29)

Shortly after:

> The term ambivalence which implies the simultaneous existence of two instinctual excitations of like content, such as, biting, looking, beating, copulating, but with contrary instinctual aims (active-passive), is mostly used in another sense, namely for the divided attitude manifested in many single instinctual impulses towards an object. When the instinctual wish exists to devour an object, the attitude of the individual who wishes this is contradictory. In the attitude where the instinctual wish in the object relationship is to devour, the tendency to incorporate the object is manifested.
>
> (Sterba, 1968 [1942], p. 29)

He also says in a footnote that 'This term, according to Ernst Bleuler [*sic*], signifies "the same thing positively and negatively felt emotionally, or positively or negatively thought or striven for".' (Sterba, 1968 [1942], p. 29, n.).

> Ambivalence signifies that two attitudes in opposition to one another, one of which can be called friendly and the other hostile, can come to pleasurable expression simultaneously towards the same object. The most marked ambivalence, that is, where the two contrary instinctual attitudes manifest the greatest difference and opposition, is the ambivalence of the second oral phase, the phase of the instinct for biting and devouring. . . . The term ambivalence is often used and characterizes very adequately certain forms of relationships between individuals.
>
> (Sterba, 1968 [1942], p. 30)

For Sterba, the primary oral phase or phase of sucking is not linked to an object but is auto-erotic, while the secondary oral phase or of biting is characterised by an ambivalent relation with objects. 'The object relationship of the second oral level can also be designated as sadistic.' (Sterba, 1968 [1942], p. 31).

Thus, Sterba characterizes ambivalence at one point as activity-passivity and at another as two antithetic attitudes, one friendly and the other hostile.

Further on, when Sterba discusses the genital phase, he says:

> we have repeatedly emphasized the fact that instincts appear in pairs of opposites. In the oral wishes, side by side with the strong wish to devour is the wish to be devoured, in the case of beating we also find the passive opposite and, at the genital level, we find masculine trends of erotogenic instinctual pleasure in the woman, while in the man we find feminine trends. This constant instinctual ambivalence manifested by sexual currents tending with opposite instinctual aims, leads us to assume that the simultaneous presence and dynamic expression of contrasting pairs of instincts is based on the general organic constitution of human beings.
>
> (Sterba, 1968 [1942], p. 53)

ψ

M. Langer, in the 'Kleinian contribution' to [the Spanish edition of] Sterba's book, says that

> Ambivalence means that the same object awakens simultaneously our love and hate. Although Abraham does not speak of Freud's new instinctive theory, presented for the first time four years previously in 1920, we believe that the concept of Eros-Thanatos dualism is implicit in the term of ambivalence and may have influenced Abraham to investigate in this line.
>
> (Sterba and Langer, 1966, p. 123)

What is emphasized in ambivalence here is more the love-hate contradiction than the activity-passivity contradiction, but ambivalence is included in both the contradiction between love and hate and the dualism between Eros and Thanatos.

M. Langer goes on to refer to the part-object, considering it the mother's breast, the father's penis or other substitutive body parts, which Abraham places no earlier than the anal stage in his scheme.

Here, the part-object is used in the sense of parts of a depositary, not in the sense I have emphasised: that of dissociation between antithetic pairs followed by directing one part of the antithetic pair towards a (part or whole) depositary, while the other part of the antithetic pair is directed to another depositary (which may also be part or whole).

However, M. Langer subsequently speaks of the first oral phase, describing defensive processes of the most primitive ego (dissociation, projection and introjection). She says that 'when the life instinct is separated from the death instinct and both are projected onto the primary and partial object, the breast, the latter is split into a good breast and a bad one.' (Sterba and Langer, 1966, pp. 126–127). Here, we see that the partial object designates not only the depositary consisting of part of a whole, but also because this depositary is experienced as two different objects, one good and the other bad, between which no unitary relation has yet been established. In these cases I believe it is better, as I said, to use the concept of divalence rather than ambivalence.

We may need to link back the concept of part-object historically to Freud's concept of component instincts, as this author ultimately does.

Studying the second oral phase, M. Langer describes how

> the mother stops being an isolated breast, face or hand and becomes a person to whom breasts, face and hands belong. Also, the breast that nourishes and the one that frustrates, the smiling face and the absent face, hands that do good and others that hurt, are finally recognised as integral parts of the same, unique mother,

and it is thus that

> the child understands, of course in his own way, that his love and hate are directed towards the same person. Thus, the dissociation yields to the ambivalent relation with the mother, which Sterba describes to us. In this ambivalence that provokes concern in the child towards the mother and anxiety for what he might have done to her and continues to do with his sadistic impulses charged with envy, jealousy and rivalry, this anxiety corresponds to and characterises the depressive position, whose achievement is the better integration of the ego and the objects and its incipient capacity to repair the damage that has been done them.
>
> (Sterba and Langer, 1966, pp. 138–139)

Here, ambivalence includes simultaneously a description of the integration of the internal object in a whole depositary, as well as the simultaneous presence in the same internal object of love and hate, which are directed towards the same person.

## Studies by other authors

Although I said that studies of ambivalence are scarce, I will refer to some. At the end, I will also mention (still fewer) works on ambiguity.

Bose, in his article 'Ambivalence' (Bose, 1949), says that Freud uses the concept especially to elucidate the relations between hate and love, and adds that in his writings we sometimes see how Freud is inclined to consider ambivalence as a fundamental trait of mental life whereas at other times he presents it as derivative from other processes, and he quotes many works by Freud in which lines of thought postulates appear.

He points out that in *Totem and Taboo* Freud states that we know nothing about the origin of ambivalence, and that in these circumstances we may take two positions: one, we may assume that it is a fundamental phenomenon of emotional life, and the other, that ambivalence was acquired from the paternal complex, in which psychoanalytic investigation of the actually present individual reveals its strongest expression.

In 'Instincts and Their Vicissitudes', Freud suggests, according to Bose, that an instinct is developed by a series of compromises between active and passive elements, and that this gives ambivalence its character. In the same work, Freud describes how the active phase of an instinct may revert to its opposite and be transformed in the subject, this reversion affecting not only activity and passivity but also emotional tone or content, as Freud describes it, in which love changes into hate. At some moment in this reversion the original object of the instinct is abandoned and replaced by the subject's self.

In *Group Psychology and the Analysis of the Ego*, Freud says that identification is ambivalent from the outset. Bose states that the concept of ambivalence becomes necessary only in cases in which opposite tendencies are working jointly and affecting behaviour. For example, a boy may love his father one day and hate him the next; this alternation of behaviour is not necessarily ambivalence, as he understands the term. Doubt is not ambivalent behaviour either, since it is a conflict on the conscious level. In true ambivalence, opposite tendencies are supposedly present, but one of the antinomic elements, at a particular moment, must necessarily be unconscious. He adds that given this unconscious element ambivalence is never an object of direct observation but must be considered an explanatory concept.

Bose decides to define ambivalence as the simultaneous presence and activity of opposite tendencies, one of which must be kept unconscious.

Freud, in 'Instincts and their Vicissitudes' is led, according to Bose, to an anomalous situation: he has to admit that in the primitive stages of libido development 'Love . . . is hardly to be distinguished from hate.' (Freud, 1915, p. 138).

Bose states that ambivalence affects *only wishes* and that it is unnecessary to discuss the opposition between hate and love as ambivalent, but that we need to consider the opposition between the wishes that lie behind this love and hate. Thus, he says that the problem of ambivalence is restricted to the domain of wishes. This restriction of the connotation of the term ambivalence, according to Bose, is the first step towards understanding the genesis of ambivalence and wishes are the only providers of motive forces of our activities, emotions and sentiments.

When we speak of opposition between love and hate, we need to observe, states Bose, that what we call love and hate are habitually very complex situations formed from wishes, feelings and emotions, and that the love-wish is not the same as the emotion of love. Thus, this opposition needs to be observed in the domain of love-wishes and hate-wishes rather than between the emotions of love and hate or between pleasure and pain.

Hence, he states that the antithesis between pleasure and pain and between hate and love does not really exist. When opposition is observed it must refer to different attitudes, independent of the affect.

Since this opposition can be observed only from the perspective of the domain of wishes, the genesis of ambivalence must be sought in mechanisms of the opposition of wishes and in the process by which one of the antinomic terms becomes unconscious.

In his conclusion, Bose states that ambivalence is not a fundamental trait of our mental life: it consists in pairs of opposite wishes. The components of the pair of wishes may alternately derive complete satisfaction from reciprocal acts and partial satisfaction with emotions of unpleasurable tone in retaliatory acts, and they do not necessarily produce states of ambivalence. Behaviours of opposing kinds that correspond to reversion of the subject-object relation are not necessarily ambivalent behaviours but, on the other hand, they should be regarded as proof of the existence of an opposition between wishes.

He concludes by saying that the primary conflict is between opposing wishes and that antitheses such as love and hate or pleasure and pain must be referred to this. Love and pleasure are the primary affects. Hate, disgust, shame, fear and pain are all products of repression. Identification, projection, introjection, reversal of an instinct into its opposite, ambivalence, conscience, moral values, sense of social propriety, etc., are better explained by assuming that conflict is produced by opposing wishes at different points in this circuit of wishes.

ψ

Stephen (1945) refers specifically to Fairbairn's 1944 article, 'Endopsychic structure considered in terms of object relationships' and he says, criticising Fairbairn, that we cannot be content with simply saying that the child becomes ambivalent:

> From the point of view of the infant himself it is a case of his mother becoming an ambivalent object, i.e. an object which is both good and bad. Since it proves intolerable to him to have a good object which is also

> bad, he seeks to alleviate the situation by splitting the figure of his mother into two objects.
>
> (Fairbairn, 1944, quoted in Stephen, 1945, p. 55)

He affirms that Fairbairn's error consists essentially in his attributing to the infant, in relation to what he calls the infant's external world, a development whose acquisition requires many years, and that many individuals never acquire it completely. According to Stephen, it must be said that the infant creates or isolates entities as he grows.

He uses the term object to denote the object of an emotion or of an instinctual impulse and the term entity to describe something that has been isolated from the rest of the external world, as we may isolate a rock, a tree or a human being and think of it as an individual unit. Fairbairn, says Stephen, thinks of the infant as having isolated that entity which we describe as his mother.

Thus, what some analysts call the bad mother is not for the child the same person as the good mother, although the good nanny may be the same person for the child as his good mother, which runs against adult opinion.

He suggests that it is much closer to the truth to say that the infant is incapable of joining what appear to him to be two separate entities into one singular unit and that reaching ambivalence means that two objects have been united in one, and that the infant then fails to hold them together.

If these viewpoints on the formation of entities are correct, it must follow that children need to go through a pre-ambivalent stage.

In this way, there can be no ambivalent conflict during the first months of life. The conflict appears only when the child has begun to adopt adult principles and to isolate entities, not according to their emotional qualities, but mainly according to their permanent physical qualities.

Expressing this in adult terms, what the adult classifies together as members of a series of experiences forming a singular entity, children classify together as members of different series. In children, the bases of classification are provided by emotions of pleasure and pain, while the adult bases it more on objective stimuli, sensations of colour, of touch, etc., separated from their immediate emotional value.

Thus far Stephen's critique. I agree with him that ambivalence does not exist from birth and that discrimination (which 'isolates entities', says Stephen) occurs with growth and makes possible the paranoid-schizoid position.

On a separate issue, the difference he establishes between the terms *object* and *entity* may correspond to our *internal object* and *depositary*.

When he says that, for the child, the bad mother is not the same as the good mother, he is pointing out what we now term divalence. However, his pre-ambivalent state is, strictly speaking, primitive undifferentiation, since ambivalence (in Abraham's scheme) includes much of what we now call divalence. Expressing this in rigorous terminology, the pre-ambivalent is divalent and the pre-divalent is ambiguity. In this respect, it is also interesting that he should point out that children classify together members of different series, since I identified this characteristic as specific to ambiguity.

ψ

Clifford Scott, in his contribution to the symposium on depressive illness, says:

> Ambivalence is a term which has been used for states in which two emotions are present at the same time, in one or other of several ways:
>
> (a) In different parts of the organism.
> (b) One emotion is in the ego and the other is in the object, internal or external, when object and ego are confused or not easily discriminated.
> (c) The state in which there is nearness to fusion of the emotions, just short of sadism or masochism.
> (d) The state in which there is nearness to an interrelationship of the emotions – nearness to a realization that the ego can rage and love, can satisfy and destroy, and that objects can also rage and love, and satisfy or destroy. The maximal states of love and hate are related to internalized, living, good, whole, continuing objects, or to internalized dead, bad, whole, continuing objects. The contrast with a continuing whole object is, of course, a split good/bad, a diffusely mutilated, a fragmented, a broken-to-bits, a discontinuous, object.
>
> The term ambivalence, as usually used, does not do justice to the complexity of the emergent state of development of which grief, depression, pining and hope are parts. [I would like to suggest a term to describe the affective aspect of this state.][220] This term is *multivalence*. It emphasizes the fact that more than two affects are involved.
>
> (Scott, 1960, p. 499)

This state, which Scott describes as multivalence, is what we refer to generally (not only for the case of depression) as the *polyvalence* of ambiguity.

However, I also disagree with Scott concerning the scope he gives to the term ambivalence, because it cannot be applied, I think, except when two emotions are present at the same time in relation to the same object, which does not occur in the cases which he describes in (a) and (b), which correspond to divalence. In the case of (c), in which he uses the word fusion instead of integration, I believe that this is also an error, since they are not

220 [This sentence was omitted from the quotation in Spanish, but is necessary for the passage to make sense.]

synonymous: if it is fusion it is a question of ambiguity, and if it is integration it is a question of resolution of ambivalence. I could also object that in the case of (b), 'when object and ego are confused or not easily discriminated', we are observing neither ambivalence nor divalence but confusion or syncretism.

Thus we see that only what Scott includes in case (d) may be considered ambivalence.

ψ

When Wisdom (1962, p. 120) discusses the problem of psychoanalytic theories on melancholia, he also begins to consider the question of ambivalence. In this article, Wisdom clarifies very well the difference between part-object and whole object in Kleinian theory and points out that 'part-object' 'refers on the one hand to parts of a person, e.g. a breast, and this was its original use' but that on the other hand it also refers to an object having only one of its qualities, good or bad. He proposes, for the sake of clarity, to distinguish the former as a 'spatial part-object' and the latter as a 'one-valued object'. Thus, a good breast and a good mother could both be one-valued objects, and in this sense, part-objects, although the former would be a spatial part-object and the other would be a spatial whole-object. The theory of the depressive position refers first to one-valued objects, whether these are spatial part-objects or whole-objects, and their integration into two-valued objects, for example, from a good breast and a bad breast into a good-and-bad breast and from a good mother and a bad mother into a good-and-bad mother. However, he also refers to part-objects and their integration into spatial whole-objects without proposing any theory for this process.

Wisdom calls the integration of part-objects into a single whole-object the *theory of the ambivalued object,* differentiating this from what he calls *the ambipotential attitude,* which refers to the attitude that the subject takes toward the object, since for him 'integration in the subject must come earlier, however little earlier, than ambivalence towards the object.' (p. 121). Thus, for him,

> an attitude of loving is experienced in conjunction with an attitude of hating, though not directed necessarily towards the same object. For convenience this combination might be called an *ambipotential attitude.*
>
> (Wisdom, 1962, p. 121)

Wisdom also says that

> an *ambivalued* object presupposes an *ambipotential* attitude. When both integrations come about there exists for the first time *ambivalence*: a positive and negative attitude towards one and the same object regarded as both good and bad. An ambivalued object and an ambipotential attitude

> are components of ambivalence and could in principle exist without it, whereas it could not exist without both of them.
>
> (Wisdom, 1962, p. 122)

I believe that the term ambivalence perfectly covers the two situations described by Wisdom and I do not think it necessary to create two different terms, one for the subject and another for the object, since whenever ambivalence is produced, it will be in a structure in which the object or objects, the ego or parts of it, and a relation between them, are always and inevitably included. In any case, his definition of ambivalence is quite clear and is also, as Wisdom emphasises, 'precisely the sense that Freud gave the term "ambivalence" when he took it over from Bleuler'. (p. 122, n. 16). This definition is the following: 'a positive and negative attitude towards one and the same object regarded as both good and bad at the same time.' When these attitudes or emotions or feelings are separated by schizoid division (dissociation) and do not appear simultaneously in relation to the same internal object and the same depositary, it is no longer, in my opinion, a question of ambivalence but of divalence.

ψ

Summarising, Wisdom identifies *spatial* part-objects and whole-objects, which may be either one-valued or two-valued. He adds what he calls the *ambipotential attitude* which refers to the subject (not to the object). For Wisdom, ambivalence only occurs when it coincides with the two-valued object (which may be spatially a part-object or a whole-object).

Although unpublished, among ourselves in recent years[221] the contribution of E. Pichon Rivière has established a clear-cut difference between internal object and depositary. This difference clears up the terminological and conceptual problem, so that part-object and whole object refer *always to the internal object*, the part-object having only one of the qualities, only one of the antithetical elements: good-bad (it may also be full-empty, attacked-protected, etc.), while the total object has both. As for the depositary, it may also be partial or total depending on whether it refers to part or to the whole, and may be 'deposited' by an internal part-object or an ambivalent (whole) object.

However, I think that Wisdom's study obliges us to extend the latter criterion, since although we call the internal object a part-object or a whole object, the former may be partial in two ways: either because the internal object implies only one antithetical term (good or bad), or because it may be an internal object incorporated as a part and not as a whole (breast, penis, etc.). For this reason, it seems convenient to preserve the terms part-object and whole object for internal objects, but within the former we may apply

221 [*i.e.* in Argentina and Uruguay]

the term spatial part-object to the internal object as part of a whole, and use the term one-valued object for the object involving a single antithetic term. To this we need to add the part-depositary, to designate a part of the external object or subject, while we propose to call it a one-valued depositary when the latter (either part or whole) is valued in a one-sided way (with love or with hate, for example) by the 'depositation' of a one-valued internal part-object. We would say the same of the ambivalent object, with which we also would always refer to an internal object which may be a *spatial* part-object or whole object. To this we would add, as we have seen, part-depositaries and whole depositaries. The latter may in turn be one-valued or two-valued (ambivalent). In this sense, I do not believe it necessary to add the concept of ambipotential attitude, since the above description and terminology now completely covers all the possibilities.

In sum, we have the following terminology: the *internal object* may be ambivalent or one-valued (one term of the divalence), but it may also be a spatial part-object or a spatial whole-object. These two latter may in turn be one-valued or ambivalent. As for the *depositary*, it may be part- or whole and both may be 'deposited' by a one-valued or an ambivalent internal object, by a spatial internal part-object or a spatial internal whole object. The latter two may in turn be either one-valued or ambivalent.[222]

## Other background literature concerning ambiguity

Of the few publications dedicated to this problem, we must begin with the chapter by Kris and Kaplan, a study on ambiguity in aesthetics (Kris and Kaplan, 1952). These authors review (p. 243) Empson's book (*Seven Types of Ambiguity*) on the role of ambiguity in poetic language. Empson describes ambiguity as: 'any consequence of language, however slight, which adds some nuance to the direct statement of prose.' (Empson, 1965 [1931]).[223] Kris and Kaplan propose to: (a) more clearly differentiate the ambiguity characteristic of poetry from ambiguity in non-poetic language; (b) study the role played by ambiguity in art as a process of re-creation and communication; (c) make explicit the standards of interpretation of the process of re-creation. These aims expressed by the authors may explain their way of approaching the problem, which is completely different from mine. For Kris and Kaplan, there is no rigidity of meaning in ambiguity or, in other terms, no constancy of response. Ambiguity, they say, does not necessarily refer to the uncertainty of meaning *but to its multiplicity*. Multiple groupings or meanings may enter into varied relations with each other. There is a

222 [See p. 272]

223 [The 2nd (1965) edition of Empson's book is cited, but the quotation by Kris and Kaplan is from the 1st (1931) edition, which Empson modified in the 2nd edition.]

continuum from one extreme where meanings are completely dissociated and inhibit one another to the other in which they are barely discriminable and reinforce each other. Along this continuum various types of ambiguity may be identified:

(a) *disjunctive ambiguity*: when we separate meanings into alternatives, which exclude and mutually inhibit each other. The most familiar case of this type of ambiguity is the oracle in which ambiguity generally resides in an equivocal construction (amphibolia) which may be interpreted in two mutually exclusive ways. This latter characteristic 'is the defining feature of the disjunctive type.' (p. 245). This type of ambiguity is also used in political discourse to elude censorship.

    Disjunctive ambiguity was used in the earliest periods of the interpretation of dreams, although more complete analysis reveals another type of ambiguity: the conjunctive.

    In relation to disjunctive ambiguity, Freud pointed out 'switch words'.[224] Latent content is an alternative meaning which excludes the manifest (initially at least); in this sense its ambiguity is disjunctive.

(b) *additive ambiguity*: two alternative but not mutually exclusive meanings which include each other to some degree. The word 'rich' [*rico*], for example, may be interpreted in terms of 'abundance', 'valuable' or 'excellent': the latter two are not mutually exclusive but superimposed.

(c) *conjunctive ambiguity*: when two meanings are effectively joined in the interpretation. Ambivalence is a conjunctive ambiguity since antithetical responses are evoked simultaneously. This type of ambiguity includes condensation in dreams, epigrams and jokes.

(d) *integrative ambiguity*: multiple meanings are evoked and support each other.

    In *Gestalt* terms, disjunctive ambiguity includes several fields that are disconnected from each other. In conjunctive ambiguity, several fields are connected but remain distinct. In integrative ambiguity, they are reconstituted or integrated into a short and complex meaning.

(e) *projective ambiguity*: when the responses vary with the interpreter: the term appears as vague and meaning is imposed (projected) by the interpreter.

ψ

As we can see, the authors apply the title of ambiguity to cover the entire spectrum of possibilities, thereby including ambivalence (conjunctive ambiguity), as well as divalence (disjunctive ambiguity) as forms of ambiguity. This way of approaching the problem, I believe, is not correct for a study like mine which tends to centre on the personality and its psychological

224 [The Spanish is followed by the English phrase in quotation marks.]

characteristics. For this reason it seems important to keep the three phenomena distinct, while recognising co-existences, transitions and transformations (or not) between them.

Subsequently, Tarachow (1965) uses the word ambiguity in the same sense as Kris and Kaplan 'in describing a characteristic of language, in that each word had a symbolic character with a wide range of responses. Each word has a *cluster* of meanings – some close, some distant, some similar, some opposite.' (Tarachow, 1965, pp. 86–87). However, he says that he does not consider the term ambiguity equal to ambivalence 'in its classical psychoanalytic sense', but uses the term ambiguity in the sense of 'two opposites which have not fused, have not modified one another', and he uses the term ambivalence to refer to 'aggression *not* modified or fused with libido.' (p. 87). He explains that for the aims of his paper, 'ambivalence is an unresolved aggression', and adds that 'ambivalence is a state of the instincts - ambiguity is a state of the ego.' (p. 87). I believe that Tarachow further confuses rather than clarifying the problem, and I think that he uses the concept of fusion erroneously as a synonym of integration or synthesis of the ego. I also consider that establishing the difference between ambivalence and ambiguity by referring the former to a state of the instincts and the latter to a state of the ego is an artifice which departs from the descriptive field and ventures into a meta-psychological and entirely speculative field.

I have already referred in Chapter 4 to the studies of M. Baranger, as well as those by H. Deutsch and D. Winnicott, which may now be linked up, I believe, with the problem of ambiguity.

# 8

# Commentary on 'The antithetical meaning of primal words'[225]

Freud begins this study (1910) with a quotation from *The Interpretation of Dreams* in which he says:

> The way in which dreams treat the category of contraries and contradictories is highly remarkable. It is simply disregarded. 'No' seems not to exist so far as dreams are concerned. They show a particular preference for combining contraries into a unity or for representing them as one and the same thing. Dreams feel themselves at liberty, moreover, to represent any element by its wishful contrary; so that there is no way of deciding at a first glance whether any element that admits of a contrary is present in the dream-thoughts as a positive or as a negative.
>
> I did not succeed in understanding the dream-work's singular tendency to disregard negation and to employ the same means of representation for expressing contraries until I happened by chance to read a work by the philologist Karl Abel ... We obtain from [the crucial passages] the astonishing information that the behaviour of the dream-work which I have just described is identical with a peculiarity in the oldest languages known to us.
>
> (Freud, 1910b, pp. 155–156)

Freud quotes Abel, who says:

> Now in the Egyptian language, this sole relic of a primitive world, there are a fair number of words with two meanings, one of which is the exact opposite of the other ...
>
> In view of these and many similar cases of antithetical meaning ... it is beyond doubt that in one language at least there was a large number of

225 Freud (1910b)

> words that denoted at once a thing and its opposite. (K. Abel).
>
> (Freud, 1910b, p. 156)

The quotation from K. Abel continues:

> Of all the eccentricities of the Egyptian vocabulary perhaps the most extraordinary feature is that, quite apart from the words that combine antithetical meanings, it possesses other compound words in which two vocables of antithetical meanings are united so as to form a compound which bears the meaning of only one of its two constituents ... So that in these compound words contradictory concepts have been quite intentionally combined, not in order to produce a third concept, as occasionally happens in Chinese, but only in order to use the compound to express the meaning of one of its contradictory parts – a part which would have had the same meaning by itself ...
>
> (Freud, 1910b, p. 157)

For Freud, the solution to this problem is easier than it seems, since our concepts derive from comparisons. He again quotes K. Abel:

> If it were always light we should not be able to distinguish light from dark, and consequently we should not be able to have either the concept of light or the word for it ... It is clear that everything on this planet is relative and has an independent existence only in so far as it is differentiated in respect of its relations to other things ... Man was not in fact able to acquire his oldest and simplest concepts except as contraries to their contraries, and only learnt by degrees to separate the two sides of an antithesis and think of one without conscious comparison with the other.
>
> (Freud, 1910b, pp. 157–158)

Freud adds that:

> According to Abel it is in the 'oldest roots' that antithetical double meanings are found to occur. In the subsequent course of the language's development this ambiguity disappeared and, in Ancient Egyptian at any rate, all the intermediate stages can be followed, down to the unambiguousness of modern vocabularies.
>
> (Freud, 1910b, p. 158)

He continues to quote Abel:

> A word that originally bore two meanings separates in the later language into two words with single meanings, in a process whereby each of the

> two opposed meanings takes over a particular phonetic 'reduction' (modification) of the original root. . . . In other words, the concepts which could only be arrived at by means of an antithesis became in course of time sufficiently familiar to men's minds to make an independent existence possible for each of their two parts and accordingly to enable a separate phonetic representative to be formed for each part.
>
> (Freud, 1910b, pp. 158–159)

Abel recalls that the philosopher Bain wrote:

> The essential relativity of all knowledge, thought or consciousness cannot but show itself in language. If everything that we can know is viewed as a transition from something else, every experience must have two sides; and either every name must have a double meaning, or else for every meaning there must be two names.
>
> (Freud, 1910b, p. 159)

Some examples are: '*altus*', which in Latin means high and deep; '*sacer*' means holy and accursed.

> Abel calls attention to further traces of ancient difficulties in thinking. Even to-day the Englishman in order to express '*ohne*' says 'without' ('*mitohne*' ['with-without'] in German), and the East Prussian does the same. The word 'with' itself, which to-day corresponds to the German '*mit*', originally meant 'without' as well as 'with', as can be recognized from 'withdraw' and 'withhold'. The same transformation can be seen in the German '*wider*' ('against') and '*wieder*' ('together with').
>
> (Freud, 1910b, p. 160)

A paragraph in the Spanish edition begins:

> According to this author, the phenomenon of the antithetical meaning can be observed in the 'oldest roots', since in the course of the language's development this ambivalence disappeared and, at least in Ancient Egyptian, it is possible to follow its evolution through all its phases, until we reach the univocality of modern vocabulary.
>
> (Freud, 1910d, p. 64, our translation)

In the English edition it reads:

> In the subsequent course of the language's development this ambiguity disappeared and, in Ancient Egyptian at any rate, all the intermediate stages can be followed, down to the unambiguousness of modern vocabularies.
>
> (Freud, 1910b, p. 158)

That is to say that the Spanish edition uses ambivalence whereas the English edition employs ambiguity, and I point this out because I believe that it is actually a case of ambiguity rather than ambivalence.[226]

The Egyptian language presents another very strange and important feature in relation to its parallel with dream-work.

> In Egyptian, words can – apparently, we will say to begin with – *reverse their sound as well as their sense.* . . .
>
> Abel tries to explain the phenomenon of reversal of sound as a doubling or reduplication of the root. Here we should find some difficulty in following the philologist. We remember in this connection how fond children are of playing at reversing the sound of words and how frequently dream-work makes use of a reversal of the representational material for various purposes. (Here it is no longer letters but images whose order is reversed.) We should therefore be more inclined to derive reversal of sound from a factor of deeper origin.
>
> In the correspondence between the peculiarity of the dream-work mentioned at the beginning of the paper and the practice discovered by philology in the oldest languages, we may see a confirmation of the view we have formed about the regressive, archaic character of the expression of thoughts in dreams.
>
> (Freud, 1910b, pp. 160–161)

Freud adds a note to the last paragraph of his article in which he says:

> It is plausible to suppose, too, that the original antithetical meaning of words exhibits the ready-made mechanism which is exploited for various purposes by slips of the tongue that result in the opposite being said [of what was consciously intended].
>
> (Freud, 1910b, p. 161)

ψ

For my part, I believe that work with the hypothesis of primitive undifferentiation and with ambiguity clarifies some characteristics of both dreams and language. When the same word expresses two contradictory senses, or an image in a dream represents two antithetical meanings, it is not a question, as Freud thinks, of having to consider a contradiction, for *this contradiction does not yet exist.* That is to say, the opposite terms have not yet been discriminated and the totality is expressed in a typical structure in which different and contradictory elements are found to be undifferentiated or in an ambiguous form; however, at that moment in the development

226 [The German is *Zweideutigkeit* (Freud, 1991, Vol. 8, p. 218).]

of the structure of the ego they are not yet discriminated as different or opposite.

If dreams dispense with 'no' as if it did not exist, this is not due to erasure of the limits of contradiction but to the fact that the ego is now functioning with a structure in which discrimination has been lost; in the case of primal words this discrimination has not yet been acquired. In this way, condensation can only be accepted in dreams if the waking state is given priority; however, this is not actually condensation but a new ego structure in which opposites are not condensed but the discrimination between them is lost.

When an element or a meaning in a dream is represented in the manifest content by an opposite wish, this is due to incipient discrimination in the ego structure and in the objects and experiences associated with it.

When, as Abel says, we find in the Egyptian language a considerable number of terms with a double meaning, each of which is exactly the opposite of the other, the double meaning exists for us but not for the ego-world structure of the early Egyptians, for whom this double meaning was not yet discriminated.

When the Egyptian language,

> quite apart from the words that combine antithetical meanings, . . . possesses other compound words in which two vocables of antithetical meanings are united so as to form a compound which bears the meaning of only one of its two constituents
>
> (Freud, 1910b, p. 157)

this is a moment of dialectical movement or transition from undifferentiation to discrimination; and I do not believe that these composed words are 'intentionally combined' (Freud, 1910b, p. 157) (as Abel affirms).

My thesis is that, starting with the initial primal undifferentiation which corresponds to a particular ego structure in which the ego is not discriminated from the non-ego and opposite objects are not discriminated, the introduction of schizoid division makes this discrimination possible, and both in the study of dreams and in the development of language we can understand that this transition from undifferentiation or ambiguity to schizoid division does not take place once and for all, but through a dialectical movement in which there are different moments.

This undifferentiation or ambiguity refers not only to meaning but to speech itself, and this explains how words may reverse both their sound and their meaning.

The experience quoted by Freud of children's pleasure in playing at reversing speech sounds is actually a learning game.

We are justified in admitting Freud's thesis regarding 'the regressive, archaic character of the expression of thoughts in dreams', but this regression is a regression of the ego to a structure and a dynamic different from the ego of waking life, which has its own laws and its own order. Therefore, whatever occurs on this regressive level of the ego during sleep cannot be explained by an alteration, condensation or any other mechanism based on the discrimination we possess in the waking state.

When Freud refers in his footnote to slips of the tongue, he does so because in slips of the tongue a destructuring of ego organization also occurs in the waking state, leading to a different structure that is undifferentiated or ambiguous.

ψ

E. Benveniste, in 'Remarques sur la fonction du langage dans la découverte freudienne' ['Remarks on the function of language in the Freudian discovery'] (Benveniste, 1956) refers precisely to the same article by Freud that I am discussing. This author affirms that:

> reasons of fact deny the credibility of the etymological speculations of Karl Abel that intrigued Freud. . . .

It is no accident that no qualified linguist, either at the time at which Abel was writing (and there were some as early as 1884) or since, supported the methods or the conclusions of the *Gegensinn der Urworte*. If one claims to trace the course of the semantic history of words and to reconstruct their prehistory, the first methodological principle is to consider the forms and meanings as attested successively at each period of history all the way back to the earliest date, and to start reconstruction from the most remote points attainable in the investigation. This brings up another principle of the comparative technique, which is to submit the comparisons between languages to regular correspondences. Abel worked without regard for these rules and assembled all the data on the basis of resemblance. (Benveniste, 1956, p. 69). Some of Abel's errors regarding data and methodology are studied by Benveniste. One of these refers, for example, to the double meaning of the word '*sacer*': sacred and accursed, words understood in opposite senses in the same language. Thus, in the Middle Ages, a king and a leper were both actually 'untouchables', but we cannot deduce from this that '*sacer*' includes two contradictory meanings;

> it was cultural conditions which determined two opposed attitudes towards the objects described as *sacer*. The double meaning attributed to Latin *altus*, 'high' and 'deep', stems from the illusion that makes us take the categories of our own language as necessary and universal.
>
> (Benveniste, 1956, p. 70)

The same errors are studied by Benveniste with respect to the English word '*without*', which does not contain a contradictory expression 'with-without'.

The meaning of '*with*' is in this case 'against' and indicates an impulse or effort in some direction. Therefore, '*within*': 'towards the interior' and '*without*': 'towards the exterior'.

Thus, affirms Benveniste, the possibility of an homology between the stages of a dream and the processes of 'primitive languages' vanishes. (Benveniste, 1956, p. 71).

Benveniste repeats:

> each language is specific, and shapes the world in its own way. The distinctions each language brings forth must be explained by the particular logic that supports them and not be submitted straight off to a universal evaluation.
>
> Let us suppose that a language exists in which 'large' and 'small' are expressed identically; this would be a language in which the distinction between 'large' and 'small' literally has no meaning and in which the category of dimension does not exist, and not a language allowing for a contradictory expression of dimension. The claim that the distinction exists but that it is not verbalized would demonstrate the insensitivity to contradiction not in the language but in the researcher, for it is indeed contradictoriness to impute to a language both a knowledge of two notions as opposite and the expression of these notions as identical.
>
> (Benveniste, 1956, p. 71)

All the observations by Benveniste concerning the errors in the evaluation of primitive language also apply to dreams, a process that was studied brilliantly by Politzer. The fundamental point is that dreams are understood by starting from a waking structure that is inherent not to dreams but to waking life. Although this procedure is legitimate in terms of our need to understand, it may by no means be accepted as legitimate in regard to the mechanisms or genesis of dreams. Benveniste concludes by affirming that

> Everything seems to take us far away from an 'actual' correlation between oneiric logic and the logic of a real language.
>
> (Benveniste, 1956, p. 72)

ψ

To this conclusion I would add that both dreams and language reflect a dialectic; in the course of its movement, undifferentiation, ambiguity, schizoid division, ambivalence and its synthesis are moments in its evolution.

# 9

# Ambiguity and syncretism in Freud's 'The "Uncanny"'[227]

At the beginning of his article (1919) Freud presents a preliminary result of his investigation, stating that:

> the uncanny is that class of the frightening which leads back to what is known of old and long familiar. How this is possible, in what circumstances the familiar can become uncanny and frightening, I shall show in what follows. . . .
>
> The German word *'unheimlich'* is obviously the opposite of *heimlich'* ['homely'], *'heimisch'* ['native'] – the opposite of what is familiar; and we are tempted to conclude that what is 'uncanny' is frightening precisely because it is not known and familiar. Naturally not everything that is new and unfamiliar is frightening, however; the relation is not capable of inversion. We can only say that what is novel can easily become frightening and uncanny; some new things are frightening but not by any means all. Something has to be added to what is novel and unfamiliar in order to make it uncanny.
>
> (Freud, 1919, p. 220)

Freud quotes Jentsch as saying that the uncanny is related to what is new, with what is unfamiliar. Freud continues:

> He [Jentsch] ascribes the essential factor in the production of the feeling of uncanniness to intellectual uncertainty: so that the uncanny would always, as it were, be something one does not know one's way about in.[228]
>
> (Freud, 1919, p. 220)

227 Freud (1919).

228 [*desconcertado* – here following Strachey's translation, but elsewhere rendered as 'bewildered'.]

Freud states that the characterization of the uncanny by the equation uncanny=unfamiliar does not exhaust the meaning of the term, and this is correct. I believe that three conditions are involved in the uncanny:

(1) An event or a thing which has been familiar and therefore well-known and discriminated up to that moment becomes undiscriminated or uncertain; in other words, *the familiar has become ambiguous* and is therefore no longer familiar.
(2) This change appears or comes about in a sudden, unfamiliar and unexpected way.
(3) We need to add another factor which I consider of greatest importance, which is the character of the ego that suffers the impact of the transformation of the familiar into the ambiguous.[229]

Evaluation of these three conditions allows us to delimit the uncanny as that which requires, aside from the first two conditions, an ego that undergoes, in most of its structure, an undifferentiation; in other words, that the ego itself is subject to a process of ambiguity. For this to occur, the ego must be, for the most part, a structure that is neither very mature nor very well integrated. With a more integrated ego, we observe perplexity or *suspense* when the ego is paralysed in the face of the unfamiliar and ambiguous. In its *bewilderment* the ego shows some degree of confusion (and not ambiguity as in the uncanny), and the same occurs in relation to what is *strange* or *mysterious*, in which the more integrated ego is able to 'face' ambiguity.

In reality, we cannot therefore speak of three isolated factors, and instead we need to think about the relation between them, since a small amount of ambiguity in a familiar phenomenon will produce the "uncanny" in an ego

229 The role of the ego is also implicated in the observation by K. Goldstein (quoted by R. Board in *Psychiatry*, 1958), that in patients with brain damage, feelings of the uncanny occur when an organism's capacities become inadequate for understanding what is happening (Board, 1958).

In *Totem and Taboo* (1913), Freud already says (before writing 'The "Uncanny"', in footnote 2. [p. 86]) that 'we appear to attribute an "uncanny" quality to impressions that seek to confirm the omnipotence of thoughts and the animistic mode of thinking in general, after we have reached a stage at which, in our *judgement* we have abandoned such beliefs.'

In his study on Count de Lautréamont, E. Pichon Rivière also points out this need for a more integrated ego: 'Therefore, the uncanny appears to be conditioned by this stage of development of our thinking, the animism that has *already been overcome* and is manifested again due to external circumstances which facilitate its reappearance.' (Pichon Rivière, 1947, p. 629, our translation). He further remarks: 'According to Freud, Hoffmann used other ego disturbances in his tales, consisting in a return to certain phases of development in the ego's experience: a regression to a period when the ego was not yet delimited from the external world and from others.' (p. 617, our translation).

that is lacking in organization, integration or maturity, whereas something quite ambiguous, even though it may appear in an unfamiliar way, may provoke a reaction of strangeness or mystery in a more mature or better integrated ego. In other cases, the ego may be integrated but susceptible to regression.

Since the ego is a dynamic structure, familiar phenomena which become ambiguous in an unfamiliar way may, depending on their intensity, reactivate immature aspects or characteristics in any subject (even with a well integrated ego), or may provoke regression in the best integrated ego. In other words, the uncanny appears when the ambiguous is able to mobilize an individual's 'syncretic ego' or non-ego: the most regressive and ambiguous or undiscriminated levels of the personality, which *tend to remain fixed and unknown, hidden behind what is well-known,* that is, behind the more integrated ego, and – in other cases – when the ego is susceptible to this kind of regression.

ψ

After describing a passage from the *Wörterbuch der Deutschen Sprache* by D. Sanders, Freud says that he notices that the word *heimlich*

> is not unambiguous, but belongs to two sets of ideas, which, without being contradictory, are yet very different: on the one hand it means what is familiar and agreeable, and on the other, what is concealed and kept out of sight.
>
> (Freud, 1919, p. 220)

> *'Unheimlich'* is customarily used, we are told, as the contrary only of the first signification of *'heimlich',* and not of the second.
>
> (Freud, 1919, p. 225)

Freud adds to this a note by Schelling,

> [which] says something which throws quite a new light on the concept of the *Unheimlich*, for which we were certainly not prepared. According to him, everything is *unheimlich* that ought to have remained secret and hidden but has come to light.
>
> (Freud, 1919, p. 225)

Here we find something important to add to the three conditions that I listed for the appearance of the uncanny. This is the fact that the uncanny is not only something familiar or well-known that becomes ambiguous but also the unfamiliar appearance of the *ambiguous that is inevitably in everything well-known.* It seems to me important to emphasize this point, since we inhabit the domain of the familiar, with discriminated objects, situations and persons. However, *within* what is discriminated, which we inhabit in a familiar or well-known way, there are always ambiguous, unknown aspects or parts that must remain hidden or secret if what happens is to continue to be familiar. In this regard, we remember Allport's opinion that 'we have to simplify in order to live,' (Allport, 1954, pp. 169–170), and Hegel's, when he says that: 'What is "familiarly known" is not properly known, just for the reason that it is "familiar".' (Hegel, 1807, p. 91).

Scientific and aesthetic investigations (I consider artistic creation to be an investigation)[230] are an attempt to know and discriminate what is unknown or undiscriminated and therefore ambiguous. It is an effort to discriminate what we believe we know and want to preserve as familiar by concealing and keeping secret or narrowing the phenomena of the world we inhabit, so that they may continue to be familiar.[231]

The Standard Edition says:

> In general we are reminded that the word *'heimlich'* is not unambiguous, but belongs to two sets of ideas, which, without being contradictory, are yet very different.
>
> (Freud, 1919, p. 224)

I quote the English translation since it introduces the expression 'unambiguous', which means that the word '*heimlich*' is ambiguous (in the Spanish translation from the German it has not been translated this way). The German-English translator adds a footnote on the following page in which he observes that according to the *Oxford English Dictionary* a similar ambiguity corresponds to the word *canny*, which may mean not only *cosy* but also *endowed with occult or magical powers.* That is, at some time the word that denotes the familiar becomes ambiguous and shifts to mean exactly its opposite. Thus, I believe that the word describing the phenomenon picks up, in its sense or meaning, the ever-present possibility that the familiar may become ambiguous, since what is familiar is – strictly speaking – only one defined or 'reduced' aspect of an uncertain or undiscriminated configuration.

230 Kris & Kaplan emphasize the creative capacity of artistic production; for Dewey aesthetic creation is one of the ways to solve problems. These aspects, as well as the one I point out, do not exclude each other.

231 To this we may add artistic manifestations which *directly express the uncanny* and with this there is a twist from art as the sweetening of the uncanny to the direct expression of it. E. Pichon Rivière in his study on the Count de Lautréamont, also points to the use of the extraordinary and of black humour as techniques to overcome or struggle against the uncanny. In the same way, H. Read (*Beauty and the Beast*) quotes a statement by Nietzsche: 'Greek art has taught us that there are no really beautiful surfaces without terrible depths.' (Read, 1966).

I wish to emphasise another interesting aspect of the ambiguity of the term *heimlich*. The text quoted above states that this word does not have a single meaning but that, not being 'unambiguous', it

> belongs to two sets of ideas, which, *without being contradictory, are yet very different*: on the one hand it means what is familiar and agreeable, and on the other, what is concealed and kept out of sight.
>
> (Freud, 1919, pp. 224–225)

I emphasise this because here Freud is pointing out (and this is conveyed by the English text) one of the fundamental characteristics of ambiguity: that two groups of ideas appear together which are *not contradictory but which are different,* and because this is the characteristic that I emphasized in an earlier chapter, affirming that ambiguity does not involve contradiction but the co-existence of different terms, which have not been discriminated from one another. I also pointed out that, in some cases, ambiguity may also include contradictory terms, but in this case the contradiction has been lost, has become 'blurred' or blunted, so that they appear to be undiscriminated and uncontradictory. Thus, what is typical in ambiguity is that there appear at the same time and in an undiscriminated manner things that are different and that have never been contradictory or if they have been, this contradiction was lost or blunted.

In this sense, in the uncanny it is not the whole of what is familiar which becomes ambiguous but what fundamentally occurs is that hidden or non-manifest aspects, *i.e.* that which has not yet been discriminated, appear *within* that which is familiar. I consider this aspect extremely important for the study of the uncanny.

Freud then quotes the *Dictionary* by Jacob and Wilhelm Grimm in which, among other definitions, they say that *heimlich* 'is also used of a place free from ghostly influences . . .' and that *heimlich* also means or has another definition: 'withdrawn from knowledge, unconscious . . .' (Freud, 1919, pp. 225–226). This emphasises that the familiar is something 'free from ghostly influences' or 'withdrawn from knowledge' or 'the unconscious': something that, though familiar on the one hand, also has an obscure part full of ghosts which constitutes the unknown, and that – in our everyday life – we are unaware that it exists *within* the familiar.

Freud ends this paragraph by saying:

> Thus *heimlich* is a word the meaning of which develops in the direction of ambivalence, until it finally coincides with its opposite, *unheimlich*. *Unheimlich* is in some way or other a sub-species of *heimlich*.
>
> (Freud, 1919, p. 226)

Here Freud characterises the word *heimlich* as meaning ambivalent ('until it finally coincides with its opposite'), whereas we now recognize it as a question of ambiguity. This superposition of ambiguity and ambivalence is quite frequent, and part of my effort in an earlier chapter was aimed at describing the difference between them. When Freud says that '[u]nheimlich is in some way or other a sub-species of *heimlich*', I understand him as saying that not only the word but the phenomenon itself also contains the hidden, the ghostly, the unknown and the undiscriminated. Its unfamiliar appearance provokes the uncanny when the ego perceiving the phenomenon is transformed into an ambiguous ego or when what is uncertain or undiscriminated also arises in the ego itself.

ψ

Continuing the investigation, Freud recalls Jentsch again, for whom the uncanny is characterized by 'doubts whether an apparently animate being is really alive; or conversely, whether a lifeless object might not be in fact animate' (Freud, 1919, p. 226), and he gives as examples the impression inspired by wax-work figures, ingeniously constructed dolls and automata, as well as the uncanny impression produced by epileptic fits and manifestations of insanity.

For Jentsch, one of the most successful procedures for easily creating the uncanny

> is to leave the reader in uncertainty whether a particular figure in the story is a human being or an automaton, and to do it in such a way that his attention is not focused directly upon his uncertainty, so that he may not be led to go into the matter and clear it up immediately. That, as we have said, would quickly dissipate the peculiar emotional effect of the thing.
>
> (Freud, 1919, p. 227)

In this quote from Jentsch, apart from some aspects already pointed out, there also appears the fact that in order to evoke the uncanny a phenomenon of doubt or uncertainty must be produced but that this must not become the main focus of attention. He thereby points out that the uncanny is different from doubt and uncertainty since, in the uncanny, the ego must not become an observer of doubt or uncertainty. This seems to me to be fundamental, since what characterizes the uncanny is not a state of doubt or uncertainty but a special disorganization (or re-organization) that is undergone by the ego, or rather, a de-structuring of the integrated ego and the formation of a new ego structure, one which is ambiguous in itself.

Freud then goes on to consider – as an example – a story by Hoffmann ('The Sand-Man') and begins by pointing out that the subject of 'the doll Olympia'

> is by [no] means the only, or indeed the most important, element that must be held responsible for the quite unparalleled atmosphere of

> uncanniness evoked by the story .... The main theme of the story is, on the contrary, something different, something which gives it its name, and which is always re-introduced at critical moments: it is the *theme of the 'Sand-Man'* who tears out children's eyes.
>
> (Freud, 1919, p. 227)

In his analysis of the story, Freud concludes that it is not a matter as Jentsch states, of 'any intellectual uncertainty' and instead he ascribes fundamental importance to the fear of losing one's eyes, 'the fear of going blind', which 'is often enough a substitute for the dread of being castrated.' Freud concludes that 'the uncanny effect of the Sand-Man [must be referred] to the castration complex of childhood.' (Freud, 1919, pp. 230–233).

In another of Hoffmann's stories, 'The Devil's Elixir', Freud studies the phenomenon of the double and points out that this ego-disturbance, which Hoffmann uses in his story, consists in '*a regression to a time when the ego had not yet marked itself off sharply from the external world and from other people*'.[232] (Freud, 1919, p. 236). Further on, Freud ties down the impression of the uncanny as something that emanates from 'the repetition of the same thing', which may also derive from the psychic life of infancy. He goes on to relate the phenomenon of the uncanny to omnipotence of ideas and says that 'everything which now strikes us as "uncanny" fulfils the condition of touching those residues of animistic mental activity within us and bringing them to expression.'[233] (Freud, 1919, pp. 240–241). He continues:

> At this point I will put forward two considerations which, I think, contain the gist of this short story. In the first place, if psycho-analytic theory is correct in maintaining that every affect belonging to an emotional impulse, whatever its kind, is transformed, if it is repressed, into anxiety, then among instances of frightening things there must be one class in which the frightening element can be shown to be something repressed which *recurs*. This class of frightening things would then constitute the uncanny; and it must be a matter of indifference whether what is uncanny was itself originally frightening or whether it carried some *other* affect. In the second place, if this is indeed the secret nature of the uncanny, we can understand why linguistic usage has extended *das Heimliche* ['homely'] into its opposite, *das Unheimliche*; for this uncanny is in reality nothing new or alien, but something which is familiar and old-established in the

232 The emphasis is mine.

233 A footnote by Freud [1919, p. 241] refers to chapter III of 'Totem and Taboo', 'where the following footnote will be found: 'We appear to attribute an 'uncanny' quality to impressions that seek to confirm the omnipotence of thoughts and the animistic mode of thinking in general, after we have reached a stage at which, in our *judgement*, we have abandoned such beliefs."

> mind and which has become alienated from it only through the process of repression. This reference to the factor of repression enables us, furthermore, to understand Schelling's definition of the uncanny as something which ought to have remained hidden but has come to light.
>
> (Freud, 1919, p. 241)

For Freud, then, the uncanny is a return of the repressed. We would now say that the uncanny is a breakdown in the splitting between the ego and the non-ego (or 'syncretic ego', which is ambiguous), and not simply a return of the repressed, and that for it to be repressed there would have to have occurred a schizoid division and therefore discrimination.[234] With this modification that I am introducing, we can better understand the imperceptible passage from the *Heimlich* to the *Unheimlich*, since within any familiar and known phenomenon there is also present something that is unknown or undiscriminated. The same occurs if we centre our attention, not now on the phenomenon but on the ego itself. The 'known' or integrated ego is supported by a non-ego, which is the 'syncretic' or ambiguous ego. This adds the understanding that the uncanny is not something familiar which has become strange by repression, but something familiar or usual that is itself what supports the ego, and from which both the ego and that which we recognise as familiar were formed through a discrimination of part of it. In the uncanny, therefore, is manifested the split-off part of the personality and of reality, which tends to remain split off because of its undifferentiated or syncretic character.

ψ

Freud writes:

> We have now only a few remarks to add – for animism, magic and sorcery, the omnipotence of thoughts, man's attitude to death, involuntary repetition and the castration complex comprise practically all the factors which turn something frightening into something uncanny.
>
> (Freud, 1919, p. 243)

All this is summarized in the sentence in which Freud writes:

> an uncanny effect is often and easily produced when the distinction between imagination and reality is effaced, as when something that we have hitherto regarded as imaginary appears before us in reality, or when a symbol takes over the full functions of the thing it symbolizes, and so on.
>
> (Freud, 1919, p. 244)

234 The theory of anxiety that Freud uses here is modified in 'Inhibitions, Symptoms and Anxiety' (Freud, 1926) and this modification lends further support to my hypothesis.

This characteristic, the disappearance of the boundary between phantasy and reality (their co-existence in an undiscriminated form), is precisely the phenomenon of ambiguity to which I believe that all the phenomena that are grouped under the heading or imprint of the uncanny can ultimately be reduced. Omnipotence of thoughts, magic, sorcery, animism, the castration complex and involuntary repetition all acquire the character of the uncanny whenever the boundaries between the familiar and the unfamiliar or between phantasy and reality disappear: when they become ambiguous phenomena and, as I said, not only when the phenomenon becomes ambiguous but when this ambiguous phenomenon is able to lead the ego itself into ambiguity; when it can cause the ego to regress to a period or stage of undifferentiation between ego and non-ego. This is precisely what characterizes what I call the glischro-caric position.

When there is no effacing of the boundary between phantasy and reality, there is no production of the uncanny, as is the case when we are squarely situated in fiction.

Freud writes:

> Our conclusion could then be stated thus: an uncanny experience occurs either when infantile complexes which have been *repressed* are once more revived by some impression, or when primitive beliefs which have been *surmounted* seem once more to be confirmed.[235]
>
> (Freud, 1919, p. 249)

All these cases involve the ego's return or regression to the glischro-caric position: there is no return of the repressed but instead a return to an ego whose structure has been superseded,[236] or the appearance of an ego that remains split off, with an undifferentiated structure.

My conclusion is also enriched by Freud's statement that:

> in the first place a great deal that is not uncanny in fiction would be so if it happened in real life; and in the second place that there are many more means of creating uncanny effects in fiction than there are in real life.
>
> (Freud, 1919, p. 249)

Thus, he points out that in artistic creation the ego is placed in a situation of particular regression or in a situation of specific knowledge that what is going to be narrated or is going to occur in the story or the literary creation

235 The emphasis is Freud's.

236 [*superadas*, the same word as Bleger has emphasised in the quotation from Freud immediately above, which Strachey in that context translates as 'surmounted'; Freud's word was *überwundene*.]

is separated or delimited from the real, and that this is not the case with the phenomenon of the uncanny that occurs in real life.

'The situation is altered,' says Freud,

> as soon as the writer pretends to move in the world of common reality. In this case he accepts as well all the conditions operating to produce uncanny feelings in real life; and everything that would have an uncanny effect in reality has it in his story.
>
> (Freud, 1919, p. 250)

I will now illustrate with a brief example from the analysis of a patient who at a certain moment has a feeling of the uncanny. She is a person with a phobic character and frequent melancholic and hypochondriac manifestations. Her few relationships are highly idealized and she also goes through life with an intense over-valuation of herself. Due to her ego limitations, she has a serious distortion of reality, of which she perceives only what coincides with her image of herself, the world and others. She has made very good progress in her psychoanalytic treatment, and recently she has begun to work through and accept that her parents, her husband, I and she herself are not as she always used to see us. This discovery of unfamiliar and unsuspected aspects in her familiar and everyday life is accompanied by a new experience of the uncanny.

I only wish to mention that there is a very close relation between the unfamiliar, as rhythm, and epileptoidia. Other patients may learn this more gradually, and consequently their 'discoveries' do not appear in a brusque and unfamiliar way. The production of these two latter characteristics depends in all cases I think on a marked epileptoid component in the personality, which makes discovery and learning appear in a sudden manner. I am here giving only an indication of the relation between the phenomenon of the uncanny and epileptoidia.

One of this patient's sessions begins with the analysis of how, when she left the previous session, she left her melancholia deposited in me. I interpret that she now allows herself to leave her melancholia deposited so that I will be worried about her, something she could never do with her parents, whom she always experienced as carefree and therefore untrustworthy.

As responses to my interpretation, the patient then remembers that I told her that next week I would not see her because I was going to interrupt my work, and she continues by associating this with her husband, saying that now she realizes that her relationship with him is uncanny;[237] that she was

237 [In Spanish the word *siniestro*, the word used to translate Freud's *unheimlich* ('uncanny'), is used in everyday speech to mean 'sinister', 'evil', 'ominous', etc. We retain the translation as 'uncanny', even though in English it sounds odd in this context, in order to maintain continuity with the preceding discussion of *unheimlich*. It would not be easy in any case to translate accurately in this context.]

discovering that the relationship with him is uncanny because she always felt quite enamoured of him and only saw his good qualities, but she now realizes how he abandons her emotionally, deprecates her and very frequently has extramarital relations, and that knowing all this gives her the impression of an uncanny relationship.

If we first take up her relationship with her husband, we see that what produces the impression of the uncanny is her discovery that her husband is an entirely different person from the way she saw him until that moment, which means that the familiar contained unknown aspects for her, so that the familiar is no longer familiar. She is entering a situation in which her husband is now a total stranger: she has a relationship with a person who is no longer that person. In other words, what is familiar, defined or known has become unknown and undiscriminated, that is, ambiguous.

However, her description of her relationship with her husband is, in the transference relation, a displacement of her feeling that the relation with me is also uncanny, since on the one hand, I tell her implicitly that she should deposit her melancholia in me and I invite her to trust me, but when I point this out to her, the relation with me also becomes uncanny since on the one hand I induce her to deposit trust and on the other I am unfaithful, because I abandon her when I interrupt my work. That is, what is familiar and customary in her relation with me has suddenly become unknown, and she feels I am no longer the same for her as before, someone she can trust, which transforms me into an ambiguous object. I appear to her as having different and contradictory characteristics that she does not yet discriminate in her relation with me. Suddenly, she no longer knows who I am: the relation with me has become an ambiguous one.

However, we may add that her relation with me is the transference repetition of her relation with her parents. With her very limited ego she attained a certain adaptation to reality and establishes familiar, known relations, but always with this great limitation of her ego and with defence mechanisms, among which idealization plays a very important part. This more integrated ego has been achieved through severe splitting from the ambiguous part of her personality, that is, with a part that is undifferentiated between ego and non-ego, or through a reactivation of the psychotic nucleus of the personality. When I tell her that she can trust me, and she remembers that I will not see her for some time, at that moment is actualised the inconsistent relation with her parents, on whom she cannot count as depositaries, that is, with a reliable symbiosis. This rupture with the depositary (her parents, me) causes a breakdown in the existing split between her more integrated ego and the psychotic part of her personality (her melancholic nucleus). This melancholic nucleus consists in the psychotic part of the personality which is deeply ambiguous or undifferentiated. When it loses the depositary it invades the ego and causes this more integrated ego to fall into a certain degree of ambiguity as well. In her life, she has developed a more integrated ego to a certain extent through the possibility of keeping her psychotic part split off and fixed in certain depositaries. However, since these depositaries (her parents) have not been reliable depositaries, the psychotic part of the personality has condensed into a nucleus: the melancholic nucleus. Sudden loss of her depositary in the transference relation prevents this melancholic nucleus from being re-introjected as such, and because of the breakdown in splitting it instead invades the more integrated ego, producing then an experience of the uncanny with the breaking in of ambiguity: that is, as a function of the ego's de-structuring towards a more primitive level of organization.

To an observer her parents' behaviour (and my own) becomes contradictory, but for her it does not: on this level of her personality she has not yet been able to discriminate contradiction, and so the latter appears to her as the actualization of her ambiguity.

I consider that this example illustrates the three basic conditions that I described at the beginning as fundamental to the phenomenon of the uncanny: the familiar has become ambiguous; this change takes place in a sudden and unexpected way; and the patient's entire ego goes into a regression that itself implies ambiguity.

# References#


Abadi, M. (1957). 'Interpretación y verbalización. La comunicación a distancia'. *Revista de Psicoanálisis*, 14: 6–12.

Abadi, M. (1961). 'La hipocondría. Proposiciones acerca de su temática inconsciente'. *Revista de Psicoanálisis*, 18: 370–373.

Abadi, M. (1962). 'El significado inconsciente de las fantasías orales'. *Revista de Psicoanálisis*, 19: 6–13.

Abbagnano, N. (1963). *Diccionario de Filosofía*. México: Fondo de Cultura Económica; originally (1961) *Dizionario di Filosofia*, Turin: Unione Tipografica-Editrice Torinese.

* Aberastury, A. et al. (1967). *Historia, enseñanza y ejercicio legal del psicoanálisis.* Buenos Aires: Omeba.

Abraham, K. (1908). 'The Psycho-Sexual Differences between Hysteria and Dementia Præcox', in *Selected Papers of Karl Abraham, M.D.* (pp. 64–79), ed. E. Jones., trans. D. Bryan & A. Strachey (1949), London: Hogarth Press.

Abraham, K. (1919). 'A Particular Form of Neurotic Resistance against the Psychoanalytic Method', in *Selected Papers of Karl Abraham, M.D.* (pp. 303–311), ed. E. Jones., trans. D. Bryan & A. Strachey (1949), London: Hogarth Press.

Abraham, K. (1921). 'Contribution to a Discussion on Tic', in *Selected Papers of Karl Abraham, M.D.* (pp. 323–325), ed. E. Jones., trans. D. Bryan & A. Strachey (1949), London: Hogarth Press.

Abraham, K. (1924). 'A Short Study of the Development of the Libido, Viewed in the Light of Mental Disorders', in *Selected Papers of Karl Abraham, M.D.* (pp. 418–479), ed. E. Jones., trans. D. Bryan & A. Strachey (1949), London: Hogarth Press.


# [*Note:* Items marked with an asterisk have been added by the Editors. *Revista de Psicoanálisis* refers to the journal of that name published by the *Asociación Psicoanalítica Argentina*. Works by Sigmund Freud are denoted by the following abbreviations: *'SE'*: Strachey, J. (ed.) (1953–1974). *The Standard Edition of the Complete Psychological Works of Sigmund Freud*, Volumes 1–24. London: Hogarth Press & Institute of Psychoanalysis; '*GS*': Freud, S. (1925). *Gesammelte Schriften*. Vienna: Internationaler Psychoanalytischer Verlag; '*GW*' for Freud, S. (1991). *Gesammelte Werke: Chronologisch Geordnet.* London: Imago Publishing Co., Ltd.; '*OC*': Freud, S. (1952–56). *Obras Completas*, 21 vols.; trans. L. López-Ballesteros y de Torres (vols. 11–17) & L. Rosenthal (vols. 18–21). Buenos Aires: Santiago Rueda.]

Adorno, T.W., Frenkel-Brunswik, E., Levinson D.J., & Nevitt, S. (1950). *The Authoritarian Personality.* New York: Harper & Row; reprinted (1993). New York: W. Norton & Company.

Alexander, E.G. & Selesnick, S.T. (1966). *The History of Psychiatry.* New York: Harper & Row.

Allport, G.W. (1954). *The Nature of Prejudice.* Cambridge, MA: Addison-Wesley Publishing Company.

Alpert, A. (1959). 'Reversibility of Pathological Fixations Associated with Maternal Deprivation in Infancy'. *Psychoanalytic Study of the Child*, 14: 169–185.

* Alsteens, A. (1984). 'Problématique narcissique et cadre analytique'. *Revue Belge de Psychanalyse*, 5: 41–62.

* Alsteens, A. (1987). 'Négativité de cadre et déploiement de la psyché'. *Revue Belge de Psychanalyse*, 11: 33–57.

Álvarez de Toledo, L. (1954). 'El análisis del "asociar", del "interpretar" y de las "palabras"'. *Revista de Psicoanálisis*, 11: 267–313; also *Revista de Psicoanálisis*, 1956, 12: 503–506.

Álvarez de Toledo, L., Grinberg, L., Langer, M. (1964). 'Terminación de análisis'. Relato oficial al *Primer Congreso Psicoanalítico Panamericano*, Mexico.

* Arbiser, S. (2003). 'A Brief History of Psychoanalysis in Argentina'. *Journal of the American Psychoanalytic Association*, 51S: 323–335.

Balint, M. (1949). 'Early Developmental States of the Ego. Primary Object Love'. *International Journal of Psychoanalysis*, 30: 265–273; reprinted in *Primary Love and Psycho-analytic Technique* (1952), London: Hogarth Press.

Balint, M. (1952). 'On Love and Hate'. *International Journal of Psycho-Analysis*, 33: 355–362; reprinted in *Primary Love and Psycho-analytic Technique* (1952), London: Hogarth Press.

Balint, M. (1960). 'Primary Narcissism and Primary Love'. *Psychoanalytic Quarterly*, 29: 6–43.

Baranger, M. (1959). 'Homosexualidad y confusión'. Buenos Aires: *Asociación Psicoanalítica Argentina.* (Unpublished.)

Baranger, M. (1960). 'Regresión y temporalidad en el tratamiento analítico'. Buenos Aires: Asociación Psicoanalítica Argentina (Unpublished). Later (1969) published in *Revista de Psicoanálisis*, 26 (2): 265–299.

Baranger, M. (1963). 'Bad Faith, Identity, and Omnipotence', in M. Baranger & W. Baranger (2009) *The Work of Confluence: Listening and Interpreting in the Psychoanalytic Field* (pp. 179–201), London: Karnac Books.

Baranger, W. (1956a). 'Asimilación y encapsulamiento: estudio de los objetos idealizados'. *Revista Uruguaya de Psicoanálisis*, 1: 26–63; also in W. Baranger, R. Zak de Goldstein & N. Goldstein (1994), *Artesanías psicoanalíticas* (pp. 26–63), Buenos Aires: Kargieman.

Baranger, W. (1956b). 'Fantasía, objetos y estructura psíquica'. *Revista Uruguaya de Psicoanálisis*, 1: 303–341; also in W. Baranger, R. Zak de Goldstein & N. Goldstein (1994), *Artesanías psicoanalíticas*, Buenos Aires: Kargieman.

Baranger, W. (1961–1962). 'El muerto vivo: Estructura de los objetos en el duelo y en los estados depresivos'. *Revista Uruguaya de Psicoanálisis*, 4: 586–603; also in Baranger, W. & Baranger, M. (1969) *Problemas del campo psicoanalítico* (pp. 217–229), Buenos Aires: Kargieman.

Baranger, W. (1962). 'Aspectos problématicos de la teoría de los objetos en la obra de M. Klein'. *Revista de Psicoanálisis*, 19: 14–19; also in Baranger, W. & Baranger, M. (1969), *Problemas del campo psicoanalítico* (pp. 97–102), Buenos Aires: Kargieman.

Baranger, M. & Baranger, W. (1961–62). 'La situación analítica como campo dinámico'. *Revista Uruguaya de Psicoanálisis*, 4 (1): 3–54; trans. S. Rogers & J. Churcher (2008) 'The Analytic Situation as a Dynamic Field', *International Journal of Psychoanalysis,* 89 (4): 795–826.

Baranger, M., Baranger, W., Fernández, A., Garbarino, M. F., Mendilaharsu, S. A., & Nieto, M. (1964). 'Mecanismos hipocondríacos normales en el desarrollo femenino'. *Revista Uruguaya de Psicoanálisis*, 6: 5–18.

Beauvoir, S. de (1947). *Pour une morale de l'ambiguité.* Paris: Gallimard.

Benedek, T. (1949). 'The Psychosomatic Implications of the Primary Unit: Mother-Child'. *American Journal of Orthopsychiatry*, 19: 642–654.

Benedek, T. (1952). 'Personality Development'. in F. Alexander & H. Ross, *Dynamic Psychiatry*, Chicago: University of Chicago Press.

Benedek, T. (1956). 'Toward the Biology of the Depressive Constellation'. *Journal of the American Psychoanalytic Association*, 4: 389–422.

Benveniste, É. (1956). 'Remarks on the function of language in Freudian theory', in (1971) *Problems in General Linguistics* (pp. 65–75), trans. M. E. Meek. Coral Gables: University of Miami Press.

Beres, D. & Obers, S. J. (1950). 'The Effects of Extreme Deprivation in Infancy on Psychic Structure in Adolescence'. *Psychoanalytic Study of the Child,* 5: 212–235.

Bergler, E. (1934). 'The Psychoanalysis of the Uncanny'. *International Journal of Psychoanalysis*, 15: 215–244.

Bergler, E. (1948). 'Three Tributaries to the Development of Ambivalence'. *Psychoanalytic Quarterly*, 17: 173–181.

* Bernardi, R. (2002). 'The Need for True Controversies in Psychoanalysis: The Debates on Melanie Klein and Jacques Lacan in the Río de la Plata'. *International Journal of Psychoanalysis*, 83: 851–873.

Bion, W. R. (1954). 'Notes on the Theory of Schizophrenia'. *International Journal of Psychoanalysis*, 35: 113–118; reprinted in *Second Thoughts: Selected Papers on Psycho-Analysis* (1967) (pp. 23–35), London: William Heinemann Medical Books; reprinted (1984), London: Karnac Books.

Bion, W. R. (1955). 'Language and the Schizophrenic', in M. Klein, P. Heimann, & R. E. Money-Kyrle (eds.) *New Directions in Psychoanalysis. The Significance of Infant Conflict in the Pattern of Adult Behaviour* (pp. 200–239), London: Tavistock Publications.

Bion, W. R. (1956). 'Development of Schizophrenic Thought'. *International Journal of Psychoanalysis*, 37: 344–346; reprinted in *Second Thoughts: Selected Papers on Psycho-Analysis* (1967) (pp. 36–42), London: William Heinemann Medical Books ; reprinted (1984), London: Karnac Books.

Bion, W. R. (1957). 'Differentiation of the Psychotic from the Non-Psychotic Personalities'. *International Journal of Psychoanalysis*, 38: 266–275; reprinted in *Second Thoughts: Selected Papers on Psycho-Analysis* (1967) (pp. 43–64), London: William Heinemann Medical Books ; reprinted (1984), London: Karnac Books.

Bion, W. R. (1958). 'On hallucination'. *International Journal of Psychoanalysis*, 39: 341–349; reprinted in *Second Thoughts: Selected Papers on Psycho-Analysis* (1967) (pp. 65–85), London: William Heinemann Medical Books; reprinted (1984), London: Karnac Books.

Bion, W. R. (1959). 'Attacks on linking'. *International Journal of Psychoanalysis*, 40: 308–315; reprinted in *Second Thoughts: Selected Papers on Psycho-Analysis* (1967) (pp. 93–109),

London: William Heinemann Medical Books ; reprinted (1984), London: Karnac Books.

Bion, W. R. (1962). 'The Psycho-Analytic Study of Thinking'. *International Journal of Psychoanalysis*, 43: 306–310; reprinted in *Second Thoughts: Selected Papers on Psycho-Analysis* (1967) (pp. 110–119), London: William Heinemann Medical Books; reprinted (1984), London: Karnac Books.

* Birksted-Breen, D. (2010). 'Is Translation Possible?' *International Journal of Psychoanalysis*, 91: 687–694.

* Blass, R. B. & Blatt, S.J. (1996). 'Attachment and Separateness in The Experience Of Symbiotic Relatedness'. *Psychoanalytic Quarterly*, 65: 711–746.

Bleger, J. (1958). *Psicoanálisis y dialéctica materialista. Estudio sobre la estructura del psicoanalisis.* Buenos Aires: Paidós.

Bleger, J. (1960). 'Estudio de la dependencia-independencia en su relación con el proceso de proyección-introyección'. *Revista de Psicoanálisis*, 17: 456–479.

Bleger, J. (1961). 'La simbiosis'. *Revista de Psicoanálisis*, 18: 361–369.

Bleger, J. (1962a). 'Estudio sobre la simbiosis en "El reposo del guerrero"'. *Revista de Psicoanálisis*, 19: 173–179.

Bleger, J. (1962b). 'Modalidades de la relación objetal'. *Revista de Psicoanálisis*, 19: 58–62.

* Bleger, J. (1963). *Psicología de la Conducta.* Buenos Aires: Eudeba.

Bleger, J. (1964a). 'Simbiosis; estudio de la parte psicótica de la personalidad'. *Revista Uruguaya de Psicoanálisis*, 6 (2–3): 159–279.

Bleger, J. (1964b). 'Simbiosis, psicopatía y manía', in Symposium *Manía y Psicopatía*, Buenos Aires: Asociación Psicoanalítica Argentina; in A. Rascovsky & D. Liberman (eds.) (1966) *Psicoanálisis de la Manía y la Psicopatía* (pp. 280–289), Buenos Aires: Paidós.

Bleger, J. (1966). *Psicohigiene y Psicología Institucional.* Buenos Aires: Paidós.

* Bleger, J. (1967a). 'Psycho-analysis of the Psycho-Analytic Frame'. *International Journal of Psychoanalysis*, 48: 511–519.

* Bleger, J. (1967b). 'Enrique Pichon Rivière, su aporte a la psiquiatría y al psicoanálisis'. *Acta Psiquiátrica y Psicológica de América Latina*, 13 (4): 346–350.

* Bleger, J. (1967c). *Simbiosis y ambigüedad: estudio psicoanalítico.* Buenos Aires: Paidós.

* Bleger, J. (1969). 'Teoría y práctica en psicoanálisis: la praxis psicoanalítica'. *Revista Uruguaya de Psicoanálisis*, 11 (3–4): 287–303. Republished in *Revista de Psicoanálisis*, 60 (4), 2003.

* Bleger, J. (1971a). 'El concepto de psicosis'. *Revista de Psicoanálisis*, 28 (1): 5–23.

* Bleger, J. (1971b). *Temas de Psicología: Entrevista y Grupos.* Buenos Aires: Nueva Visión.

* Bleger, J. (1971c). 'Cuestiones metodológicas del psicoanálisis', in D. Ziziemsky (ed.), *Métodos de Investigación en Psicología y Psicopatología*, Buenos Aires: Nueva Visión.

* Bleger, J. (1973a). 'Ambiguity', in S. Arieti (ed.) *The World Biennial of Psychiatry and Psychotherapy*, Vol. 2, New York: Basic Books.

* Bleger, J. (1973b). 'La identidad del adolescente', in J. Bleger et al., *La identidad en el adolescente*, Buenos Aires: Paidós, pp. 9–14.

* Bleger, J. (1973c). 'Duelo y sus vicisitudes'. *Minerva Psiquiátrica Argentina*, 2 (6).

* Bleger, J. (1974). 'Schizophrenia, Autism, and Symbiosis'. *Contemporary Psychoanalysis*, 10: 19–25.

* Bleger, J. (1989). *Psicoigiene e Psicologia Istituzionale.* Loreto: Edizione Lauretana.

* Bleger, J. (2011). *Psicoigiene e Psicologia Istituzionale.* Molfeta: Edizione La Meridiana.

* Bleger, L. (2009). 'La séance psychanalytique de José Bleger'. *Revue Belge de Psychanalyse*, 55: 9–10.

Bleger, L. de Storch (1964). 'Algunos problemas transferenciales en la psicopatía', in Symposium *Manía y Psicopatía*, Buenos Aires: Asociación Psicoanalítica Argentina; in A. Rascovsky & D. Liberman (eds.) (1966), *Psicoanálisis de la Manía y la Psicopatía* (pp. 259–264), Buenos Aires: Paidós.

Bleger, L. de Storch & Bleger, J. (1960). 'Consideraciones sobre algunas psicosis en la adolescencia'. Mar del Plata: Segundo Congreso Argentino de Psiquiatría.

Bleger, L. de Storch & Bleger, J. (1962). 'Algunas correlaciones entre Freud, M. Klein y Fairbairn'. *Revista de Psicoanálisis*, 19: 63–65.

Bleger, J., Bleger, L. de Storch, García Reinoso, D. & García Reinoso, G. de T. (1966). 'Psicopatía como déficit de personificación', in A. Rascovsky & D. Liberman (eds.), *Psicoanálisis de la Manía y la Psicopatía* (pp. 265–271), Buenos Aires: Paidós.

* Bleger, J., Cvik, N. & Grunfeld, B. (1973). 'Perversiones'. *Revista de Psicoanálisis*, 30 (2): 351–366.

Bleuler, E. (1911). *Dementia Praecox or the Group of Schizophrenias*; trans. J. Zinkin (1950), New York: International Universities Press.

* Blomfield, O. H. D. (1992). 'Bleger's Extension of Kleinian Theory: Some Developmental and Transferential Implications'. *Melanie Klein and Object Relations*, 10 (1): 62–88.

Blum, G. S. (1953). *Psychoanalytic Theories of Personality*. New York: McGraw-Hill Book Company, Inc.

Board, R. (1958). 'Intuition in the Methodology of Psychoanalysis'. *Psychiatry*, 21(3): 233–9.

Bonnard, A. (1958). 'Pre-Body-Ego Types of (Pathological) Mental Functioning'. *Journal of the American Psychoanalytic Association*, 6: 581–611.

Bose, G. (1949). 'Ambivalence'. *Samiksa*, 3 (2): 55–75.

Bowlby, J. (1958). 'The Nature of the Child's Tie to his Mother'. *International Journal of Psychoanalysis*, 39: 350–373.

Bowlby, J. (1960). 'Separation Anxiety'. *International Journal of Psychoanalysis*, 41: 89–113.

Breuer, J. & Freud, S. (1893–95). *Studies on Hysteria. SE*, 2

Brody, M. W. (1956). 'Clinical Manifestations of Ambivalence'. *Psychoanalytic Quarterly*, 25: 505–514.

Bunker, H. A. (1948). 'Note on an Ambivalent Dream'. *Psychoanalytic Quarterly*, 17: 389–390.

Burke, E. (1756). *On the Sublime and the Beautiful*, in (1961) *The Harvard Classics*, vol. 24, New York: P. F. Collier & Son.

Burlingham, D. T. (1935). 'Child Analysis and the Mother'. *Psychoanalytic Quarterly*, 4: 69–92.

Burlingham, D. T., Goldberger, A. & Lussier, A. (1955). 'Simultaneous Analysis of Mother and Child'. *Psychoanalytic Study of the Child*, 10:165–186.

Bychowsky, G. (1945). 'The Ego of Homosexuals'. *International Journal of Psychoanalysis*, 26: 114–127.

Campo, A. J. (1963). 'Introduccíon al estudio genético y evolutivo de la omnipotencia'. *Revista de Psicoanálisis*, 20, 4: 357–374; republished in A. J. Campo (1993), *Teoría, clínica y terapia psicoanalítica, 1957–1991* (pp.79–100), Buenos Aires: Paidós.

Cesio, F. (1958). 'La reacción terapéutica negativa'. *Revista de Psicoanálisis*, 15: 293–299.

* Cesio, F. (1981). 'Historia del movimiento psicoanalítico latinoamericano'. *Revista de Psicoanálisis*, 38 (4): 695–713.

Christoffel, H. (1952). 'Le problème du transfert'. *Revue Française de Psychanalyse*, 16 (1–2): 178–203.

* Civitarese, G. (2004). 'Vincolo simbiotico e setting'. *Rivista di Psicoanalisi*, 50: 1117–1147 trans. P. Slotkin (2010), in *The Intimate Room: Theory and Technique of the Analytic Field*. London: Routledge.

Colby, K. M. (1949). 'Human Symbiosis'. *Psychiatry*, 12 (2): 135–139.

* Cruz Roche, R. (1992). 'The Autistic-Contiguous Position'. *International Journal of Psychoanalysis*, 73: 363.

* Cucurullo, A., Faimberg, H., & Wender, L. (1982). 'La psychanalyse en Argentine', in R. Jaccard (ed.) *Histoire de la psychanalyse*, vol. 2. Paris: Hachette.

Davanzo, H. (1962). 'A Contribution to the Analysis of Resistances in Neurotic Dependence'. *International Journal of Psychoanalysis,* 43: 441–447.

Delacroix, H. et al. (1952). *Psicología del lenguaje*. Buenos Aires: Paidós; originally in French as *Psychologie du langage* (1933), Paris: Librairie Felix Alcan.

Deutsch, H. (1942). 'Some Forms of Emotional Disturbance and their Relationship to Schizophrenia'. *Psychoanalytic Quarterly*, 11: 301–321.

* Donnet, J. L. (1973). 'Le divan bien tempéré'. *Nouvelle Revue de Psychanalyse*, 8: 23–49

Empson, W. (1965 [1931]). *Seven Types of Ambiguity*. Harmondsworth: Penguin Books.

Erikson, E. H. (1959). *Identity and the Life Cycle*. Psychological Issues Monographs, vol. 1, New York: International Universities Press.

* Etchegoyen, R. H. (1991). *The Fundamentals of Psychoanalytic Technique*, trans. P. Pitchon. London: Karnac Books.

* Etchegoyen, R. H. & Zysman, S., (2005a). 'Melanie Klein in Buenos Aires: beginnings and developments'. *International Journal of Psychoanalysis*, 86 (3): 869–894.

* Etchegoyen, R. H. & Zysman, S. (2005b). 'Psychoanalysis in Latin-America: an Approximation to the History and Ideas', in S. Lewkowicz & S. Flechner, *Truth, Reality, and the Psychoanalyst* (pp. 1–22), London: The International Psychoanalytical Association.

Evelson, E. (1958). 'Una experiencia analítica. Análisis simultáneo de hermanos mellizos'. *Revista de Psicoanálisis*, 15: 16–21.

Fairbairn, W. R. (1940). 'Schizoid Factors in the Personality', in (1952) *Psychoanalytic Studies of the Personality* (pp. 3–27), London: Tavistock Publications.

Fairbairn, W. R. (1941). 'A Revised Psychopathology of the Psychoses and the Psychoneuroses', in (1952) *Psychoanalytic Studies of the Personality* (pp. 28–58), London: Tavistock Publications.

Fairbairn, W. R. (1943). 'The War Neuroses', in (1952) *Psychoanalytic Studies of the Personality* (pp. 256–287), London: Tavistock Publications.

Fairbairn, W. R. (1944). 'Endopsychic Structure Considered in Terms of Object Relationships'. *International Journal of Psychoanalysis*, 25: 70–92.

Fairbairn, W. R. (1952). *Psychoanalytic Studies of the Personality*. London: Tavistock Publications.

Fairbairn, W. R. (1954). 'Observations on the Nature of Hysterical States'. *British Journal of Medical Psychology*, 27: 105–125.

Federn, P. (1953). *Ego Psychology and the Psychoses*. New York: Basic Books.

Fenichel, O. (1926). 'Identification', in (1954) *The Collected Papers of Otto Fenichel* (pp. 97–112), New York: Basic Books.

Fenichel, O. (1946). *The Psychoanalytic Theory of Neurosis*. London: Kegan Paul, Trench, Trubner & Co.

Ferenczi, S. (1913). 'Stages in the Development of The sense of Reality', in (1950) *First Contributions to Psycho-Analysis* (pp. 213–239), London: Hogarth Press.

Ferenczi, S. (1926). 'The Problem of Acceptance of Unpleasant Ideas. Advances in Knowledge of the Sense of Reality', in (1950) *Further Contributions to the Theory and Technique of Psychoanalysis* (pp. 366–379), London: Hogarth Press.

Ferrater Mora, J. (1941). *Diccionario de Filosofía.* México: Atlante; republished (1965), Buenos Aires: Editorial Sudamericana.

Ferschtut, G. (1963). 'Intelectualización, verbalización y cambio de idioma'. Buenos Aires: *Asociación Psicoanalítica Argentina.*

Ferschtut, G. & Serebriany, R. (1964). 'Notas sobre la simbolización en la psicopatía', in Symposium *Manía y Psicopatía,* Buenos Aires: Asociación Psicoanalítica Argentina; in A. Rascovsky & D. Liberman (eds.) (1966) *Psicoanálisis de la Manía y la Psicopatía* (pp. 301–309), Buenos Aires: Paidós.

Fliess, R. (1961). *Ego and Body Ego.* New York: Schulte Publishing Company.

Fontana, A. E. (1959). 'Vinculaciones de la fantasía de regresión intrauterina con la hipocondría y la psicopatía'. *Revista de Psicoanálisis,* 16: 226–241.

Foulkes, S. H. (1937). 'On Introjection'. *International Journal of Psychoanalysis,* 18: 269–293.

Freeman, T. (1959). 'Aspects of Defence in Neurosis and Psychosis'. *International Journal of Psychoanalysis,* 40: 199–212.

French, T. M. & Kasanin, T. (1941). 'Psychodynamic Study of the Recovery of Two Schizophrenic Cases'. *Psychoanalytic Quarterly,* 10: 1–22.

Frenkel-Brunswik, E. (1949). 'Intolerance of Ambiguity as an Emotional and Perceptual Personality Variable'. *Journal of Personality,* 18: 108–143.

Frenkel-Brunswik, E. & Sanford, R. N. (1950). 'La personalité antisémite'. *Les Temps Modernes* (Oct.): 577–602.

Freud, A. (1936). 'The Ego and the Mechanisms of Defense', in (1966) *The Writings of Anna Freud,* vol. 2, New York: International Universities Press.

Freud, A. (1946). 'The Mutual Influences in the Development of Ego and Id'. *Psychoanalytic Study of the Child,* 7: 31–41.

Freud, A. & Burlingham, D. (1942). *Young Children in War-time. A Year's Work in a Residential War Nursery.* London: George Allen & Unwin.

Freud, A. & Burlingham, D. (1944). *Infants without Families.* New York: International University Press.

Freud, S. (1892–93). 'A Case of Successful Treatment by Hypnotism'. *SE,* 1: 117–128.

Freud, S. (1893 [1888–1893]). 'Some Points for a Comparative Study of Organic and Hysterical Motor Paralyses'. *SE,* 1: 157–172.

Freud, S. (1894). 'The Neuro-Psychoses of Defence'. *SE,* 3: 45–61.

Freud, S. (1900). *The Interpretation of Dreams. SE,* 4–5.

Freud, S (1901). *The Psychopathology of Everyday Life. SE,* 6.

Freud, S. (1905a). 'Fragment of an Analysis of a Case of Hysteria'. *SE,* 7: 3–122.

Freud, S. (1905b). *Three Essays on the Theory of Sexuality. SE,* 7: 125–245.

Freud, S. (1905c). *Jokes and Their Relation to the Unconscious. SE,* 8.

Freud, S. (1907). *Delusions and Dreams in Jensen's Gradiva. SE,* 9: 3–95.

Freud, S. (1909). 'Notes upon a Case of Obsessional Neurosis'. *SE,* 10: 153–318.

Freud, S. (1910a [1909]). *Five Lectures on Psycho-Analysis. SE,* 11: 1–56.

Freud, S. (1910b). 'The Antithetical Meaning of Primal Words'. *SE,* 11: 155–161.

Freud, S. (1910c). 'A Special Type of Choice of Object made by Men (Contributions to the Psychology of Love, I)'. *SE,* 11: 165–175.

Freud, S. (1910d). 'Sobre el sentido antitético de las voces primitivas'. *OC,* 18: 59–67.

Freud, S. (1911). 'Formulations on the Two Principles of Mental Functioning'. *SE,* 12: 213–226.

Freud, S. (1912a). 'On the Universal Tendency to Debasement in the Sphere of Love (Contributions to the Psychology of Love, II)'. *SE,* 11: 177–190.

Freud, S. (1912b). 'The Dynamics of Transference'. *SE,* 12: 97–108.

Freud, S. (1913). *Totem and Taboo. SE,* 13: 1–161.

Freud, S. (1914a). 'Remembering, Repeating and Working-Through (Further Recommendations on the Technique of Psycho-Analysis, II)'. *SE,* 12: 145–156.

Freud, S. (1914b). 'On Narcissism: An Introduction'. *SE,* 14: 67–104.

Freud, S. (1915). 'Instincts and their Vicissitudes'. *SE,* 14: 109–140.

Freud, S. (1916–17). *Introductory Lectures on Psycho-Analysis. SE,* 15–16.

Freud, S. (1919). 'The "Uncanny"'. *SE,* 17: 219–256.

Freud, S. (1920). *Beyond the Pleasure Principle. SE,* 18: 7–64.

Freud, S. (1921). *Group Psychology and the Analysis of the Ego. SE,* 18: 67–143.

Freud, S. (1923a). *The Ego and the Id. SE,* 19: 3–66.

Freud, S. (1923b [1922]). 'Remarks on the Theory and Practice of Dream-Interpretation'. *SE,* 19: 109–121.

Freud, S. (1923c). 'A Seventeenth-Century Demonological Neurosis'. *SE,* 19: 69–105.

Freud, S. (1924a). 'Neurosis and Psychosis'. *SE,* 19: 149–154.

Freud, S. (1924b). 'The Economic Problem of Masochism'. *SE,* 19: 157–170.

Freud, S. (1924c). 'The Loss of Reality in Neurosis and Psychosis'. *SE,* 19: 183–190.

Freud, S. (1925). *Gesammelte Schriften.* Vienna: Internationaler Psychoanalytischer Verlag

Freud, S. (1926). *Inhibitions, Symptoms and Anxiety. SE,* 20: 77–174.

Freud, S. (1927). 'Fetishism'. *SE,* 21: 147–158.

Freud, S. (1928 [1927]). 'Dostoevsky and Parricide'. *SE,* 21: 173–194.

Freud, S. (1930). *Civilization and its Discontents. SE,* 21: 57–146.

Freud, S. (1931). 'Female Sexuality'. *SE,* 21: 221–244.

Freud, S. (1933). *New Introductory Lectures On Psycho-Analysis. SE,* 22: 1–182.

Freud, S. (1937). 'Analysis Terminable and Interminable'. *SE,* 23: 211–253.

Freud, S. (1940a [1938]). *An Outline of Psychoanalysis. SE,* 23: 141–207.

Freud, S. (1940b [1938]). 'Splitting of the Ego in the Process of Defense'. *SE,* 23: 271–278.

Freud, S. (1940–41 [1892]). 'Sketches for the "Preliminary Communication" of 1893'. *SE,* 1: 147–154.

Freud, S. (1952–56). *Obras Completas,* 21 vols., trans. L. López-Ballesteros y de Torres (vols. 11–17) & L. Rosenthal (vols. 18–21). Buenos Aires: Santiago Rueda.

Freud, S. (1991). *Gesammelte Werke: Chronologisch Geordnet.* London: Imago Publishing Co., Ltd.

Fromm-Reichmann, F. (1939). 'Transference Problems in Schizophrenics'. *Psychoanalytic Quarterly,* 8: 412–426.

Garbarino, H. (1962). 'Mecanismos confusionales en un paciente histérico'. *Revista de Psicoanálisis,* 19: 80–85.

Garbarino, H. (1965 [1962]). 'Un núcleo confusional: el muerto vivo'. *Revista Uruguaya de Psicoanálisis,* 7: 119–137.

Garbarino, M. F. de (1961–1962). 'Disociación y confusión'. *Revista Uruguaya de Psicoanálisis,* 4: 417–452.

García Reinoso, D. (1956a). 'Cuerpo y mente'. *Revista de Psicoanálisis*, 13: 312–319.

García Reinoso, D. (1956b). 'Sobre el esquema corporal'. *Revista de Psicoanálisis*, 13: 536–539.

García Reinoso, D. (1961). 'Consideraciones sobre el duelo'. *Revista de Psicoanálisis*, 18: 139–155.

Garma, A. (1944). 'La realidad exterior y los instintos en la esquizofrenia'. *Revista de Psicoanálisis*, 2, 1: 56–82.

Garma, A. ( 1945). 'La génesis del juicio de realidad'. *Revista de Psicoanálisis*, 2, 3: 423–438.

Geleerd, E. R. (1946). 'A Contribution to the Problem of Psychoses in Childhood'. *Psychoanaytic Study of the Child*, 2: 271–291.

Giovacchini, P. L. (1958). 'Mutual Adaptation in Various Object Relationships'. *International Journal of Psychoanalysis*, 39: 547–554.

Glover, E. (1930). 'Grades of Ego Differentiation'. *International Journal of Psychoanalysis*, 11: 1–11.

Glover, E. (1943). 'The Concept of Dissociation'. *International Journal of Psychoanalysis*, 24: 7–13.

Glover, E. (1949). *Psycho-Analysis*. London: Staples Press.

Glover, E. (1955). *The Technique of Psychoanalysis.* New York: International Universities Press; London: Baillière, Tindall & Cox.

* Godfrind, J. (1983). 'Symbiose et Ambigüité de José Bleger'. *Revue Belge de Psychanalyse*, 2: 79–89.

* Godfrind, J. (1991). 'De l'utilisation du cadre: les objets inanimés'. *Revue Belge de Psychanalyse*, 18: 83–102.

Goldstein, K. (1950). *Trastornos del lenguaje.* Barcelona: Científico-Médica; originally (1948) *Language and Language Disturbances: Aphasic Symptom Complexes and their Significance for Medicine and Theory of Language,* New York: Grune & Stratton.

* Green, A. (1975). 'The Analyst, Symbolization and Absence in the Analytic Setting (On Changes in Analytic Practice and Analytic Experience)'. *International Journal of Psychoanalysis*, 56: 1–22.

* Green, A. (2005). 'The illusion of common ground and mythical pluralism'. *International Journal of Psychoanalysis*, 86: 627–632.

Greenacre, P. (1952). *Trauma, Growth and Personality*. New York: Norton.

Greenacre, P. (1959). 'Certain Technical Problems in the Transference Relationship'. *Journal of the American Psychoanalytic Association*, 7: 484–502.

Greenacre, P. (1961). 'Considerations regarding the parent-infant relationship'. *International Journal of Psychoanalysis,* 31: 571–584.

Grinberg, L. (1957a). 'Perturbaciones en la interpretación por la contraidentificación proyectiva'. *Revista de Psicoanálisis*, 14 (1–2): 23–30.

Grinberg, L. (1957b). 'Revisión de los conceptos sobre magia y omnipotencia'. *Revista de Psicoanálisis*, 14 (3): 11–22.

Grinberg, L. (1958). 'Aspectos mágicos en la transferencia y en la contratransferencia'. *Revista de Psicoanálisis*, 15: 341–368.

Grinberg, L. (1962). 'Aspectos normales y patológicos del sueño'. Rio de Janeiro: IV Congreso Psicoanalítico.

Grinberg, L. (1963). 'Psicopatología de la identificación y contraidentificación proyectivas y de la contratransferencia'. *Revista de Psicoanálisis*, 20 (2): 113–123.

Grinberg, L. (1964). 'Relación objetal y modalidad en las identificaciones proyectivas en la manía y la psicopatía'. In Symposium *Manía y Psicopatía*, Buenos Aires: *Asociación*

*Psicoanalítica Argentina*; in A. Rascovsky & D. Liberman (eds.) (1966) *Psicoanálisis de la Manía y la Psicopatía* (pp. 138–148), Buenos Aires: Paidós.

Grinberg, L. & Liberman, D. (1964). 'Identificación proyectiva y comunicación en la situación transferencial'. Symposium *Manía y Psicopatía*, Buenos Aires, *Asociación Psicoanalítica Argentina*; in A. Rascovsky, D. Liberman (eds.) (1966), *Psicoanálisis de la Manía y la Psicopatía* (pp. 109–118), Buenos Aires: Paidós.

Guiraud, P. (1955). *La Sémantique*. Paris: Presses Universitaires de France.

Guntrip, H. (1961). *Personality Structure and Human Interaction*. London: Hogarth Press.

Hacker, F. J. (1962). 'The Discriminatory Function of the Ego'. *International Journal of Psychoanalysis,* 43: 395–405.

Handelsman, I. (1965). 'The Effects of Early Object Relationships on Sexual Development – Autistic and Symbiotic Modes of Adaptation. *Psychoanalytic Study of the Child*, 20: 367–383.

Hartmann, H. (1947). On Rational and Irrational Action', in G. Róheim (ed.) *Psychoanalysis and the Social Sciences*, vol. I, New York: International Universities Press.

Hartmann, H. (1950). 'Comments on the Psychoanalytic Theory of the Ego'. *Psychoanalytic Study of the Child*, 5: 74–96.

Hartmann, H. (1952). 'The Mutual Influences in the Development of Ego and Id'. *Psychoanalytic Study of the Child,* 7: 9–30.

Hartmann, H. (1956a). 'The Development of the Ego Concept in Freud's Work'. *International Journal of Psychoanalysis*, 37: 425–438.

Hartmann, H. (1956b). 'Notes on the Reality Principle'. *Psychoanalytic Study of the Child*, 11: 31–53.

Hartmann, H. (1958 [1939]). *Ego Psychology and the Problem of Adaptation*. New York: International Universities Press.

Hartmann H., Kris E. & Loewenstein R. M. (1946). 'Comments on the Formation of Psychic Structure'. *Psychoanalytic Study of the Child*, 2: 11–38.

Hegel, G. W. F. (1807). *Phenomenology of Mind*, trans. J. B. Baillie (1910). London: Macmillan; revised edition (1931); reprinted (1967), New York: Harper and Row.

Hegel, G. W. F. (1816). *Science of Logic*, trans. A.V. Miller (1969), Foreword by J. N. Findlay, London: G. Allen & Unwin.

Heimann, P. (1942). 'Contribution to the Problem of Sublimation and its Relation to Processes of Internalization'. *International Journal of Psychoanalysis*, 23: 8–17; reprinted in (1989) *About Children and Children-No-Longer* (pp. 26–45), London: Tavistock/Routledge.

Heimann, P. (1949). 'Some Notes on the Psychoanalytic Concept of the Introjected Object'. *British Journal of Medical Psychology*, 22 (1–2): 8–17; reprinted in (1989) *About Children and Children-No-Longer* (pp. 61–72), London: Tavistock/Routledge.

* Heimann, P. (1950). 'On Counter-Transference'. *International Journal of Psychoanalysis*, 31: 81–84.

Heimann, P. (1952). 'Certain Functions of Introjection and Projection in Early Infancy', in M. Klein, P. Heimann, S. Isaacs & J. Riviere (eds.), *Developments in Psychoanalysis* (pp. 122–168), London: Hogarth Press.

Heimann, P. (1955). 'A Contribution to the Re-evaluation of the Œdipus Complex', in M. Klein, P. Heimann & R. Money-Kyrle (eds.), *New Directions in Psychoanalysis* (pp. 23–38), London: Tavistock Publications.

Hendrick, L. (1951). 'Early Development of the Ego'. *Psychoanalytic Quarterly,* 20: 44–61.

Hesnard, A. (1957). *Psychanalyse du lien interhumain.* Paris: Presses Universitaires de France.

Hinsie, L. E. & Campbell, R. J. (1960). *Psychiatric Dictionary.* New York: Oxford University Press.

Hoffer, W. (1950). 'Development of the Body-Ego'. *Psychoanalytic Study of the Child,* 5: 18–23.

Hoffer, W. (1952). 'The Mutual Influences in the Development of Ego and Id'. *Psychoanalytic Study of the Child,* 7: 31–41.

Jackson, D. (1960). 'The Monad, the Dyad, and the Family Therapy of Schizophrenics', in A. Burton (ed.), *Psychotherapy of the Psychoses* (pp. 318–328), New York: Basic Books.

Jacobson, E. (1954). 'The Self and the Object World'. *Psychoanalytic Study of the Child,* 9: 75–127.

Jacobson, E. (1957). 'On Psychotic Identifications'. *International Journal of Psychoanalysis,* 35: 102–108.

Jacobson, E. (1964). *The Self and the Object World.* London: Hogarth Press.

Jacques, E. (1951). *The Changing Culture of a Factory,* London: Tavistock Publications.

Jacques, E. (1955). 'Social Systems as a Defence against Persecutory and Depressive Anxiety', in M. Klein, P. Heimann & R. Money-Kyrle (eds.), *New Directions in Psychoanalysis* (pp. 478–498), London: Tavistock Publications.

Jones, E. (1953). *Sigmund Freud: Life & Work,* Volume 1: *The Young Freud.* London: Hogarth Press.

Jones, E. (1955). *Sigmund Freud: Life & Work,* Volume 2. *Years of Maturity.* London: Hogarth Press.

Jones, E. (1957). *Sigmund Freud: Life & Work,* Volume 3: *The Last Phase.* London: Hogarth Press.

* Kaës, R. (ed.) (1979). *Crise, rupture et dépassement: analyse transitionnelle en psychanalyse individuelle et groupale.* Paris: Dunod.

Kaiser, S. (1958). 'Disturbances in Abstract Thinking and Body-Ego Formation'. *Journal of the American Psychoanalytic Association,* 6: 628–652.

Kaiser, W. (1957). *The Grotesque in Art and Literature.* Dayton: Morningside Books.

Kanner, L. (1935). *Child Psychiatry.* London: Baillère, Tindall & Cox.

Kanner, L. (1972 [1935]). *Child Psychiatry.* Fourth Edition. Springfield, ILL: C.C. Thomas.

Kasanin, J. S. (1944). *Language and Thought in Schizophrenia.* Berkeley: University of California Press.

Khan, M. (1960). 'Clinical Aspects of the Schizoid Personality'. *International Journal of Psychoanalysis,* 41: 430–436; also in (1974) *The Privacy of the Self* (pp. 13–26), London: Hogarth Press.

Klein, M. (1930). 'The Importance of Symbol-Formation in the Development of the Ego', in *Love, Guilt & Reparation, 1921–1945* (pp. 219–232). London: Hogarth Press.

Klein, M. (1932). *The Psycho-Analysis of Children.* Reprinted (1975), London: Hogarth Press.

Klein, M. (1933). 'The Early Development of Conscience in the Child', in (1975) *Love, Guilt and Reparation, 1921–1945* (pp. 248–257), London: Hogarth Press.

Klein, M. (1940). 'Mourning and its Relation to Manic-Depressive States', in (1975) *Envy and Gratitude and Other Works 1946–1963* (pp. 344–369), London: Hogarth Press.

Klein, M. (1945). 'The Œdipus Complex in the Light of Early Anxieties', in (1975) *Love, Guilt and Reparation, 1921–1945* (pp. 370–419), London: Hogarth Press.

Klein, M. (1946). 'Notes on Some Schizoid Mechanisms', in (1975) *Envy and Gratitude and Other Works 1946–1963* (pp. 1–24), London: Hogarth Press.

Klein, M. (1952a). 'Some Theoretical Conclusions Regarding the Emotional Life of the Infant', in (1975) *Envy and Gratitude and Other Works 1946–1963* (pp. 61–93), London: Hogarth Press.

Klein, M. (1952b). 'The Origins of Transference', in (1975) *Envy and Gratitude and Other Works 1946–1963* (pp. 48–56), London: Hogarth Press.

Klein, M. (1955a). 'The Psycho-Analytic Play Technique: Its History and Significance', in (1975) *Envy and Gratitude and Other Works 1946–1963* (pp. 122–140), London: Hogarth Press.

Klein, M. (1955b). 'On Identification', in (1975) *Envy and Gratitude and Other Works 1946–1963* (pp. 141–175), London: Hogarth Press.

Klein, M. (1957). *Envy and Gratitude,* in (1975) *Envy and Gratitude and Other Works 1946–1963* (pp. 176–235), London: Hogarth Press.

Klein, M. (1958). 'On the Development of Mental Functioning', in (1975) *Envy and Gratitude and Other Works 1946–1963* (pp. 236–246), London: Hogarth Press.

Klein, M. (1959). 'Our Adult World and its Roots in Infancy', in (1975) *Envy and Gratitude and Other Works 1946–1963* (pp. 247–263), London: Hogarth Press.

Kohut, H. (1966). 'Forms and Transformations of Narcissism'. *Journal of the American Psychoanalytic Association*, 14: 243–272.

Koolhaas, G. (1958). 'El origen psicótico de las neurosis'. *Revista Uruguaya de Psicoanálisis*, 2: 406–451.

Kris, E. & Kap1an, A. (1952) 'Aesthetic Ambiguity', in E. Kris, *Psychoanalytic Explorations in Art,* New York: International Universities Press.

Lagache, D. (1952). 'Le problème du transfert'. *Revue Française de Psychanalyse*, 16: 1–2, 5–122.

Lagache, D. (1955). 'La personnalité et les relations avec autrui'. *Bulletin de Psychologie*, 8 (3).

Lagache, D. (1961). 'La psychanalyse et la structure de la personnalité'. *La Psychanalyse*, 6: 5–54.

Lalande, A. (1953). *Vocabulario Técnico y Crítico de la Filosofía*. Buenos Aires: El Ateneo; originally (1946) *Vocabulaire technique et critique de la philosophie* (5th edition); reprinted (1991) Paris: Presses Universitaires de France.

Langer, M. (1957). 'La interpretación basada en la vivencia contratransferencial de conexión o desconexión con el analizado'. *Revista de Psicoanálisis*, 14: 31–38.

Langer, M. (1966). 'Aporte kleiniano'. In R. Sterba, M. Langer, *Teoría psicoanalítica de la libido y aporte kleiniano* (pp. 121–156), Buenos Aires: Hormé.

Langer, S. K. (1954 [1942]). *Philosophy in a New Key: A Study in the Symbolism of Reason, Rite, and Art.* Cambridge: New American Library.

Leenhardt, M. (1979 [1947]). *Do Kamo: Person and Myth in the Melanesian World.* Chicago: University of Chicago Press.

Lévi-Strauss, C. (1962). *Le totemisme aujourd'hui.* Paris: Presses Universitaires de France; trans. R. Needham (1963) *Totemism*, Boston: Beacon Press.

Lévi-Strauss, C. (1964). *La pensée sauvage.* Paris: Plon; trans. J. Weightman & D. Weightman (1966) *The Savage Mind.* Chicago: Chicago University Press.

Lévy-Bruhl, L. (1910). *Les fonctions mentales dans les sociétés inférieures.* Paris: Presses Universitaires de France.

Lévy-Bruhl, L. (1922). *La mentalité primitive*. Paris: Alcan.

Lewin, K. (1935). *A Dynamic Theory of Personality*. New York & London: McGraw Hill Book Company.

Liberman, D. (1956). 'Identificación proyectiva y conflicto matrimonial'. *Revista de Psicoanálisis*, 13: 1–20.

Liberman, D. (1957). 'Interpretación correlativa entre relato y repetición'. *Revista de Psicoanálisis*, 14: 55–62.

Liberman, D. (1958). 'El autismo transferencial. El mito de Eco y Narciso'. *Revista de Psicoanálisis*, 15 (4): 368–385.

Liberman, D. (1962). 'Comunicación extraverbal y situación analítica'. Rio de Janeiro: 4° Congreso Psicoanalítico Latinoamericano.

Liberman, D. (1963). *La comunicación en terapéutica psicoanalítica*. Buenos Aires: Eudeba.

Liberman, D., Ferschtut, G. & Sor, D. (1961). 'El contrato analítico'. *Revista de Psicoanálisis*, 18: 85–98.

Lidz, R. W. & Lidz, T. (1954). 'Therapeutic Considerations Arising from the Intense Symbiotic Needs of Schizophrenia Patients', in E. B. Brody & F. C. Redlich, *Psychotherapy with Schizophrenics*, New York: International Universities Press.

Lieber, L. R. (1960). 'THE Great Discovery of Modern Mathematics'. *General Semantics Bulletin*, 26–27.

Limentani, D. (1956). 'Symbiotic ldentification in Schizophrenia'. *Psychiatry*, 19: 231–236.

Little, M. (1958). 'On Delusional Transference'. *International Journal of Psychoanalysis*, 39: 134–138.

Little, M. (1960). 'On Basic Unity'. *International Journal of Psychoanalysis*, 41: 377–384.

Loewald, H. W. (1951). 'Ego and Reality'. *International Journal of Psychoanalysis*, 32: 10–18.

Lounsbury, F. G. (1963). 'Linguistics and Psychology', in S. Koch, *Psychology: A Study of a Science*, vol. VI (pp. 553–582), New York: McGraw-Hill.

Luchina, I. L. & Wender, L. (1964). 'Yo motor, aprendizaje y duelo'. *Revista de Psicoanálisis*, 21: 227–238.

Mahler, M. (1952). 'On Child Psychosis and Schizophrenia'. *Psychoanalytic Study of the Child*, 7: 286–305.

Mahler, M. (1958). 'Autism and Symbiosis, Two Extreme Disturbances of Identity'. *International Journal of Psychoanalysis*, 39: 77–83.

Mahler, M. (1960). 'Perceptual De-differentiation and Psychotic "Object Relationship"'. *International Journal of Psychoanalysis*, 41: 548–553.

Mahler, M. (1961). 'On Sadness and Grief in Infancy and Childhood: Loss and Restoration of the Symbiotic Love-Object'. *Psychoanalytic Study of the Child*, 16: 332–351.

Mahler, M. (1963). 'Thoughts About Development and Individuation'. *Psychoanalytic Study of the Child*, 18: 307–324.

Mahler, M. & Elkish, P. (1953). 'Some Observations on Disturbances of the Ego in a Case of Infantile Psychosis'. *Psychoanalytic Study of the Child*, 8: 252–261.

Mahler, M. & Furer, M. (1960). 'Observations on Research Regarding the Symbiotic Syndrome of Infantile Psychoses'. *Psychoanalytic Quarterly*, 29: 317–327.

Mahler, M. & Furer, M. (1963). 'Certain Aspects of the Separation-Individuation Phase'. *Psychoanalytic Quarterly*, 32: 1–14.

Mahler, M. & Goslinger, B. J. (1955). 'On Symbiotic Child Psychosis: genetic, dynamic and restitutive aspects'. *Psychoanalytic Study of the Child*, 10: 195–212.

Mahler, M., Furer, M. & Settlage, C. F. (1959). 'Severe Emotional Disturbances in Childhood', in S. Arieti, *American Handbook of Psychiatry* (pp. 816–839), New York: Basic Books.

Mahler, M. S., Ross, J. R., Jr. & De Fries, Z. (1949). 'Clinical Studies in Benign and Malignant Cases of Childhood Psychosis (Schizophrenia-Like)'. *American Journal of Orthopsychiatry*, 19: 295–304.

* Maldavsky, D. (1973). 'Lista cronológica de la obra de José Bleger'. *Revista de Psicoanálisis*, 30 (2): 591–601.

Marty, P. (1958). 'The Allergic Object Relationship'. *International Journal of Psychoanalysis*, 39: 98–103.

* Marx, K. (1844). 'Economic and Philosophical Manuscripts', in (1975) *Marx/Engels Collected Works*, Vol. 3. London: Lawrence & Wishart.

Maurel, H. (1954). *Le thème de protection et la pensée morbide.* Paris: Presses Universitaires de France.

Mendilaharsu, G. (1964). 'Vínculo simbiótico-parasitario e identidad'. *Revista Uruguaya de Psicoanálisis*, 6: 127–157.

Merleau-Ponty, M. (1945). *Phenomenology of Perception,* trans. C. Smith (1962), New York: Humanities Press; and trans. revised F. Williams (1981); reprinted (2002), London: Routledge & Kegan Paul.

Merleau-Ponty, M. (1951). 'The Child's Relations with Others', trans. W. Cobb, in J. Edie (ed.) (1964) *The Primacy of Perception* (pp. 96–155), Evanston: Northwestern University Press.

Merleau-Ponty, M. (1960). *Signs.* Trans. R. McCleary (1964), Evanston: Northwestern University Press.

Milner, M. (1952). 'Aspects of Symbolism in Comprehension of the Not-Self'. *International Journal of Psychoanalysis*, 33: 181–194.

Minkowski, E. (1953). *La schizophrénie.* Paris: Desclée de Brouwer.

Minkowski, E. (1960). *La esquizofrenia.* Buenos Aires: Paidós.

* Minkowska, F. (1923). 'Recherches généalogiques et problèmes touchant aux caractères (en particulier à celui de l'épileptoidie)'. *Annales Médico-Psychologiques*, (2): 149–170.

* Minkowska, F. (1956). 'L'épilepsie essentielle, sa psychopathologie et le test de Rorschach', in F. Minkowska & E. Minkowski (eds.) *Le Rorschach, à la recherche du monde des formes.* Etude No. 3. Paris: Desclée de Brouwer.

* Mitrani, J. L. (2001). *Ordinary People and Extra-Ordinary Protections: A Post-Kleinian Approach to the Treatment of Primitive Mental States.* Hove, East Sussex: Brunner-Routledge.

Modell, A. H. (1961). 'Denial and the Sense of Separateness'. *Journal of the American Psychoanalytic Association,* 9: 533–547.

Mom, J. (1956a). 'Consideraciones sobre la disociación en la obesidad'. Buenos Aires: Asociación Psicoanalítica Argentina.

Mom, J. (1956b). 'Algunas consideraciones sobre el concepto de distancia en las fobias'. *Revista de Psicoanálisis*, 13: 430–435.

Mom, J. (1957). 'Algunas consideraciones sobre la interpretación de las fobias'. *Revista de Psicoanálisis*, 14: 63–71.

Mom, J. (1960). 'Aspectos teóricos y técnicos en las fobias y en las modalidades fóbicas'. *Revista de Psicoanálisis*, 17: 190–218.

Mom, J. (1962). 'Consideraciones sobre el concepto de fobia en relación con algunos aspectos de la obra de M. Klein'. *Revista de Psicoanálisis*, 19: 26–33.

* Mom, J. (1982). *Asociación psicoanalítica argentina 1942–1982*. Buenos Aires: Asociación Psicoanalítica Argentina.

* Moreno, J. H. (1995). 'Psychoanalysis In Argentina'. *Journal of the American Psychoanalytic Association*, 43: 641–644.

Morris, C. (1946). *Signs, Language and Behavior.* New York: Prentice Hall.

Nieto, M. (1964). 'Fantasía de la cloaca y confusión'. *Revista Uruguaya de Psicoanálisis*, 6: 83–90.

Nunberg, H. (1931). 'The Synthetic Function of the Ego'. *International Journal of Psychoanalysis*, 12: 123–140.

Nunberg, H. (1951). 'Transference and Reality'. *International Journal of Psychoanalysis*, 32: 1–9.

* Ogden, T. H. (1989). 'On the Concept of an Autistic-Contiguous Position'. *International Journal of Psychoanalysis*, 70: 127–140.

Osgood, C. E. (1963). 'Psycholinguistics', in S. Koch, *Psychology: A Study of a Science,* vol. VI (pp. 244–316), New York: McGraw Hill.

Palacios, A. (1965). 'La relación temprana de objeto y sus manifestaciones transferenciales'. *Cuadernos de Psicoanálisis*, 3: 263–279.

Pappenheim, E. & Sweeney, M. (1952). 'Separation Anxiety in Mother and Child'. *Psychoanalytic Study of the Child*, 7: 95–114.

Paz, C. A. (1964). 'Actualización: el paciente fronterizo ("The Borderline Case") en la psicología actual y su importancia en psicoanálisis'. *Revista de Psicoanálisis*, 21: 239–258.

Peto, A. (1961). 'The Fragmentizing Function of the Ego in the Transference Neurosis'. *International Journal of Psychoanalysis,* 42: 238–245.

Peto, A. (1963). 'The Fragmentizing Function of the Ego in the Analytic Session'. *International Journal of Psychoanalysis*, 43: 328–338.

Pichon Rivière, A. (1958). 'La dentición, la marcha y el lenguaje en relación con la posición depresiva'. *Revista de Psicoanálisis*, 15: 41–48; trans., 'Dentition, Walking, and Speech in Relation to the Depressive Position', *International Journal of Psychoanalysis*, 39: 167–171.

Pichon Rivière, E. (1943–1944). 'Los dinamismos de la epilepsia'. *Revista de Psicoanálisis*, 1: 340–381.

Pichon Rivière, E. (1944–1945). 'Patogenia y dinamismos de la epilepsia'. *Revista de Psicoanálisis*, 2 (4): 615–625.

Pichon Rivière, E. (1947). 'Lo siniestro en la vida y la obra del Conde de Lautréamont'. *Revista de Psicoanálisis*, 4 (4): 1–65. Also in (1970) *Del Psicoanálisis a la Psicología Social.* (2 Vols.). Buenos Aires: Galerna; and in M. Pichon Rivière (ed.) (1992), *Psicoanálisis del Conde de Lautréamont*, Biblioteca de Psicoanálisis, Buenos Aires: Argonauta.

Pichon Rivière, E. (1952). 'Quelques observations sur le transfert chez des patients psychotiques'. *Revue Française de Psychanalyse*, 16 (1–2): 254–262; also in Spanish, (1961) 'Algunas observaciones sobre la transferencia en pacientes psicóticos', *Revista de Psicoanálisis*, 28 (2); republished in (1977) *La psiquiatría, una nueva problemática. Del psicoanálisis a la psicología social II* (pp. 366–375), Buenos Aires: Ediciones Nueva Visión.

Pine, F. & Furer, M. (1963). 'Studies of the Separation Individuation Phase'. *Psychoanalytic Study of the Child*, 18: 325–342.

Pizzolanti, C. P. de (1965). 'Vivencias transferenciales simbióticas en el momento de terminación de un análisis'. *Revista Uruguaya de Psicoanálisis*, 7: 139–197.

Plata mujica, C. (1960). 'El fenómeno del doble y sus relaciones con el psiquismo fetal', in A. Rascovsky, *El psiquismo fetal,* Buenos Aires: Paidós, 120–148.

* Plotkin, M. (2001). *Freud in the Pampas. The Emergence and Development of a Psychoanalytic Culture in Argentina.* Stanford: Stanford University Press.

Polito, R. C. (1963). 'Análisis de un psicótico'. *Revista de Psicoanálisis,* 20: 133–146.

Polito, R. C. (1966). 'Análisis de un estado hipocondríaco'. Buenos Aires: Asociación Psicoanalitica Argentina.

* Politzer, G. (1928). *Critique des Fondements de la Psychologie.* Paris: Les Éditions Rieder.

Politzer, G. (1965–66). *Escritos psicológicos de Georges Politzer,* trans. E. Ramos, ed. J. Bleger, 3 vols. Buenos Aires: Jorge Alvarez.

Pollock, G. H. (1964). 'Simbiosis y neurosis simbiótica'. *Revista Uruguaya de Psicoanálisis,* 6: 281–346; trans. 'On Symbiosis and Symbiotic Neurosis', *International Journal of Psychoanalysis,* 45: 1–30.

Przyluski, J. (1940). *La participation.* Paris: Presses Universitaires de France.

Racker, G. T. (1958). 'El cajón de juguetes del niño y el cajón de fantasías del adulto'. *Revista de Psicoanálisis,* 15: 49–54.

Racker, G.T. (1959). 'Autismo transferencial y la interpretación como objeto transicional'. Buenos Aires: Asociación Psicoanalítica Argentina.

* Racker, H. (1953). 'A Contribution to the Problem of Counter-Transference'. *International Journal of Psychoanalysis,* 34: 313–324.

Racker, H. (1960). *Estudios sobre técnica psicoanalítica.* Buenos Aires: Paidós.

* Racker, H. (1968). *Transference and Countertransference.* The International Psycho-Analytical Library, 73: 1–196. London: Hogarth Press & Institute of Psycho-Analysis.

Rapaport, D. (1959). 'A Historical Survey of Psychoanalytic Ego Psychology'. *Psychological Issues,* 1: 15–17.

Rascovsky, A. (1957). 'Esquema de la organización del psiquismo fetal'. *Revista de Psicoanálisis,* 14: 402–409.

Rascovsky, A. (1958). 'Desenvolvimiento primitivo del individuo'. São Paulo: 2° Congreso Psicoanalítico Latinoamericano.

Rascovsky, A. (1960). *El psiquismo fetal.* Buenos Aires: Paidós.

Rascovsky, A., Liberman, D. et al. (1966). *Psicoanálisis de la Manía* y *de la Psicopatía.* Buenos Aires: Paidós.

Read, H. (1966). *La bella y la bestia.* Buenos Aires: Eudecor.

Real Academia Española (1956). *Diccionario de la lengua española.* Madrid: Espasa-Calpe.

Reider, N. (1953). 'A Type of Transference to Institutions'. *Bulletin of the Menninger Clinic,* 17: 58–73.

Resnik, S. (1955). 'Sindrome de Cotard y despersonalización'. *Revista de Psicoanálisis,* 12: 80–101.

* Resnik, S. (1970). 'Syndrome de Cotard et dépersonnalisation'. *L'Information Psychiatrique,* 46 (5): 461–474.

* Resnik, S. (1978). *Personne et psychose: études sur le langage du corps.* Paris: Payot.

* Resnik, S. (2001). *The Delusional Person: Bodily Feelings in Psychosis.* London: Karnac Books.

Rickman, J. (1926–27). 'A Survey: The Development of the Psycho-Analytical Theory of the Psychoses, 1894–1926'. *British Journal of Medical Psychology,* 6 (4): 270–94; 7: 94–124, 321–74; reprinted in (1957) *Selected Contributions to Psychoanalysis* (pp. 224–383), London: Hogarth Press.

Rickman, J. (1940). 'On the Nature of Ugliness and the Creative Impulse', in (1957) *Selected Contributions to Psychoanalysis* (pp. 68–89), London: Hogarth Press.

Ritvo, S. (1962). 'Report of Panel on Object Relations'. *Journal of the American Psychoanalytic Association*, 10: 102–117.

Riviere, J. (1936a). 'A Contribution to the Analysis of the Negative Therapeutic Reaction'. *International Journal of Psychoanalysis*, 17: 304–320.

Riviere, J. (1936b). 'On the Genesis of Psychical Conflict in Early Infancy'. *International Journal of Psychoanalysis*, 17: 395–422. Also in J. Riviere (ed.) (1952), *Developments in Psychoanalysis*, London: Hogarth Press.

Riviere, J. (1937). 'Hate, greed and aggression', in M. Klein & J. Rivière (eds.) *Love, Hate and Reparation*, London: Hogarth Press.

Rochefort, C. (1958). *Le repos du guerrier*. Paris: Éditions Bernard Grasset, trans. L. Bair (1962 [1960]) *Warrior's Rest*. London: The New English Library Limited.

Rodrigué, E. (1955a). 'El objeto de amor primario'. *Revista de Psicoanálisis*, 12 (3): 415–421.

Rodrigué, E. (1955b). 'The analysis of a three-year-old mute schizophrenic'. In M. Klein, *New Directions in Psychoanalysis* (pp. 140–179), London: Tavistock Publications.

Rodrigué, E. (1955–56). 'Revisión del simbolismo'. *Revista de Psicoanálisis*, 12: 522–532; 13: 70–76.

Rodrigué, E. (1956). 'La concepción del mundo en el autismo'. *Revista de Psicoanálisis*, 13: 383–387.

Rodrigué, E. (1965). 'El contexto de la transferencia'. Buenos Aires: Asociación Psicoanalitica Argentina. Also in (1966) *El contexto del proceso analítico* (pp. 202–232), Buenos Aires: Paidós.

Rodrigué, E. (1966). 'La naturaleza y la función de los símbolos', in (1966) *El contexto del proceso analítico* (pp. 79–107), Buenos Aires: Paidós.

Rodrigué, E. & Rodrigué, G. T. (1966). *El contexto del proceso analítico*. Buenos Aires: Paidós.

Rolla, E. (1963). 'Etapas en el trabajo de simbolización'. *Revista de Psicoanálisis*, 20: 70–75.

Rolla, E. (1966). 'Uso de modelos mentales y de la dosificación de la interpretación en el estudio y tratamiento de las fobias'. Buenos Aires: Asociación Psicoanalitica Argentina.

Rosen, V. H. (1958). 'Abstract Thinking and Object Relations'. *Journal of the American Psychoanalytic Association*, 6: 653–671.

Rosenfeld, H. (1947). 'Analysis of a Schizophrenic State with Depersonalization'. *International Journal of Psychoanalysis*, 28: 130–139; also in (1965) *Psychotic States* (pp. 13–33), London: Hogarth Press.

Rosenfeld, H. (1950). 'Notes on the Psychopathology of Confusional States in Chronic Schizophrenia'. *International Journal of Psychoanalysis*, 31: 132–137; also in (1965) *Psychotic States* (pp. 52–62), London: Hogarth Press.

Rosenfeld, H. (1952a). 'Notes on the Psychoanalysis of the Superego Conflict in an Acute Schizophrenic Patient'. *International Journal of Psychoanalysis*, 33: 111–131; also in (1965) *Psychotic States* (pp. 63–103), London: Hogarth Press.

Rosenfeld, H. (1952b). 'Transference-Phenomena and Transference-Analysis in an Acute Catatonic Schizophrenic Patient'. *International Journal of Psychoanalysis*, 33: 457–464; also in (1965) *Psychotic States* (pp. 104–116), London: Hogarth Press.

Rosenfeld, H. (1958). 'Some Observations on the Psychopathology of Hypochondriacal States'. *International Journal of Psychoanalysis,* 39: 121–128.

Rosenfeld, H. (1962). 'The Superego and the Ego Ideal'. *International Journal of Psychoanalysis,* 43: 258–263; also in (1965) *Psychotic States* (pp. 144–154), London: Hogarth Press.

Rosenfeld, H. (1964). 'On the Psychopathology of Narcissism: a Clinical Approach'. *International Journal of Psychoanalysis,* 45: 332–337; also in (1965) *Psychotic States* (pp. 169–179), London: Hogarth Press.

Rosenfeld, H. (1965). 'The Psychopathology of Hypochondriasis', in (1965) *Psychotic States* (pp. 180–199), London: Hogarth Press.

Royer, G. (1963a). 'Dificultades en el duelo en relación con los procesos de diferenciación e individuación'. Buenos Aires: Asociación Psicoanalítica Argentina.

Royer, G. (1963b). 'La Metamorfosis'. *Revista de Psicoanálisis*, 20: 253–267.

Rubinfine, D. L. (1962). 'Maternal Stimulation'. *Psychoanalytic Study of the Child*, 17: 265–282.

Sachs, H. (1947). 'Observations of a Training Analyst'. *International Journal of Psychoanalysis,* 16: 151–156.

Sanford, B. (1952). 'An Obsessional Man's Need to be "Kept"'. *International Journal of Psychoanalysis,* 33: 144–52; also in M. Klein, P. Heimann & R. Money-Kyrle (1955), *New Directions in Psycho-Analysis* (pp. 266–281), London: Tavistock Publications.

Sartre, J. P. (1948). *Being and Nothingness.* Trans. E. Hazel (1958), London: Routledge.

Saussure, F. de (1916). *Course in General Linguistics*, Eds. C. Bally & A. Sechehaye, trans. R. Harris (1983), La Salle, ILL: Open Court.

* Scharff, D. E. (2011). 'The Concept of the Link in Psychoanalytic Therapy'. *Couple and Family Psychoanalysis*, 1 (1): 34–48.

Schöne, M. (1947). *Vie et mort des mots.* Paris: Presses Universitaires de France.

Scott, C. (1960). 'Depression, Confusion and Multivalence'. *International Journal of Psychoanalysis*, 41: 497–503.

Searles, H. F. (1955). 'Dependency Processes in the Psychopathology of Schizophrenia'. *Journal of the American Psychoanalytic Association*, 3: 19–66; also in (1965) *Collected Papers on Schizophrenia and Related Subjects* (pp. 114–156), London: Hogarth Press.

Searles, H. F. (1963). 'Transference Psychoses in the Psychotherapy of Schizophrenia'. *International Journal of Psychoanalysis,* 44: 249–281; also in (1965) *Collected Papers on Schizophrenia and Related Subjects* (pp. 654–716), London: Hogarth Press.

Searles, H. F. (1965). *Collected Papers on Schizophrenia and Related Subjects.* London: Hogarth Press.

Segal, H. (1950). 'Some Aspects of the Analysis of a Schizophrenic'. *International Journal of Psychoanalysis*, 30: 268–78; also in (1981) *The Work of Hanna Segal* (pp. 101–120), New York: Jason Aronson.

Segal, H. (1952). 'A Psycho-analytic Approach to Æsthetics'. *International Journal of Psychoanalysis*, 33: 196–207; also in M. Klein, P. Heimann & R. Money-Kyrle (1955), *New Directions in Psycho-Analysis* (pp. 384–407), London: Tavistock Publications.

Segal, H. (1956). 'Depression in the Schizophrenic'. *International Journal of Psychoanalysis*, 37: 339–343; also in (1981) *The Work of Hanna Segal* (pp. 121–130), New York: Jason Aronson.

Segal, H. (1957). 'Notes on Symbol Formation'. *International Journal of Psychoanalysis*, 38: 391–397; also in (1981) *The Work of Hanna Segal* (pp. 49–64), New York: Jason Aronson.

Segal, H. (1964). *Introduction to the Work of Melanie Klein*, London: Heinemann.
Serebriany, R. (1962). 'Detención del tiempo, angustia claustrofóbica y actuación'. *Revista de Psicoanálisis*, 19: 218–233.
Serebriany, R. (1965). 'Contribución al estudio de la confusión'. Buenos Aires: Asociación Psicoanalítica Argentina.
Shaw, G. B. (1916). *Pygmalion*. New York: Brentano.
Silbermann, I. (1957). 'Two Types of Preœdipal Character Disorders'. *International Journal of Psychoanalysis,* 38: 350–358.
Smolensky, G. (1962). 'La disociación. Comprensión de sus dinamismos a través de los conceptos de M. Klein'. *Revista de Psicoanálisis*, 19: 135–139.
Smolensky, G. (1965). 'Evolución clínica y mecanismos de defensa. Integración, confusion y regresión'. *Revista de Psicoanálisis*, 22: 284–291.
Soifer, R. (1961). 'Símbolo. Notas para una semántica psicoanalítica'. *Revista de Psicoanálisis*, 19 (3).
* Sosnik, R. (2011). 'Simbiosis y Ambiguedad [Symbiosis and Ambiguity] by José Bleger'. *Journal of the American Psychoanalytic Association*, 59: 847–858.
Sperling, O. (1944). 'On Appersonation'. *International Journal of Psychoanalysis*, 25: 128–132.
Sperling, O. (1949). 'The Role of the Mother in Psychosomatic Disorders in Children'. *Psychosomatic Medicine*, 11: 377–385.
Sperling, O. (1950). 'Children's Interpretation and Reaction to the Unconscious of their Mother'. *International Journal of Psychoanalysis*, 31: 36–41.
Sperling, O. (1959). 'A Study of Deviate Sexual Behaviour in Children by the Method of Simultaneous Analysis of Mother and Child', in L. Jessner & E. Pavenstedt (eds.), *Dynamic Psychopathology in Childhood*, New York: Grune & Stratton.
Spinoza, B. (1677). *The Ethics*, trans. R.H.M. Elwes (1883). London: George Bell and Sons.
Spitz, R. (1947). 'Anaclitic Depression'. *Psychoanalytic Study of the Child*, 2: 313–342.
Spitz, R. (1955). 'The Primal Cavity'. *Psychoanalytic Study of the Child*, 10: 215–240.
Spitz, R. (1957). *No and Yes*. New York: International Universities Press.
Spitz, R. (1961). 'The Psychogenic Diseases in Children'. *Psychoanalytic Study of the Child*, 16: 332–351.
* Steiner, J. (1993). *Psychic Retreats*. London: Routledge.
* Steiner, J. (1994). 'Patient-Centered and Analyst-Centered Interpretations: Some Implications of Containment and Countertransference'. *Psychoanalytic Inquiry*, 14: 406–422.
Stephen, A. (1945). 'A Note on Ambivalence'. *International Journal of Psychoanalysis*, 26: 55–58.
Sterba, R. F. (1968 [1942]). *Introduction to the Psychoanalytic Theory of the Libido*. New York: Nervous and Mental Disease Monographs.
Sterba, R. & Langer, M. (1966). *Teoría psicoanalítica de la libido y aporte kleiniano*. Buenos Aires: Hormé.
Stierlin, H. (1959). 'The Adaptation to the "Stronger" Persons Reality. Some Aspects of the Symbiotic Relationship of the Schizophrenic'. *Psychiatry*, 22: 55–65.
Stoll, W. A. (ed.) (1959). *Congress Report: 2nd International Congress for Psychiatry, Zurich (Switzerland), September 1st to 7th 1957*. Zürich: Füssli.
Strachey, J. (1934). 'The Nature of the Therapeutic Action of Psychoanalysis'. *International Journal of Psychoanalysis,* 15: 127–159.

Strachey, J. (ed.) (1953–1974). *The Standard Edition of the Complete Psychological Works of Sigmund Freud*, Volumes 1–24. London: Hogarth Press & the Institute of Psychoanalysis.

Strachey, J. (1955). 'Editor's Introduction'. In J. Breuer, & S. Freud, (1893–95) *Studies on Hysteria. SE,* 2: ix–xxviii.

* Taiana, C. (2006). 'The Emergence of Freud's Theories in Argentina: Towards a Comparison with the United States'. *Canadian Journal of Psychoanalysis*, 14: 269–295.

Tarachow, S. (1962). 'Interpretation and Reality in Psychotherapy'. *International Journal of Psychoanalysis*, 43: 377–387.

Tarachow, S. (1965). 'Ambiguity and Human Imperfection'. *Journal of the American Psychoanalytic Association*, 13: 85–101.

* Tylim, I. (1996). 'Psychoanalysis in Argentina: A Couch with a View'. *Psychoanalytic Dialogues*, 6: 713–727.

Uexküll, J. von (1957). 'A Stroll Through The World of Animals and Men'. In Schiller, C. H., *Instinctive Behaviour* (pp. 50–80), New York: International Universities Press.

Ullmann, S. (1962). *Semantics: An Introduction to the Science of Meaning*. Oxford: Basil Blackwell.

* Ungar, V. (2005). 'Child and adolescent psychoanalysis in Latin America'. In S. Lewkowicz & S. Flechner (eds.), *Truth, Reality, and the Psychoanalyst* (pp. 237–59), London: The International Psychoanalytical Association.

Usandivaras, R. (1956). 'Sobre la vivencia de lo maravilloso en algunas fobias'. *Revista de Psicoanálisis*, 13: 436–443.

* Vezzetti, H. (1996). *Aventuras de Freud en el pais de los argentinos*. Buenos Aires: Paidós.

Waelhens, A. de (1951). *Une philosophie de l'ambigüité*. Louvain: Publications Universitaires de Louvain.

Wallon, H. (1934). *Les origines du caractère chez 1'enfant*. Reprinted (1973), Paris: Presses Universitaires de France.

Weiland, H. (1966). 'Considerations of the Development of Symbiosis, Symbiotic Psychosis and the Nature of Separation Anxiety'. *International Journal of Psychoanalysis*, 47: 1–5.

Weiss, E. (1947). 'Projection, Extrajection and Objectivation'. *Psychoanalytic Quarterly*, 16: 357–377.

Weiss, E. (1948). 'Proyección, extrayección y objetivación'. *Revista de Psicoanálisis*, 5 (4): 984–1002.

Weiss, J. (1965). 'Clinical and Theoretical Aspects of "As If" Characters'. *Journal of the American Psychoanalytic Association*, 14: 569–590.

Wender, L. (1965). 'Reparación patológica y perversión'. Buenos Aires: Asociación Psicoanalitica Argentina.

* Wender, L. et al. (1992). 'Argentina'. In P. Kutter (ed.) *Psychoanalysis International, A Guide to Psychoanalysis Throughout the World* (vol. 2). Stuttgart & Bad Cannstatt: Frommann-Holzboog.

Werner, H. (1940). *Comparative Psychology of Mental Development*. New York: International Universities Press.

Winnicott, D. W. (1945). 'Primitive Emotional Development'. *International Journal of Psychoanalysis,* 26: 137–143; also in (1958) *Collected Papers* (pp. 145–156), London: Tavistock Publications.

Winnicott, D. W. (1949). 'Hate in the Countertransference'. *International Journal of Psychoanalysis*, 30: 69–74; also in (1958) *Collected Papers* (pp. 194–203), London: Tavistock Publications.

Winnicott, D.W. (1953). 'Transitional Object and Transitional Phenomena'. *International Journal of Psychoanalysis,* 34: 89–97; also in (1958) *Collected Papers* (pp. 229–242), London: Tavistock Publications.

Winnicott, D.W. (1956). 'On transference'. *International Journal of Psychoanalysis*, 37: 386–388; also in (1958) *Collected Papers* (pp. 295–299), London: Tavistock Publications.

Winnicott, D.W. (1957). 'The Capacity to be Alone'. *International Journal of Psychoanalysis*, 39: 416–420; also in (1965) *The Maturational Processes and the Facilitating Environment* (pp. 29–36), London: Hogarth Press.

Winnicott, D. W. (1960). 'The Theory of the Parent-Infant Relationship'. *International Journal of Psychoanalysis*, 41: 585–595; also in (1965) *The Maturational Processes and the Facilitating Environment* (pp. 37–56), London: Hogarth Press.

Wisdom, J. O. (1962). 'Comparison and Development of the Psycho-Analytical Theories of Melancholia'. *International Journal of Psychoanalysis,* 43: 113–132

Zazzo, R. (1953). 'Stages of Psychological Development of the Child'. In J. M. Tanner & B. Inhelder (eds.) *Child Development,* First Meeting of the World Health Organization, Geneva (pp. 161–181). London: Tavistock Publications.

# Index